AMERICAN HIGHER EDUCATION

AMERICAN HIGHER EDUCATION

A History

CHRISTOPHER J. LUCAS

ST. MARTIN'S GRIFFIN
NEW YORK

AMERICAN HIGHER EDUCATION

COPYRIGHT © CHRISTOPHER J. LUCAS, 1994.

ALL RIGHTS RESERVED. PRINTED IN THE UNITED STATES OF AMERICA.

NO PART OF THIS BOOK MAY BE USED OR REPRODUCED IN ANY MANNER
WHATSOEVER WITHOUT WRITTEN PERMISSION EXCEPT IN THE CASE OF
BRIEF QUOTATIONS EMBODIED IN CRITICAL ARTICLES OR REVIEWS. FOR
INFORMATION, ADDRESS ST. MARTIN'S PRESS, 175 FIFTH AVENUE, NEW
YORK, N.Y. 10010.

DESIGN BY DIGITAL TYPE & DESIGN.

LIBRARY OF CONGRESS CATALOGING-IN-PUBLICATION DATA

LUCAS, CHRISTOPHER J.
  AMERICAN HIGHER EDUCATION: A HISTORY / CHRISTOPHER J. LUCAS.
       P.   CM.
  INCLUDES BIBLIOGRAPHICAL REFERENCES AND INDEX.
  ISBN 0-312-12294-2 (CLOTH)
  ISBN 0-312-12945-9 (PAPER)
  1. EDUCATION, HIGHER--UNITED STATES--HISTORY. I. TITLE.
  LA226.L83 1994
  378.73--DC20   94-17001
                                                       CIP

10 9 8 7

Contents

PART 1:
HISTORICAL ORIGINS AND ANTECEDENTS

PART 2:
AMERICAN HIGHER EDUCATION: THE FORMATIVE PERIOD

PART 3
AMERICAN HIGHER EDUCATION:
MATURATION AND DEVELOPMENT

PART 4
CONTEMPORARY CHALLENGES AND ISSUES

Acknowledgments

Special thanks are owed to Michael Schwartz, Robert Young, and Kim Sebaly, who kindly consented to review and critique preliminary manuscript drafts; to Frederick Chambers, James White, Clifton Goine, Carol Flynne, Karen Stauffacher, Bart Cohen, and Averil McClelland for invaluable assistance and suggestions with source materials; to Normand Bernier, who reviewed the text and contributed a number of valuable ideas; to Karen Courchaine for encouragement; to Diane Damicone, Leanne Hoopnagle, and Sonja Bennett for clerical support; and to Laura Heymann and Jennifer Farthing of St. Martin's Press.

Grateful acknowledgment is made for permission to quote briefly from the following:

Official Knowledge, by Michael Apple, by permission of Routledge

Turmoil on the Campus, Edward J. Bander, ed., by permission of H. W. Wilson Company

An Aristocracy of Everyone, by Benjamin Barber, by permission of Ballantine

The Good Society, by Robert N. Bellah, et al., by permission of Random House/Vintage

Habits of the Heart: Individualism and Commitment in American Life, by Robert N. Bellah, et al., copyright © 1985 The Regents of the University of California

Debating PC: The Controversy Over Political Correctness On College Campuses, Paul Berman, ed., by permission of Bantam Doubleday Dell Publishing Group

Education Without Impact, by George H. Douglas, copyright © 1992 by George H. Douglas. Published by arrangement with Carol Publishing Group. A Birch Lane Press Book.

Illiberal Education: The Politics of Race and Sex on Campus, by Dinesh D'Souza, copyright © 1991 by Dinesh D'Souza. Reprinted with the permission of The Free Press, a division of Macmillan, Inc.

The University: An Owner's Manual, by Henry Rosovsky, by permission of W. W. Norton and Company

Killing the Spirit: Higher Education In America, by Page Smith, by permission of Viking Penguin

Introduction

Criticizing colleges has always amounted to something of a national pastime, dating back practically to the colonial era. Yet in the waning years of the twentieth century, public disaffection with American higher education seems to have generated a cacophony of popular criticism almost without historical precedent. Its tone, at any rate, seems more strident and acerbic than almost anything heard in recent memory. In early 1994, Patrick Terenzini and Ernest Pascarella ("Living with Myths, Undergraduate Education in America," *Change* 26, January/February 1994: 28–32) reviewed an impressive body of research literature calling into question some of the most fundamental precepts and assumptions underlying American academe. The hallowed tenet that institutional prestige and reputation reflect genuine educational quality, they asserted, had not been substantiated by recent findings. On the contrary, by almost any meaningful indicator of effective teaching or academic achievement, educational "quality" was not found to be closely associated with any given academic school's repute or standing in the traditional institutional hierarchy. Lackluster performance was in evidence at prestigious schools; and otherwise mediocre colleges might be blessed with many first-rate instructors and high-achieving students.

Similarly, the long-cherished assumption that good teachers tend to make for good researchers and vice versa did not seem to be borne out by the evidence. Although some researchers were judged to be effective teachers, the association of teaching skills and those abilities required for pursuing a research agenda was not especially close. Again, the comfortable bromide that traditional methods of instruction provide proven, effective ways of teaching, they argued, was incapable of withstanding close scrutiny. The lecture method in particular, long a pedagogical mainstay of the collegiate classroom, reportedly was found to be inferior in comparison with other nontraditional expedients emphasizing small-group discussion, individualized study, auto-tutorial instruction, role-playing, micro-drama, and the like. In short, or so it appeared, nothing was as it had seemed.

Long-established academic patterns have come in for renewed criticism, among them the apparent inability of American colleges and universities to graduate more than 50 percent of those admitted to pursue a degree. Half of those entering college full-time do not secure a degree within five years, noted the prestigious Wingspread Group on Higher Education, in an "open letter" entitled *An American Imperative: Higher Expectations for Higher*

Education (Washington, D.C.: Johnson Foundation, 1993). "Our education system," its authors observed, "is better organized to discourage students—to weed them out—than it is to cultivate and support our most important national resource, our people" (p. 5). As another observer noted with considerable understatement (Ted Marchese, "Getting the Baldrige Right," *Change* 26, January/February 1994: 4), "A system that brings just half the talent it enrolls through to the degree, and just half of whose graduates achieve [satisfactory] literacy levels . . . on the National Assessment of Educational Progress, has plenty of room for improvement."

A common response to critics who allege that "mass higher education" poses a contradiction in terms has been that American postsecondary education offers students of solid ability but limited means academic opportunities lacking virtually anywhere else in the world. The American system is populist, egalitarian and democratic, or so it is claimed, insofar as it offers practically everyone a chance to pursue academic credentials. But in the 1990s even this cherished assumption about equality of opportunity was being challenged. Typical was the finding advanced by Thomas P. Wallace ("Public Higher Education Finance," *Change* 25, July/August 1993: 57) who reported that "of the individuals receiving baccalaureate degrees by age 24 between 1985 and 1989, 56.3 percent were awarded to individuals from the top income quartile." Only 5.6 percent of the degrees, it was found in a major study cited, went to those in the bottom income quartile. Further, approximately one half of the first-time, full-time freshmen attending selective-admissions public universities in 1990 were reported to have family incomes of more than $60,000, while 24 percent came from families earning less than $35,000. In short, contrary to official mythology, ability to pay still seems to be a more important determinant of access to higher education than has been generally acknowledged.

Possibly the most fundamental assumption about American higher learning called into question in recent years has had to do with academic quality. Claims that students are poorly educated or are underachieving are hardly new, of course. But in the 1990s hard evidence was mounting to buttress claims of serious academic shortcomings. "In the past," noted the Wingspread Group, "our industrial economy produced many new and low-skill jobs and provided stable employment, often at high wages, for all. Now the nation faces an entirely different scenario: a knowledge-based economy with a shortage of highly skilled workers at all levels and a surplus of unskilled applicants scrabbling to earn a precarious living." The Wingspread authors added ominously, "Many of those unskilled applicants are college graduates, not high school dropouts."

Reiterating the familiar complaint about students who seem to want "the credential without the content, the degree without the knowledge and effort it implies," *An American Imperative* went on to observe: "The simple fact is that some faculties and institutions certify for graduation too many students who cannot read and write very well, too many whose intellectual depth and breadth are unimpressive, and too many whose skills are inadequate in the face of the demands of contemporary life" (p. 1). The "harsh truth," the document's authors avowed, concealed behind the large numbers who receive associate's and bachelor's degrees each year, is that "a significant minority of these graduates enter or reenter the world with little more than the knowledge, competence, and skill we would have expected in a high school graduate scarcely a generation ago" (p. 2).

Evidence to bolster the Wingspread Group's allegations was not difficult to uncover. A 1993 National Adult Literacy Survey (NALS), for example, found that surprisingly large numbers of college graduates were unable to use basic skills involving reading, writing, computation, and elementary problem-solving in everyday situations. Part of the problem, as suggested by a 1992 analysis of college transcripts conducted by the United States Department of Education, was the lack of system or rigor in collegiate curricula: 26.2 percent of recent bachelor's degree recipients had not earned a single undergraduate credit in history; 30.8 percent had not studied mathematics of any kind; 30.6 percent earned no credits in either English or American literature; and 58.4 percent had left college without any exposure to a foreign language. American higher education, complained the Wingspread Group, "now offers a smorgasbord of fanciful courses in a fragmented curriculum that accords as much credit for 'Introduction to Tennis' and for courses in pop culture as it does for 'Principles of English Composition,' history, or physics, thereby trivializing education— indeed, misleading students by implying that they are receiving the education they need for life when they are not" (p. 5).

The major thesis of the Wingspread manifesto was phrased in the bluntest of terms: "A disturbing and dangerous mismatch exists between what American society needs of higher education and what it is receiving. Nowhere is the mismatch more dangerous than in the quality of undergraduate preparation provided on many campuses. The American imperative for the 21st century is that society must hold higher education to much higher expectations or risk national decline" (p. 1). In dozens of books, articles and research studies produced throughout the 1990s, much the same theme has been enunciated time and time again.

Partly overlooked in the midst of heated debate has been the ineluctable fact that higher education in the United States in the latter half of the twentieth century has undergone a momentous transformation, a development largely unremarked upon in terms of its overall scope and significance. Considered as a whole, the changes that have occurred amount to a fundamental transmutation of American academe, a shift whose character and meaning, arguably, have not yet been fully assessed. Within the brief span of scarcely more than two generations, for example, the total number of post-secondary institutions has more than doubled, from around 1,600 on the eve of America's entry into World War II to almost 3,400 today. Nearly half of the colleges and universities operating in the 1990s did not even exist fifty or sixty years ago—which is to say, about 1,500 new collegiate institutions have appeared on the scene since 1945. Whereas schools hosting a few hundred students were the norm in the late 1930s, and institutions with upwards of 10,000 collegians enrolled were considered exceptional, by the mid-1980s more than a few campuses were attracting over 50,000 students at a time. Universities with student bodies exceeding 9,500 had enrolled only a fifth or less of all students attending college in the years immediately prior to World War II. By the mid-1980s at least 80 percent of all those attending college were enrolled in a school boasting more than 10,000 students.

Fewer than 1.5 million students were enrolled in college during the academic year 1939–40. In the last decade of the 1900s, enrollments numbered in excess of 13 million. Public colleges and universities, which barely outnumbered private schools in enrollment in 1940 or thereabouts (representing no more than a third of all colleges then in existence), today account for around 85 percent of all students attending college. Likewise indicative of a monumental shift has been the explosive growth of two-year colleges. In 1940–41, no more than 100,000 students were attending junior or community colleges, which numbered a few hundred at most. By the early 1970s, more than a thousand community colleges, over three-quarters of them publicly assisted, had opened their doors. Enrollment grew fivefold within the span of a single decade. By the closing years of the twentieth century, it was estimated that nearly 5 million students were enrolled in some 1,200 two-year schools, a few of which boasted enrollments in excess of 25,000.

Accompanying these enrollment increases have been profound changes in the composition of the American student body. Prewar undergraduate students were predominantly male (about 60 percent overall), overwhelmingly white (approximately 97 percent), and drawn mainly from middle or upper-class social backgrounds. Most students accepted into college throughout the late 1930s and early 1940s had placed in the upper third to upper fourth of their high-school graduating classes and had qualified for admittance under selective-admission policies of varying stringency. Most subsequently attended school full-time, lived on a residential campus, and pursued a liberal-arts curriculum bounded by numerous common course requirements (or, alternatively, a pre-professional course of study preparatory to a finite number of learned specializations). Among those completing the baccalaureate degree, the overwhelming majority did so within the traditional four-year period. Fewer than an estimated 100,000 students in 1940 elected to pursue a post-baccalaureate degree.

The Servicemen's Readjustment Act of 1944—popularly dubbed the G.I. Bill of Rights—more than any other single initiative, brought massive changes to higher education in the postwar era. Within a year following the cessation of hostilities, returning war veterans had begun flocking to the nation's campuses: ultimately some 2.2 million in all. By 1948 veterans were already responsible for almost half of the country's total collegiate enrollment; and their numbers were to prompt the beginnings of the greatest expansion colleges and universities had yet experienced. Contrary to some expectations, veterans quickly established themselves as serious students. Older, more mature and experienced for the most part than the collegians of the preceding decade, servicemen (and women—about 60,000 of them) indelibly altered the meaning and purpose of a college education. Attending college for them was neither primarily a rite of passage to adulthood nor an interval of leisurely intellectual contemplation and self-discovery. Still less did college mark an interim devoted to post-adolescent pranks and boisterous diversions. Completing a college education now came to represent climbing another rung on the ladder of opportunity, a necessary preparation for the challenge of making one's way in the new world of corporate business and industry.

If government-sponsored research on college campuses throughout the war years marked the first tentative step toward increased federal involvement in higher education, the G.I. Bill represented the next chapter of an evolving "partnership" between academe and the national government. A third phase began with passage of the National Defense Act of 1958, enacted at the height of official hysteria over the Soviets' successful launching of Sputnik. Over the course of the next decade, a flood of new legislation poured over scores of sleepy bucolic campuses, transforming them into bustling research and development centers sustained with federal largesse. Government-backed student loans, fellowships, and research grants became more plentiful and easier to obtain. Libraries, classrooms, laboratories, and residence halls sprang up everywhere—most of them ultramodern glass and concrete high-rise blocks overshadowing the stately neo-Gothic spires and quaint faux-colonial edifices of yesteryear. Meanwhile, whole new campuses were springing into existence to keep pace with expanding enrollments—a net increase of no less than 5 million students between 1960 and 1970 alone as postwar "baby boomers" came of age. Attending college was clearly no longer the exclusive prerogative of a privileged few. It was now seen as a necessary and almost inevitable prerequisite for success in modern mass society.

Beginning in the late sixties and early seventies, women, blacks, and other minorities in ever increasing numbers began attending college. Of the three and a half million new students enrolled in the 1970s, for example, well over three-fourths were female; and within a few short years women for the first time outnumbered their male counterparts on campus. What was valid for undergraduates held true among graduate students as well. Graduate enrollments more than tripled between 1940 and 1960 and exceeded a total of 1 million by 1970. By 1980, the number of women candidates for advanced degrees had equaled that of men. African Americans, historically underrepresented on campus in proportion to their numbers within society at large, were similarly enrolled in increasing numbers, beginning in the mid-sixties. By 1980 they numbered more than a million, representing close to 10 percent of all students attending college. In the mid-1980s, according to some estimates, both women and blacks in higher education had achieved rough proportional representation relative to the nation's population. Fully 40 percent of all African Americans attending college, however, were enrolled in two-year schools. About one in every five was attending a predominantly or historically black institution.

By the mid-nineties, the shape of higher learning in America bore scant resemblance to the overall pattern predominating a quarter-century before. Traditional students had dwindled in numbers, their places now occupied by a new breed of "nontraditional" collegians. By 1994 there were more women than men among the almost 14 million students enrolled on campuses across the country. Close to 45 percent were over the age of 25, including an estimated 300,000 over the age of 50. Minority Americans of varied hues and origins constituted about one-fifth of all enrollments in higher education.

Almost half of all college students were attending school part-time and intermittently rather than full-time and without interruption. The typical college undergraduate more often than not was holding down a part-time job or was even employed full-time while pursuing his or her college degree. Thanks in part to an explosive growth in the number and size of large urban commuter campuses, there were more students living at home or off-campus than there were in dormitories or in fraternity and sorority houses. Married students or single parents with children to support while attending school had become commonplace. In stark contrast with the past, fewer than one-third of undergraduate college students toward the close of the century had declared a major in the liberal arts; and nearly 60 percent were pursuing occupational or professional studies, many of which had not been enshrined within a collegiate degree program or had even existed two or three decades previously. Whether or not academic leaders in the 1990s were responding adequately to the unique needs of nontraditional students, in the minds of some critics at least, remained very much an open question.

Demographic shifts aside, many other major changes marked the transformation of academe throughout the last decades of the twentieth century. Some were both far-reaching and profound in their potential implications for the century ahead. Small, private liberal-arts colleges (the less prestigious among them at least) faced an uncertain future as they witnessed a continuing decline in their share of student enrollments. Dwarfed by burgeoning numbers of institutional colossuses devoted to research, professional or technical training, and public service, undergraduate institutions pledged exclusively to undergraduate teaching were cast on the defensive. Prospects for their very survival appeared extremely problematic in the eyes of many. Simultaneously, if there had ever been a time when a consensus prevailed about the central core of liberal study appropriate to baccalaureate-level studies, in the aftermath of the tumult and student disruptions of the 1960s, it seemed obvious that any such consensus had long since suffered erosion.

Attempts to "democratize" colleges and universities, to make them less elitist and restrictive in character, symbolized by the abandonment of selective-admission policies and their replacement by systems allowing open admissions, troubled many observers. So far as populist reformers were concerned, opening up the colleges to new students was a measure long overdue. Detractors, on the other hand, lamented what they characterized as a loss of standards and a consequent dilution of "higher" learning. The much-touted "knowledge explosion" of the postwar era likewise reworked higher learning in unexpected ways, spawning a bewildering multitude of new disciplines and subdisciplines competing for space within already overcrowded curricula. Prospects for restoring some type of common learning to undergraduate education as the antidote to fragmentation and excessive specialization thus appeared doubtful at best. Increasing impersonality and bureaucracy necessitated by skyrocketing enrollments likewise spelled a palpable loss of academic community, a sense of shared purpose and identity within academic institutions.

Overall, it must be observed, the character of American higher education toward the close of the twentieth century is radically different from what it once was a scant few decades ago. In the first place, the picture nowadays is not that of a "system" so much as it is of an untidy array of small liberal-arts colleges, two-year community colleges, technical institutes, local and regional universities, and sprawling research universities, both public and private, with different but overlapping identities, missions, and functions. Second, students who attend colleges today do not much resemble so-called traditional collegians: they pursue academic credentials under radically dissimilar circumstances; and they seek degrees with expectations and needs quite unlike those prevailing in a bygone era. Third, for good or for ill, postsecondary curricula have been transformed. Courses of instruction are broader, more varied, and more specialized than ever before. Fourth, in some cases the linkages between academics and occupations have been drawn tighter; and career-related considerations seem to loom larger in the minds of many than ever before. The very notion of a curricular "core" or of common learning of any sort whatsoever has been thrown into dispute. Fifth, the typical collegiate environment bears scant resemblance to the one experienced by college students of an earlier generation. There is less paternalism and more freedom, but there is also more technocratic rationality and bureaucratic machinery with which to contend. The role of local, state, and federal government in academe is likewise larger and more important than in the past. Finally, societal expectations and aspirations for higher education are broader, more insistent, and more intrusive than ever before. Accordingly, standards or criteria for judging the performance of colleges and universities have also changed.

Clearly, the closing years of the century mark an opportune time for taking stock, for reassessing the past performance and future prospects of higher education in the United States, with a view toward understanding how it has come to assume the form or shape it now displays. The aim, of course, is not to contrast the present unfavorably with an imagined idyllic past. Still less is it to minimize current shortcomings in American higher education by measuring them against the array of more modest precedents afforded by the historical record. Rather, the need is to create a sense of context, a setting within which both continuities and essential discontinuities with the past may be examined fruitfully.

A few disclaimers and caveats regarding the present historical account of the development of higher education appear to be in order. Retracing historical ground covered by previous authors, it should be emphasized, poses a daunting prospect. Students of the history of American higher education have not lacked for source materials; and in point of fact, several excellent studies have appeared over the years. Among them must be counted Frederick Rudolph, *The American College and University: A History* (1962); John S. Brubacher and Willis Rudy, *Higher Education in Transition: A History of the American Colleges and Universities, 1636–1976* (1976); and Laurence Veysey, *The Emergence of the American University* (1965). Each in its own way has long been considered a standard reference in the field. Also helpful has been the compendium of source materials assembled some few years ago for the Association for the Study of Higher Education (ASHE) by Lester F. Goodchild and Harold S. Wechsler, *The History of Higher Education* (1989). Many other, more specialized studies might be mentioned as well.

The presumption behind the writing of this particular work has been that it might be possible to generate something more concise and less voluminous than previous works, even while extending and updating, rather than attempting to supplant them. The aim, in sum, has been to offer a more "accessible" historical account, useful chiefly for nonspecialists and a more general readership than the audiences for which earlier studies were intended, though without sacrificing essential material.

Accordingly, this is an historical narrative not overburdened with the extensive detail and technical analysis appropriate to a more specialized study. Some material is synopsized from standard works in the field, revised and added to as necessary. Works by Veysey and Rudolph especially have been relied upon extensively, not so much in matters of interpretation or analysis, but more as references and guides to anecdotes and illustrative "quotable quotes." The author's indebtedness in this respect to earlier histories is expressly and gratefully acknowledged.

Most of the discussion is framed by composites rather than specific institutional examples or illustrations—hence considerable detail is left out when the picture is painted with very broad brush stokes. Major references drawn upon are cited in the Sources and References section, and should be consulted for additional background reading. Throughout, a conscientious effort has been made to incorporate new scholarship and insights from a rich and growing literature previously unavailable. Formerly, it was said, the history of education was treated at too primitive a level to be of much interest to professional historians. Unquestionably, that harsh judgment is no longer warranted. There exists an abundance of first-rate material from which to draw, much of which informs the present narrative.

A conscientious attempt has been made to deploy a frame of reference generous enough to accommodate several different discussions of institutional structure and organization, curricula and instruction, governance questions, sometimes the particulars of faculty and student life, and issues of basic social purpose and function. However, no single architectonic theme, no grand interpretive synthesis, is advanced in an effort to comprehend the whole. Any such project extends far beyond the ambition of this work.

At a point in time when cultural inclusivity has become increasingly *de rigueur* in historical writing, it may be worth emphasizing the point that no attempt has been made to construct a true "global" history of higher education. Thus, the great imperial libraries and teaching institutions traditionally associated with China's successive dynasties from the Sui-T'ang era onward are not cited. Nor is any account provided of oral teaching and devotional centers nurtured by the Vedantist and so-called heterodox philosophic schools of ancient and pre-modern India. Only cursory attention is given to Nestorian and, later, Muslim *scriptoria* that stretched across the Near and Middle East from the Persian court to Samarkand and Baghdad between the tenth and thirteenth centuries. Immense centers of higher learning that once flourished in the principal West African cities of Jenne, Gao, and Timbuktu under the Songhay imperium from the thirteenth to the late sixteenth century are similarly left unmentioned.

These omissions are in no way intended to denigrate or deny the fact that great centers of advanced learning have existed at various historical points, in many different cultures around the world. The unabashedly "Eurocentric" focus of the present work derives, rather, from a felt need to confine the narrative to a discussion of the historical antecedents of American higher education and its subsequent development down to the present time. The historical fact of the matter is, American colleges and universities are mainly an outgrowth of, and elaborations upon, European and English traditions, and behind them, those of Greco-Roman civilization—not African, Indian, or Chinese. Moreover, understanding and appreciation for how the past has shaped the texture of American academic life at the end of the twentieth century are—and should be seen to be—logically independent of any given individual's racial or ethnic background, ideological predilections, or gender.

Standard histories of American higher education typically begin with the colonial period—which, one supposes, is a bit like coming in for the end of the third act of a play. The very earliest colleges in North America in fact were very much a product of European social forces and cultural movements underway well before the early 1600s; and those in turn were outgrowths of trends at work since the time of the late Renaissance, and so on. Consequently, Part I of the present work opens with a necessarily cursory look to beginnings in remote antiquity, then traces the evolution of institutions of higher learning throughout the classical and Hellenistic periods, and on into the high Middle Ages. The origins of the first European universities are treated, as well as their subsequent evolution and permutations from the thirteenth to the early eighteenth centuries. Discussion of the development of modern European higher education is broken off at the point where the focus of the narrative turns to colonial North America. It would require separate volumes to examine European institutions of higher learning over the past two centuries in any meaningful way.

Part II offers an overview of American colonial and antebellum colleges from the early 1600s through to the midpoint of the nineteenth century. For the post–Civil War period, the subsequent narrative analyzes formative events and circumstances surrounding the emergence of comprehensive land-grant institutions, sectarian or denominational colleges, and the beginnings of the prototypical American university.

Part III is given over to the main outlines of the history of American academe in the twentieth century, from the opening years of the 1900s and the appearance of large corporate research institutions of higher learning through to the century's closing decade. Finally, in Part IV, contemporary criticisms of colleges and universities in the United States are briefly examined and assessed in a concluding historical retrospective.

Lastly, it needs to be said, there is no tacit assumption behind this brief work that American institutions of higher learning somehow represent a "culmination" of what has gone before. For its intended readership, the central question that drives the narrative to follow is simply: *What preceded American higher education within the Western cultural tradition and how did the modern American college or university subsequently come to be what it is today?* Every effort has been made to make the account accessible to anyone minimally conversant with the social and intellectual history of Western civilization. More important still, as a social and intellectual history, rather than an institutional chronicle, the effort throughout has been to keep the narrative reasonably compact. The extent to which all of these aspirations have been achieved satisfactorily, of course, must be left ultimately to the judgment of readers.

PART I

HISTORICAL ORIGINS
AND ANTECEDENTS

1

Higher Learning in Antiquity

BEGINNINGS: THE OVERCONFIDENT CANDIDATE

"From your childhood to your adult age you have been reposing in [school]," the teaching master reminds one of his older students. "Do you know the scribal art you have pursued?" The student retorts confidently, "What would I not know? Ask me, and I will supply you the answer." The senior scholar is skeptical. He predicts—correctly, as it turns out—that his boastful protégé has an inflated estimation of his own scholarly attainments. A long and difficult examination ensues.

The hapless student fares poorly. Throughout the course of the interrogation, set in a school courtyard, the aspiring scribe is required to translate back and forth between two quite dissimilar languages, one archaic and the other vernacular. He is tested over several different kinds of calligraphy and esoteric scripts. There are questions pertaining to various classes of clergy and the ranks within other types of professions. Others treat the preparation of official documents and seals in excruciating detail. He is required to analyze a long list of song categories and problems of choral direction. At one point, the master asks the candidate to explicate technical details of the "tongues," or technical terminologies, employed by priestly officials, silversmiths, jewelers, shepherds, and master shippers. Mathematical problems dealing with the proper allocation of foodstuffs and conducting land surveys are dealt with at length. Finally, there are questions of technique in playing different musical instruments.

At this point the examinee abandons his faltering efforts and turns upon his teacher, accusing him of lack of thoroughness in his instruction. Attempting to shift the blame for his lackluster performance to his mentor, the student berates the teacher for not having prepared him sufficiently. The teaching master responds with a sharp rejoinder. "What have you done, what good came of your sitting here? You are already a ripe man and close to being aged! Like an old ass you are not teachable anymore. Like withered grain you have passed the season. How long will you play around?"

His harangue continues in the same vein at length. Then, apparently relenting, he breaks off to extend the failed candidate some hope for his future. "But, it is still not too late," he observes sternly. "If you study night and day and work modestly and without arrogance, if you attend to your colleagues and teachers, you still can become a scribe! Then you can share the scribal craft which is good fortune for its owner, a good spirit leading you, a bright eye, possessed by you, and that is what the palace requires."

The so-called *Examination Text A* from which the above exchange is drawn is of historical interest on several counts. Dating back to between 1720 and 1625 B.C. (and purportedly reflecting a still earlier period in ancient Sumer, around 2300–2100 B.C.), this particular Babylonian document constitutes one of the very earliest pieces of evidence for institutionalized "higher learning" in remote antiquity.[1] It serves also to reveal something of the complexities of a long and demanding course of studies, a regimen Sumero-Akkadian students were obliged to master before attaining full-fledged status as scribes (Sumerian: *umbisag,* or more commonly, *dubsar;* in Akkadian, *tupsarru,* literally, "tablet-writer").[2] As the composition itself attests, a long preparatory period of study and training was required before a candidate was examined over his mastery of the vaunted "scribal arts" (Sumerian: *namdubsar;* Akkadian: *tupsarrutu*) and could be considered a true *dubsar gagazu* (Akkadian: *upsarr mudû*), a "scribe rich in scholarship."[3]

THE TABLET-HOUSE OF ANCIENT MESOPOTAMIA

Both textual and archaeological evidence attest to the existence of scribal institutions of learning flourishing all along the axis of the *al-Jarirah* or "island" formed by the Tigris and Euphrates Rivers by no later than the second half of the third millennium B.C., several centuries before the appearance of their counterparts among the Egyptians. The emergence of formal schooling in ancient Mesopotamia may be accounted for by the early development of large-scale cereal agriculture (supplemented by horticulture and animal husbandry). It in turn must have necessitated a developed "storage economy," complete with means for recording wages and rations, registering land titles and rentals, crop payments, transfers of staples and materials, and similar transactions. At the center of this complex economic circulation system stood the temple, which served also as the pivot of the broader social and political order. These autarchic "landed sanctuaries" or cultic preserves would have been supported by extensive land holdings, the management of which required a literate class of administrators.

Writing fragments unearthed from the archaic temple of E-Anna in Uruk, to cite a case in point, reveal the presence of such a literate class well established by the midpoint of the third millennium, and further open up the possibility of organized instruction conducted under temple auspices. Overall, it can be assumed that the invention of cuneiform was at once the necessary and sufficient condition for the emergence of a literate bureaucracy. The scribal class, in turn, represented a functional response to the need for efficient record-keeping within an ever-increasing system of administrative control.[4]

Likewise supportive of the growth of a scribal caste was the ascendancy of the royal court as a major center of power. Mesopotamian courts, no less than temples, required the service of literate bureaucrats for conducting affairs of state (correspondence, tax collections, conscriptions, and so on), and correlatively, schools in which to prepare scribes for their multiple tasks. The many economic, political, administrative, and literary tablets recovered so far suggest that the number of scribes, of varying ranks and titles, who practiced their craft in the service of temple and court from Sumerian times onward must have run into the many thousands. Included among their numbers were "junior" and "high" scribes, both public and private copyists, liturgical specialists, assorted cultic functionaries, administrative factotums, commercial letter-writers, notaries, seal inscribers, stele engravers, registrars, land surveyors, court advisors, royal secretaries, diplomatic envoys, and many other classes of court retainers.[5]

"Tablet writers," it is plain, considered themselves members of an intellectual elite (*dumu gir*), and perhaps justifiably so. Undoubtedly the high scarcity value of literacy translated into special standing, as suggested both by the range of important occupations open to them exclusively, and by a common scribal boast that they alone were fit to dispense counsel, or *nagida* (Akkadian: *masartu*), to kings and other members of the reigning aristocracy. Generally speaking, if the literati were not themselves members of the ruling class, at least they enjoyed the patronage and respect of the rich and powerful.

The school in which scribes received their training was called the "tablet house" (Sumerian: *édubba;* Akkadian: *bît-tuppi*).[6] By the middle of the third millennium B.C. such preparatory institutions were scattered across the entire *wadi arifidan* or "twin rivers basin" of the Tigris and Euphrates. There were thriving enterprises in Uruk, Ur, Shuruppak, Isin, Larsa, Nippur, Babylon,

Saduppûm, Kish, Sippar, Mari—in virtually every major metropolitan center throughout the whole region. Model lessons and compositions recounting aspects of school life supply surprisingly detailed if not always coherent indications of how the *édubba* was staffed, the nature of the instruction offered, and the content of the curriculum. Assisting the tablet-house "father" (*adda édubba*) or "master" (*ummia; ummianu*) was a *sêsgal* or "elder brother," a clerk (*ugula*) and a "proctor" (*lu gisshurra*), not to mention several teachers of the various specialized subjects comprising the curriculum. Apparently the *édubba* course of instruction was as far-ranging and comprehensive as it was difficult. Scattered references throughout the corpus of Sumerian schoolhouse literature make mention of a diverse array of subjects: accounting, geometry, musical notation, law and legal phraseology, grammar, poetry, history, courtly and priestly etiquette, and much else besides.[7]

Thus, it is apparent that the comprehensive and far-reaching nature of the course of studies mandated for graduation required many years to complete. School instruction began at a relatively early age and could continue in many cases on through adolescence and well into adulthood.[8] The latter portion of instruction and study, resting as it did on a preparatory foundation consisting of years of training within a formal institution of learning, may justifiably be considered "higher education," of a type roughly comparable with that developed elsewhere at later dates in antiquity. Whether conducted in a temple with its adjacent library or within the precincts of a royal place, specialized or advanced training in mathematics, literature, possibly law, medicine, and theology was in fact both characteristic of, and ultimately indispensable to, the shaping and maintenance of the earliest literate civilization to emerge at the dawn of recorded history.

ADVANCED LEARNING IN EGYPT

The historical priority of Sumer over Egypt in the development of high civilization is generally acknowledged by most scholars.[9] By what period of time the former preceded the emergence of an indigenous Nile River culture remains largely speculative, however. As in Sumer, both temple and palace as economic and social institutions were to play important roles in the emergence of a maturing Egyptian civilization. Systems for reckoning and writing made their appearance early on, sometime in the third millennium. Unfortunately, direct evidence for some form of organized instruction is largely lacking for the period of the Old and Middle Kingdoms (c. 2700–1800 B.C.). So-called wisdom literature, most notably three pieces, the *Hymn to the Nile*, the *Instruction of Amenemhet*, and *Instruction of Duauf*, imply that at least some scribal schools were functioning toward the end of the Old Kingdom, particularly as temple agencies.[10] Additional evidence from a slightly later date indicates they had grown considerably in numbers and importance by the time of the outset of the Empire (c. 1570 B.C.). The expansion of a bureaucracy of priests and scribes to service the administrative needs of an ever-expanding imperium thereafter rather strongly suggests the prevalence of training institutions, as in Mesopotamia. Also as was the case in Sumer, scribes came to enjoy close associations with the ruling classes; and the prestige attached to the rank of a high-ranking scribe was considerable.

More basic still to the attraction of the scribal vocation, for those capable of deciphering the mysteries of writing, was that it offered one of the few alternatives to a life of arduous manual labor. Numerous passages in the *Instruction of Duauf,* for example, drive home the point that a scribe's life is infinitely to be preferred over that of the common laborer. The artisan must constantly wield his chisel; the farmer's neck and back strain with his heavy loads; the cobbler spends his life cutting and tearing leather; a smith sweats at his furnace, "stinking more than fish offal." But in contrast, "no scribe lacks sustenance, the things of the king's house; Mesekhent [the goddess of birth] has prescribed success to the scribe; at the head of the officials is he set; and his father and mother give thanks." The aspiring student scribe is advised to discipline himself and to live as an ascetic: "Rest content with your diet. If three loaves satisfy you, and you drink two pots of beer, and the belly is not yet content, fight against it. . . . Speak no hidden words and utter no insolent words. . . . Set not your heart on pleasures, or you will be ruined." Further advice is offered: "Acquire for yourself this great calling of a scribe; pleasant and abounding in possessions are your palette and papyrus roll, and blissful will you be every day. . . . Be a scribe who is free from forced labor and protected from all [burdensome] work." A scribe need not dig with a hoe for his living, and he does not need to carry a basket. The scribe, the reader is reminded, "directs every work that is in this land."[11]

Entry to the scribal craft probably was gained by apprenticeship, through private tutoring, or most typically by attending a temple school, referred to by the colloquial title "House of Books." The most common forms of scribal instruction were likely of a quite rudimentary character, aiming at little more than students' acquisition of basic literacy skills. But scattered references to a "House of Life," some dating back to the Old and Middle Kingdoms and others to the period following the reign of Rameses III (1195–1164 B.C.), suggest that some students progressed far beyond. Presumably only a small number of scribal scholars of exceptional ability entered upon the more extensive courses of higher study in astrology, medicine, liturgy, and theology.[12] Again, specific details are lacking.

The House of Life, such as that excavated at Tell El-'Armana and dating to the Eighteenth Dynasty (1570–1305), sometimes was a part of a much larger complex of administrative edifices, including both a temple and a palace. Likely to be found in every major city, the House of Life probably combined the functions of a royal mortuary, a *scriptorium* for the copying of documents, a library, and a center for learned discussion among scholars. Less clear is the extent to which it may also have served as a teaching institution. The situation respecting a select few endowed temple schools points more clearly to the existence of centers for higher instruction in ancient Egypt. At Heliopolis, Karnak, Memphis, and Heracleopolis, for example, it is almost certain that priest-scholars were afforded opportunities to devote themselves to advanced study in the several branches of mathematics, astronomy, medicine, physics, cultic arts, and other higher disciplines.

THE SOPHISTS OF CLASSICAL GREECE

As depicted in Plato's *Protagoras,* the appearance of the sophists (*sophisai*), or teachers of "wisdom," in fifth-century B.C. Athens was heralded by intense excitement among the city's youth.[13] Here were the first full-time teachers, scholars who insisted on being paid handsomely for their labors, savants who offered systematic instruction and a defined course of instruction in those practical arts needed for making one's way in the world. This, after all, was a society that had never known much in the way of organized education, excepting the efforts of aristocrats' tutors, paramilitary drillmasters, and humble, much-ridiculed schoolmasters of elementary writing. Understandably then, the arrival from the Greek colonies in Italy and Asia Minor of a class of peripatetic professors who put on brilliant forensic demonstrations, who conducted sample lectures in the *agora,* or marketplace, and had their virtues lavishly touted by the students who accompanied them in their wanderings, must have been electrifying. Skeptics might complain that all such self-styled wise men were frauds and charlatans, that they "made the worse appear the better cause," that they were lacking in scruples. But to the crowds of eager youths who gathered to hear them hold forth, the sophists seemed to offer an irresistible opportunity to acquire a useful brand of wisdom: the learning needed to arm oneself for political strife and to prepare for a public career.

It was an opportune time. Athens at the midpoint of the fifth century B.C. was in the midst of a major political, social and economic efflorescence. Hard on its triumph over Persian invaders and its rise to a preeminent position as leader of the Greek states, Athens had emerged in the first half of the century as a burgeoning commercial and maritime metropolis. Advances in ship-building, navigation, agricultural technology and commerce were bringing unprecedented prosperity. The coming to power of a middle class encouraged a more fluid, egalitarian order; and the city's citizenry already was experimenting with democratic self-government. Increased contacts with foreign peoples and cultures had conferred a new urban sophistication or worldliness as well. In short, the age of Pericles and the building of the Parthenon marked a new era of social transformation and cultural creativity.

Accompanying these changes was a nascent spirit of questioning and skepticism. The shift in speculative thought was away from the mythic worldview of the past and toward critical analysis and reflection upon the world of human affairs. The old Homeric sense of a moral order governing the cosmos, an impersonal fate that preserved the natural equilibrium of things amidst change, was giving way before an awakened interest in observation and analysis. Belief in the Olympian pantheon likewise was being seriously undermined; and a more secular spirit was clearly abroad in the land. "Concerning the gods," as one of the early sophists declared, "I have no means of knowing whether they exist or not, nor of what form they are; for there are many obstacles to such knowledge, including the obscurity of the subject and the shortness of human life."[14]

To the sophists, arid disputations over the ultimate nature of reality as advanced by Thales, Anaxamander, Leucippus, Democritus, Anaxagoras, Heraclitus, Zeno—indeed, of all the speculative philosophers of the past— seemed increasingly irrelevant. In the sophists' view, the intellectual chaos generated by the old cosmologies, each particular theory contradicting or negating its competitors, was neither plausible to common sense nor applicable to practical human needs. As the Roman writer Cicero put it much later, speaking of the sophists, they "brought philosophy down from heaven to the dwellings of men." Possibly there were no transcendent truths, these teachers of wisdom conjectured, no ultimate norms or ethical standards. If religious beliefs, political institutions, and rules of moral conduct are all humanly created conventions, if social conventions are merely local and not universal, then conceivably all standards of good and bad, right and wrong, of morality and immorality should be considered equally unsubstantial and ephemeral.

Further, given the now-apparent unreliability of sensory experience, perhaps all understanding is only a matter of subjective opinion. Everyone creates his own reality. Genuine objectivity is impossible. And if everything is relative, then the only knowledge worth possessing is that which serves the individual. The effort that had gone previously into understanding the cosmos, it was argued increasingly, might now more productively be applied to human affairs, to ethics and politics. Correlatively, the aim of human thought should be to serve human needs; and only personal or individual experience was thought to afford a basis for achieving that aim. Each person therefore should be advised to rely upon his own powers and abilities to make his way through the world.

What the sophists urged upon their listeners were the practical arts of oratory and rhetorical persuasion, as well as an array of studies in history, music, and mathematics. In a culture that had always valued fluency and style in forensic debate, speech-making, and the like, here was precisely the sort of training by means of which a young man could improve his life chances. No longer bound by social class or the circumstances of birth, provided he applied himself, any ambitious student might aspire to better himself and ultimately achieve high position within the social order. Students signed up in droves to sit at the feet of these new teachers.

"Human excellence," proclaimed Protagoras (481–411 B.C.), a recent arrival from Abdera on the Thracian coast, "is the proper care of one's personal affairs, so as best to manage one's own household, and also of the state's affairs, so as to become a real power in the city, both as a speaker and man of action."[15] Despite its novelty, so bold a declaration must have exercised a powerful appeal in a society where the spoken word potently molded public opinion. Because any aspirant to power had to be an effective speaker if he was to be heard in the courts and halls of government, Protagoras advised the importance of the study of language—grammar, etymology, syntax—and its uses in rhetoric. Such studies would assist each student to clarify and shape his thoughts and enable him to express them eloquently.

Briefly, Protagoras' dictum, "Man is the measure of all things," presaged the message of all the later sophists to follow. Truth, goodness, justice, or beauty are relative to particular human interests and needs. Hence there can be only particular truths valid for a given time and place. Morality varies from one society to another. There are no absolute canons of right and wrong decreed in the heavens to fit all cases; private judgment alone must determine what is fitting and appropriate in any given instance or situation. It is incumbent upon each individual accordingly to erect a personal standard of authority through his own careful reflection and judgment. The means to establish the measure of all things follow from the study of logic and oratory.

Those who followed after Protagoras extended much the same message. Among the more celebrated teachers of wisdom were Gorgias of Leontini, the Sicilian ambassador to Athens (c. 427 B.C.) who possibly had been influenced by the rhetoricians Tisias and Corax of Syracuse; Prodicus of Ceos, who stressed the importance of literary studies; Euenos of Paros; such lesser lights as Antiphon, Prodicus, and Thrasymachus; Hippias of Elis, a prominent rhetorician who professed to teach a kind of polymathy or compendium of all popular knowledge that allegedly traded scope for depth; and Hippias' two most important successors, Euthydemus and Dionsodorus, both of whom enjoyed fame as teachers of a special method of disputation that reputedly allowed one to hold sway without having mastered much detailed knowledge at all.

Delicately balancing a healthy ethical common sense against crass opportunism, the sophists quickly gained in popularity. It was almost as though the young men who were drawn to them sensed that opportunities for success in public life, now so enlarged and exacting, could be seized successfully only by attending to their message. The question of the day had become, What kind of education is needed for helping the individual secure political advantage in public affairs? And to that query the sophists had an unequivocal answer: *rhetoriké,* the study of the arts of persuasion.

Learning was not inexpensive. As their public acceptance increased, so too did the fees they charged for lecturing, ranging from the not inconsiderable sum of one-half to four drachmae. Admission to "popular" lectures (*epideixeis*) open to the *hoi polloi* ("the entire populace") was the least expensive; those admitted to an extended sequence of private lectures were apt to be charged much more, up to one thousand drachmae. When a certain Demosthenes offered two hundred for one-fifth of the course of studies given by one distinguished orator, for example, the latter is recorded as having replied haughtily, "I cannot cut my course into slices; the finest fish are sold whole." Poor students, inspired by the hope of a future return on their investments, were reportedly forced to go to extreme lengths and to make great sacrifices in order to raise the necessary tuition.

On the positive side, the education purveyed by the sophists offered a more popular and democratic form of instruction than the Greek city-states had ever known before. The curriculum in its essential outlines was much broader and more comprehensive than any previously available, emphasizing logic, grammar, rhetoric, oratory, eristics and dialectics as the subjects most useful in preparing young men for public careers. But it went far beyond extended training in the technicalities of public address alone. Though no two sophists sponsored exactly the same program, their instruction typically encompassed a wide range of subjects, including oftentimes trenchant commentary on contemporary public affairs. As a group, the sophists tended to condemn the institution of slavery; they ridiculed the chauvinistic pretensions of the Athenians; and they often preached against the follies of war. In other words, the sophists were iconoclasts. The way in which the new teachers were willing to tackle social issues frontally, while attacking the conventions of the old order, could not help proving irresistible to a younger generation.

On the other hand, early on "sophistry" evidenced the symptoms of superficiality and the pedantic shallowness for which it would soon become notorious. It was one thing to affirm, as did Hippias, that it is logically possible to learn to argue for or against any formal proposition whatsoever. It was quite another, perhaps, to require students to memorize set speeches verbatim, together with lists of prepared questions and answers on both sides of a given argument, without necessarily insisting on genuine comprehension and understanding from them. The latter practice, it might be observed, was to lead eventually among other things to a proliferation of the infamous *technai,* or handbooks on rhetoric and grammar, so much disdained for their lifeless artificiality by later generations of scholars.

Not surprisingly, it was almost inevitable that the relativism, skepticism, and radical individualism of the sophists should have aroused strenuous opposition from guardians of the old order. So far as traditionalists were concerned, when itinerant teachers questioned both the authority and the very existence of the gods, it was evident the very foundations of Hellenic culture itself were under attack. If there are no ultimate truths accessible to human reason, as the sophists rather clearly implied, and if goodness and justice are simply matters of subjective preference or taste, then religion, morality, the state, indeed society itself, were endangered. Also, the sheer rhetorical virtuosity of the sophists aroused special ire. A sophistic character in Aristophanes' play *The Clouds,* for example, boasts, "I mean to say, we argue up or down—Take what you like—It comes to the same end."

Reaction to the intellectual challenge posed by the sophists was not long in coming. The response was exemplified most clearly in the life and teachings of the Athenian philosopher Socrates (c. 469–399 B.C.), whose intellectual "midwifery" was directed to a goal diametrically opposed to that of the sophists, namely, the uncovering of transcendent knowledge quite distinct from mere opinion.[16] In common with the sophists (with whom he was initially confused by his detractors), Socrates insistently sought answers to questions that had not been posed before and sought to undermine conventional beliefs and assumptions. Likewise, he shared a conviction that the purpose of philosophy was the proper conduct of one's life, not special insight into the nature, origin or constitution of the cosmos. Where he differed fundamentally was in what he considered the appropriate goal of human inquiry. The sophists professed to teach others how to live successfully in a world where all knowledge was considered relative and all moral standards mere conventions. The Socratic aim, however, was to discern a morality separate and apart from subjective preference. What it sought, in the final analysis, was a knowledge of how life should best be lived without primary regard for personal advantage. Furthermore, unlike the sophists, Socrates offered his instruction free of charge.

The form of argument he developed and with which his name is most closely associated, the so-called Socratic method, usually took the shape of a conversation or "dialectic." His characteristic strategy was to engage a listener on a topic and then request that some critical term be defined more carefully. When a provisional definition was proposed by one of his students, Socrates would then relentlessly analyze one by one the implications inherent in the definition or argument under scrutiny. Successive attempts to define the essence of that something—the meaning, for instance, of "courage" or "virtue" or "beauty"—were rejected as too vague, or too broad, or too narrow, or as inherently self-contradictory. The objective throughout was never merely destructive. Rather, Socrates' aim was to produce a consistent idea of universal validity, one capable of withstanding all further criticism. The truth of anything, Socrates taught, resides not in individual perceptions, as Hippias and others had claimed, but in the element common to all perceptions, the concept or definition. Thus, ethical relativism holds that virtue varies according to place, time, or circumstances. There can be no universal morality. But if one could attain a definition of, say, virtue holding true under all conditions, he claimed, then one could judge each individual's actions insofar as they accorded with or contradicted the universal concept of virtue. The generalized principle of "virtue" in and of itself could then be shown to be binding upon all who aspire to be virtuous. The final measure would not be private opinion, but objective truth.

Socrates' life, as is well known, ended in martyrdom. Never popular in his role as gadfly, incessantly puncturing the pretensions of the rich and powerful, forever sowing doubt and confounding those who claimed to be wise, it was not long before Socrates began to attract powerful enemies. Particularly insofar as he insisted that knowledge could not be purchased secondhand like a prepackaged commodity (as the sophists seemed to promise) and that true wisdom was won from within only by critical self-reflection and intellectual struggle, his was bound to be a minority voice. Socrates' injunction to "know thyself" and his declaration that the unexamined life is not worth living were hardly likely to endear him to the masses either. In the end, caught up in a political backlash of intrigue, he was forced to drink the hemlock. Recounting the final death scene, Plato's *Phaedo* has a character observe, "This . . . was the end of our friend, a man, we should say, who was the best of all his time that we have known, and moreover, the most wise and just."

PHILOSOPHIC SCHOOLS

Neither Socrates' instruction nor that of his sophist opponents required the benefit of an actual physical facility. A small space in the open marketplace of the city, or perhaps within the colonnades of a nearby temple where one might find shelter from the sun, usually sufficed for a teaching master, surrounded by his band of students. With Plato (c. 428–348 B.C.), however, who was Socrates' most famous pupil, may be found one of the first instances of a literal "school" devoted expressly to higher learning among the ancient Greeks.

Following an eventful career as a world traveler and would-be advisor to several successive rulers in Sicily, Plato had returned to his native Athens in midlife to devote himself to teaching. Around 388 and for the next four decades until his death, he offered instruction in or near a school (*gymnasion*) located some two miles northwest of the city. Situated in a grove dedicated to the early folk hero Academus, the school had long been known popularly as the Academy. Plato's institution apparently inherited the same name, an appellation it was to bear thereafter throughout the many centuries of its existence.

In his early writings, according to one interpretation at least, Plato's teachings differed little from those of Socrates. Considered as a whole, however, the *corpus Platonicum* evolved into a much more ambitious and comprehensive philosophic program than anything contemplated by "the wisest man in Athens." In common with his mentor, he rejected the sophists' claim that man is the measure of all things. But in rejecting relativism, Plato went on to construct a grand metaphysical and ethical system guided by a vision of a just and harmonious social order.[17] Within an ideal state, he taught, education would become a tool for sorting and screening people according to their respective abilities, inclinations, and natures. The bulk of the state's citizenry would be simple artisans, shopkeepers, and the like. A separate class of warriors would be assigned the task of serving as guardians, protecting the state from its enemies and ensuring internal order. A third class of philosophers, guided by perfect knowledge of the arts of governing, would be set to rule.

Unlike Socrates, Plato came to believe that only a select few were capable of casting off the chains of myth and superstition in order to achieve true wisdom. The culmination of years of arduous study and analysis, Plato argued, was a kind of supra-rational, intuitive apprehension of a transcendent reality wholly unlike that disclosed by ordinary sensory experience. Only the "philosopher-king" (or queen), he concluded, was competent to discern the true archetypal Forms or Ideas from which sensory particulars within the empirical world ultimately derive. Thus guided and inspired by knowledge of the Good in and of itself, those entrusted to govern in an ideal state would rule with perfect justice for all.

The Academy in which Plato conversed with his disciples evolved over an extended period into a major classical center of learning.[18] Little is known about the formal curriculum in Plato's own time. Presumably it included dialectic (the study of discussion, discourse, forensic debate, and formal argumentation), mathematics, and metaphysics. Nor are there reliable indications of precisely how instruction was managed within the Academy. Plato himself apparently gave few formal lectures. Note-taking, he once insisted, is simply a mnemonic device to preserve pseudoknowledge; whereas truth, once grasped, requires no aids to memory and will forever be remembered.[19] Most likely, such teaching as was done was conducted through oral questioning and responding, or some other form of dialectic. If there were formal presentations at all, judging from the evidence left by former students, they would have dealt primarily with geometry, advanced mathematics, and number theory.[20]

Upon Plato's death, the estate was bequeathed to Plato's nephew, Speusippos (348–270 B.C.), under whose tenure the school seems to have lapsed into relative obscurity.[21] The Academy regained some of its old vigor and fame when it passed into the hands of Arcesilaus (315–240 B.C.) who assumed control around the year 270. A third revival ensued a half century or so later with the accession of Carneades of Cyrene (ć. 214–129 B.C.). He was followed in turn by Clitomachus, of whom little is known, and he subsequently by a certain Philo of Larissa. In 88 B.C. the Academy came under the directorship of another illustrious figure, Antiochus, and entered upon yet another period of prosperity and influence. All told, the Academy was to remain in operation for a full nine centuries, until its final closing in A.D. 529.[22]

The second major school of philosophy in Athens (in the dual sense of a systematic body of thought and a literal institution in which its teaching was housed) was that of Aristotle (384/3–322 B.C.).[23] He was born in the Greek city of Stagira in Chalcidice, not far from the Macedonian court at Pella. In the year 366 B.C., when he was eighteen, Aristotle arrived at the Platonic Academy where he remained for almost two decades. After Speusippos assumed the directorship of the school upon Plato's death, Aristotle reportedly took leave for the island of Lesbos where he pursued his interests in medicine and marine biology. Thereafter, according to traditional accounts, he sojourned at the court of Hermias and subsequently served for several years as tutor to Alexander, son of the Macedonian monarch Philip. Around 335–334 B.C. Aristotle returned to Athens, which by now was firmly under Macedonian control. There in a rented building adjacent to the *gymnasion* known as the Lyceum (*Lykeion*), he founded his own teaching institution, quite possibly under the direct patronage of his protégé Alexander.[24]

For Plato, the architectonic purpose of philosophic study was to produce enlightened rulers and political advisors. Aristotle's goal, however, was in certain respects far more disinterested. For him, the pursuit of knowledge for its own sake, without regard to extraneous considerations, seems to have been paramount. His works on methods of inquiry, for example, consisting of the *Categories, On Interpretation, Prior Analytics,* and the *Posterior Analytics* (collectively known as the *Organon*) treat issues of epistemology; of the nature of knowing and of knowledge; syllogistic reasoning; induction; and procedures for the scientific demonstration of empirical truths. His *Physics* develops an elaborate theory of causation and an account of changes in the phenomenal world; while the *Metaphysics* sets forth his views on the constitution of reality (one differing considerably from the Platonic view). Elsewhere, as in the *Ethics* and *Politics,* Aristotle turned to an analysis of the organization and grounding of values in the human world. Of greatest interest perhaps, historically speaking, has been the Aristotelian account of excellence, or intellectual "virtue" (*areté*), as freedom from the merely vegetative and appetitive modes of human existence.[25]

From the outset, the Aristotelian Lykeion seems to have enjoyed great success. Of particular note were the tree-lined walks traversing the school's grounds, from which the school derived the popular name of the Peripatos (*peripateo,* "I walk"). Plato's school had tended to emphasize mathematical and logical studies. Teaching in Aristotle's Lyceum, however, seems to have concentrated more upon biology, physics, ethics, politics, logic, and rhetoric. Some have suggested that a formal curriculum or sequence of studies evolved, consisting, first, of the natural sciences, and only secondly the normative disciplines of ethics, politics, and rhetoric.

Whatever the truth of the matter, Aristotle taught at his school for about twelve years, until shortly after Alexander's untimely death, whereupon he was forced to flee an anti-Macedonian uprising in Athens. Aristotle eventually sought sanctuary at Chalcis, in Euboea, where he died the year following, in 322 B.C. Meanwhile control of the Lyceum had passed to Theophrastus of Lesbos (371–287).[26] He in turn was succeeded by Eudemus of Rhodes, a specialist in astronomy and mathematics; then by Straton of Lampsacus, after which time both the school's reputation and its original founder's influence gradually began to wane.[27]

A third major school of philosophy, together with an informal institution for the propagation of its doctrine, traces back to a certain Antisthenes (c. 440–390 B.C.), a contemporary and reputed associate of Socrates, who had studied under Gorgias and then struck out on his own as a teacher of rhetoric. After Socrates died, Antisthenes is said to have opened a school of philosophy in the *gymnasion* of the Cynosarges, from which derived the term "Cynicism" to identify his precepts and teachings. Of Antisthenes' own views little is known, other than an injunction to his followers to seek the highest good, which is a virtuous life, and to shun a life of unbridled desire.[28] Diogenes of Sinope, a disciple of Antisthenes, developed the school of thought in a new direction, one predicated upon the untrustworthiness and fallibility of all human knowledge. Sometime around 310 the school attracted the support of a young Cypriot merchant by the name of Zeno of Citium (c. 336–264 B.C.). Having studied for a time under the Cynics, Zeno eventually disassociated himself from them and opened his own school among the colonnades *(stoai)* of the Athenian marketplace. As was customary, the term "Stoa" came into use to refer to the teachings of Zeno's followers, including Cleanthes of Assus (331–232 B.C.) and Chrysippus of Tarsus (c. 280–207 B.C.), among many others. The term "Porch" *(poecile)* became the traditional poetic reference to the place of instruction associated with Stoic teachers.

Interestingly enough, it was the Stoic philosophy that proved most enduring in the Hellenistic period and that was to find widest acceptance, for example, among the Roman intelligentsia in succeeding centuries. Stoicism as a school of thought resists succinct characterization.[29] In brief, Stoic philosophers taught that the cosmos is an ever-changing flux known but imperfectly through human sense impressions. Behind its apparent fluidity and chaos, however, there operate lawlike regularities ordained by an intelligent Providence. By seeking to understand the ordering processes under which the world operates, a wise person through rational reflection and contemplation attains to a knowledge of that which is true, virtuous, and beautiful. The proper end of human existence is to live a life in harmony with nature. Happiness and ultimate fulfillment stem from an acceptance of what life brings, whether it be painful or pleasurable. Such disciplines as grammar, dialectic, rhetoric, logic, poetry, and music should be regarded as useful means to this supreme end: a life lived in accordance with the dictates of reason.[30]

The fourth philosophical school of the period was that of Epicurus (342–270 B.C.), a native of Athens. In the year 306, having returned from a teaching position at Mytilene, he opened a place of instruction in his home on the outskirts of the city, in a suburb called Melite. Celebrated for its beautiful cultivated grounds, it rather quickly came to be known as the *Kepos,* or "Garden." Here men and women alike were invited to gather for instruction, scholarly discussion, and leisurely reflection. Epicurean thought was highly eclectic, unsystematic, often mystical in its character. Basically, a central theme was the quest for human happiness. True "joy" *(hēdonē)* in life—hence the term "hedonism" to characterize Epicureanism—was considered to come not from attempting to satisfy bodily pleasures, but, rather, from the more austere pursuit of emotional tranquility and the inexhaustible mental pleasures of the soul.[31] Self-discipline, avoidance of the distractions of earthly pleasures, and spiritual concentration—these were the means by which the highest and most satisfying forms of happiness could be secured. Although the original Garden of Epicurus closed temporarily in the year 79 B.C., after having been guided under some fourteen different directorships, the influence of its founder was to outlast the institution itself by many centuries.[32]

THE HELLENISTIC PERIOD

Even before Plato's death, growing disunity among the Greek city-states had increased their vulnerability to external threats, most notably that posed by the expansion-minded Macedonians. By the middle of the fourth century when the threat could no longer be ignored, it was too late. The major military debacle suffered by the Greeks at Chaeronea in 338 B.C., for example, for all intents and purposes spelled the end of Greek independence and the establishment of Macedonian hegemony throughout Hellas. Yet even after the ancient city-states lost their sovereignty, the classical culture they had nurtured was being dispersed or exported throughout the eastern Mediterranean world by Alexander the Great. Nor did his premature death halt the process. The emergence of Hellenistic culture, very much rooted in that of classical antiquity but enriched and extended by contacts with the peoples of the Near East, proceeded largely unimpeded by the disintegration and division of the short-lived Alexandrian imperium.[33] Scores of major municipal centers, for example, rather quickly evolved from sleepy provincial outposts into bustling cultural centers in their own right: Antioch in Syria; Seleucia on the Tigris; Pergamon; Jerusalem; and Pelusium, Oxyrhynchus, Ptolemais, and Alexandria in Egypt, the last-named founded by Alexander himself in 332 B.C. Nevertheless, all of the important elements of Greek "civilization" (*oikoumene*) continued to hold sway, regardless of who actually held the reigns of political power, whether it was the Seleucids in the east, the Ptolemies in Egypt, or the Macedonian *diadochi,* or generals, in Greece itself. Ultimately, of course, even the mighty Romans who alone eventually achieved the goal of unified control over the entire Mediterranean basin, were to succumb to the allure of Greek culture, or *paideia,* even as they impressed upon it the flavor of their own history and institutions.

Details on the precise shape of institutionalized higher learning from the third and second centuries B.C. onward into the period of Roman domination tend to be somewhat sketchy. It is known there existed a number of major philosophic enclaves, each offering a definite course of study, such as those established in Delphi, Beirut, Antioch, Rhodes, and Pergamon.[34] Most were direct offshoots of the original philosophical schools of Athens. With the passage of time, however, some of the philosophical schools appear to have lost much of the originality and breadth of vision of their respective founders, evolving instead into tight semireligious communities separated from the ongoing life of society. In later centuries, under Roman rule, such schools came to resemble evangelical centers more than academic institutions in any traditional sense. Something of the sort is indicated, for instance, by the tendency of their graduates to venture forth proselytizing, organizing rituals, and caring for adherents of the various sects. Whatever their specific character, philosophical schools ministered to the needs of a relatively small intellectual class.

How women were educated, and to what degree, at any time throughout the entire Greco-Roman period still remains something of a mystery. Tantalizing clues abound in scattered references to females who were obviously well versed in Greek culture, to women who were celebrated as philosophic disputants, renowned for their wit and polished literary style, and who otherwise won acclaim for their accomplishments. Aristodama of Smyrna, who gave recitations of her poetry throughout Greece and was accorded many honors, supplies a case in point. Again, among the *hetairai,* or "courtesans" who formed a special social class of their own, mention is made of highly respected and well-educated women such as Thais, Diotima, Thargelia, Leontium, Aspasia, and quite a number of others. Many philosophers, like Epicurus, did not hesitate to admit women into their schools; and the practice may have been more widespread than has heretofore been suspected.

Far more influential than the philosophic strand were the oratorical or rhetorical traditions of Greek learning, so vividly illustrated by the continued existence of hundreds of rhetorical schools scattered throughout the Hellenistic world.[35] As it happened, the practices and customs of Greek elementary and intermediary schooling had survived virtually intact in all the Hellenistic states. Private schools presided over by *grammatistes* taught simple reading, writing and mathematical calculation. Poorly linked or articulated with elementary grammar schools were intermediate-level institutions conducted by the grammarian, or *grammatikos.* Higher or advanced education, properly speaking, overlapped to an indeterminate extent with secondary education, and was centered in the public *gymnasion,* each typically consisting of an open-air atrium or courtyard (*palaistra*) at the center, surrounded by a colonnaded walkway forming a square or rectangle, around the borders of which were arranged the enclosed *exhedrae,* or "theater halls," which saw service as classrooms. Other recesses were reserved for oiling rooms and steam baths.

As in the original Athenian model, public involvement in the life and operations of schools of all levels was cursory at best. Typically, each city had an education "director," or *gymnasiarchos,* assisted by a subordinate deputy known as the *paidonomos.* Together, they presided over the formal governance and general administration of the city's educational endeavors. Apparently, courses of advanced instruction, some extending upwards of five or more years, were sometimes conducted in public buildings and under public auspices. Equally common, however, were entrepreneurial or private-venture schools.

Whatever the precise circumstances of the case, when a youth had successfully completed his literary and grammatical studies under the *grammatikos*, he would leave to seek instruction with a specialist in oratorical eloquence, the rhetor. An aggregation of disciples attracted to a common master was referred to poetically as a "chorus" or *thiastos*, or "fraternity." The popularity of rhetorical schools, which were to be found in practically every major town and city, is difficult to account for, given the radically altered changes that had transpired since their inception. Rhetoric as a subject of instruction had been highly functional when city-states were democratic and autonomous. Yet long after the fifth century, when independent city-states were virtually nonexistent and oratory no longer served directly for social advance and preferment, the rhetoricians continued to practice their craft. Moreover, they continued to attract large student followings. So deeply ingrained was the notion in Greek culture of the importance of speaking with grace and eloquence that rhetorical schools flourished unabated.

Still, testimony to the growing aridity and social irrelevance of the rhetors is not lacking. In fact, evidence abounds that the models for good speaking rhetoricians increasingly employed were at once pretentious and divorced from the practicalities of cultural life. The *Master of Rhetoric* authored by the Roman satirist Lucian, for example, affords a case in point as it ridicules professorial foibles.[36] The work opens with a speaker declaring, "You ask, my boy, how you can get to be a public speaker, and be held to personify the sublime and glorious name of 'sophist.'" With heavy-handed irony the speaker continues, "Life, you say, is not worth living unless when you speak you can clothe yourself in such a mantle of eloquence that you will be irresistible and invincible, that you will be admired and stared at by everyone."

The narrative continues with words of advice: "Bring with you, then, as the principal thing, ignorance; secondly, recklessness, and thereto effrontery and shamelessness. Modesty, respectability, self restraint and blushes may be left at home, for they are useless and somewhat of a hindrance to the matter at hand. But you need a very loud voice, a shameless singing delivery, and a gait like mine. . . . Have also many attendants, and always a book in hand." Further, "you must pay special attention to outward appearance, and to the graceful set of your cloak. Then cull from some source or another fifteen, or anyhow not more than twenty, Attic words, drill yourself carefully in them, and have them ready at the tip of your tongue."

As Lucian extends the burlesque, his character advises a would-be rhetorician to acquire the trappings of scholarship: "Hunt up obscure, unfamiliar words, rarely used by the ancients, and have a pile of these in readiness to launch at your audience," he advises. "The many-headed crowd will look up to you and think you amazing and far beyond themselves in education. . . . If you commit a solecism or a barbarism, let shamelessness be your sole and only remedy, and be ready at once with the name of someone who is not now alive, and never was, either a poet or a historian, saying that he, a learned man, extremely precise in his diction, approved the expression."

Besides the philosophical and rhetorical schools, a third type of institution of higher learning prevalent throughout the Hellenistic period was, for want of any better designation, the scholarly "research center." Illustrative examples include major teaching and research complexes at Ephesus, Smyrna, Rhodes, Pella, Cos, and Pergamon, to name only the more prominent. Foremost among them, however, and far surpassing all others in its longevity, influence and scale was the famous "Temple of the Muses" (*Mouseion*) or Museum, at Alexandria on the Egyptian coast. Located in a city whose inhabitants eventually numbered nearly a million or more people by the first century, Alexandria was a model of urban planning, boasting spacious paved streets laid out in regular order, an excellent harbor to facilitate maritime commerce and trade, and numerous parks, monuments, and temples. It was a fitting site for one of the most brilliant centers of learning of the entire Hellenistic world.[37]

The Alexandrian Museum was formed under the first two Ptolemaic rulers, Ptolemy Soter (d. 283 B.C.) and his son and successor, Ptolemy Philadelphus (d. 247 B.C.). Its first director (*prostates*) was the Aristotelian scholar Demetrius of Phaleron (c. 345–283 B.C.) who had studied under Theophrastus at the Athenian Lyceum. After Demetrius fell from favor, he was replaced by Zenodotus of Ephesus, then by Callimachus of Cyrene who arrived during the reign of Ptolemy II, though it is uncertain whether the latter served formally as a director. Thereafter, leadership passed into the hands of the scholar Lycophron, to Apollonius of Rhodes, and then to Eratosthenes of Cyrene (c. 275–195 B.C.). The latter was succeeded by the grammarian Aristophanes of Byzantium (c. 260–183 B.C.) and thereafter by a long line of less well-known successors.

Endowed as a storehouse for manuscripts, much like the ancient Mycenaean storehouses or the great seventh-century library at Nineveh under Ashurbanipal, the *Mouseion* attracted large numbers of scholars across the Greek world. According to the contemporary writer Strabo, the complex was part of the royal palace of the capitol, and boasted "a public walk, an [amphitheater] with seats and a large house which is the common mess-hall of the men of learning. . . ." Under successive enlargements, its facilities included copying rooms, botanical and zoological gardens, and a massive library, the largest of its kind in antiquity. Less flattering in his description of the institution's operations was the report of Timon in his *Satirical Poems*. "In this populous Egypt of ours, " he observed, "there is a kind of bird-cage called the Museum where they fatten up any amount of scribblers and readers of musty tomes who are never tired of squabbling with each other."[38]

The roster of intellectual luminaries attracted to the Museum was extensive: Archimedes of Syracuse; the geometer Euclid; Herophilus of Chalcedon, who founded a medical school early in the third century; Erasistratus of Ceos, his contemporary, who was a specialist in anatomy; the geographer Strabo of Pontus; and countless others. The Museum's chief attraction to scholars, of course, was its collection of manuscripts, including thousands of papyrus scrolls gathered by agents all over the Mediterranean and Near Eastern world. Subjects treated included all of the major disciplines and fields of knowledge: astronomy, poetry, grammar, mathematics, medicine, natural history, philosophy, philology, and so on. Estimates of the total number of holdings, including Babylonian, Indian, Egyptian, Greek, and Hebraic works, vary considerably. Some accounts, beginning with the great catalogue, the *Pinakes* (Greek: *pinax,* tablet), cite upwards of 400,000 unsorted titles and 90,000 catalogued works, besides an additional 120,000 single books housed in smaller collections in the Temple (known as the "Daughter Library" and the *Serapiana,* or *Serapeum*). If we recall that all books in antiquity had to be laboriously reproduced by hand, the extent of the Museum's holdings is all the more impressive.

Scholars who inhabited the Museum's communal college were primarily academics engaged in full-time investigation and research. From their ranks flowed a steady outpouring of commentaries, textual glosses, and original writings in all fields of knowledge. So far as is known, resident scholars were not obliged to give lectures or otherwise involve themselves in the actual work of teaching. Nevertheless, many did so on a voluntary basis. It is in this sense that the Alexandrian *Mouseion* qualifies as a center of higher learning, as does the Museum and Library at Antioch, founded under Seleucid patronage during the reign of Antiochus the Great (223–187 B.C.) under the directorship of Euphorion of Euboea.

The chief competitor and rival to the Museum at Alexandria was its counterpart at Pergamon in Asia Minor.[39] Although the exact date of its founding remains unknown, toward the end of the third century B.C. its library holdings had grown sufficiently extensive to arouse jealousy in Alexandria. Sometime toward the end of Eratosthenes' reign in Alexandria, the rivalry had grown in intensity to the point of open political hostility. Seeking to preserve the preeminence of the Alexandrian Museum, for example, the Egyptian monarch Ptolemy Epiphanes went so far as to declare an embargo on papyrus, the

essential writing material required for augmenting Pergamon's library holdings. In response, it is said, during the reign of Eumenes II (197–159 B.C.)
when the Stoic philosopher Crates of Mallos had begun directing rhetorical
and grammatical studies at the Museum and building up its holdings, scholars
turned to parchment and vellum derived from animal skins for the copying of
documents. By the first century B.C. the Library's collection numbered over
200,000 volumes.

Ranking slightly behind Alexandria and Pergamon as a scholarly enclave
but more active as a teaching center was a school of higher studies established
at Rhodes in the first century B.C. Among its more illustrious students are
counted Aeschines, Mark Antony, Pompey, Julius Caesar, Cicero, Brutus,
Cassius and Dionysius Thrax.

ROMAN HIGHER EDUCATION

"Among the Greeks," Cicero once observed, "some devote themselves with
their whole soul to the poets . . . and to the arts which mold the mind of youth
to humanity and virtue. The children of the Romans, on the other hand, are
brought up that they may one day be able to be of service to the fatherland, and
one must accordingly instruct them in the customs of the state, for that I hold
to be the highest wisdom and virtue." The contrast between Greek and Roman
can easily be exaggerated, but it points to a real difference. Lagging some two
or three centuries in their cultural development, the Romans finally accepted
Hellenic traditions, but only when their own native ideals were crumbling in
the face of the more luxuriant, sophisticated culture to which they had exposed
themselves in the process of building an empire. Cicero was essentially correct
in claiming that the Roman mind was more prosaic, practical, and severe than
the Greek. It revered law and order, duty to the state, ancestral traditions, and
the ideal of self-sufficient dignity. The popular ideal among the Romans was
one of masculine vigor, an ideal which tended to produce a proud, overbearing, and sometimes cruel and rapacious people. And perhaps it may be observed
that it was this fundamental difference of national temperament or character that
explains why the indigenous Roman civilization could never fully accept the
Hellenistic outlook. If the Romans ultimately embraced the culture of their subject people, it was as a graft on a very homely Roman stock. The fruit of that
grafting was something subtly different from either original Hellenic classicism
or its Hellenistic outgrowth and expansion.

In the mid-third century Rome headed a proud and confident state dominating all of the Italian peninsula, its appetite whetted for still further conquest.
First Carthage, seat of the vast Phoenician empire extending along the African
coast, succumbed, followed by Macedonia, Syria, Greece, and most of Egypt

as well as the other states bordering the eastern Mediterranean. Yet in the process, even as the Hellenistic world was brought to its knees and fell under the heel of the Roman legions, the Hellenization of Roman life proceeded apace. Imported slaves and returning soldiers brought back with them all of the important elements of Greek learning—philosophy, arts and sciences, rhetoric, grammar—"pouring in as a great flood," as Cicero described it. Even though Romans disdained their conquered subjects as inferiors, they instinctively acknowledged the superiority of Greek culture. Neither the fulminations of traditionalists like Cato the Elder nor the force of official edicts availed to stem the tide of Hellenistic influence.

The cultural conquest of the Romans was most vividly illustrated by changes in Roman education. Whereas the indigenous Romans undoubtedly had rudimentary schools for the teaching of basic literacy sometime prior to the third century B.C., not until much later did they require or even desire much more in the way of formal institutions of learning. But when changes did come, they were adapted more or less directly from the customs and usages of Hellenistic Greeks. The Greek elementary school became the Roman *ludus* ("play") school, complete with the *ludi magister* or *litterator* as a humble teacher of the rudiments of literacy. By the late third century, it was already common for sons of the more privileged classes to pass on then to the instruction offered by the better-paid *grammaticus* (the nearly exact counterpart to the Greek *grammatikos*), where they were introduced to the study of literature in both Latin and Greek, along with work in geography, music, mathematics, geometry, and astronomy. Works by Homer, Aesop, Horace, Terence, Sallust, Livius, Virgil, and Cicero, among others, soon established themselves as school classics. Later, as courses of instruction were expanded, the work of the *grammatici* began to impinge upon, or overlap with, more advanced studies. For older youths, studies in grammar, rhetoric, and dialectic were developed, followed by extended instruction in geometry, arithmetic, astronomy, music, medicine, and architecture.

By late Republican times, in the second and first centuries B.C., rhetorical studies had achieved a degree of popularity and acceptance to the point where the Roman Senate itself grew alarmed. In an edict dating to 161 B.C., for example, it issued one of several solemn proclamations on the subject: "It is reported to us that certain persons have instituted a new kind of discipline; that our youth resort to their schools; that they have assumed the title of Latin rhetoricians; and that young men waste their time there, whole days together. . . . These innovations, contrary to the customs and instructions of our ancestors, we neither approve nor do they appear to us good. Wherefore it appears to be our duty that we should notify our judgment both to those who keep such schools and those who are in the practice of frequenting them, that they meet our disapprobation."

But as the Roman observer Suetonius remarked, in a classic understatement: "However, by slow degree, rhetoric manifested itself to be a useful and honorable study, and many persons devoted themselves to it both as a means of defense and of acquiring reputation." Owing to the influence of Crates of Mallos, the Stoic Panaetius of Rhodes (c. 180–111 B.C.), Diogenes, Critolaus, and many others who flocked to Rome, and in increasing numbers remained for a time to teach, rhetors' schools of the type found elsewhere throughout the Hellenistic world steadily gained in popularity.

The Roman version of the Greek rhetorical school was virtually indistinguishable from the original model. Most were private ventures, though with the passage of time more and more fell under public patronage and limited control. (In the latter instance, as in Rome and elsewhere, state or municipal involvement at first was confined mainly to the assignment of *exhedras,* arranged like miniature theaters opening out onto the porticos of the public forum.) The rhetor, or *magister dicendi,* enjoyed far more status and prestige than did his colleagues at the lower school levels; and he was apt to command, for example, a salary as much as four times that earned by the lowly grammarian. What *rhetores* offered was a more or less standardized course of studies in correct linguistic usage, essay writing, literary exegesis, and the composition of declamations, the last of which were practiced by those intending to win success in the courts. Declamations typically were of two types: the *suasoriae* (arguments for alternative courses of action in response to a specified hypothetical situation) and the *controversia,* or legal cases, where the speaker was obliged to build an argument on behalf of a fictitious civil or criminal suit.

Intellectually, efforts were made to integrate the rhetorical arts within a much broader curriculum framed and informed by ethical considerations. "No one," Cicero insisted in his *De Oratore,* "can hope to be an orator in the true sense of the word unless he has acquired knowledge of all the sciences and all the great problems of life." Similarly, the first-century rhetorician Quintilian proclaimed in the preface to Book I of his *Institutio Oratoria* that his intent was to outline the education of the perfect orator. The first essential, he avowed, is that such a person should be a virtuous individual distinguished by moral goodness as well as exceptional powers of speech. The ideal orator, he continued, is a citizen who can be entrusted with the management of any public or private enterprise, who can offer wise counsel to representatives of the state, who can establish good government by his legislation and correct it by his judgments. In short, the orator must be a moral philosopher in the truest sense, as well as one well versed in the theory and practice of public speech.

Some who enrolled in the rhetorical schools undoubtedly professed the ideal of acquiring *humanitas,* the broad culture defining a well-rounded individual.[40] Yet, one suspects, taking into consideration the deeply ingrained Roman concern for practicality and narrow utilitarianism, most who sought to become skilled orators hoped to profit eventually in the marketplace from the training they received.

Wherever Roman control penetrated, rhetorical schools followed, not simply within the urban centers of the Near East but to the north and west as well. Both Massila and Autun in Gaul had such schools not long after Julius Caesar's conquests, as did Bordeaux; and rhetors were to be found plying their trade by the third century A.D. in places as far distant as the northern provincial towns of Britain. Accompanying the dispersion of rhetorical and philosophical schools in the later centuries of Roman rule was a growing tendency on the part of state authorities to attempt to regulate their operations more closely. In earlier times, local municipal authorities had been allowed to set salaries and to proscribe excessive fees. But by the late third century, that authority had been seriously undermined. Constantius Chlorus, for example, is recorded as having fixed the salary paid to Eumenius, head of the school at Autun. Again, Emperor Julian in 362 A.D. went even further in claiming the right to appoint candidates to specific professorships, a prerogative previously not contemplated by his predecessors. "I command," he further declared, "that if any man should wish to teach, he shall not leap forth suddenly and rashly to this task, but he shall be approved by the judgment of the municipal senate and shall obtain the decree . . . with the consent and agreement of the best citizens." Likewise, salaries were determined by the state for teachers in the schools of Smyrna, Ephesus, Tarsus, and Antioch. An imperial edict by Gratian in 376 left towns free to appoint their own teachers but stipulated what salaries would be paid. Finally, an edict of Theodosius and Valentinian in A.D. 425 went further still in forbidding the opening of any school except by imperial rescript.

THE HELLENISTIC DECLINE

From the first century A.D. onward, if not before, the satirical writer Lucian was joined by many others in complaining about growing degeneracy among the professorate and the artificiality of what was taught in higher schools. The Stoic writer Persius (A.D. 34–62), for one, was unsparing in his criticism of literary mannerism and the banality of the literature so often produced by school graduates. His first *Satire,* for example, derided the typical hack poet as "some fellow with a purple mantle round his shoulders lisping out with a snuffle some insipid trash about a Phyllis or a Hypsipyle or some other dolorous poetic theme, mincing his words, and letting them trip daintily over his palate." The historian Cornelius Tacitus (c. A.D. 55–115) in his *Dialogus de Oratoribus* offered an equally vigorous denunciation of the deterioration of academic studies so much in evidence already in his own time. Deploring what he considered excessive reverence for form coupled with a disregard for actual content, he issued a trenchant attack on the superficiality of theme and manner of delivery characteristic of most orators.

Juvenal's seventh *Satire* likewise is a biting indictment of a system of education devoid of social purpose or application to daily life. Assailing the scholars of the various disciplines in turn, he challenged the historian: "And is your labor more remunerative, you writers of history? More time, more oil, is wasted here; regardless of all limit, the pages run up to the thousands; the pile of paper is ever mounting to your ruin. So ordains the vast array of facts, and the rules of the craft. But what harvest will you gather, what fruit, from the tilling of your field?" The same critical theme was sounded in later centuries, with the loudest criticisms reserved for the consciously archaic style cultivated by scholars, and for the *crambe*—literally, "rehashed"—codifications of pedantry that allegedly passed for real knowledge within school curricula.

Despite the schools' supposed irrelevance, Gregory of Nazianzen (A.D. 329–390) offered especially vivid testimony to the rivalry that existed among supporters of various professors in any given city. "Most of the young enthusiasts for learning, noble and lowborn alike, become demented partisans of their professor," he reported. "Like those who have a passionate love of racing can scarcely contain themselves, but copy all the gestures of the jockeys, or bet upon the horses entered for the prize, although they hardly have the wherewithal to live themselves; so the students show a similar eagerness for their teachers and the masters of their favorite studies." Students went to extraordinary lengths to augment their own numbers. "They post themselves over the city, on the highways, about the harbor, on the tops of the hills, nay, in every isolated spot; they importune every passerby to join their faction. As each newcomer disembarks, he falls into their hands; they carry him off at once to the house of some countrymen or friend, who is bent on trumpeting the praises of his own professor, and by that means gaining his favor or exemption from his fees."

Confirming testimony is supplied in the writings of Libanius of Antioch (A.D. 314–392), a private teacher himself, who had studied and taught in Athens and in Constantinople, then in Nicomedia, across the Propontine Sea on the coast of Bithynia, before returning to his native Antioch. While living abroad, he noted, he had witnessed scenes where competing hordes of students loyal to different masters would descend upon some unwary new arrival to the city and fight with one another to take him prisoner until he declared his preference for a teacher. Once committed, the novice would then be led to the public baths for an initiation ceremony, followed by a lavish feast to celebrate his choice (usually at the newcomer's expense, if possible). Sometimes, Libanius wrote, riots would break out as rival gangs armed with rocks and clubs fought each other in the streets over the right to abduct a prospective addition to their ranks. When outbreaks occurred, no one was safe until the authorities intervened.

The general picture Libanius paints is one of disorder and chaos. Wherever there were schools, the resulting influx of students generated a carnival-like atmosphere. If not attending lectures or studying, he observed, students tended to give themselves over to gambling, whoring, horse racing, ball games, drinking, and playing practical jokes of one kind or another upon the hapless local citizenry. It was a constant struggle to maintain law and order; and authorities frequently found it necessary to imprison or fine the worst offenders.

Private teachers, dependent upon fees to augment the meager salaries permitted by civil authorities, tacitly condoned the recruitment of new students. Libanius reports, for example, the case of one schoolmaster from nearby Phoenicia who, while traveling abroad, received a dispatch urging him to return home quickly before all of his students were stolen from him by his competitors. Libanius himself had experienced problems in attracting enrollments until he rented a stall in the marketplace where he could conduct his classes. Even then he labored at a disadvantage, because unlike many of his rivals, he was not yet authorized to teach in the municipal *Mouseion*. Not until he had secured a municipal appointment was he entitled to a favored location within the shelter of the city's governmental center, or *bouleterion*. Even then, rival rhetoricians continued to harass him and make his life miserable.

The professorial life, he confided to his readers, was not all that the uninitiated imagined. "Be not misled by names like those of orators and professorial chairs, but listen to the truth from one who knows it well," he advised. "Some even now have no dwellings of their own, but . . . live in hired lodgings; or if anyone has bought a little house, it is still so mortgaged that the owner has more anxiety than if he had never bought it." The high cost of living led many professional schoolteachers to remain single: "One rhetorician counts himself a fortunate man because he has only a single child; another thinks his numerous family a real misfortune; the prudent avoid marriage altogether." Professors' economic circumstances, Libanius implied, had deteriorated: "In former days, the schoolmen used to stroll into the goldsmiths' shops, and talk freely with the craftsmen, finding fault with the workmanship of one, or pointing out the finer tooling, or praising them for promptitude, or blaming them if they were too slow." But no longer. "Now they have to deal mainly with the bakers, to whom they owe the very bread they eat; they have to promise that they will soon pay, and beg a little more meantime; they are driven to grievous straits, for they would gladly shun the shops, because they are ashamed to owe them money, but are forced by hunger to go to them again."

Indebtedness was allegedly chronic. "As the debt goes on increasing always, and no funds come in to meet it, they curse their literary craft, and carry to the bakers the earrings or necklace of their wives; they must not think what present they can give them to replace it, but only what other ornament there is to sell." As Libanius recounts it, at the end of a long hard day at school, the masters did not hasten back to their humble lodgings to enjoy their leisure as one might expect, but lingered on in their lecture halls, "because they know that they will feel their misery more at home." Exchanging stories of their woes offered scant comfort or solace: "They sit down and talk and bemoan their wretchedness to one another, but each finds that however piteous his tale, he has something worse to hear."[41]

EARLY CHRISTIAN LEARNING

The growing cultural challenge to Hellenism posed by Christianity was a gradual phenomenon in the Roman world, and did not become explicit until sometime late in the third century A.D. But even as the mighty Roman imperium began to crumble and decay, Christian communities were gaining in both strength and numbers. The Roman decline was almost imperceptible at first. It accelerated noticeably during the reigns of Severus (A.D. 193–211) and his son Caracalla (A.D. 211–217), and the trend was never reversed thereafter. From without came hordes of barbarians who sought to settle inside the empire's far-flung borders. As events would show, they could neither be bought off nor driven back. Internally, as imperial institutions began to weaken, the realm was wracked by almost constant political intrigue and upheaval. Roman coinage was debased; the army grew ever more undisciplined; and both the moral authority and political efficacy of the organs of centralized rule deteriorated. By the time of Emperor Diocletian's accession to the throne, Rome was firmly in the grip of an absolute despot.

Emperor Constantine's decision to found a new imperial capital in the East was partly an attempt to reverse the threatened disintegration of the ailing empire, but it was already too late. By A.D. 395 centrifugal pressures had led to the *de jure* division of the *imperium Romanum* into two autonomous parts, headed by two theoretically equal and independent monarchs. In the Greek East, détente with imperial Byzantium was achieved for a period of some three hundred years, albeit at great cost. In the Latin West, after Theodosius, titular authority continued until almost the end of the fifth century. Each successive ruler who came to power, however, seemed to enjoy less prestige and power than his predecessors. When the end finally came, the collapse of imperial authority was as total as it was irreversible.

Meanwhile, alternately tolerated and persecuted by civil authorities, communities of Christian adherents continued to practice their faith. Yet even as late as the fourth century when Constantine's celebrated Edict of Milan (A.D. 313) legalized Christianity and accorded it equal rights with official paganism, no single, unified church existed. Doctrinal consensus, a common body of canonical writings, some uniform system of ecclesiastical ranks and titles, a centralized governing structure to undergird official orthodoxy—all were lacking. Among other problems, communication among local churches tended to be fitful and sporadic at best. As a result, each separate metropolitan see at Antioch, Alexandria, Ephesus, Caesarea, Constantinople, Aquileia, Arles, Milan, Rome, and elsewhere pursued its own interests more or less independently of all others, proselytizing and organizing as its leaders saw fit.

The challenge for Christians throughout the first century or so had been simply one of collective survival in the face of a hostile, fundamentally uncomprehending world. In the second century, however, prominent Christian figures began turning their attention to an equally urgent intellectual task, that of apologetics. The basic problem in defining and defending Christian teachings was that virtually all had been preserved not in Aramaic or Hebrew languages but in Greek. The question then was how to reconcile Christian faith with Greco-Roman secular learning, how to render the content of religious belief in some form intelligible and persuasive to a culture shaped by Hellenistic paganism. To be sure, there were many Christian intellectuals who denied any such need. In their view, the realms of faith and reason had to be kept utterly separate and apart. Some—including large numbers of Latin Christians in the West, most particularly the church leader Tertullian—counseled disengagement from the world, and urged that secular learning be avoided altogether lest it contaminate doctrinal purity. Others, most particularly syncretist church leaders who had been steeped in Hellenistic thought before their conversion to the new faith, insisted that the reconciliation of religious faith with reason was easily accomplished—that, indeed, there was no inherent contradiction whatsoever to be resolved. Essentially, or so they argued, Hellenic learning afforded the means for completing, illuminating and, in the final analysis, confirming the truth of Christian teachings. Ironically enough, practically all the major protagonists, whatever their respective persuasions, framed their arguments in language and intellectual forms acquired in pagan schools.

Christian schooling, when it existed at all, was rudimentary at best. In the first century A.D. catechumenal instruction was sometimes offered by local communities of believers for prospective initiates as a means of encouraging adherence to a common set of doctrines and precepts. Later, simple catechetical courses of study relying upon a question and answer format were devised to help prepare evangelists for the task of seeking out new converts. Otherwise, Christians continued to attend Greek schools and built up no independent educational system of their own.

On the other hand, with the passage of time a few institutional centers devoted to the study of Christian doctrine did begin to appear. In Alexandria, for example, by the second and third centuries, groups of Christian students were taking up the pagan custom of gathering around masters for instruction, as illustrated in the case of Titus Flavius Clement (c. A.D. 153–215) and his student Origen (185–253), who directed a famous catechetical school within the city.[42] In the fourth century in Constantinople, Emperor Jovian (r. 363–364) reportedly authorized the establishment of an unnamed Christian institution of advanced learning "in the auditorium of the capital" to which scholars from throughout Christendom were drawn in large numbers. Otherwise there were relatively few Christian institutions of learning to be found in either the West or the East until the fifth century or thereabouts.

Throughout, periodic efforts were made to retain some semblance of state control over education and to initiate needed school reforms. During the reign of Valens (364–378), for instance, several edicts were issued relating to the need to maintain high academic standards; and in 369 the emperor decreed the tightening up of qualifications for the position of "philosopher," in a document which alludes to the "filthy crowd" that had "usurped the garb of philosophers." Impostors and charlatans, he declared, were to be banished forthwith and compelled to return to their respective municipalities of origin. The next year, in 370, Valens issued an order requiring students arriving in Rome or Constantinople to register their academic credentials and testimonials to good character with the master of tax assessment before seeking admission for study in some specialized discipline. The imperial tax service was further charged with general superintendence over all other matters relating to students. Authorities were made responsible, among other things, for seeing to it that students were well housed, that they remained attentive to their studies, and that they avoided all licentious behavior. Offenders were ordered to be flogged in public and then placed on board the next ship to be returned home. Monthly checks had to be made on each and every student, proper records maintained, and an annual report of all inquiries forwarded for imperial review.

Similar efforts resumed under Theodosius (r. 408–450) a half century later. Once again, charlatans and pretenders were to be prohibited from teaching. The so-called Capital School was reorganized and reformed. Regulations were issued governing the conduct of professors, including a prohibition against their renting out rooms to students in their own private homes. Each approved teaching master was to be assigned a designated location for lecturing so as to ensure order and any unseemly competition for available spaces. Awards were to be bestowed upon deserving professors "if they demonstrate that they are living a praiseworthy life, with approved morals, if they have shown skill in teaching, their eloquence in speaking, their subtlety in interpretation, and their fluency in dissertation."

Continuing imperial decline rendered efforts to supervise academic life ever more difficult. Justinian's successors from the sixth century onward were preoccupied with larger matters that only worsened over time, including Lombard advances into Italy and Slavic occupations of Thrace and Thessaly. Meanwhile, to the East, matters were equally desperate. In the year 612 Persian invaders fell upon Byzantium and were turned back only after protracted struggle. Two decades later, following the death of the prophet Mohammed, Arabic forces to the south launched the first of several campaigns of expansion, eventually extending their control as far north as Tarsus and Antioch. In 677 the great eastern capital at Constantinople was itself besieged by a Moslem fleet, and only desperate measures sufficed to avert a near-total Arab victory.

Constant warfare took a heavy toll so far as the preservation of Hellenistic learning was concerned; and the decline evident in Justinian's time was to continue unchecked throughout the seventh and eighth centuries and on into the ninth.[43] Only within scattered communities established by Nestorian Christians in Edessa, Nisibis, and Seleucia, deep within the emergent Islamic empire of the time, were efforts successful to maintain both Christian culture and ancient Greek learning. Interestingly, Moslem leaders proved themselves remarkably tolerant in this respect, allowing scholars to continue building up collections of works in mathematics, science, medicine, and philosophy.

Matters improved somewhat between the mid-ninth and eleventh centuries in Constantinople, where a major revival of learning took place. Beginning under the Amoran dynast Michael III (r. 842–867) and the combined patronage of his chief minister and regent, Caesar Bardas, and the patriarch Photius (810–891), a new school of higher learning was founded in the rooms of the Magnaura Palace (hence known thereafter as the School of Magnaura). Headed by a "principal" (*oekonemikos didaskalos*), the institution was endowed with chairs of geometry, philosophy, philology, and astronomy, and subsidiary professorships in music, arithmetic, grammar, law and medicine. Equally distinguished was the revived Capital School of Constantinople under Constantine IX (r. 1042–1055) where advanced learning was organized around two faculties: law and philosophy. Here admission was free to qualified students;

professors were paid from the public treasury; and the school's reputation for preparing lawyers and civil officials was unexcelled. At its inception, direction of the law faculty was entrusted to a famous legal scholar by the name of John Xiphinus (1018–1078) who was appointed head (*nomophylax*), while the head of the philosophy faculty went to his close friend and colleague, Constantius Pellus (1018–c. 1080), under whose stewardship the school propagated a major revival of Platonic and Neo-Platonic studies. Records of particular institutions aside, evidence that the study of letters remained lively in the late eleventh century comes from an account authored by Anna Comnena, the well-educated daughter of Emperor Alexius I (r. 1081–1118) who reported that schools were flourishing at the time of her father's accession to the throne.

In the West, a linear pattern of incremental educational decline was more pronounced from the fifth century onward. By the year 410 the Western empire had fallen completely under non-Roman domination and was isolated from Eastern influences and controls. Elementary *ludi* schools disappeared, as did the grammar schools, along with most higher instruction in the few rhetorical and philosophical schools remaining. For a time general learning was sustained in a few isolated Mediterranean settlements (Avignon, Marseilles, and Lérins) that had been left untouched by barbarian incursions. Elsewhere, some few efforts were mounted to reverse deterioration under such leaders as the Frankish king Clovis (r. 481–511), the Gothic monarch Euric (d. 473), and briefly under Theodoric and the mid-sixth-century ruler Chilperic I, not to mention Alfredus in England and Charlemagne in Frankland somewhat later, but these were exceptions to the general rule.[44]

Likewise, many of the early monastic communities at Milan, Vercelli, Vivariium, and Monte Cassino, among others, began taking up educational work, if only reluctantly. But as a rule, from the sixth century onward and for several centuries to come, the situation grew ever more barren. By the eighth century, if not before, the Latin Church had come to exercise a monopoly on all learning, now conducted under the auspices of local churches and monasteries and considerably reduced in its breadth of aim and the scope of its content. Of the din and clamor of the Latin and Greek rhetoricians, the endless disputations of the classical philosophers in their amphitheaters, or of hordes of eager students gathered at the feet of the countless orators that had once thronged the marketplace of every major city, nothing remained.

2

From Cathedral Church Schools to Universities

THE EARLY MEDIEVAL WASTELAND

Cultural and intellectual recovery in the early Middle Ages was a slow, painstaking process. By the end of the seventh century most of Europe lay in ruins. Antique monuments were destroyed; the old Roman roads, which had once afforded efficient transport had long since fallen into disrepair; whole cities had crumbled; and the past was largely forgotten. To the hordes of Vandals, Goths, Huns, Visigoths, Franks, and Saxons that had once overwhelmed the tottering Roman Empire now succeeded roving bands of indigenous brigands, mercenaries, and feudal barons. Innumerable local wars ravaged the land; and law and order ceased to exist. The great masses of the peasantry could hope for little more than subsistence, even as the rich and powerful preyed upon them at will. The nobility, meanwhile, retreated into the safety of its walled fortresses and castles. The long night of the Dark Ages had fallen.

Even within monastic enclaves where the tattered remains of ancient learning sometimes had been preserved, classical thought and culture were ignored. Competent scholars were far and few between; resources were scarce; and most of the original classical texts comprising the bulk of Greco-Roman learning had been lost.[1] With the exception of a very small learned minority, literacy—where it existed at all—was minimal at best. Moreover, the absolute primacy of Christian faith over secular concerns asserted throughout the early Middle Ages discouraged much interest in worldly matters. Clerics and monks for their part were absorbed with meditation upon the Scriptures, by means of which it was believed the soul might hope to attain salvation in the afterlife. Heaven, so to speak, absorbed the energies and attention of the devout. Any compelling curiosity about nature, science, literature, or philosophy was more or less effectively curbed. The sole and self-sufficient intellectual task worthy of scholarly human endeavor, it was held, was to contemplate the ways of God and the mysteries of Christian doctrine. All else was considered mere "vanity" or the work of the devil.[2]

CATHEDRAL CHURCH SCHOOLS

It was not until the early eleventh century that medieval Europe began to embark upon its recovery from centuries of invasion and disorganization. Technical innovations in agriculture and the mechanical arts were bringing a new level of affluence. Populations increased. Cities and towns started expanding; and a dynamic new middle class, organized for production and social purposes into guilds, communes, and fraternities, began making its influence felt. By the century's midpoint, the paternalistic authority of all-powerful vassals and lords had started to give way to systems of legal rights and obligations of a much more secular cast. Trade and commerce within and beyond the continent had quickened. Renewed contacts with the startlingly alien culture of Byzantium and beyond were beginning to spell a radical expansion of medieval Europe's intellectual horizons.[3]

As Western civilization underwent transformation, the Church's formerly rigid antipathy toward pagan writings and secular learning softened. Its intellectual and spiritual hegemony by now firmly established, non-Christian culture no longer seemed to pose so large a threat to the Church's authority. Intellectual accommodation seemed all the more possible if classical literature could somehow be assimilated within the Christian ambit. As a result, secular learning was no longer as devalued as it had been formerly; and clergy were allowed to peruse whatever few copies of ancient pagan manuscripts they could find, dissecting them for whatever wisdom they afforded. Over time, ecclesiastical officials came to view themselves as benevolent patrons of the new scholarship then spreading slowly across the continent, a revival inspired by texts imported from Arabic and Byzantine sources to the east and from Moorish sources across the Pyrenees in the south.

Symbolic of the Church's changing attitude was a proclamation issued in the year 1079 by Pope Gregory VII. Henceforth, he announced, bishops everywhere were ordered to have the *artes litterarum* taught at their churches. Similar in its tone was an official injunction issued by the Third Lateran

Council in 1179: "Since the Church of God, like a good and tender mother, is obliged to provide for the spiritual and bodily needs of the poor in order that they may not be deprived of the opportunity of reading . . . in every cathedral church, schools shall be reopened." Therefore, it was directed, "Let some sufficient benefice be set aside in every cathedral church for a master who shall teach the clergy of the same church and poor scholars *gratis,* whereby the need for a teacher shall be met and the way to knowledge opened to learners."[4]

Both edicts simply ratified practices already established. Informal instruction within the cathedrals of bustling towns and at highway crossroads had been offered for some time previously. The major difference was that formerly teaching had encompassed little more than the rudiments of literacy for training parish priests and for choristers who assisted in the singing of the Mass. Now, however, various popes and councils throughout the late eleventh and early twelfth centuries were reaffirming the obligation for major cathedral churches to educate the clergy in their own schools, and, further, to formalize and expand the curricula they offered. No longer was instruction to be confined solely to devotional manuals, patristic writings, scriptural collections, and the text of papal bulls or ecclesiastical councils. The course of studies presided over by the *magister scholarum* or *scholasticus caput scholae* was to embrace the full spectrum of the Seven Liberal Arts—a division of subject matter inherited from a traditional classification system devised by antique encyclopedists. Included were the subjects of both the *trivium* (grammar, rhetoric, and dialectic) and the *quadrivium* (arithmetic, music, geometry, and astronomy).[5]

Cathedral church schools grew in numbers: in Paris at the Augustinian Abbey of the Canons Regular of St. Victor, at the Church of St. Geneviève on the left bank of the Seine; within the Paris Cathedral astride the Île de la Cité; in the city of Rheims under Abbot Gerbert (c. 980), who later was anointed Pope Sylvester II; at Fleury in Orléans under the famous Abbot Abbo; under Fulbert at the Cathedral of Chartres in the early eleventh century; in practically all of the major cities of the Rhine; and in Belgium and elsewhere as well.[6] Epitomizing a larger, more generous attitude toward the full panoply of classical studies gaining currency was advice urged by Hugh of St.Victor (d. 1141): "Learn everything; later you will see that nothing is superfluous." The true purpose of studying philosophy, theology, physics, mathematics, logic, mechanics, and all of the liberal arts, he avowed, was "to pave the way for the mind to penetrate to the full knowledge of philosophical truth" and "to restore God's image in us."

SCHOLASTIC SCHOLARSHIP

What had begun as a mere trickle of foreign learning in previous centuries became a flood of new materials in the twelfth and thirteenth. Among them,

Latin translations of Aristotle's *Metaphysics,* the *Physics,* and *De Anima* were warmly received, as were Arabic commentaries on Neo-Platonic and Aristotelian philosophy. To a slightly lesser degree, other works of Greek science, notably those of Ptolemy, also received a hearing. Medieval theologians for some time had been seeking ways of joining faith with reason so that the divinely revealed truths of Christian dogma could be explicated and defended with the aid of rational analysis. Philosophy was understood as the hand-maiden of theology, as human reason was taken to be the interpreter of faith. Reason was thereby subordinate to faith. With the introduction of the richly textured works of Aristotle in logic, demonstration and formal proof, such work among the early scholastic philosophers and theologians further intensified. Anselm (1033–1109), Archbishop of Canterbury, typified the intellectual shift most clearly. On the one hand, he declared, "I do not seek to know in order that I may believe, but I believe in order than I may know." Or, again: "The Christian ought to advance to knowledge through faith, not to come to faith through knowledge." On the other hand, he added, "It seems to me a case of negligence if, after becoming firm in our faith, we do not strive to understand what we believe."

The evolution of cathedral church schools into universities was tied closely to the rise of scholasticism (from *scholasticus*) and the development of theology as a systematic discipline. As an intellectual movement, scholastic learning traced its origins back to the ninth century. It was to reach its greatest height with Thomas Aquinas in the thirteenth; and it subsequently entered upon a marked decline in the fifteenth century and thereafter.[7] As methodology, scholasticism was distinguished by a specific form of syllogistic reasoning worked out among the masters of the cathedral schools. It began in the efforts of such scholars as John Scotus Erigena to reconcile the many obvious contradictions in Christian doctrine revealed through the conflicting pronouncements of popes, assemblies, bishops, and church councils. Bishop Anselm, for one, confidently proclaimed that true religion and true philosophy had to be in agreement; logical analysis of the latter clarifies the former. Complicating the task, however, was the dispute into which he fell with a learned contemporary by the name of Roscellinus of Compiène (1050–1106). The issue at stake was a highly technical one, even though for a time it came to dominate the entire medieval philosophical arena.

Briefly, following the Neo-Platonist writer Porphyry, Anselm argued the "realist" position that ideas or concepts—not individual, particular things apprehended by the senses—possess ontological reality, that is, they are the true constituents of what exists. Roscellinus, following Aristotle, argued the contrary "nominalist" position that only individual, concrete entities have existent reality, and concepts as such are simply abstractions generated by human reasoning from experience. The more important consequence of the realist-nominalist controversy lay not so much in the respective theoretical implications scholars derived from each position, but, rather, from the fact that for the first time theological questions were brought forward for sustained and intensive formal analysis in systematic fashion. Much of the disputations that followed among the ranking theologians and philosophers of the day would be conducted in Europe's leading cathedral church schools.

LEARNED WOMEN

The emergence of cathedral institutions as major centers for learning, interestingly, had a decidedly deleterious effect upon educational opportunities for medieval women. There is little question that at least some females in the Middle Ages were literate, and a few (so far as one can judge by piecing together allusions to their accomplishments in surviving records and letters) were extremely well educated.[8] Adalperga, daughter of the last Lombard monarch, Desiderius, in the eighth century, was widely commended for her learning and wisdom; Irmintrude, spouse of Charles the Bald, was fully literate, an unusual accomplishment in her time; and Adela, daughter of William the Conqueror in the eleventh century, was celebrated as a woman of culture and erudition. So too was Alix of Chartres, the daughter of Eleanor of Aquitaine. In common with their male peers, young girls occasionally did sit for instruction in monastic or conventual schools. More often, particularly if they were part of the nobility, they were tutored at home or within the royal court. Charlemagne's sister, Gisela, and his daughter, Rectruda, for example, both received instruction at the palace school founded by Alcuin and were literate, as was the Carolingian empress Judith.

Education offered in lower schools did not extend in most cases beyond rudimentary reading and writing. However, it must be remembered that the same restriction held true for most of the laity in general. Some references dating to the thirteenth and fourteenth centuries attest to the existence of schoolmistresses at work, as in the archives of Paris for the year 1292 and again in 1380. Moreover, it is known that some coeducational schools existed throughout the medieval period, if only because periodically there were prohibitions issued against them. (Traditionally the Church held that gender commingling was to be avoided whenever possible.) Some girls' schools run by convents offered much more than basic letters, and were presided over by abbesses renowned for their erudition, including Anstrude of Laon, Gertrude of Niville, Bertille of Chelles, and Hilda of Hartlepool, to cite only a few examples. At Chelles in the eighth century and at Masseyk in the ninth, certain women's convents had acquired excellent reputations as learning centers. By the eleventh and twelfth centuries, references to learned nuns become more frequent, as in the case of Diemud of Wessobrunn (c. 1057–1130); Herrad of Landsberg, the abbess of Hohenburg from 1167 to 1195; and Hildegard of Bingen (founder of a major convent at Rupertsberg in 1147).

When knowledge accumulated to the point where it could no longer be encompassed within the liberal arts program of the monastic and conventual schools, a select few cathedral church schools began their transformation into true universities. Ultimately, of course, they were to develop full-fledged courses of instruction in the specialized areas of law, medicine, and theology, from which graduates went on to pursue careers in government, the church, teaching, and other professions. Professionals received their degrees by examination and usually were not allowed to practice without the official sanction of a license. But since women were not allowed to attend universities, the net result was to constrict even further whatever educational opportunities they might have enjoyed. Needless to add, their exclusion likewise meant that careers in law, medicine, or theology—with very rare exceptions—were for them closed off forever.

Accounting for the exclusion of women in late medieval Europe is not difficult. Their marginality, so to speak, stemmed from a number of social, economic, and cultural factors, foremost among them perhaps the fundamental misogyny of the early Church fathers themselves. A judgment offered by the Apostle Paul that women could learn but under no circumstances should be allowed to teach affords an especially vivid illustration: "A woman must be a learner, listening quietly and with due submission. But I suffer not a woman to be a teacher, nor should a woman [be allowed to] usurp a man's authority, but must remain silent" (*I Tim.* 2:11–13). Likewise, the Aristotelian view of women as basically "defective males" had proved enduring, reinforced by a Thomistic precept that the teleological end of true womanhood is procreation—that the female's highest function is one of sexual generation. Hence any woman who excelled intellectually blurred her gender identity and invited alarm or scorn— to her contemporaries she represented almost a hermaphroditic figure: male by intellect, female in body and spirit, less than a male but not fully a female. The medieval woman thus faced two choices: in the Italian idiom, *maritar o monacar,* marriage or the convent. For learned women it could be an agonizing dilemma. The former meant social acceptance but typically the abandonment of academic pursuits. The latter spelled abandonment of the world.

There were other, more specific reasons for excluding women from universities. It was widely believed, for example, that a female student's chastity would be at risk from a male teacher. (Here traditionalists could and did invoke the experience of Abelard and Héloïse: the pedagogical relationship that turned into a secret love affair between master and pupil, the resulting pregnancy, their secret marriage, his castration at the hands of her outraged uncle, their separate retirements into monastic seclusion—this was a cautionary tale not easily ignored.)[9] Also, or so it was assumed, the classical arts curriculum was unfit for female scrutiny because it included tales of illicit love, explicit sexuality, and bawdy humor—elements sure to corrupt a woman's tender sensibilities.

All proscriptions notwithstanding, and despite prohibitions against women in academe, there may have been occasional exceptions. The actual historicity of a certain Trotula who was said to have served as a member of the medical school at Salerno in the eleventh or twelfth century is open to some question, as is the story of a woman professor by the name of Novella who was reported to have lectured at Bologna in law. The latter, the daughter of Giovanni d'Andrea, a famous professor of canon law at Bologna in the early fourteenth century, tradition held, lectured in her father's absence standing behind a veil or curtain so as not to distract the male students with her beauty. More reliable are accounts of a woman named Dorotea Bocci who taught medicine and moral philosophy at Bologna in 1390; of a certain Constanza Calenda who lectured on medicine in the fourteenth century; and of Allesandra Giliani (c. 1326) whose task it was to dissect human cadavers and prepare them for anatomical demonstrations.[10] There may have been others as well, but they serve chiefly as exceptions to prove the rule that women were prevented from studying and taking university degrees and hence pursuing careers in teaching or some other academic profession.

TEACHING GUILDS: THE NATIONS AT PARIS

Fundamentally, the medieval university as an institution of higher learning grew out of the more advanced courses of instruction evolving within the cathedral church school. What it provided, essentially, was an organized meeting place for students and masters drawn together by a common interest in learning. During its formative period, almost any academic gathering was commonly referred to as a *studium* ("place of study"), or less frequently, a *discipulorum,* an association of persons devoted to scholarly pursuits. When it happened that one or more teachers in specialized disciplines became sufficiently renowned to attract large numbers of students from well beyond the cathedral school's immediate precincts, however, the term *studium generale* came into usage. It served basically to distinguish the larger, more "general" or "international" place of study from a strictly local institution. Only much later on, in the fifteenth century or so, was the term *universitas*—originally referring to an association or corporation of a kind common in medieval life—employed restrictively to refer to a teaching-learning community. The term *universitate* sometimes was used also to designate an association of teaching masters or a guild or society of students. Later on, when scholastic guilds and *studia* fused (essentially becoming identical), the term *universitas* replaced *studium* and thus acquired the modern meaning of "university."[11]

No two *studia generalia* evolved in precisely the same way. A common pattern across northern and central Europe, as at Paris, was for the masters or professors affiliated with a cathedral's *studium* to organize themselves into guilds, very much resembling those that had long dominated any other craft or profession, whether an association of vintners, cobblers, brewers, glass-blowers, or some other recognized trade. Teachers' guilds, or "nations" (*nationes*), as they were known, initially were voluntary associations of scholars who shared a common ethnic or regional identity and a common vernacular language. Toward the midpoint (1245) of the thirteenth century, for example, there were four nations officially acknowledged at Paris: French, Normand, English, and Picardian. Why only four nations were recognized is not clear, since the geographical localities represented by each ranged widely. The French nation included not only local Parisian scholars and surrounding regions, but also teachers from Spain, Italy, Greece, and all of Eastern Europe. The Norman nation enrolled those coming from the north of France and the Low Countries. The English nation accepted members from the British Isles, but likewise from Holland, the Germanies, Denmark, Sweden, Norway, and from the Hungarian and Slavic countries, and on.[12]

Masters' nations at Paris, it should be emphasized, functioned only as formal subdivisions with a larger "arts faculty," consisting of all teachers who specialized in the teaching of the subjects comprising the *trivium* and the *quadrivium*. Teachers of theology or law were grouped as separate faculties. (Unlike the arts faculty, none was subdivided into nations.) Ultimately, the so-called "lower" or "inferior" courses of study offered by the arts faculty came to be viewed as preparatory for, and prerequisite to, admission to the "higher" or more advanced, specialized courses of instruction organized under the law, medicine, or theology faculties. Many who taught within the Faculty of Arts were themselves simultaneously enrolled as students who were pursuing advanced degrees in one or another of the higher faculties. It was a usage very much like that of the modern university in which graduate students are employed as assistants to teach undergraduates.

Each of the four nations comprising the arts faculty at the Parisian *studium generale* in the early thirteenth century was a separate association or entity unto itself, with its own designated members, official seal, revenues, patron saints, elected officials, and respective sphere of jurisdiction.[13] Heading each nation was an elected "proctor" or "rector"—in the 1200s the two titles seem to have been used interchangeably. The proctor's chief task was to function as the nation's general treasurer. To him fell also the obligation to enforce the many rules and regulations governing members of the nation and the students they instructed. Assisted by a *receptor,* or "receiver," of the various dues and fines collected, the proctor presided over weekly meetings of the nation's assembly, during which time business was conducted regarding classroom maintenance, airing of student infractions of rules, the scheduling of special lectures, and similar matters. Besides his management of the assembly, the proctor was expected to serve as a recorder of the meeting's minutes.

Other officials important to the nation included an elected major *bedellus,* or "beadle," and sometimes a subordinate "sub-beadle." The beadle (roughly, "attendant"), who was referred to as "a common servant of all the masters," served as a ceremonial master-of-arms at assembly meetings and was privileged to serve as the official mace-bearer who headed the many elaborate processionals that typically punctuated academic routines. Whereas the proctor served only briefly for a month's (renewable) term, the beadle was elected on an annual basis, as was the receptor. Among his other duties, this last-named official superintended the nation's observances of feast days and kept account of revenues received from the payment of membership admission fees.

Heading the arts faculty as a whole was an official functionary elected by all the masters or teaching regents of its constituent nations. As chief administrative officer of the faculty's larger assembly (as distinct from the weekly assemblies of each member nation), the rector's obligation, in cooperation with the four proctors, was to preside at an executive council. The council, in turn, furnished a forum for reviewing various proposals forwarded by proctors on behalf of their respective nations (or the subdivisions thereof). It customarily met on a bimonthly basis. On alternate weeks, the entire faculty assembly took up and deliberated upon recommendations and other matters submitted to it for consideration by the executive council. Issues discussed pertained chiefly to courses of studies in the arts, qualifications for the arts degree, and standards and procedures governing the conferral of teaching licenses.

Collective meetings of all the faculties of the *universitas magistrorum et scholarium studii Pariensis,* as it was now known, were conducted weekly. Proceedings of the University Assembly resembled the meetings of the nations or of the arts faculty as a body. Corresponding to the executive council of the faculty of arts was a general University Council, in later years consisting of the deans of the faculties of law, medicine, and theology, the proctor or rector of the arts faculty, and an elected chief rector who by the late 1300s was serving as head of the university as a whole, including its so-called higher faculties.

From the year 1219 onward, more often than not it was the chief presiding officer of the arts faculty who won election as university rector. Selected either by proctors or by electors chosen by the nations, the university's ranking officer served for no more than a three-month term at a time. An acceptable candidate, as was often the case, might be retained through several successive elections, however. Full recognition of his special standing as a representative for the entire university came only gradually—sometimes grudgingly—from the ranks of the several faculties.[14]

From the very beginning, frictions within and among the nations were pronounced. Feuds and factional rivalries were especially well represented at Paris. "They wrangled and disputed not merely about the various sects or about some discussions," one chronicler reports, "but the difference between the countries also caused dissensions, hatreds and virulent animosities among them, and they impudently uttered all kinds of affronts and insults against one another. They affirmed that the English were drunkards and had tails; the sons of France proud, effeminate, and carefully adorned like women. They said that the Germans were furious and obscene at their feasts; the Normans, vain and boastful; the Poitevins, traitors and always adventurers. The Burgundians they considered vulgar and stupid. The Bretons were reputed to be fickle and changeable. . . . The Lombards were called avaricious, vicious, and cowardly; the Romans, seditious, turbulent, and slanderous; the Sicilians, tyrannical and cruel; the inhabitants of Brabant, men of blood, incendiaries and brigands and ravishers; the Flemish, fickle, prodigal, gluttonous, yielding as butter, and slothful."[15]

At Paris and within most of the other French medieval *studia generalia,* nations as distinguishable units within a university's governance structure retained their separate identities for many centuries thereafter. Not until their official suppression in the early seventeenth century and formal abolition by royal decree late in the eighteenth did they finally disappear from the academic scene altogether.

STUDENT NATIONS: BOLOGNA

Whereas the nations at Paris were controlled by teaching masters, a quite different situation prevailed in other fledgling universities elsewhere, most notably to the south in Bologna. Nations there made their appearance at the beginning of the thirteenth century not as masters' guilds, but as students' *collegia,* that is, associations of foreign (i.e., non-Bolognese) apprentice-scholars. Formed for purposes of collective security and protection, student nations basically originated as fraternal organizations of out-of-town students who had banded together for mutual aid against sometimes hostile local authorities.

As a city and cultural center, Bologna owed its growth in large measure to the intellectual revival that had swept through Europe in the eleventh and twelfth centuries. Located at the center of the main roads that led from the Lombard plain to Tuscany and central Italy, and those connecting the Adriatic provinces of northern Italy with the Tyrrhenian provinces to the south, Bologna afforded an ideal meeting place for students and scholars from all of southern Europe.[16] Around the year 1100 a famous scholar by the name of Irnerius (Warnerius) established within the municipal precincts a school for the teaching of the liberal arts and of Roman civil law. His efforts were paralleled by those of a younger contemporary, the monk Gratian of the Camaldunensian monastery of St. Felix nearby, who won renown as a teacher of canon or church law. Together, they and their colleagues offered a comprehensive course of studies extending from elementary grammatical studies and simple composition all the way through juridical rhetoric and other advanced subjects. Over the next thirty years or so their teaching grew in prestige and academic reputation, thereby laying the foundation for the fame Bologna would later enjoy as a center for legal studies. Precisely when the Bolognese *universitas* as such was founded remains in dispute.[17] In 1158 the German Emperor Frederick Barbarossa granted a charter that implied special rights and privileges to the local *studia* in Bologna, of which there were at least three. By the year 1215, over a half century later, little question remains but that a full-fledged university was then in operation.

Students of canon and civil law early on formed their own nations, based on the specific regions from which they had originated. By the late 1200s Bologna's non-Italian nations included the French, Spanish, Provençal, English, Picard, Burgundian, Poitevin, Tourainian, Norman, Catalonian, Hungarian, Polish, German, and Gascon. Sometime over the course of the century following, all of these smaller guilds or nations coalesced to form two linked "universities." The first, the *universitas ultramontanorum,* consisted of students coming from "over the mountains" in the Italian north—in other words, non-Italian foreigners. In 1265 the fourteen nations of the *ultramontane* university were reduced to thirteen; in 1432 records show there were sixteen. The other, the *universitas citramontanorum,* was comprised by four nations of students native to the Italian peninsula and its nearby islands, including Sicily. Its groupings included those made up of students from Rome, Campania, Tuscany, and Lombardy. By 1400 there were three nations: Lombard, Tuscan, and Roman, each with multiple subdivisions. Only local Bolognese students remained unorganized as a separate nation.

The formation and emergence to power of student nations did not go unopposed. Bolognese officials, for example, struggled long and hard to prevent the growth of student groupings, claiming that their members "did not make a class by themselves but were only pupils of the doctors of the law." Faced at one point with demands for dissolution, students appealed to Pope Honorius III (1216–1227), who offered their respective nations protection and legal standing. When local civil authorities at last realized that the formation of nations could not be prevented, and cognizant of the economic advantages of hosting large numbers of students in the city, they reversed themselves and offered special inducements such as exemption from local military service and taxes to their members.

Each of the nations shared in the university's academic life through their elected representatives in university assemblies, where the actual governance of the *studium* occurred. The German nation had two elected proctors; while the single elected heads of all the other nations were called *consiliarii,* or "counselors." Each *consiliarius* belonged to a university-wide senate presided over by a rector, who was elected by its members. The typical pattern was for the office of rector to rotate among the various nations, so that all would be assured adequate representation of their respective interests. The primary executive duty of the rector—to which he was bound by solemn oath—was to exercise both civil and criminal jurisdiction over students and professors (though this authority was often vigorously challenged). He acted also as an arbiter in disputes between the teaching masters and students, convened examinations, presided at graduations, and otherwise performed the ceremonial duties of his office.

Assisting the rector were several other classes of officials. They included *syndics,* or auditors; *massarii,* or treasurers; beadles and subordinate beadles, custodians, recorders, and various other student-elected functionaries. Surviving records fail to indicate clearly how various tasks and administrative responsibilities were apportioned among the many classes of academic factotums. The general pattern they suggest is one of a pyramidal hierarchy, with ceremonial functions clustered at the apex but with real power retained by students' nations at the base.

In stark contrast with the pattern of academic control by faculties that was evolving among the northern universities, in Bologna the Ultramontanes and the Citramontanes jointly came to exercise near complete control over all facets of the three original institutions that eventually came together to form a single *studium generale.* Although the teaching masters had formed a *collegium* or guildlike "college" of their own, its authority seems to have been largely ceremonial. Real power was exercised exclusively and collectively by the students' nations.

Teaching doctors in consequence were reduced to an almost incredible state of subservience. It was the students through their representatives who hired and fired the faculty, fixed their salaries, required each professor to swear allegiance and obedience to whatever statutes were enacted, granted and limited leaves of absence, and in other ways controlled even the smallest details of daily academic life. Committees of secret student informers, for example, maintained close surveillance over their teachers; and reports of infractions were delivered to the rector and the *consiliarii* within three days for disposition. Offenses for which a master might be fined or even dismissed included failure to begin a lecture at the appointed hour, not finishing a presentation on schedule, digressing from the announced topic or subject or showing signs of unpreparedness, neglecting to employ the approved disputation method, leaving the most important points of a lecture until its conclusion when students were beginning to wander out, and so forth. Students at Bologna tended to be somewhat older than those attending northern universities, which explains in part how they came to exercise more influence and institutional control.

Other southern universities followed Bologna's organizational and governance structure. Students at Padua, for instance, also elected their *consiliarii,* as did those attending the Florentine *studium generale* established in 1321. In Orléans, proctors elected by their respective nations chose a rector in precisely the same manner as was done at Bologna. Other universities organized by nations included major *studia* at Pisa, Ferrara, Perugia, Salamanca in Spain (founded between 1220 and 1230 by Alfonso IX of León), Lérida, and elsewhere across southern Europe.

Whatever their particular organizational structures, universities of all types proliferated throughout Europe at an increasing rate between the thirteenth and fifteenth centuries. By the year 1500 it has been estimated there were at least seventy-nine in operation. Some were short-lived; others proved more enduring. In Italy, in addition to those already cited, the more important higher *studia* included institutions in Reggio, Vicenza, Padua, Vercelli, Arezzo, Siena, Florence, and Naples, as well as the *universitas* at Bologna and several in Rome. In Spain and Portugal, practically every state could claim at least one university: Palencia-Valladolid in Castile, Salamanca in Leon, Huesca in Aragon, Lérida in Catalonia, and Lisbon in Coimbra. German universities were equally numerous, including schools at Prague (founded 1347), Vienna (1365), Cologne (1388), Erfurt (1379–1392); and after 1400, at Würzburg, Leipzig, and Rostock. The university at Cracow was chartered in 1364; Buda followed shortly thereafter, in 1389. Upsala and Copenhagen hosted the two most important medieval universities in Scandinavia. In the late 1400s new universities appeared in Scotland, including St. Andrews, Aberdeen, and Glasgow. The two most important institutions in England, of course, were Oxford and Cambridge.

APPRENTICE SCHOLARS AND MASTERS

Inasmuch as Latin was the exclusive language of instruction in medieval universities, minimal proficiency in the ancient tongue of Cicero and Virgil was prerequisite to admission for higher studies. One directive of the period stipulated that anyone seeking university admission had to be able to "read, sing and construe well and also compose twenty-four verses on one subject in one day" in Latin. Sometimes towns and cities themselves sponsored public grammar schools where preparatory studies could be undertaken. In other places, as in Germany, universities often seem to have operated their own ancillary schools in which youths might seek necessary tutelage. Again, most collegiate or parish church schools in smaller towns and villages could supply the essentials of ecclesiastical Latin, which usually sufficed for a student's immediate needs.[18]

The average age of an entering student was probably no more than fifteen or sixteen. The first challenge awaiting him upon arrival in the city was to find suitable lodgings—in a comfortable suite of rooms if he were affluent, more likely a tiny garret in some wretched inn if he were poor. Selecting a place to live was likely to pose a significant problem for any youth without friends or compatriots to offer counsel, particularly since the university offered entering students little more than facilities for lectures and practically no official guidance whatsoever as to how to get settled into its routines. In Paris, most students took rooms along the infamous Vicus Stramineus, or Rue de Fouarre (Straw Street), so-named for the straw-strewn floors of its lecture halls where students reposed. Low rents were the district's chief advantage. In all other respects, the narrow rows of ramshackle frame houses, always damp and leaking, overrun with vermin, icy cold in winter and stifling hot in summer, offered few attractions.[19]

Fending off the clamoring hordes of students that often hung about the inns awaiting each new arrival was a formidable challenge. Hired by masters as "chasers" or recruiters, each would set upon the newcomer, urging that he enlist under a particular teacher, all the while deriding the merits of his competitors. Free demonstrations and lectures or tuition discounts were offered as inducements; and if the recruiter was successful in signing up someone on the spot he could expect a hefty commission as reward. A thirteenth-century manual of advice to students stressed the importance of delaying a final decision of which teaching master to select for at least three days, and urged each new student to attend several different teachers' lectures before making a final choice.

The next step was for the student to present himself before the official representative of the nation appropriate to his place of origin (if attending a *universitas* organized on the model of Bologna) or, as at Paris (where the *studium* was organized by masters' guilds), to the rector of the arts faculty. If found proficient in Latin and deemed sufficiently well grounded in the fundamentals to attend lectures, the student was required to swear an oath of allegiance to the ranking officials and statutes of the university or, depending upon the school, to the members and representatives of his nation. Upon payment of a required matriculation fee, he was admitted forthwith as an apprentice-scholar, fully entitled to whatever privileges and immunities pertained thereto.

Once formalities were concluded, the new student was visited by a delegation of his peers and subjected to supposedly good-natured horseplay and hazing.[20] Immediately thereafter he was required to host as sumptuous an initiation banquet for his tormentors as his means would allow. The *Manuale Scholarium* of 1481 at Heidelberg includes a rather horrific account of the many indignities heaped upon the *bejaunus* ("yellow-billed"), or fledgling scholar. Rites of passage went well beyond ridicule or mere name-calling. In several instances, it is recorded that the initiate was smeared with excrement, soaked in urine, or forced to ingest a strong cathartic, meanwhile being whipped or beaten about the head. University officials tried repeatedly to abolish the more brutal forms of hazing, but to little avail.[21] Typical was a statute of Leipzig, issued in 1495: "Each and every one attached to this university is forbidden to offend with insult, torment, harass, drench with water or urine, besprinkle or defile with dust or any filth, mock by whistling, accost with a terrifying voice, or dare to molest in any way whatsoever . . . any who are called *beani*."[22] Similarly, complaints were often made about the excessive expenses entailed in mounting the overly extravagant initiation feast demanded for the occasion. Nevertheless, the student custom of requiring expensive banquets was almost impossible to eradicate.

In its early days, the university had all it could do to enforce its own regulations and statutes. Medieval disciplinarians were forever wrestling with problems caused by students roaming the streets after curfew, forgetting to keep doors locked, or neglecting their studies for the brothels and taverns.[23] Sometimes teams of "wolves" (*lupi*), or student informers, were appointed to enforce the exclusive use of Latin rather than the vernacular among students, and to report other infractions of the rules as necessary.[24]

The cost of city living and the many demands made upon a student's slender purse were apt to come as a shock. A student at Oxford writing home to his father for money—in uncommonly bad Latin—tried to explain. "I am studying," he emphasized, "with the greatest diligence, but the matter of money stands greatly in the way. . . . It is now two months since I spent the last of what you sent me. The city is expensive and makes many demands; I have to rent lodgings, buy necessaries, and provide for many other things. . . . Wherefore I respectfully beg your paternity that by the prompting of divine pity you may assist me, so that I may be able to complete what I have well begun."[25]

So common were pleas for funds from impoverished students that a common saying had it, "A student's first song is a demand for money, and there will never be a letter which does not ask for cash."[26] Especially irksome to parents were requests from those whose academic and personal conduct left much to be desired. One father, patience exhausted, wrote to his errant son, "I have recently discovered that you live dissolutely and slothfully, preferring license to restraint and play to work and strumming a guitar while the others are at their studies, whence it happens that you have read but one volume of law while your more industrious companions have read several." He concluded, "Wherefore I have decided to exhort you herewith to repent utterly of your dissolute and careless ways, that you may no longer be called a waster and your shame may be turned to good repute."

Similar in tone is a letter written by a parent who had been informed by his son's teacher that the young student might benefit by a judicious parental admonition to mend his ways. Not wishing to disclose the source for his information, the parent wrote, "I have learned . . . from a certain trustworthy source . . . that you do not study in your room or behave in the schools as a good student should, but play and wander about, disobedient to your master and indulging in sport and in certain other dishonorable practices which I do not now care to explain by letter." The customary exhortation to the youth to apply himself more diligently followed.

A composite of university life indicates upwards of four to five years elapsing between a student's initial admission and the series of academic trials required for his obtaining the medieval equivalent of the baccalaureate degree.[27] In the interim, the apprentice attended lectures, participated in class disputations, and listened to disputations among the teaching masters.[28] Eventually, having satisfied the professor under whom he had worked that he was adequately prepared, a candidate presented himself for his first qualifying examination. A panel of examiners appointed by his nation within the arts faculty then passed on his fitness by interrogating him over a set list of titles. The student had to affirm under oath that he had in fact faithfully attended lectures and had studied to requisite standards selected portions of the works of Aristotle, Boethius, Donatus, and other authorities included within the arts curriculum. Depending on the time and place in question, the "responsion" at which the student was questioned by a master to determine his preparedness for further examination seems to have been held in the month of December preceding Lent, during which period weekly "determinations" of candidates were conducted.

The rituals of formal determination were apt to be elaborate in the extreme. Those selected as examiners had to swear solemnly that they would judge impartially, that they would not succumb to pressure exercised by a master on behalf of one of his candidates, and that no one because of his class or social standing would receive special consideration. For their parts, both the master and his candidate had to affirm that the examiners' decision, no matter what the outcome, would never be appealed to higher university authorities. Evidence that the proprieties of the occasion were sometimes honored only in the breach comes from the frequency with which complaints were heard of influence-peddling and bribery. Authorities tried to curb the worst excesses, but instances of students tendering sums to the examining masters "for their consolation and honor" were not uncommon.

The actual form of the examination was a series of formal disputations. These had to commence prior to the Wednesday following the first week of Lent, and had to be concluded on a specified date before Easter. If the judgment was a favorable one, the title *baccalaureus,* or "bachelor," a "beginner," was formally bestowed, indicating the candidate's determination to continue on for the actual degree. Upwards of two more years of study were required before this aim could be actually accomplished.

The final "determination," a series of stylized disputations that culminated in the formal bestowal of the bachelor of arts degree, or *baccalaureat,* was likewise an elaborate affair.[29] Custom dictated that the candidate announce the specific theses he intended to defend well in advance. Invitations to attend were sent out in hopes of attracting as large an audience as possible. If at the time the exercises began the number of those present was judged insufficient, tradition required that passersby from the streets be hauled in, by force if necessary, and made to witness the proceedings! Alternatively, raiding a rival determiner's audience for the same purpose was not unknown. The ensuing demonstrations were high theater, sometimes lasting for hours on end, and were much beloved by spectators. Inceptions, it might be said, were considered an important form of entertainment as well as instructive for future candidates. According to eye-witness accounts, verbal jousting between a candidate and his opponents took place "amid loud clamor on the part of the audience, and on the part of the combatants, with a great shaking of heads and stamping of feet, and extending of the fingers, a waving of hands, and contortions of the body as though they were crazed." Assuming the final outcome was judged satisfactory, the former "beginner" now at last joined the ranks of full-fledged bachelors of arts. Graduation was marked as at previous points in his progression with a celebratory feast for friends and teachers.[30]

Almost immediately thereafter a major career decision had to be made. A student could elect to conclude his studies and seek a position as a teacher in some outlying rural school where the demand for bachelors was strong. Or he could decide to remain for further study. If he chose to continue on for his master's degree in arts, further years of study, lecture, and disputation awaited him. Once again, the course of studies stretching out ahead was prescribed in great detail. Included were selected works of Aristotle, Priscian, Boethius, Ovid, Euclid, Vitellio, Ptolemy—a regimen encompassing all of the major elements of philosophy, poetry, rhetoric, arithmetic, music, geometry, astronomy, natural science, ethics, and logic that comprised medieval arts and letters. Depending on how well the student was already acquainted with the contents of the scholarly canon, anywhere from another six months to three or more years of additional study would be necessary.

Occupying an intermediate point between the bachelorship and receipt of a mastership was the licentiate, or permission to teach. In the period when universities were first forming, a teaching license was granted by ecclesiastical authorities only after the applicant had successfully completed yet another series of examinations or disputations. Examining board members were selected from the various nations. Once again the successful candidate took an oath of obedience to the rector and to the nations' proctors, swore that he would neither offer nor accept bribes, and promised that he would be responsible for the payment of any and all fees mandated.

Licensure was a major milestone in a scholar's career, marked by a procession of candidates in full academic garb (sometimes in order of merit or academic distinction), accompanied by the rector and proctors, who were preceded by the beadles, the entire entourage wending its way to the residence of the local bishop or chancellor. Each candidate was then presented to the official before whom the student knelt as the license was conferred. Once the ceremony was concluded and substantial fees paid, each candidate was expected to help defray the expense of an evening meal—or at least to pay for the wine consumed, which was expected to be of good quality.

Inception as a master of arts proceeded along the same lines as the baccalaureate determination. After having performed meritoriously in a series of disputations and having sworn the usual oaths of loyalty and fidelity, the candidate was ceremoniously inaugurated into the fellowship of masters. On the evening before his inception, the student participated in a disputation; the next morning he delivered a graduation lecture. There followed the actual inauguration ritual itself. The new graduate was now granted the symbols of his newly acquired office: his master's round cap (the *pileum*) or the *biretta* (a square cap with a tuft), a book from the presiding regent, and a kiss of fellowship. Hereafter he was entitled to don standard academic garb, consisting of a long outer garment closed in front (the *tabard*), a longer robe (the *toga*), and a still more distinctive *cappa,* or cope, the wearing of which was restricted to formal occasions.

Thereafter, predictably, a banquet was held to celebrate and mark the occasion. Reporting on the results of one student's inception to his parents, a professor at

Bologna by the name of Buoncompagno proudly testified, "Your son has held a glorious disputation, which was attended by a great number of teachers and scholars. He answered all questions without a mistake. Moreover, he celebrated a famous banquet, at which both rich and poor were honored as never before, and he has duly begun to give lectures which are already so popular that others' classrooms are deserted and his own are filled."

ADVANCED STUDIES: HIGHER FACULTIES

Graduated masters had several choices. Those for whom the degree was the termination of their academic career usually sought ecclesiastical or civil service posts. Others departed for teaching positions at the leading *studia* in their home states. Still others elected to continue teaching within the faculty of arts. Of these, most were intending to present themselves for still further study in one or another of the so-called "higher" faculties of theology, law, or medicine.

Writing at the end of the twelfth century, the English scholar Alexander Neckham, who had studied at Paris, testified that at his *alma mater,* "the arts flourish, theology reigns, the [canon] laws are holding their own, jurisprudence shines, and medicine grows vigorously." Of these, however, theology certainly ranked highest in importance—so much so that Paris came to be popularly dubbed "the Mount Sinai" for instruction in theological studies. The theological course at Paris was a lengthy one, reportedly requiring more than a decade to complete. It apparently was divided into at least two or three successive stages, each defined by the particular works studied, and by a concluding series of examinations or public disputations.

While many details remain in question, the first period of study at Paris and elsewhere seems to have occupied between four and six years. It culminated in an exercise where the candidate for progression had to articulate and defend two theses assigned in advance before a convocation of masters elected to represent a given *collegium,* or "college," which, as at Florence, consisted of all the professors of the particular discipline. There followed a formal "deposition," or testimonial to the candidate's ability, good moral character, and religious piety. If the judgment handed down was a favorable one, a license was granted allowing the applicant to lecture as a "regent" or "regent master." In the latter phase of his studies, the licentiate again participated in a similar series of disputations, called *puncta,* before finally achieving the status of doctor in theology.[31]

If Paris was the preeminent center for theology, Salerno in Italy and Montpellier in southern France early emerged as leading institutions for medical studies. Just as the growth of theology as a systematic discipline was shaped by the disputations of leading scholastics inspired by new translations of Aristotle, medicine owed its growth as a field of study and scholarship in part to an influx of new learning from outside Europe. With the arrival in the mid-eleventh century at Salerno of the famous refugee monk Constantius Africanus, for example, translations of the works of Galen, Hippocrates, Isaac Judaeus, and the Arabic physician Avincenna, among others, soon stimulated major interest in medical research. By 1231 when Emperor Frederick II, king of Sicily, confirmed the legal authority of the Salerno *studium,* it was already a flourishing medical teaching center. Much the same could be said also of the university at Montpellier, chartered in 1170 by Count William VIII of Montpellier.[32]

Precisely how advanced training in medicine was linked to a preparatory education in the liberal arts is not clear, either at Paris or in other *studia* where medical studies became well known. At Bologna, a student desiring to pursue medical studies had to be at least twenty years of age, give evidence of "sufficient" grounding in the arts, and had to be able to attest to having studied a stipulated number of medical texts as well as having attended specified medical lectures. At Paris the requirements were similar. Generally speaking, requirements for advanced studies included a stipulated minimum age for candidacy, a defined period of preparatory instruction, and familiarity with recognized texts in the field. Medical students followed much the same pattern of studying, hearing lectures, disputing, responding, and so forth, as did liberal arts and theology students. Actual clinical work, in the modern sense, was notably absent; only in later centuries apparently were students afforded opportunities to conduct dissections or otherwise apply and extend their bookish studies in practical ways.

Possibly the fact that knowledge of ancient Roman law was never completely extinguished in Italy helps explain the early medieval revival of legal studies at Pavia, Ravenna, Rome, and Bologna.[33] Assisting the process was the growth of independent Italian city-states after the tenth century, which in turn gave rise to the need for legal assistance in administering municipal governments. Whatever the specific factors at work, the development of legal studies paralleled closely that of theology and medicine as university subjects. Inerius's lectures at Bologna on the *Code,* the *Digest,* and the *Institutes* of Justinian (together, the *Corpus Juris Civilis*) probably contributed more than anything else to the prominence of law studies in that city, although Gratian's compilation of Church canon law, the *Decretum,* was likewise undoubtedly influential.

Candidates for a degree in either canon or civil law engaged in a lengthy sequence of lectures and disputations, of defenses and argumentation, thesis presentations and refutations very much resembling that required of medical or theological degree candidates. Ten years were needed to complete a so-called double doctorate in both civil and ecclesiastical law. A lesser period was required for completing the course of studies in just one or the other specialization. At

Bologna, a doctoral applicant first presented himself for an initial examination before the local archdeacon, during which he was interrogated on points of law previously assigned by an assembly of doctors. His performance was judged by those convened, and if he had performed satisfactorily, the candidate was probated as a doctor.[34]

The initial or "private" examination was followed by a "public" examination, called the *conventus*. This second review usually was held in the cathedral before a large audience. Here the candidate was obliged to read and defend a legal thesis against opponents selected from among the student body. The successful candidate thereupon received formal licensure and the official insignias of his new standing. Afterwards, the triumphant graduate proceeded in company with friends and teachers on a processional through the city. Then came a banquet for colleagues and associates. The entire proceeding was inordinately costly to the new graduate. Customary expenses included substantial fees, gifts for lesser university officials, and sometimes, according to set statutes, large sums of money to the archdeacon and specified teaching doctors. The outlay was so great, according to reports, that some candidates had to delay their final *conventus* for years in order to save up enough to defray its cost.

UNIVERSITY INSTRUCTION

Prior to the invention of the printing press and movable type, books were few and prohibitively expensive. University teachers consequently had to rely heavily upon oral lecturing, leaving students to transcribe notes as best they could. Copies of such few texts as could not be dispensed with were acquired personally by students only at great cost and not without difficulty. Around 1274 at Bologna, for instance, local authorities attempted to address the problem of booksellers (*stationarii*) in the city who were allegedly overpricing their wares or had little to sell. "For the common profit of the scholars and the *studium*," they declared, "we order the booksellers neither to sell copies of textbooks and of commentaries nor to alienate them in any way to *studia* of other cities. . . . Furthermore, we order the booksellers to have their copies [for sale] well corrected and amended and to make copies from these amended texts when the students ask for them." The instructions concluded, "For the copying, they should charge what they had been used to charge hitherto, and not more."[35]

Library collections were scanty and not always accessible to students. At medieval Oxford, regulations were issued as follows: "Since in the course of time the great number of students using the library is in many ways harmful to the books and since the laudable purpose of these desiring to profit [by reading them] is often defeated by too much disturbance of noisy people, the university has ordered and decreed that only graduates and people in religious orders who have studied philosophy eight years shall study in the library of the university." Thus, lower students were effectively denied any access to the collection whatsoever. "Also," it was announced, "for the better protection of the books, the university has ordered and decreed that all the university graduates and others defined as such in the statutes who may enter . . . must take an oath . . . that when they enter the common library for the sake of study, they will handle the books they consult decently and not inflict any harm on them by tearing out or ruining layers or single pages of the book."[36]

A student's daily routine began about 4:00 A.M. each weekday with Mass. The first "ordinary" lecture attended would commence at 5:00 or 6:00, and last about two hours. Customarily, lecturing broke off by 9:00 in the morning, and was followed by two "extraordinary" or "review" lectures in the afternoon, extending perhaps until around 4:00 or 5:00 P.M. A student would join in disputations until suppertime; later he would attend an organized recitation or a review session, or perhaps go off to read on his own. He retired by 9:00 in the evening. Holding ordinary lectures in the very early morning, before dawn, apparently was a deliberate expedient. At Paris, the custom was intended to force lecturers to speak extemporaneously in the dark, without notes or a candle for illumination. In some recorded instances, professors were expressly forbidden from bringing a lamp to the lecture hall.

A typical lecture in, say, canon law was organized around a specific portion of some standard text—perhaps Gratian's *Decretals*—together with its many interlinear glosses and commentaries or side notes by other authorities. The master would seat himself at the rostrum, and students gathered around followed the lecture from their own copies of the text. Students who lacked a text to consult took notes. The central question under consideration might be "Whether or not it is to be permitted that priests should read secular literature." The master would treat two contrary theses—that the reading of "heathen" literature by the clergy was allowable, and that such knowledge of pagan learning should be proscribed. Gratian's preliminary conclusion on the matter was analyzed. Then, systematically, the lecture would proceed to marshal arguments from other learned authorities on both sides of the issue and treat each in exhaustive detail. Finally, the lecturer would draw his own settled conclusions and draw out whatever legal ramifications followed from them.

An often-cited example of how medieval university lectures were organized comes from a account (1250) of a certain Petrus Peregrossi, professor of law at Bologna, who previewed for his students the plan he would follow in teaching the *Corpus Juris Civilis:* "It is my intent," he announced, "to teach you faithfully and in a kindly manner, in which instruction the following order has customarily been observed. . . . First, I shall give you the summaries of each title [of the law] before I come to the text. Second, I shall put forth well and distinctly and in the best terms I can, the purport of each law. Third, I shall read the text in order to correct it. Fourth, I shall briefly restate the meaning. Fifth, I shall solve conflicts, adding general matters . . . and subtle and useful distinctions and questions with the solutions, so far as divine Providence shall assist me." He added, "And if any law is deserving of a review by reason of its fame or difficulty, I shall reserve it for an afternoon review."[37]

The "extraordinary" lecture or "repetition" assumed different forms. An ordinance for Louvain in 1476 stipulated its conduct as follows: "After the midday repast, each one having brought to the table his books, all the scholars of the faculty together, in the presence of a tutor, shall review that regular lecture; and in the review the tutor shall employ a method which will enable him by discreet questioning of every man to find out if each of them listened well to the lecture and remembered it and which will also recall the whole lecture by having its parts recited by individuals. And if watchful care is used in this, one hour shall suffice." But some lecturers balked at offering repetitions without extra compensation. "Next year," one professor announced to his students, "I expect to give ordinary lectures well and lawfully as I always have, but no extraordinary lectures, for students are not good payers, wishing to learn but not to pay, as the saying is: 'All desire to know but none to pay the price.'"[38]

Opinion differed on the best way of delivering a lecture. Some masters preferred to speak at a brisk conversational pace, a rate that made students' notetaking virtually impossible. Others were willing to dictate from their notes so that students could take down a complete transcription of everything said. For obvious reasons, students tended to prefer the latter approach, despite the fact that authorities strongly disapproved. Thus, at Paris in 1355, legislation was enacted requiring teaching masters to swear formally that they would adhere to the first method; and anyone failing to comply was to be deprived for a year "from lecturing and from honors, offices and other advantages of our faculty." For second-time offenders, the penalty was doubled. Anticipating a strong negative reaction from students, the officials who issued the proclamation further declared: "Moreover, listeners who oppose the execution of this our statute by shouting, hissing, noise-making, or throwing stones by themselves or by their . . . accomplices or in any other way, we deprive of and cut off from our company for a year and for each relapse we increase the penalty double and quadruple."[39]

The oral disputation was a still more important tool for learning throughout the thirteenth and fourteenth centuries. In its simplest form a master would pose a question on a given topic to a student. A respondent was selected (or perhaps the teacher himself served in the role) whose task it was to counter the first disputant's arguments and to propose alternative views. Informal proceedings—

and sometimes more formal ones—were accompanied by shouts of encouragement from excited spectators when a protagonist scored a telling point, or by derisive hissing from the company assembled when the debater's performance was judged incompetent. In the more elaborate form of the disputation as an examination, the candidate was assigned to defend a particular thesis or position at some length before a board of examiners, and to respond to whatever objections and difficulties were brought against it by antagonists appointed for the task. By the 1400s, the disputation was in widespread use in all universities and far overshadowed the lecture as a means of instruction.

THE STRUGGLE FOR IMMUNITIES AND EXEMPTIONS

However lowly his origins or how desperately poor he might be, the university student occupied a unique position in medieval society. All medieval scholars and students were referred to colloquially as "clerks" (*clerici*) and were considered members of the lay clergy, as confirmed by their tonsures (i.e., the crown of the head shaven in a neat circle). Civil and ecclesiastical officials alike usually were disposed to place students under protection as a special class, and to grant them privileges and immunities not normally extended to others.[40] Thus, for example, in an age when travel was hazardous and fraught with peril, authorities did what they could to protect students coming to and from their places of study: "We in our loving kindness," reads one decree, "do grant to all scholars who are traveling for the sake of study and especially to professors of divine and sacred law, this privilege: Both they and their messengers are to come in security to the places in which the studies are carried on and there they are to abide in security." A royal guarantee of safe passage and exemption from taxes was extended by Philip VI of France (1328–1350) in a proclamation dating to the year 1341. "To the aforesaid masters and scholars [at Paris] now in attendance at the university, and to those who are hereafter to come to the same university, or who are actually preparing in sincerity so to come, also while [they are] staying at the university, or returning to their own homes," the king announced, "we grant . . . that no layman, of whatever condition or prominence he may be, whether he be a private person, prefect or bailiff, shall disturb, molest, or presume otherwise in any way whatsoever to seek to extort anything from the aforesaid masters and scholars in person, family or property, under pretext of toll . . . tax customs, or any such personal taxes, or other personal exaction of any kind."

Immunity from the jurisdiction of local civil courts (*privilegium fori*) ranked as an extremely important right. A charter issued by Emperor Frederick I (1152–1190) in 1158 and confirmed by Pope Alexander III (1159–1181), for example, allowed students to decide whether they would be disciplined by their own teaching masters for any offense they might commit or submit themselves to the judgment of ecclesiastical authority. Almost identical was a reaffirmation of the same privilege as issued in the year 1200 by Philip Augustus of France (1180–1223) to students at Paris.

Equal in importance was exemption from out-of-town ecclesiastical courts, "the right of not being summoned outside" (*jus non trahi extra*). Pope Innocent IV (1243–1254), for one, confirmed the exemption for Parisian students as follows: "To the masters and scholars at Paris. So that you may pursue your studies more freely and be less occupied with other affairs, we . . . grant you the privilege of not being summoned by apostolic letters beyond the limits of the city of Paris regarding questions that have arisen within the city limits."[41]

Besides whatever privileges were granted by monarchs, emperors, or popes, students sometimes sought to exact special favors from local municipal authorities too. Considering the strained relations that usually prevailed between "town and gown," whatever concessions students were able to wrest from townspeople were apt to be significant. Records of medieval university life rather clearly leave an impression of near-constant anarchy and disorder. Even under the best of circumstances, an influx of youthful, high-spirited students within a city's precincts (ranging from a few hundred up into the thousands) carried with it the potential for trouble. Little was heard of the quiet, conscientious scholars who spent their days poring diligently over their studies, of a type immortalized in Chaucer's portrait of the "clerk of Oxenford" in his *Canterbury Tales*.[42] Its archaisms preserved intact, the following passage from the Prologue describes a thin, sober-minded student, one wholly absorbed in philosophical studies, forever borrowing funds from his friends in order to add to the meager stock of books kept at bedside, taciturn but well-spoken, indifferent to matters of dress or worldly goods, an intellectual of whom Chaucer wrote, "Gladly would he learn, and gladly teach":

> A Clerk ther was of Oxenford also,
> That un-to logik hadde long y-go.
> As lene was his hor as is a rake,
> And he was nat right fat, I undertake;
> But loked holwe, and ther-to soberly.
> Full thredbar was his overest courteby;
> For he had geten him yuet no benefice,
> Ne was so worldly for to have offyce.
> For him was lever have at his beddes heed
> Twenty bokes, clad in blak or reed,
> Of Aristotle and his philosophye,
> Than robes riche, or fithele, or gay sautrye.

But al be that he was a philosophre,
Yet hadde he but litel gold in cofre;
But al that he mighte of his freendes hente,
On bokes and on learnge he it spent,
And bisily gan for the soules preye
Of hem that yaf him wher-with to scoleye.
Of studie took he most cure and most hede.
Noght o word spak he more than was nede,
And that was seyd in forme and reverence,
And short and quik, and full of hy sentence,
Sounginge in moral vertu was his speche,
And gladly wolde he learne, and gladly teche.

But if the image of the student as scholar devoted to academic pursuits represented one part of the picture, there was another: that of the medieval university student as wastrel, vagabond, and incorrigible troublemaker. Conspicuous for their outrages, for instance, were the boisterous gangs of clerks that reportedly roamed the city's crowded streets and narrow alleys at all hours, accosting innocent townfolk as they passed. Burghers complained incessantly about pickpockets, about students gambling in public places, about stone-throwing incidents, vandalism and destruction of private property, about loud singing and quarrelsome tavern brawls. Students were notorious for cruel practical jokes, for sticking out their tongues and making faces at people, for singing baudy songs calculated to offend the sensibilities of the pious, for playing tambourines and guitars long past curfew. In 1269 at Paris, an official complained that students "by day and night atrociously wound and slay many, carry off women, ravish virgins, break into houses" and commit "over and over again robberies and many other enormities hateful to God." Further, he alleged, "They quarrel among themselves over dogs, women, or what-not, slashing off one another's fingers with their swords, or, with knives in their hands and nothing to protect their tonsured pates, rush into conflicts from which armed knights would hold back."[43]

Officials meted out harsh penalties when law and order were threatened, but sometimes to little effect. Typical was a statute for keeping the peace enacted at Oxford in 1432 by university authorities. "Since the unrestrained continuance in this University of execrable dissensions, which increase vices and idleness, has almost blackened its charming manners, its famous learning and its sweet reputation," it was observed, "and since there is no better punishment than a fine which in these days is more dreaded than anything, it is thought that imposing such a fine on the disturbers will be the quickest way to curb them, the Masters of the University unanimously order and decree that whoever is lawfully convicted of disturbing the peace, shall be fined according to the quantity and quality of his crime, over and above the usual penalties."

But students for their part had their own grievances as well. There were constant complaints of rapacious landlords charging excessive rents, of innkeepers who served sour ale and watered their wine, and merchants who allegedly cheated their customers at every turn. Citizens who unceremoniously dumped slops and the contents of chamber pots from their windows into the open sewers below were especially criticized. Equally offensive were the butchers who slaughtered livestock within city walls, leaving entrails and offal to accumulate in piles along public thoroughfares to attract vermin and swarms of flies. And when students' demands for redress of their grievances were ignored or rebuffed, they not infrequently resorted to violence.[44]

If ecclesiastical authorities did not intervene to rectify matters, secular officials did not hesitate to issue admonitions and ultimatums of their own. In 1231, for example, the Crown dispatched a lengthy missive to the mayor and bailiffs of Cambridge urging them to control student rents or face the prospect of the loss of economic benefits associated with hosting a major *studium* of scholars and students. "You are aware," the king reminded the mayor, "that a multitude of scholars from divers parts, as from this side of the sea as from overseas, meets at our town of Cambridge for study, which we hold a very gratifying and desirable thing, since no small benefit and glory accrue therefrom to our whole realm; and you, among whom these students personally live, ought especially to be pleased and delighted at it." He continued, "We have heard, however, that in letting your houses you make such heavy charges to the scholars living among you, that unless you conduct yourselves with more restraint and moderation towards them in this matter, they will be driven by your exactions to leave your town and, abandoning their studies, leave our country, which we by no means desire."

Whenever tensions between townfolk and students erupted, the result was tantamount to open warfare. Not infrequently it happened that the two opposing factions set upon one another with pikes, cudgels, swords, and pails of boiling water for days on end, and no one was safe in the streets. The most infamous example occurred on the feast day of St. Scholastica at Oxford in 1354. This particular riot started, as had many previously, as a tavern brawl. It soon spilled over into the streets. University officials sounded the alarm. Armed to the teeth, crowds of students set out to do battle. Door-to-door fighting raged on for two full days. Scholars were dragged from their hiding places and ruthlessly butchered; clerics were literally seized while officiating at the altar; some students were flayed alive in the public square. When the battle finally subsided and peace was restored, it appeared at first the townsfolk had carried the day. One eyewitness account reported: "Some twenty inns or halls were pillaged. Scholars were killed or wounded; their eatables and drinkables plundered; their books torn to pieces; the halls themselves fired." But the town's victory, such as it was, proved short-lived. In the end, it was the university that under royal decree won the right to regulate weights and measures in the marketplace, to fix rents, and to set up university courts to punish merchants accused of cheating their customers.

Far and away the most important privilege won by the university was the right to control the licensing of teachers. Traditionally, licensure had been the sole and exclusive prerogative of the Church; and ecclesiastical officials stoutly opposed the masters' guilds when they began insisting upon the right to establish their own rules for the admission of new members. The problem first assumed urgency at Paris where the ranking archdeacon of the cathedral had long held undisputed authority to grant teaching licenses. However, his sovereignty in this respect was limited by statute solely to the area under his direct jurisdiction, the Île de la Cité and the bridges over the Seine leading to the island. But as the *studium* grew larger, attracting increasing numbers of students, it spilled over into adjacent districts. There, along Straw Street, for example, recent graduates of the arts faculty who intended to continue studying in one of the higher faculties now found it profitable to begin teaching younger students on their own, without benefit of formal licensure. Rather quickly the teaching masters set about the task of putting their own house in order, laying down rules governing the qualifications of those who would be allowed to teach. Church officials moved just as promptly to counter the growing power of the masters' guilds, which they regarded as a direct threat to their own authority. Meanwhile, allegations were heard that ecclesiastical officials were charging unreasonable fees for licenses and that they all too readily accepted bribes in exchange for the coveted license, without regard for an applicant's scholarly qualifications.

In the confrontations that ensued, Church leaders sometimes went so far as to brandish the threat of outright excommunication. Appeals were sent to Rome. An interim step was taken by Pope Alexander III at the Third Lateran Council in 1179 when he issued a papal bull that inaugurated several important reforms but still reserved licensure as the exclusive right of the Church. Protests continued. Finally, in 1215 Pope Innocent III suggested a compromise that in effect legitimized the guilds' right to set licensing standards, though reserving the actual right of bestowal to chancellors or other high cathedral officials. In 1233 when Gregory X founded the University of Toulouse, he declared that any graduate master was entitled to teach in any other *studia* without further examination—the *jus ubique docendi,* the "right to teach anywhere." Some faculty guilds continued to insist upon a "resumption" (*resump-*

tio), that is, a formal disputation conducted by a newcomer before he was admitted to their ranks from another institution. Nevertheless, over time the *jus ubique docendi* was included within the founding charters of universities; and faculties embraced it because it confirmed their control over the conditions under which licensure was initially granted. Bologna was granted the right to establish its own teaching qualifications in 1291; Paris had the same privilege conferred by Nicholas IV in 1292; and it became the common pattern in most of the medieval universities established thereafter.

UNIVERSITY MIGRATIONS

Because the medieval university lacked fixed facilities of its own, only renting lecture halls and lodgings as needed, the act of suspending lectures and moving the entire *studium* to a new location was always a distinct possibility, as some towns and cities learned to their chagrin. Even the prospect of the sudden departure of hundreds, perhaps thousands, of students and their professors was a potent threat to any city whose economic vitality depended on the university's presence. For precisely this reason, the right to strike (*cessatio*), sometimes referred to as the *suspendium clericorum,* or "boycott," was an extremely important legal privilege wrested by the university from civil and ecclesiastical authorities. Thus, if local officials with whom the academics happened to be at odds failed to redress grievances, it was a relatively simple matter for the entire scholarly community to pull out and seek more congenial surroundings elsewhere.

Cities often bid against one another for the advantage of hosting a university, a situation some *studia* were quick to exploit. In the year 1228, for example, the city fathers at Vercelli offered students and scholars from Padua several powerful inducements to migrate to their city, including a promise of rent controls, exemption from local taxes, fixed-interest loans, and the use of several of the finest houses in the city as lecture halls.[45] In Bologna, officials grew alarmed over the tendency among the professors to seek out the highest bidders. Despite a decree from Pope Honorius III in 1217 that sought to invalidate municipal regulations against a *studium* emigrating to another town, city officials persisted in their efforts. Typical was a law enacted in 1227 requiring every master to take an oath that he would remain to teach for a minimum of two years. As late as 1432, Bolognese authorities were still attempting to prevent any teaching doctor over the age of fifty from departing for the purpose of lecturing elsewhere. Further, for anyone convicted of involvement in a conspiracy to relocate the local university to a competing city, the penalty under law was death.

The right of *cessatio* at Paris was won only as the outcome of a long and bitter struggle. A major step was taken in 1215 when Robert de Courçon laid down a series of famous statutes granting local teaching masters authority "to make among themselves or with others agreements and regulations" pertaining to rents and housing. Included among the privileges extended was conditional approval for the right to suspend lectures. A papal bull issued in 1231 by Pope Gregory IX (1227–1241), entitled the *Parens Scientiarum* ("Mother of Sciences"), went even further.[46] In response to disturbances that had led to a mass exodus of scholars from Paris to Rheims, Orléans, Toulouse, Angiers and other French cities, Gregory sought to stem the tide by placating those who had remained. Henceforth, he announced, the right to boycott would be protected as a means of redressing complaints arising from an unlawful imprisonment, injury or mutilation of a student, or out of any refusal upon the part of local authorities to enact and enforce rent controls. "Unless the injury ceases when you remonstrate," the pope informed the scholars, "you may, if you judge it wise, suspend your lectures immediately."

The specific events to which Pope Gregory responded had begun two years earlier (1229) in a major outbreak of hostilities between gown and town. It started, as had a previous uprising in the year 1200, with a tavern fight. An argument between students and an innkeeper over the wine bill turned into a general brawl. The tavern owner called in reinforcements and the students were summarily ousted from the premises. The next day the students returned, their numbers augmented by new recruits. Descending upon the tavern, they beat the keeper senseless and then sallied forth in search of new conquests. The local governor sent in mercenaries to help quell what had now degenerated into a full-scale riot. Protests were made on both sides. As the fighting raged on, appeals were carried to the queen regent, Blanche of Castile. She promptly called out troops who took their revenge by beating up an allegedly innocent band of students at play outside the city's walls. The savage attack left several students dead in the fields. The masters protested to the papal legate and the royal court, but their pleas fell on deaf ears. Finally, on the Monday of Easter week, April 16, 1229, the professors voted to close the university down for six full years.

Across the channel, the English king, Henry III, hearing of the turmoil at Paris, sought to take advantage of the situation by extending the following invitation:

> Greetings to the masters and the whole body of scholars at Paris. Humbly sympathizing with the exceeding tribulation and distresses which you have suffered at Paris . . . we wish by our pious aid, with reverence to God and His Holy Church, to restore your status to its proper condition of liberty. Wherefore we have concluded to make known to your entire body that if it should be your pleasure to transfer yourselves to our kingdom of England and to remain there to

study we will for this purpose assign to you cities, boroughs, towns, whatsoever you may wish to select, and in every fitting way cause you to rejoice in a state of liberty and tranquility which should please God and fully meet your needs.[47]

As it happened, a fairly large *studium generale,* described as a place where distinguished doctors had gathered about them "students of great fame and note," had been operating at Oxford since at least 1167, if not earlier.[48] Why Oxford had been chosen as a university site remains something of a mystery, since there already were important cathedral church schools at Exeter, Salisbury, Lincoln, and Canterbury. Whatever the reasons, Oxford early on had acquired a reputation for excellence in the teaching of theology and civil law. To this university came many scholars and students fleeing the Parisian riots of 1229. With them they brought their academic customs, titles, and ceremonies, many of which were eventually adopted at Oxford.

Meanwhile, internal difficulties some years before at Oxford had given rise to yet another mass exodus of scholars who "spun off" to found a new university of their own, this time at Cambridge in the marshlands of East Anglia.[49] As at Paris, the migration came about indirectly as the result of a pitched battle in 1209 between Oxford townsfolk and students. An innocent woman's death, allegedly at the hand of students, had led to widespread disorder and rioting. Two or three scholars were hanged for their crimes. The university suspended its operations in protest. Lengthy negotiations ensued, the result being that in 1214 townsmen who had participated in the lynching were required as penance to make a barefoot procession to the graves of their victims.

Similar incidents transpired throughout the remainder of the century, but always with the same result: repeated confirmation of the university's legal right to suspend lectures when officials deemed it necessary. Northampton's university between 1238 and 1264 was the product of migrations from Oxford and Cambridge, as was a *studium* at Salisbury that only lasted until about 1278. Ironically enough, by the time the right to threaten *cessatio* was no longer in dispute, the university's ability to wield it with any effect had lessened considerably. The chief cause at work was a loss of potential mobility brought about as the result of the growth of endowed residential halls, or colleges, within the *universitas* itself.

COLLEGES

As early as the twelfth century there were strong pressures encouraging the development of student houses or "hospices" (*hospitia*) in which students could be housed under the watchful eye of university officials.[50] Most originated within existing hostels, sometimes in hospitals with extra beds to spare.

The earliest *hospicium* was a simple affair, consisting of eighteen beds reserved for students under the terms of an endowment provided in 1180 by a certain Jocius de Londoniis to the Hospital of the Blessed Mary of Paris, known more commonly as the Hôtel Dieu. Students who lodged there were subject to no special regulations or supervision beyond those imposed upon ordinary patients. A half century or so later this simple college had evolved into an independent community with a building of its own. It maintained its existence until 1789 as a consolidation of other small *hospitia* and was called the College of Louis the Grand. Endowments supplied by other philanthropists, including Count Robert of Dreux, Étienne Belot, several abbots from Cluny and Clairvaux, and Robert de Sorbon, the canon of Cambrai and later of Paris (from whom the modern Sorbonne derives its name) supported other independent colleges in years following. The College of Ave Maria at Paris, for example, was one of the earliest of two dozen or so such institutions established at Paris in the first half of the fourteenth century.

For university officials and students alike, the advantages of living in *collegia* became obvious. Students benefited because they could live four or five to a room, take their meals in common, and enjoy the protection afforded by controlled rents. University officials, ever anxious to keep their charges out of trouble, likewise appreciated the opportunities for adequate supervision thereby afforded. At Sorbon's institution, for example, stringent rules were enforced. "No student shall bring friends [*extraneos*] frequently to drink at the expense of the community; if he does he has to defray the costs," it was ordered. "No student shall have the keys to the kitchen. No woman of whatever status shall eat with students in their chambers. If anyone does this he must pay the fixed penalty." Further, it was decreed, "If a student attacks, knocks down or severely beats one of the students he has to pay one sester of wine to his fellows, and this wine ought to be of a better to best quality."

In England, Walter de Merton was among the first (c. 1250) to recognize the need to provide lodgings for senior students attending Oxford who otherwise lacked proper accommodations. Much the same was provided for younger students by William of Wykeham (1324–1404) who founded the College of St. Mary of Winchester at Oxford. Such simple dormitories evolved over time into quite elaborate institutions, each with its own special rights and privileges, and eventually its own distinctive character. When masters and senior students or fellows began to tutor the younger boys and arranged disputations and exercises for them in-house instead of within a separate lecture hall, the pattern was set for officials to dispense with outside instruction entirely. In effect, over time colleges collectively came to constitute the university itself. Whereas residential colleges of this type generally died out on the continent, they gradually became a standard feature of English universities. By the sixteenth and seventeenth centuries, English colleges were semi-autonomous corporations, each headed by a principal elected by his peers to administer the college's internal affairs. Once colleges invested in fixed dwellings, it might be noted, they of course lost their physical mobility, as did the university as a whole.

THE CONTRIBUTION OF THE MEDIEVAL UNIVERSITY

Their real and undoubted contributions notwithstanding, it would be misleading to assume a simple linear descent from the universities of the Middle Ages to their contemporary counterparts. In point of fact, the historical lineage is somewhat discontinuous and indirect in certain respects. The most obvious difference is one of architecture. Not until Tudor times did Oxford and Cambridge, for example, begin to acquire the elaborate neo-Gothic edifices for which they would become famous. The prototypical medieval university in its formative period, it should be recalled, lacked physical facilities or a campus as such: there were no carefully manicured lawns and greens, no quadrangles—indeed, no fixed buildings at all.

Secondly, it is difficult to discern much substantive connection between the curriculum or plan of studies common in the medieval university and that of a present-day institution of higher learning. At most, the principle was preserved that instruction in various sciences, arts and letters (the *trivium* and the *quadrivium*), the rough equivalent of "undergraduate" studies, were commonly regarded as preparatory to higher, or more advanced "graduate" professional study in some specialized discipline (civil and canon law, medicine or theology). Nor is one able to find in the medieval university much of the notion of liberal learning for its own sake, or for the promotion of the "well-rounded" individual as a major educational consideration. The medieval university was first and foremost a professional school for a select few discrete professions. On the other hand, to the extent that the modern university has become increasingly "professional" or "vocational" in its orientation—emphasizing careerism and occupationally relevant instruction—it probably has come to resemble its medieval forbear to a greater extent than ever before.

Thirdly—an admittedly minor point—whereas medieval schoolmen made full use of academic regalia, including gowns or robes and special caps, the paraphernalia commonly worn at commencement ceremonies and processionals in modern universities did not win widespread acceptance until the nineteenth century at the very earliest. Thus, the historical accuracy and longevity of garb worn today have been greatly exaggerated. The truth of the matter is that contemporary ceremonial robes and hats bear scant resemblance to those favored in medieval times.

Fourthly, while it is true that much of the nomenclature of academic titles—proctors, rectors, chancellors, deans, presidents, and so forth—has survived, there is little correspondence between how such titles were applied in the late Middle Ages and such titular designations as they find use today. A better correspondence between the medieval and modern university is illustrated in the continued use of such terms as bachelor of arts, master's degree, and doctor of philosophy, the Ph.D. The clearest link between the two institutional types inheres in the sense of corporate institutional identity, together with an elaborate system of rights, privileges, prerogatives, and special forms of academic authority.

Such caveats notwithstanding, the importance of the universities as an element of medieval culture can scarcely be exaggerated. As many commentators have noted, universities did help shape the progress and intellectual development of Europe more powerfully than did any other cultural institution of the time. It was in the universities that knowledge was organized, preserved, and transmitted. As a center of learning where learning was advanced, stimulated, and codified, the university served as an oasis of intellectual freedom in an age profoundly suspicious of the slightest taint of heresy. It was the one place where forbidden or suppressed questions could be discussed (albeit not without attempts at interference) with what hostile critics termed "brazen impudence." There was virtually no question too thorny, no problem touching upon the most fundamental issues of life too sacrosanct to be posed and examined within its halls. Only in the university could there emerge the twin traditions of *Lehrfreiheit* ("freedom to teach") and *Lernfreiheit* ("freedom to learn") essential to its mission.

Needless to add, the development of intellectually free universities did not proceed without strong opposition. An address in 1290 before an ecclesiastical council by Pope Boniface VIII offers a revealing example. On that occasion the prelate vigorously chided the teaching masters at Paris for their seeming disrespect for established orthodoxy. "At Rome," Boniface declared, "we account them more foolish than the ignorant, men who have poisoned by their teaching not only themselves but also the entire world. You masters of Paris have made all your learning and doctrine a laughingstock. . . . It is all trivial. . . . To us your fame is mere folly and smoke."[51] To this might be added countless other examples of efforts by external authorities, both ancient and modern, to denigrate the work of universities and to disparage the efforts of those who have served within them.

Nevertheless, when universities were successful in fending off those who sought their intellectual domestication, they served in their own time as vital and energetic catalysts for learning.[52] Above all, although few could have predicted it in advance, the rise of the universities effectively spelled the end of the Church's monopoly on teaching and learning. Once securely established, universities did not hesitate to intervene in public affairs, to air grievances before kings and popes alike, to offer advice, and to pass upon a variety of important legal and religious questions. Europe's intellectual center of gravity thus shifted inexorably from the monastic community to the schools, from monks to professors; and hence, in a very real if indirect way, helped usher in the modern age.

3

Post-Medieval Academe: Evolution and Estrangement

CLASSICISM AND ITALIAN HUMANISM

The medieval poet Guillaume de Guilleville's declaration, "Your life here is but a pilgrimage," crystallizes with exceptional clarity the basic temper of the Middle Ages. The true significance of earthly life—or so it was held— was that its character determined the fate of one's soul struggling on a perilous journey toward heaven or hell. The hazards en route were manifold, for legions of darkness—incubi, succubi, undines, witches, sylphs, and other horrors—sought by devious means to ensnare the unwary and lead them to perdition. Hell's denizens were even reputed to assume the alluring forms of saintliness and purity in order better to outwit the pious. But the traveler's allies were equally potent. Guardian angels forever hovered nearby to intercede on one's behalf; and the merciful Virgin could be relied upon to protect sinners from the spirits of malediction or God's stern wrath. Mother Church—God's earthly custodian of souls—stood vigilant meanwhile to protect her righteous and obedient children. And when the Day of Judgment arrived, the wicked would be thrown into eternal torment, but the souls of the virtuous, now purified and sanctified, would ascend into the heavens, there to dwell in eternal bliss.[1] This, in essence, encapsulated the officially sanctioned medieval worldview, a compound of popular piety, conventional religiosity and institutionalized precept.

Even as this medieval vision was being rationalized in the *Summa* of Thomas Aquinas (1225–1274) and celebrated in the *Divina Commedia* of Dante Alighieri (1265–1321), however, an intellectual shift of major proportions was taking place. It was a development stimulated in part by many of the same social, economic, and political forces that had contributed to the previous cultural synthesis. Hence, use of the traditional term, "Renaissance," (literally, *re-naissance,* or "rebirth") to denote the rise of worldliness that characterized much of Europe from the mid-fourteenth century onward is misleading if it suggests a sudden cultural revival unrelated to such forces as the growth of politically emancipated towns, increase in trade, the replacement of guilds by independent bankers and entrepreneurs, and so on.[2] In point of fact, out of the later High Middle Ages and its feudal order grew cities, leagues, states, international commerce, a new merchant class, parliaments, corporate liberties, early forms of constitutional government, important technological innovations, and much else besides, all of which helped to shape and define the cultural transformation suggested by the term "rebirth."[3]

Traditional scholarship, it must be said, has tended to exaggerate the novelty of the Renaissance in relation to the age immediately preceding. Jacob Burckhardt's classic 1860 study, *The Civilization of the Renaissance in Italy,* for example, represents the rebirth as a decisive break with the medieval past.[4] As the opening chapter of the modern era, Burckhardt claimed, the Renaissance was a revolt against the asceticism, collectivism, and authoritarianism of the Middle Ages. A more balanced view would acknowledge fundamental continuities between the Europe of the 1200s and the next two centuries following, even with due allowance for important differences as well.[5] Perhaps the most defensible generalization is that the dawning era was a time when European culture had reached a level of complexity, sophistication, and expansiveness such that it could no longer be contained within old thought forms and strictures. New paradigms were needed. By the midpoint of the 1300s or thereabouts, at any rate, the thousand-year medieval gestation and maturation of the West was about to assert itself in a series of enormous cultural convulsions that would give birth to the modern world.

A key to understanding the shift to secularism and worldliness exemplified by the Renaissance is to be found in the emergence of a new consciousness: expansive, rebellious, energetic and creative, individualistic, ambitious, curious, self-confident, and skeptical in character. This quickening spirit tended to look not to otherworldly concerns and salvation in the afterlife, but increasingly, rather, to the full and rich possibilities for human fulfillment in this world. Pico della Mirandola's *Oration on the Dignity of Man,* for illustration, has God address humanity with a reminder of its potential for self-enhancement and development:

"We have set thee at the world's center that thou mayest from thence more easily observe whatever is in the world. We have made thee neither of heaven nor
of earth, neither mortal nor immortal, so that with freedom of choice and with
honor, as though the maker and molder of thyself, thou mayest fashion thyself
in whatever shape thou shalt prefer." Human existence thus was to be appreciated for its inherent value, having its own significance or importance independent of some otherworldly spiritual destiny; and humankind was free to make of
its freedom whatever it willed.[6]

Paradoxically, burgeoning confidence in human potency to refashion the self
and the natural world typical of Renaissance thought came to fruition against
the background of a series of unmitigated disasters, and it thrived despite continuous social upheaval. Beginning at the middle of the fourteenth century
(1348), the black plague swept across Europe, taking with it upwards of a third
of the continent's entire population.[7] The Hundred Years War between England
and France (1337–1453) proved an interminable and ruinous conflict. Equally
vicious wars ravaged Italy throughout the same period. Severe economic
depressions succeeded one another with monotonous regularity; as did
internecine religious warfare and political conspiracies throughout the length
and breadth of Western Christendom. Gross superstition flourished. For years
on end, the reign of terror inaugurated under the Inquisition held sway, and the
fires of the auto-da-fé burned brightly. Bitter ecclesiastical struggles became
almost routine; famine and pestilence were realities faced daily by thousands;
and—as if domestic violence and unrest were not enough to occupy people's
energies—beyond loomed the ever-present specter of Turkish hordes threatening to overwhelm Europe at any time. As for the Church, long a symbol of
stability and order, to increasing numbers of critics, it appeared to have grown
irremediably corrupt and sclerotic, utterly devoid of whatever spiritual
integrity it might have once possessed.

Against a backdrop of violence and social chaos, a determined revolt against
the cramping narrowness of medievalism and an insistent demand for a larger
and fuller life proceeded unimpeded nevertheless.[8] For Francesco Petracco
(1304–1374), better known as Petrarch, the preceding millennium since the
decline of Rome had been little more than a "dark" interregnum between the
golden age of Greece and Rome and his own time.[9] For him and many of his
contemporaries, the single most pressing intellectual challenge facing the
"modern" world accordingly was to recover and revivify that classical past,
to animate it and give it life once again in the historical present. Medieval
schoolmen had long been at work rediscovering and integrating ancient works.
But now Petrarch drastically shifted the tone and focus of this work of intellectual reclamation. Rather than concentrating more or less exclusively on

Aristotelian logic and philosophy in order to place them in the service of Christian truth, after the fashion of the medieval scholastics, Petrarch sought to retrieve the larger corpus of classical belle lettres for its own sake: poetry, philosophy, essays, histories, biographies, letters—the full genius of classical thought in all of its literary and aesthetic expressions.

"I am still in the thrall of one insatiable desire which hitherto I have been neither able nor willing to check," Petrarch confided to a correspondent around the year 1346. "I cannot get enough books. It may be that I have already more than I need, but it is with books as it is with other things: success in acquisition spurs the desire to get still more."[10] In company with other scholars such as Lovato, a learned judge from Padua (1241–1309), and his associate, Albertino Mussato (1262–1329), Petrarch set about the task of finding and absorbing whatever literary classics of antiquity had survived over the centuries. His efforts were to help inaugurate a fashion for discovering and collecting ancient manuscripts that spread rapidly throughout Italy.[11] Cathedral church-houses and monasteries in Pomposa, Naples, Ravenna, and elsewhere were combed assiduously for surviving scraps of text authored by such classical luminaries as Cicero, Virgil, Horace, Livy, Plato, and Homer. More and more scholars took up the search; and each new discovery was greeted with intense excitement. No longer absorbed with the syllogistic hairsplitting and cerebral analysis of the medieval scholastics, Renaissance scholarship now undertook the gargantuan task of collating, editing, correcting, and translating texts comprising an entire literary heritage, a long-lost legacy heretofore neglected and unappreciated. Henceforth, Renaissance humanists avowed, *studia humanitatis*—studies of humanity—would take their legitimate place alongside *studia divinitatis* as a legitimate end of scholarly inquiry.

Many others joined in the search for the classical past. Their ranks included, among the more distinguished, Giovanni Boccaccio, Leonardo Bruni d'Arezzo, Jacopo di Agnolo da Scarperia, and Pietro Paolo Vergerio, as well as countless others. With the arrival in Italy of the Byzantine scholar Manuel Chrysoloras (1350–1415), who taught classical Greek in Florence toward the close of the 1300s, Greek studies received new impetus; and by the end of the fourteenth century, a general revival of classical learning was well established, both in Greek and Latin, in most of the major Italian city-states.[12] Among them, Florence quickly established itself as the main center of classical humanistic studies, or *litterae humaniores,* its prominence owed in no small measure to the patronage of the de' Medici family and certain leading church officials.[13] But civil and ecclesiastical leaders in other states likewise acted as patrons for the new learning: in Ravenna, Venice, Naples, Rome, and other cities. All told, the quest to recover the major classics of antiquity became the major intellectual preoccupation of fourteenth- and fifteenth-century Italy. Inevitably, within the space of a few short decades, Italian humanism and its ideals began to extend its influence northward into the rest of Europe, albeit assuming sometimes a rather different character or orientation in the process of its dispersion.[14]

At the same time, a creative outburst of vernacular literature by authors infected with the humanistic spirit was making itself felt. The new literary wave, thoroughly courtly and aristocratic in its origins, was led by Naples, Florence, and Ferrara, in defiance of a tradition that had long considered the vernacular unsuited for literary usage. The *novelle,* or short story form, became immensely popular, as did the pastoral romance and the romantic epic. Boccaccio's *Ameto* and the *Ninfale Fiesolano,* not to mention his *Decameron,* were widely admired as exemplars for the new genres, and both his prose and poetry found avid audiences nearly everywhere. So too did Sannazaro's *Arcadia* as a model for the pastoral romance. The case for using the vernacular instead of medieval Latin was indisputably advanced also with the publication of epics by Pulci, Boiardo, and Ariosto.

Interestingly, among Italian humanists, men by no means enjoyed a monopoly on learning. Women too were reasonably well represented among the ranks of humanist correspondents, letter-writers, poets, and literary authors.[15] Especially in northern Italy, upper and middle class families were inclined to seek much the same education for their daughters as for their sons; and in more than a few cases women well versed in literary and artistic pursuits won high respect for their intellectual accomplishments.[16] Notable examples included Constanza Varano, Cecilia Gonzaga, and Vittoria Colonna—each the product of a prominent ruling family. Sometimes fathers took a direct hand in educating a talented daughter, as was the case with Alesandra Scale who was trained by her father, Bartolommeo of Florence. Laura Cereta studied with her father, Silvestro; and Caterina Caldera received her tutelage at the hands of her father Giovanni, a noted physician of the day.

In other instances, women renowned for their letters, orations, dialogues, treatises and poetry had received their education from private tutors. The three famous Nagarola sisters (Angela, Isotta, and Ginevra) of Verona were taught by Martino Rizzoni, himself a student of the great Guarino Beronese. Cassandra Fedele was taught by Gasparino Borro. Olimpia Morata studied alongside her two brothers under the direction of a house tutor. Others included Maddalena degli Scrovegni; Battista Malatesta; Niccolosa Castellani Sanuti; Ippolita Sforza, daughter of Francesco Sforza, the duke of Calabria and king of Naples; Cassandra Fidelis of Venice; Alessandra Scala of Florence; Francesco Filelfo; Lianoro Lianori of Bologna; and Angelo Poliziano. Two others of a slightly later date deserving mention were Olimpia Morata of Ferrara and Elena Lucrezia Cornaro Piscopia.

ACADEMIES AND THE IDEAL OF THE COURTIER

Southern or Italian humanism attained its greatest heights in the latter part of the Quattrocento and the first half of the Cinquecento following (fourteenth and fifteenth centuries, respectively).[17] Universities had proliferated over the preceding two centuries—at Bologna, Padua (founded c. 1222), Vicenza (1202), Vercelli (1228) and Naples (1224), followed by Reggio, Perugia, Verona, Piza, Siena, Florence, Pavia, and Padua, and in a few other northern Italian cities about a hundred years later.[18] Yet ironically it was not until toward the close of the fifteenth century that humanist doctrines began to make their way into the universities, and even then the influence was a limited one. Most of the Italian *studia* had continued to develop more or less independently along the lines of their original medieval traditions, and they remained thereafter largely unaffected by the ferment of classical learning. The reasons for their relative isolation from the main currents of Renaissance thought are somewhat complex and not easily summarized. Most were strictly local municipal institutions of little distinction or reputation.[19] A majority adhered closely to a strictly professional preparatory role emphasizing law, theology, or medicine. Literary studies consequently found little space in their curricula, even within the arts faculties, whose members remained devoted to the traditional disciplines of the *trivium* and *quadrivium*.

Rebuffed by the universities, Italian Renaissance humanism found a far more congenial home instead in a new network of alternative institutions of higher learning called, simply, academies.[20] Lacking the inhibiting traditions of medieval organization and methodology characteristic of the *studia,* humanist academies came to play a major role in the popularization and dissemination of neoclassical learning. (In the early seventeenth century they were to play an identical role in the spread of scientific learning as well.) Academies as a rule were not teaching institutions in the conventional sense of the term, since they offered neither organized courses of instruction nor formal academic degrees. Rather, they evolved as strictly voluntary associations of scholars who shared a common interest in literary studies and exegetical pursuits.

Under the patronage of Cosimo de' Medici (r. 1434–1464) and his grandson Lorenzo (r. 1469–1492) who installed a certain Marsilio Ficino in the Villa de' Careggi in Florence, the earliest and most important of these associations was chartered as the Accademia Platonica, in self-conscious imitation of the original Platonic Academy.[21] Other associations of *literati* and *dilettanti* soon followed: the Accademia dei Filleleni in Venice, the Accademia degli Infiammati in Padua, the Accademia degli Affidati in Pavia, and the Accademia Firentina and the Accademia della Crusca, both in Florence. Later additions to the roster, including the famous Accademia dei Lincei ("Academy of the Lynx-eyed"), founded at Rome in 1601; and the Accademia del Cimento ("Academy of Experimentation"), were more closely oriented toward scientific rather than literary studies. In each case, however, the Italian academies served an important function in furnishing a forum where learned amateurs could meet to converse on cultural and intellectual matters of common interest.

New schools were created under humanistic inspiration. Certainly the best known of these was the *Casa Giocosa,* or "Pleasant House," founded by Vittorino da Feltre (1378–1446), tutor to the family of Gianfrancesco Gonzaga of Mantua.[22] Here students were exposed to Latin and Greek literature, history, philosophy, poetry, music—the whole conjoined with games and healthy physical exercise, as suggested by the practices of courtly life in the major Italian city-states. In time the House of Joy, and a few other experiments like it, acquired reputations rivalling those of many of the Italian *studia.* As Guarino Guarini (1370–1460), court tutor at Ferrara, put it, the educational task was to train the whole person, body, mind, and spirit, and thereby prepare each individual to live as full and rich a life as possible.

Pietro Paolo Vergerio (1349–1420) of Padua summed up the aim of humanistic learning. A good education, he declared in *On Liberal Studies* (1401), is one that "calls forth, trains and develops those highest gifts of body and of mind, which ennoble men and are rightly judged to rank next in dignity to virtue only." In agreement with Guarino who insisted that knowledge of Greek and Latin were essential marks of an educated person, Vergerio went even further in declaring that the ideal type was best represented by Cicero's statesman and Quintilian's "good man skilled in speaking." The purpose of an education was to arm one for life's struggles, to prepare for engagement with the world, to become involved effectively in commercial enterprise and social service. In fleshing out their portrait of the ideally educated person, it was only natural perhaps that the Italian classicists should have recourse to the examples of the highest civilization they knew, the Greco-Roman. What better way, they must have asked themselves, to usher in a new golden age than to endeavor to produce leaders for their own time in the mold of the orators, rhetoricians, and statesmen of ancient Rome? And if the world had grown, so to speak, ever more "Machiavellian," all the more reason to appeal to the humanistic wisdom of antiquity as a guide to high-minded action and the practice of civic virtue.

To the medieval notion of educating men in the knightly skills of running, riding, jousting, swordsmanship, swimming, and dancing, humanist educators grafted the idea of literary training also. If one was to serve his ruler effectively in some administrative or diplomatic office, humanist theorists believed, it was imperative that the person be a well-rounded individual, one thoroughly conversant with literary, historical, philological, and philosophical studies. Training in courtly manners was also essential. The *Libro del Cortegiano* ("The Book of the Courtier") of Baldessare Castiglioni (1478–1529) supplied something close to a definitive statement of this Italian Renaissance educational ideal.[23] The real need, Castiglioni argued, was to adapt teaching and learning to the needs of the laity, the overwhelming majority of which were destined to become neither clerks nor scholars, but citizens and secular men of affairs.[24] The "manly" arts of hunting, weaponry, the equestrian arts, and so forth were all important, he emphasized, but they needed to be supplemented with systematic instruction in the literary arts, broadly defined. A gentleman should both speak and write with force and eloquence, based on thorough acquaintance with such fundamental studies as history, poetry, ethics, grammar, logic, and composition. He should be adorned with letters and well versed in the social etiquette governing court life. But, as he implied repeatedly, such an education could not be had from traditional schools, universities included. Institutions in which students' time was monopolized by old barren grammatical and rhetorical studies, where barbarous medieval Latin held sway over the purer Ciceronian style of antiquity, and where learning was exclusively bookish and academic were unfit to meet the preparatory needs of the true gentleman-courtier. Personal experience, travel, private tutors, secular court schools, and academies—these were the proper means of receiving a fit education.

NORTHERN HUMANISM

The revival of classical studies in northern Europe between the fifteenth and seventeenth centuries bore little resemblance in style or tone to the Italian Renaissance of which it was basically an offshoot. North European humanism evidenced little of the sheer exuberance of its Italian counterpart, much less of the latter's expansive interest in nature and humanity, and scarcely anything at all of the radical individuality and heaven-storming promethean spirit that had so characterized Italian city life in the fourteenth and fifteenth centuries. What northern scholars eventually found instead in the revival of classical studies was a source of inspiration for the ideals of sobriety, moderation, and decorum. More conventional and religious in its aspirations, northern humanism thus sought not the zestful rejection of tradition and authority but, rather, a reaffirmation of the classical notions of balance, restraint, and harmony. Its goal, one might say, was not the maximal self-realization of the secular individual *per se,* but the cultivation of a *pietas literata,* or "lettered piety," the hoped-for outcome of a proper synthesis of classical learning and Christian religiosity.[25]

Humanistic studies of the latter sort were first introduced by a Spanish scholar, Mebrissensis, at Seville and Salamanca around 1473. Humanism also made considerable headway at the University of Alcalá under the patronage of Cardinal Francisco Ximénez. Two students of Italian scholarship, Thomas Linacre (1460–1524) and William Grocyn (1446–c. 1514) brought Greek learning to Oxford where it was well received, eventually attracting the support of Thomas More (1478–1535), John Colet (1466–1519), William Lily, and other leading English scholars and academicians.[26] The first German of note to study in Italy, Peter Luder (1415–1474), met with less success in attempting to awaken an interest in classicism at Erfurt and Leipzig in the mid-fifteenth century. More influential were two learned Dutch scholars, Johann Wessel (1420–1489) and Rodolphus Agricola (1443–1485), who contributed to the early emergence of Heidelberg as a haven for humanist studies. Similarly, in the free cities of Flanders and Holland, humanistic learning was accorded a warm welcome, as illustrated in the work of Alexander Hegius, rector of a well-known school at Deventer between 1465 and 1498, and that of the illustrious statesman and scholar Desiderius Erasmus (1466–1536).[27] Other early northern humanists of note included Jean Luis Vives (1492–1540), Johannes Reuchlin (1455–1522), and Beatus Rhenanus, each of whom in varying ways were instrumental in popularizing Renaissance ideals.

Eminent scholars such as Guillaume Budé (1468–1540), Jacques Lefevre d'Etaples (1450–1536) and Robert Gaguin similarly sought to introduce classical humanistic studies into France. In contrast to the reaction in the Low Countries, they met with an indifferent response for the most part; which is to say, the new learning and the conception of social life that accompanied it were much slower to establish themselves among the French than elsewhere. Opposition was centered chiefly in the University of Paris, which had long been dominated by a conservative Aristotelian scholasticism and for which it was much criticized by the likes of Pierre de la Ramé (1515–1572) and François Rabelais (1495–1553).

As it happened, the literary revival of modest proportions that did take place in France was stimulated mainly as a by-product of invasions into Italy launched by Charles VIII and Louis XII between 1494 and 1512. From a purely political perspective, the temporary occupations of the cities of Naples, Florence, Rome, and Milan were an abysmal failure. Culturally, however, they were important as the retreating French armies carried the new learning back home. Libraries, a royal press, and schools were set up to promote humanist thought when Francis I took the throne (r. 1515–1517) resolving to support arts and letters. Typical of the work being done was the reorganization by André Gouvéa of a town school at Bordeaux in the early 1500s. The Collège de Guyenne, as it was called, soon became reputed for its extensive library holdings, well-trained teachers, and a liberal curriculum rarely equalled north of the Alps.[28] At a higher level the famed Collège de France at Paris opened its doors in 1530 to offer instruction in Latin, Greek, and even Hebrew as well as mathematics, the latter still a considerable novelty as a subject of instruction in higher education. It was in fact a direct imitation of the Collegium Trilingue at Louvin which had been founded the year previous as a school for Biblical studies in Latin, Hebrew, and Greek. The Collège de France (also known as the Collège Royale) within a matter of just a few years was also offering rhetoric, civil law, philosophy, mathematics, botanical studies, medicine and surgery, and even Arabic.[29]

Lesser municipal colleges spread across southern France (though not in the north where religious controversies attending the outbreak of the Reformation made the founding of schools almost impossible). Indicative of the official favor Renaissance learning was winning among the nobles classes was the appointment of the humanist Budé as royal librarian in 1522. His dictum that everyone, kings included, should devote themselves to the liberal culture of Greek and Latin literature won widespread assent in courtly circles.

The recalcitrance of French schoolmen to embrace humanistic studies did not go unremarked. Rabelais, for one, was quick to poke fun at the reluctance of professors in universities to incorporate classical languages and literature within their teaching. Even when they did so, however, their seeming preoccupation with form over content, style over substance, led Michel de Montaigne (1533–1592) in an essay *On Pedantry* to complain: "We are constantly asking about a man, Does he know Greek or Latin? Can he write in verse or prose? What is really important is whether he has grown better or wiser; and that is overlooked." The problem, as Montaigne saw it, was that efforts were directed to the memory while leaving understanding and conscience empty. "Like birds which go forth from time to time to seek for grain and bring it back to their young in their beaks without tasting it," he observed sarcastically, "our pedants go gathering knowledge from books and never take it further than their lips before disgorging it." And what is worse, he added, students "are no better nourished by it than they are themselves. It passes from one person to another and only serves to make a show or to provide entertainment. What wonder is it that the youth who returns home after spending fifteen or sixteen years in such vain learning is only more foolish and overbearing for all his Latin and his Greek?"[30]

HUMANISM AND THE UNIVERSITIES

As was the case in Italy, whereas humanism was widely disseminated across northern Europe over the course of the fifteenth century and by the early

1500s had achieved the status of a major intellectual movement or style, Renaissance studies had not to any great extent yet penetrated established institutions of higher learning.[31] The German states provide a striking example of the seeming paradox of universities springing up in ever increasing numbers while remaining largely unaffected by new currents of thought.[32] In the fourteenth century there were five German universities in regular operation: Prague (founded around 1346), Vienna (1365), Heidelberg (1386), Cologne (1388), and Erfurt (1392). Shortly thereafter, Leipzig (1409) and Rostock (1419) were added to the list. Subsequent fifteenth-century additions came with the founding of Griefswald, Freiburg, Basel, Ingolstadt, Trèves, Maintz, Tübingen, Wittenberg, and Frankfurt an der Oder. Of these, only a handful fully embraced classical studies as elements of their respective curricula: Tübingen, Leipzig, Heidelberg, and Vienna. They were followed a bit later in piecemeal fashion by Wittenberg, Königsberg, Marburg, and Jena. In virtually every instance where humanism successfully penetrated academic cloisters, infiltration typically depended upon the efforts of individual scholars of sufficient reputation to overcome faculty resistance. Recalcitrant traditionalists who clung to the well-entrenched scholastic model of higher learning (as Johannus Reuchlin, for example, was to discover in his celebrated struggle to introduce the study of Hebrew) were not easily persuaded to broaden the cultural and intellectual basis of their instruction.

Renaissance learning fared better in England, where, as previously noted, it was first introduced at Oxford in the early sixteenth century by Linacre, Grocyn, and Colet.[33] Even so, humanistic studies failed to make much headway outside certain of the colleges at Oxford and Cambridge. Not until Henry VIII began to lend support for a literary revival at court did their popularity and acceptance begin to increase. Among the gentry at large, opinions toward the new learning differed greatly. Intellectual and cultural conservatives still held to the notion that knightly skills sufficed to define the gentleman. Others, such as the King's Secretary, Richard Pace, argued the need for a more literate and academically educated gentry. The latter position was given its most forceful expression in a very influential work of the time, *The Boke named the Governour,* penned in 1531 by Thomas Elyot, son of one of Thomas More's friends and a former pupil of Thomas Linacre.[34] The governing class of England, Elyot argued at length, needed to be persuaded to educate itself for public life and for assisting in the work of administration and government. In order to do so, its members were to steep themselves in literary, historical and philosophical studies. If they failed to do so, as Roger Asham pointed out in *The Schoolmaster* (1570), they would have to expect to see "meaner men's children" secure positions in those governmental offices which had customarily gone to members of the nobility.[35]

Needless to add, then—as in all times—there were those who were profoundly skeptical of the need for bookish learning of any sort whatsoever. A
character representing an English country gentleman, as depicted in Nicholas
Breton's *The Court and Country* (1618), for example, is made to observe,
"Now for learning, what your need is thereof I know not, but with us we can
learn to plough and harrow, sow and reap, plant and prune, thrash and fan, win-
now and grind, brew and bake, and all without books; and these are our chief
business in the country." The rustic then asks rhetorically, "Then what should
we study for, except it were to talk with the man in the moon about the course
of the stars? No, astronomy is too high a reach for our reason: we will rather
sit under a shady tree in the sun to take the benefit of the cold air, than lie and
stare upon the stars to mark their walk in the heavens, while we lose our wits
in the clouds. . . . But for great learning, in great matters, and in great places,
we leave it to great men. If we live within the compass of the law, serve God
and obey our king, and as good subjects ought to do, in our duties and our
prayers daily remember him, what need we more of learning?"[36]

The basic problem so far as institutions of higher learning were concerned,
reformers agreed, was they had long functioned almost exclusively as preparatory schools for scholastic clerics. It appeared to follow that universities
would not easily be transformed into places where society's future secular
leaders might obtain a liberal education. Francis Bacon (1561–1626) in *The
Advancement of Learning* was outspoken in his criticism of the universities for
their alleged neglect of the arts and sciences as a foundation of common
learning. "This dedication of colleges . . . to the use only of professory learning has not only been inimical to the growth of the sciences," he lamented, "but
has also been prejudicial to states and governments. From thence it proceeds
that princes when they have to choose men for business of state find a wonderful dearth of able men around them; because there is no collegiate education designed for these purposes, where men naturally so disposed and affected
might . . . give themselves especially to histories, modern languages, books
of policy and civil discourse; whereby they might come better prepared and
instructed to offices of state." Bacon concluded his diatribe questioning
"whether the readings, disputations, and other scholastic exercises anciently
begun, and since continued up to our time, may be profitably kept up, or
whether we should rather abolish them and substitute better."

THE INNS OF COURT

In point of fact, several alternatives to university-based instruction already
existed in fifteenth- and sixteenth-century England.[37] Sir John Fortesque, Chief
Justice of the realm between 1442 and 1461, in *De Laudibus Legum Anglae*

(c. 1468–1471) explained why it was that the so-called "Inns of Court" near London, for example, had won increasing popularity as places of higher education for sons of the gentry.[38] "In the universities of England the sciences [i.e., various branches of knowledge] are not taught unless in the Latin language," he noted. Since England's legal statutes historically had been recorded and codified in French and English as well as Latin, "they could not be conveniently learned or studied in the universities." However, Fortesque reported, "those laws are taught in a certain public academy . . . situated near the king's courts, where these laws are pleaded and disputed from day to day, and judgments are rendered in accordance with them by the judges, who are grave men, mature, expert and trained in those laws. So those laws are read and taught in these courts as if in public schools, to which students of the law flock every day in term-time. . . . There are in this academy ten lesser inns, and sometimes more, which are called inns of Chancery. To each of them at least a hundred students belong, and some of them a much greater number. . . . These students are, indeed, for the most part, young men, learning the originals and something of the elements of law, who, becoming proficient therein as they mature, are absorbed into the greater inns of the academy, which are called the Inns of Court. Of these greater inns there are four in number, and some two hundred students belong in the aforementioned form to the last of them."

Fortesque emphasized the point that only the rich and well-to-do could afford to pursue legal training in the Inns of Court. "There are not many who learn the laws in the inns except the sons of nobles. For poor and common people cannot bear so much cost for the maintenance of their sons." He added, "And merchants rarely desire to reduce their stock by such annual burdens. Hence it comes about that there is scarcely a man learned in the laws to be found in the realm, who is not noble or sprung of noble lineage."

By Fortesque's time the Inns had expanded to become more than a school of law. Instruction in the humanities was offered as well. "In these greater inns," he wrote, "indeed, and also in the lesser, there is, besides a school of law, a kind of academy of all the manners that the nobles learn. There they learn to sing and to exercise themselves in every kind of harmonics [i.e., choral singing]. They are also taught there to practice dancing and all games proper for nobles, as those brought up in the king's household are accustomed to practice." Admission for study was highly regarded as an avenue for professional advancement. "Scarcely any turbulence, quarrels, or disturbance ever occur there," the Chief Justice emphasized, "but delinquents are punished with no other punishment than expulsion from communion with their society, which is a penalty they fear more than criminals elsewhere fear imprisonment and fetters. For a man once expelled from one of these societies is never received into the fellowship of any other of those societies. Hence the peace is unbroken and the conversation of all of them is as the friendship of united folk."[39]

THE IMPACT OF CONFESSIONALISM

"Whoever examines the principles upon which that religion Christianity is founded," Machiavelli observed in 1513, "and sees how widely different from those principles its present practice and application are, will judge that her ruin or chastisement is near at hand." His judgment was eerily prophetic: just four years later Martin Luther posted his Ninety-five Theses at Wittenberg, and within a single generation half of Europe had abandoned Roman Catholicism for Protestantism.

The proximate causes of the Reformation were multiple. The papacy's clumsy, often heavy-handed attempt to finance the architectural and artistic monuments of the High Renaissance by the theologically dubious means of selling spiritual indulgences counted foremost among them. So too did the blatant buying and selling of lucrative ecclesiastical offices among the clergy. The secular aspirations and political machinations of such popes as Sixtus IV, Alexander VI, and Leo X added to an already volatile mix. The unedifying spectacle of a great schism (1378–1417) between two rival popes, one at Avignon and the other at Rome, each bitterly hurling accusations of heresy at one another, hardly helped bolster the Church's faltering prestige and authority either. Nationalist sentiment and regional rivalries certainly played a part in paving the way also, as did the spirit of individualism, skepticism, and secularism fomented by Italian humanism. Whatever the complex interplay of forces at work, it is enough to observe that when Luther was led step by step from forensic protest against abuses to open rebellion, culminating in his official excommunication in 1521, large portions of northern and western Germany were fully prepared to follow his reformist crusade out of the Church.[40] The outbreak soon spread to Denmark, to Sweden, and the Netherlands. Meanwhile, independent sectarian movements already had arisen in Switzerland under Ulrich Zwingli (1484–1531) and John Calvin (1509–1569), in Scotland under John Knox (1505–1572), and in England.

The paradox of the confessional revolts inheres in the contrast between what religious reformers intended and the actual practical consequences of their work. The Protestant movement was essentially primitivist in its intent, urging a return to the original standards of the Bible and the usages of the earliest Christian communities. Luther, Calvin, and Zwingli would have been astonished and puzzled by the extent to which their labors ultimately contributed to the growth of individualism, for none of them was an individualist in the modern sense; to the growth of nationalism, since each sought to restore Christian unity; or to the secularization of society, since their shared aim was precisely the opposite. Nevertheless, their decisive assertion of rebellious individualism, of personal conscience, of critical private judgment against the monolithic authority of the Roman Church opened up the way for religious pluralism, early forms of private capitalism, and rampant nationalism. The resulting empowerment of the various separate states and nations of Europe, in the final analysis, had the effect of destroying forever the medieval ideal of a unified Western Christendom.

The influence of confessionalism upon schooling generally and higher education in particular differed greatly, depending on time and place. Luther's call for a reformation of the schools as an essential part of the greater Reformation upon which Germany had embarked, for instance, met a ready response from princes and scholars who had adopted the Protestant faith.[41] Thanks to the untiring efforts of such Lutheran reformers as Philip Melanchthon, Johann Sturm, and Johannes Bugenhagen, each a humanist scholar in his own right, considerable progress was made in expanding opportunities for popular instruction.[42] But though much attention was paid to university reform as well, dramatic changes were far and few between. Humanist learning allied with Protestant theology might have made for a creative synergy. In actual fact, however, the characteristic stress among Protestant zealots upon "lettered piety" (*pietas literata*) carried with it a tendency toward degeneracy and formalism even when liberal studies did find a place in university teaching. And when they did not, universities persevered in their traditional task of preparing clerks for service to church or crown. Teaching as a prospective career for university graduates continued to offer the least desirable option, reminiscent of a comment by Jerome of Prague over a hundred years before (1416), who had reported that if a student "had no other means of livelihood, he had to go to the towns and villages and earn his living by teaching in some private school."

For his part, Luther was unsparing in his criticism of the universities of his own time, calling them "asses' stalls" and "devils' schools." They were, he exclaimed, dens of murderers, temples of Moloch, synagogues of corruption, "nests of gloomy ignorance" grown moribund under the weight of scholasticism and unbending tradition; and "nothing more hellish . . . ever appeared on earth . . . or ever would appear." Writing in 1524, he commented at length on all the signs of educational decline apparent around him, best illustrated, he felt, by the "deplorable example of the universities . . . in which men have not only undermined the gospel, but have, in addition, so corrupted the Latin and German languages that the miserable folk have been fairly turned into beasts, unable to speak or write a correct German or Latin, and well-nigh lost their natural reason to boot." Ever intemperate in expressing his views, Luther felt universities were "only worthy of being reduced to dust."

Where Calvinism predominated, similar efforts were undertaken to initiate educational reforms. French Huguenots founded no fewer than eight universities, not to mention almost three dozen secondary-level colleges in the sixteenth and early seventeenth centuries. Universities in Leyden, Amsterdam, Utrecht, and Groningen were all infused with the Swiss reformer's version of Christian piety and classical learning. Similar initiatives were launched too in the several Scandinavian states.

Protestant attempts to reorganize and reconceptualize higher learning on the twofold basis of humanism and religion prompted a similar effort on the part of Catholic educators, which attained several striking successes in the Catholic countries of southern Europe where Protestantism had made few inroads. The Society of Jesus founded by the Spanish noble Inigo Lopez, or Ignatius of Loyola (1491–1556), early on took the lead in building up a system of "colleges," universities, and training seminaries. By 1600 the Jesuits had established over two hundred such institutions; and their number was to double in the next century alone. Northern France, Belgium, Austria, Hungary, and Poland were the chief beneficiaries of the Jesuits' reforming efforts. Other Catholic teaching orders, including the Piarists, the Jensenists, and the Dominicans, were not long in following suit. Collectively, they were to play a critical role in spearheading the Church's struggle to regain territories lost to the Protestants, to repel their advances in countries beginning to waver, and to counter their missionary efforts among those who remained faithful to Rome. The building up of Jesuit colleges and universities, each boasting a three-year course in philosophy and science, followed by a four-year higher course of studies in theology, excited the envy of those otherwise harboring little sympathy for the Jesuits' goals.[43] As the Protestant Francis Bacon observed ruefully in an often-quoted remark, "They are so good that I wish they were on our side" (*Talis quum sis, utinam noster esses*).

Reform in England, of course, proceeded largely from political, not religious motives. In 1530 Henry VIII petitioned Rome for permission to divorce Catherine of Aragon and to marry Anne Boleyn so that a legitimate male successor to the throne would be assured. The pope's politically motivated delay outraged the king to the point where all ties with the Roman Church were severed. Parliament's Act of Supremacy of 1554 in effect conferred upon the reigning English monarch titular leadership of a new Church of England. The Treasons Act enacted shortly thereafter gave Henry a free hand against all opponents of what pundits promptly dubbed "a papacy without the pope." The English Church assumed functions formerly exercised by the Catholic; in many cases the same priests were retained in parish churches. Alterations in doctrine and ritual were minimal. Queried as to how he had survived the shift, one anonymous cleric who had begun his career as an ordained Catholic priest and ended up as an Anglican explained, "I was rather as a supple willow, bending in the breeze, than a sturdy oak, disposed to be broken in the storm."

Henry's successor, Edward VI, perpetuated the new order. The Uniformity Acts of 1552 required everyone, clergy and teachers alike, to swear allegiance to the national Church and abide by its dictates. Succeeding years witnessed a religious narrowing of all instruction to guarantee orthodoxy among the populace. Teachers had to be licensed by the Church and were obliged to conform in every particular to the precepts and authority of the Anglican faith. An attempt at Catholic restoration (1553–1558) proved to be only an interlude, and was followed by the thorough Protestantization of the English Church under Queen Elizabeth I (r. 1558–1608). Anglican control remained firm throughout Elizabethan times, and ruthless measures were made to stamp out both Catholic and Puritan loyalties within the universities. Elizabeth's Supremacy Acts of 1559 and 1563 and the Act of Uniformity, for example, strictly prohibited Catholics and evangelical dissenters either from enrolling in or graduating from Oxford or Cambridge. Following the civil war of 1642–1649, when Oliver Cromwell (1599–1658) became Lord Protector of the Commonwealth, Puritanism flourished openly within university cloisters for a time, only to undergo repression once again with the Restoration of 1660 and the reign of Charles II. The so-called Clarendon Codes enacted between 1662 and 1665 once again required all office-holders to swear fealty to the sovereign as dual head of both church and state: "Which said declaration and acknowledgment," it was ordered, "shall be subscribed by every of the said masters and other heads, fellows, chaplains, and tutors of, or in any college, hall, or house of learning, and by every . . . professor and reader in either of the universities, before the vice-chancellor of the respective universities."[44]

One significant consequence of conformity legislation, together with supporting statutes drawn up by Oxford and Cambridge that excluded all religious nonconformists, was that non-Anglican clergymen and members of the laity were effectively precluded from attending universities. A further result was the appearance of dissenting academies. Over seventy were eventually established, of which at least three dozen or so offered theological training in addition to a wider general education. Prominent academies included institutions at Hoxton, Taunton, Kibworth, Northhamton, Warrington, and Leicestershire, among others. So successful were these alternative institutions that over time they began to attract Anglican applicants as well as the sons of nonconformists. Beyond preparation for the ministry, leading academies offered a more utilitarian curriculum or course of studies than that found in the universities, encompassing history, geography, and modern as well as classical languages. In a later phase of their existence, botany, zoology, chemistry, anatomy, hydrology, meteorology, cartography, astronomy, trigonometry, and algebra likewise were added. Additionally, a major advantage of the typical dissenting academy was that it was perceived to offer the advantages of a residential education at only a small fraction of the cost of studying in a university.

In countries where Protestantism emerged triumphant, England most particularly, the single greatest change within the universities brought about by the Reformation was the abolition of canon (i.e., Church) law as a subject of study and the abrupt elimination of degrees awarded in canon law. With a single stroke, an entire profession was wiped out, not to mention the oldest and most important course of professional preparation formerly offered within the universities. The study and practice of common civil law, the profession for which one was educated at the Inns of Court, suddenly surpassed canon law as the most powerful legal career. Henceforth too, while clergymen would continue to receive their training in the universities, they would be trained as parish clergy, not as canon lawyers or monastic leaders. This shift from the collegiate ideal of the cleric-scholar to the lay professional was a momentous one, carrying with it far-reaching consequences for the basic purposes, general character, essential spirit and substance of institutions of higher education.[45]

The very meaning of attending a university was transformed.[46] To pursue higher studies now became more a matter of confirming one's social status and class, or of moving toward higher social rank, than a matter of direct professional preparation and advancement within the Church. Rather quickly the composition of university students changed. With the growth of the idea that learning was no longer a matter solely for clerks, but an adornment of refined gentlemen, admission to a university became attractive to both the sons of the gentry as well as the nobility. On the other hand, it lessened prospects for the poorer classes— seventeenth-century registrars at Cambridge, for example, reveal that fewer than a third of all entrants were listed as the sons of shopkeepers, artisans, yeomen, farmers, or husbandmen. The overwhelming majority was comprised by sons of the landed gentry and the wealthy urban bourgeoisie. And even as academic studies grew more secular in orientation, it became apparent that the intentions of those who flocked, for example, to Oxford and Cambridge, were oftentimes more social than academic. William Harrison's *Description of England,* published in 1577, supplies a vivid and revealing picture of how a new generation of students was affecting university life.[47]

"In my time," he reported, "there are three noble universities in England, to wit, one at Oxford, the second at Cambridge, and the third in London; of which, the first two are the most famous . . . for . . . in them the use of tongues, philosophy, and the liberal sciences, besides the profound studies of the civil law, physic, and theology, are daily taught and had." Harrison noted approvingly that unlike continental institutions, English universities had become relatively orderly places of instruction: "The manner to live in these universities, is not as in some other of foreign countries we see daily to happen, where the students are enforced for want of houses, to dwell in common inns and taverns, without all order or discipline. But in these our colleges we live in such exact order, and under so precise rules of government." Enrollments, he noted, were substantial: "In most of our colleges there are also great numbers of students, of which many are found by the revenues of the houses, and others by the purveyances and help of their rich friends; whereby in some one college you shall have two hundred scholars, in others a hundred and fifty . . . and in the rest less numbers."

Harrison felt the college system, together with close supervision of students' daily routines, sufficed to further the university's objectives. "There is moreover in every house a master (or provost)," as he described it, "who hath under him a president, and certain censors or deans, appointed to look to the behavior and manners of the students there, whom they punish very severely if they make any default, according to the quantity and quality of their trespasses. . . . In each of these also they have one or more treasurers whom they call bursars besides other officers, whose charge is to see unto the welfare and maintenance of these houses." Further, "Over each . . . also there [are] several chancellor[s], whose offices are perpetual, howbeit their substitutes, whom we call vice-chancellors, are changed every year, as are also the proctors, taskers, masters of the streets and other officers for the better maintenance of their policy and estate."

Harrison conceded that a university education lay well beyond the means of people of modest means. "It is in my time," he commented, "a hard matter for a poor man's child to come by a fellowship (though he be never so good a scholar, and worthy of that room). . . . It is lamentable to see what bribery is used; for yer the scholar can be preferred, such bribage is made, that poor men's children are commonly shut out, and the richer sort received . . . and yet being placed, most of them study little other than histories, tables, dice, and trifles, as men that make not the living by their study the end of their purposes, which is a lamentable learning. Besides this, being for the most part either gentlemen, or rich men's sons, they oft bring the universities into much slander. For, standing upon their reputation and liberty, they ruffle and roist it out, exceeding in apparel, and banting riotous company (which draweth them from their books unto other trade)."

Harrison's account yields an interesting account of the typical progression of university studies. Each college, he explained, had its own "professor or readers of the tongues and several sciences . . . that is to say, of divinity, of the civil law, physic, the Hebrew, and the Greek tongues." Regardless of the college in which a student initially enrolled, the sequence thereafter was much the same: "The first degree, is that of the general sophisters, from whence, when they have learned more sufficiently, the rules of logic, rhetoric, and obtained thereto competent skill in philosophy, and in the mathematicals, they ascend higher unto the estate of bachelors of art, after four years, of their entrance into their sophistry. From thence also giving their minds to more perfect knowledge in some or all the other liberal sciences and the tongues, they rise at the last (to wit, after other three or four years) to be called masters of art, each of them being at that time reputed for a doctor in his faculty, if he profess but one of the said sciences (besides philosophy) or for his general skill, if he be exercised in them all. After this they are permitted to choose what other of the higher studies them liketh to follow, whether it be divinity, law, or physic; so that being once masters of art, the next degree . . . is the doctorship belonging to that profession."

Harrison was critical of "perpetual students" who overextended their studies and refused to move on to make way for others. As he phrased it acidly, "The most part of students do commonly give over their wonted diligence, and live like drone bees on the fat of colleges, withholding better wits from the possession of their places, and yet doing little good in their own vocation and calling."[48]

EMPIRICISM AND SCIENTIFIC INQUIRY

The origins of the critical spirit of questioning and inquiry that marks the modern age are traceable back as far as the twelfth-century revival of learning and the founding of universities. It found new expression in the Renaissance rejection of medievalism and the awakened interest among humanists in ancient literature. Applied to geography and commerce, the same impulse toward discovery led to an expansion of trade and the development of better navigational routes across the globe. The Protestant Reformation and Catholic Counter-Reformation were similarly natural outgrowths or products of the impetus for reform. In politics, the modern temper spelled the end of feudalism and the rise of the absolutist territorial nation-state. Above all, by the 1600s, critical inquiry applied to the investigation of natural phenomena led to the rise of science and the development of empirical methodology.

Throughout the sixteenth century, even as doctrinal struggles and military conflicts raged across Europe, scholars increasingly had begun questioning the traditional framework of explanation derived from scholastic Aristotelianism and searching for a better understanding of the physical universe. Something of the shift in attitude and interest within the span of a very few short decades is revealed in the contrast of Francis Bacon's complaint in 1605 that "matters mechanical" were esteemed "a kind of dishonour unto learning to descend to inquiry or meditation upon" with Joseph Glanville's rejection of traditional speculative thought sixty years later. "The unfruitfulness of those methods of science," he observed in 1668, "which in so many centuries never brought the world so much practical, beneficial knowledge as would help toward the cure of a cut finger, is a palpable argument." Another indication of the same shift in thinking comes from a letter written by John Ray in 1690. "No wonder [the ancients] should outstrip us in those arts which are conversant in polishing and adorning their language, because they bestowed all their time and pains in cultivating them," he observed. "But those arts are by wise men censured as far inferior to the study of things, words being but the picture of things."

In historical retrospect, it is not difficult to identify some of the factors at work that contributed to the scientific revolution in Western thought. In spite of its indifference to scientific learning, medieval Christianity had endorsed the Hellenic idea of a rationally-ordered world that was intelligible, in principle at least, to human reason. Scholasticism encouraged the conceptual precision that would later become the hallmark of empirical investigation. The Renaissance revival of antique texts and philosophies certainly whetted intellectual appetites, especially the Pythagorean and Platonic revivals of fifteenth-century Italy. Humanist thought also helped clear the way for scientific research by removing the stigma of sin from the natural world, nicely revealed in a popular expression that God's word could be read in the Book of Nature as well as in the Bible. Indirectly, the Reformation contributed to scientific progress by reducing the miraculous elements of Christianity and by Protestant attacks upon Aristotelian dogma.[49] Without question the expansion of geographical knowledge also was tied to attitudes favoring new forms of learning. As Bacon put it, "By the distant voyages and travels which have become frequent in our times, many things in nature have been laid open and discovered which may let in new light."

Surprisingly, the emergence of modern science and scientific method occurred during the midst of the confessional atmosphere of hatred, suspicion, and distrust, at a time when scientists' theories were assailed as heretical and their methods denounced as devilish art. The most famous example of how scientific inquiry evolved came from the first challenge to the old Ptolemaic cosmology posed by the posthumous publication at Nuremberg in 1543 of *De Revolutionibus Orbium Coelestium* by the German-Polish ecclesiastic Nicholas Copernik, or Copernicus (1473–1543). It was, the author stated, an attempt to discover "a more rational" system for explaining planetary motion. For advocating the Copernican hypothesis that the sun, not the earth, occupies the center of the solar system—denounced as an affront to the Christian affirmation of humankind's central place in the universe—the Dominican monk Giordano Bruno was burned at the stake. A Danish investigator, Tycho Brahe (1546–1601) extended and refined the work of Copernicus, whose work in turn was expanded upon by his brilliant assistant, Johann Kepler (1571–1630). Experimental confirmation for the heliocentric theory eventually was forthcoming from a professor at Pisa, Galileo Galilei (1564–1642). For his advocacy of the Copernican theory, it will be recalled, Galileo eventually was brought up before the Inquisition and forced to recant his alleged error as "absurd in philosophy" and "expressly contrary to Holy Scripture."[50]

Any remaining doubts over the basic validity of the Copernican view were dispelled with the publication of the *Principia* (1687) by the English mathematician Isaac Newton (1642–1727). The significance of Newton's contribution, of course, was that it illustrated how a mathematical method of investigation could be applied to a whole range of empirical questions and thereby generate laws or rules of enormous predictive validity. The *Principia,* in other words, laid out for all to see how science worked: deriving principles from an careful analysis of observed facts, deducing probable or likely consequences following from the principles, and experimenting to validate those deductions, such that the initial hypotheses were either confirmed or invalidated. Not without reason, Alexander Pope was moved to declare in a paroxysm of enthusiasm, "Nature and Nature's laws lay hid in night; God said, 'Let Newton be,' and all was light."

Coincident with advances registered by cosmologists were systematic explications of scientific methodology and empiricism (from the Greek: *empeiria,* or "experience"). Francis Bacon's *Novum Organum* (1620), as a case in point, went to great lengths to show how the logic of induction lay at the heart of the scientific enterprise. French philosopher René Descartes's *Discourse upon Method* (1637) similarly sought to sketch out the ligaments of a "universal mathematics" that would be, its author declared, "a more powerful instrument of knowledge than any other that has been bequeathed to us by human agency, as being the source of all others." In concert with other prophets of the new science, Bacon and Descartes thus produced a sweeping panoramic view of nature unlike anything imagined before. However incomplete and mechanistic were initial formulations of empirical science, they offered up the possibility of comprehending the whole of reality within a consistent, cumulative, and reliable framework of lawlike regularities. As Descartes confidently proclaimed, "Give me extension and motion, and I will construct the universe." Reflective of how attitudes were changing was the remark of the Countess in a dialogue by the French writer Fontenelle. "I perceive," the character observes, "philosophy is now become very mechanical. I value [this universe] the more since I know it resembles a watch, and the whole order of nature the more plain and easy it is, to me it appears the more admirable."

Scientific ideals quickly captivated the imagination of seventeenth-century Europe's intellectual classes. Robert Boyle's *The Skeptical Chemist* (1661) and Fontenelle's *Plurality of Worlds* (1686) were but two examples of how popular literature of the day brought scientific thought to wider attention. New intellectual homes for sharing scientific knowledge were founded, among them the Royal Society in London, the Berlin Academy, the Academy of Sciences in Paris, and the so-called Lyncean Academy in Rome, of which Galileo was an early member. The concept of "science" itself underwent a transformation and constriction of meaning, the term now referring not to any branch of learning generally but, instead, to exact and certain knowledge apprehended by the mind (Descartes), measured mathematically (Newton), and demonstrated by experimentation (Galileo). As the meaning of the term changed, scientific distrust of unproven hypotheses had the further effect of emphasizing the importance of the *utility* of knowledge. "The end of knowledge," insisted Thomas Hobbes, "is power, and the scope of all speculation is the performance of some action, or thing to be done."

UNIVERSITY SOMNOLENCE AND STAGNATION

Internecine struggles consequent on the Reformation that culminated in the bloody Huguenot wars in France, the Thirty Years War in Germany, and sectarian strife in England, which led to the so-called Glorious Revolution of 1688 (in which William and Mary were installed on the throne in conjunction with parliamentary rule), exacted a heavy toll on Europe, leaving its constituent nations exhausted and depleted. That institutions of higher learning continued to function at all, much less expand, between the late sixteenth century and the end of the eighteenth century in the midst of such unrelenting turmoil appears somewhat remarkable.[51] The Peace of Westphalia (1648), for example, was intended to put an end to a century of religious fratricide, but in fact what followed was yet another hundred years of strife and unremitting intolerance. Depopulated, impoverished, and unable to summon the energy and resources needed for major reform, most of the nations of Europe could do little to extend educational work at any institutional level. Meanwhile universities had all they could do simply to survive. As an Oxford vice-chancellor sometime around 1643 lamented, surveying the impact of constant civil unrest and warfare on the university, "We will hang our harps on the willows and now at length bid a long farewell to learning."[52]

Not surprisingly, universities displayed little interest in scientific discoveries. Just as traditional institutions of higher education had been slow to incorporate elements of humanist scholarship within their programs, universities tended once again to insulate themselves from the ferment surrounding new forms of knowledge. English schools under the direct influence of Bacon and Newton did show some interest in the physical and biological sciences, but otherwise European universities were not at all receptive. The seventeenth century has rightly been called the era of the "territorial-confessional" university. All factors considered, it was an age in which institutions of higher learning were still dominated by a preponderance of theological concerns, where their respective regional identities were pronounced, and where they continued to serve narrow sectarian interests or the policies of the respective states in which they were located. The only reform movement of any consequence of the period took place in Germany, symbolized by the founding of the University of Halle in 1694, which justifiably has been termed "the first modern university." Halle's distinction in this regard proceeded from the fact that it was the earliest institution of record to authorize vernacular instruction in mathematics and some of the sciences. Göttingen (founded in 1737) and later Erlangen were the only other major academic institutions to follow Halle's lead.

Overall, excluding Halle and a few other illustrious exceptions, it seems fair to claim that the long span between the latter half of the fifteenth century and the end of the eighteenth century represented a genuine nadir for European universities everywhere.[53] At the very least it can be said that few commentators harbored many illusions about the degree and extent of academic decline, about the general torpor and decadence into which institutions of higher learning had fallen, or the pervasiveness of their stagnation, which by the end of the seventeenth century cut across all regional and national borders.[54] Typical in character were complaints about the relaxation of manners and morals at Oxford toward the end of the 1600s. "Before the war," one critic observed, "we had scholars that made a thorough search in a scholastical and polemical divinity, in humane authors, and natural philosophy. But now scholars study these things not more than what is just necessary to carry them through the exercises of their respective Colleges and the University." The writer continued, "Their aim is not to live as students ought to live, viz., temperate, abstemious, and plain and grave in their apparel, but to live like gentlemen, to keep dogs and horses, and to turn [away from] their studies." Students, it was alleged, were "rude, rough whoremongers, vain, empty, careless."[55] Nor were the teaching masters held in higher regard. On numerous occasions in fact, detractors echoed complaints issued by Erasmus a century earlier that university professors were prone to giving themselves over to the most unprofitable and vicious quarrels imaginable. Scholars, Erasmus had claimed, "fight until the heat of argument leads to slanders and blows. Their weapons are not daggers but venomous pens. They tear one another with taunts."

Wherever one looked, the picture was much the same. In Spain, the number of full-fledged universities had increased from two in the mid-fifteenth century to nineteen by the opening of the seventeenth. At Salamanca, Alcalá, and Valladolid, the three leading imperial universities, enrollments swelled as sons of the Castilian nobility sought preference and careers in the royal bureaucracy. Collectively, however, the three came to exercise a virtual monopoly on the routes to prestigious professional careers in law and civil administration. Other Spanish universities, strictly local or regional in character, sought to break the monopoly and lure away students from the more prestigious national schools by offering lower examination and graduation fees. To the extent they succeeded, in the final analysis they turned themselves into diploma mills. Meanwhile, whether in a provincial or national university, the prevailing pattern was one of widespread corruption as faculties grew preoccupied almost exclusively with fee collecting. High student attrition could be accounted for not as a result of academic rigor in programs of studies, but by the fact that degrees and licenses were awarded less on the basis of merit and more on that of ability to pay. Nepotism also grew rampant, to the point where political connections, not academic ability, became the controlling consideration in the hiring of teachers. Even where academic routines were maintained with some semblance of integrity, the focus remained upon narrow legalistic training and office-seeking.[56]

The situation in France was more complex. The same intellectual stagnation that prevailed elsewhere certainly affected French universities as well, most of which by the mid-1600s had degenerated into little more than Latin secondary schools.[57] On the other hand, there did exist by way of compensation a lively movement involving the founding of single-purpose establishments where advanced studies could thrive: in the Académie de Danse (founded in 1661), the Académie des Inscriptions et Belles-Lettres (1663), the Académie des Sciences (1666), the Académie de Musique (1669), and the Académie d'Architecture (1671). A revived Collège de France flourished, offering for a time a substantial competitive threat to the Université de Paris; and in the Académie Montmor, founded in the 1640s, scientific studies were vigorously pursued.[58]

German universities registered few improvements.[59] The only significant development of note was the gradual replacement of the traditional *lectio*—the interpretation of standard texts according to a set formula—by the seminar format and the modern lecture in which a given subject was systematically presented. Over time the shift was made from Latin to vernacular German as the standard language of instruction. Otherwise until the early eighteenth century, there was little to commend Germanic institutions to those interested in modern literary and scientific studies. So low had the reputation of even the younger universities fallen that scholars of outstanding ability, like Leibnitz, were reluctant to be associated with them in any way whatsoever. Records of university life in seventeenth-century Italy are woefully incomplete, though there too the same recession typical in the German states appears to have prevailed. (Deserving of mention, however, from the annals of the University of Padua is a citation recording that a certain Elena Cornaro was the first woman to be awarded a doctorate in philosophy, on June 25, 1678.) In Scotland, the condition of universities at Aberdeen, Glasgow, and Edinburgh was fairly robust, indicated in part by the appearance of numerous intellectual debating societies, students' literary clubs, political associations, and alumni fraternities.[60]

Elsewhere, the picture was less bright. Most of the leading European universities were urban institutions situated in quite unspectacular settings, wholly lacking in quadrangles, dormitories, and teaching halls. Neither faculties or rectors were much interested in attending to the bothersome logistics of housing, feeding, and supervising students who, consequently, were left mainly to their own devices. The sole exception on the continent was France, where residence halls resembling the English college system had begun to emerge at certain institutions. And although usages differed somewhat from country to country, rarely was there a requirement that the university student complete an undergraduate liberal arts curriculum or some systematic preparatory course before gaining admission to advanced professional studies. As during the Middle Ages, completing syllabi and attending a requisite number of lectures, not the accumulation of course credits, were controlling considerations in determining academic advancement. Disputations had begun to die out, however, and in their place universities tended to depend upon comprehensive written or oral examinations.

University desuetude continued into the eighteenth century. Judging from reports emanating from Oxford and Cambridge in England in the early 1700s, professors had long since ceased to attend to their academic duties on a regular basis.[61] Many—perhaps most—of the College Fellows apparently were content to live a life of ease, tutoring their students in pleasant but desultory fashion; and they showed little interest in engaging in research themselves or conducting independent scholarly inquiry. Professors, it would seem, were reluctant to offer regular lectures or to conduct rigorous examinations—the inevitable result of which was that undergraduates could survive and graduate with an absolute minimum of effort. Furthermore, even as judged by the standards of the day, drinking, gambling, and sloth among the student body had reportedly attained epidemic proportions. "Dens of mutton-tuggers" and "nurseries of wickedness" were among the kinder epithets applied by critics to the universities of the time.[62]

So great was the disrepute into which English institutions of higher learning had fallen by the eighteenth century that many of the wealthy classes preferred to rely upon a combination of private tutors and the so-called "Grand Tour" for the education of their sons.[63] To the degree that universities had become "schools of vice," as Lady Leicester of Holkham Hall in Norfolk put it, foreign travel under the supervision of a tutor recommended itself as a preferable way of completing a young gentleman's education. In 1764, Richard Hurd, Bishop of Worcester, put the arguments for and against foreign travel as a means to the education of English gentlemen into the form of an imagined dialogue between Lord Shaftesbury and the philosopher John Locke. The former character argues the case for travel over university studies: "To put the case at the best, suppose [the young man] to have been well whipped through one of our public schools, and to come full fraught, at length with Latin and Greek, from his college. You see him now, on the verge of the world, and just ready to step into it. But, good heavens, with what principles and manners! His spirit broken by the servile awe of pedants, and his body unfashioned by the genteeler exercises! Timid at the same time, and rude; illiberal and ungraceful! An absurd compound of abject sentiments, and bigoted notions, on the one hand; and of clownish, coarse, ungainly demeanour, on the other! In a word, both in mind and person, the furthest in the world from any thing that is handsome, gentlemanlike, or of use and acceptation in good company!"[64]

Hurd's "Lord Shaftesbury" sums up his case with a critique of the universities. "The contemplation of these defects carries me still further; to the source and foundation of them all: the present state of Erudition, as we see it managed in certain sublime seats and authorized nurseries amongst us." A long series of rhetorical questions follow: "And would you invite our liberal and noble youth to resort thither? Could you expect that their free spirits would stoop to be lectured by bearded boys, or that their minds could ever be formed and tutored by such pedants in a way that fits them for the real practice of the world and of mankind? Have we not long enough submitted to the inconveniences of this monkish education?" Shaftesbury urges his antagonist to "look on the generality of those persons who have had their breeding in those seminaries." He concludes, "What principles in morals, in government, in religion have sprouted thence! What dispositions have we known corrupted by their discipline! What understandings perverted by their servile and false systems! Has truth, or liberty, or reason fair play from that quarter?"

Historian Edward Gibbon (1737–1794) had been enrolled briefly at Oxford in 1752 at Magdalen College. Reflecting back upon the experience years later in his autobiography, Gibbon spoke approvingly of certain features of English university life, especially when compared with those prevalent on the continent. "A traveller who visits Oxford or Cambridge is surprised and edified by the apparent order and tranquility that prevail in the seats of the English muses," he observed. "In the most celebrated universities of Holland, Germany, and Italy, the students, who swarm from different countries, are loosely dispersed in private lodgings at the houses of the burghers; they dress according to their fancy and fortune; and in the intemperate quarrels of youth and wine, their swords, though less frequently than of old, are sometimes stained with each other's blood. The use of arms is banished from our English universities; the uniform habit of the academics, the square cap and black gown, is adapted to the civil and even clerical professions. . . . Instead of being scattered in a town, the students of Oxford and Cambridge are united in colleges; their maintenance is provided at their own expense, or that of the founders; and the stated hours of the hall and chapel represent the discipline of a regular and, as it were, a religious community. The eyes of the traveller are attracted by the size or beauty of the public edifices; and the principal colleges appear to be so many palaces, which a liberal nation has erected and endowed for the habitation of science."

Yet concealed behind the impressive facade, Gibbon found dry-rot within. Looking back, the fourteen months he had spent at Magdalen he considered "the most idle and unprofitable" of his entire life. "These venerable bodies," he alleged, "are sufficiently old to partake of all the prejudices and infirmities of age. The schools of Oxford and Cambridge were founded in a dark age of false and barbarous science; and they are still tainted with the vices of their origin. Their primitive discipline was adapted to the education of priests and monks; and the government still remains in the hands of the clergy, an order of men whose manners are remote from the present world. . . . The legal incorporation of these societies by the charters of popes and kings had given them a monopoly of the public instruction; and the spirit of monopolists is narrow, lazy, and oppressive."

Gibbon's estimation was that little had changed since. "The greater part of the public professors have for these many years given up altogether even the pretense of teaching," he asserted. "The fellows or monks of my time were decent easy men, who supinely enjoyed the gifts of the founder; their days were filled by a series of uniform employments; the chapel and the hall, the coffeehouse and the common room, till they retired, weary and well satisfied, to a long slumber." Professorial indolence was objectionable enough in its own right, he felt, but it created an environment in which scarcely any learning took place at all. "From the toil of reading, or thinking, or writing they had absolved their conscience; and the first shoots of learning and ingenuity withered on the ground, without yielding any fruits to the owners or the public."[65]

UNFULFILLED PROMISES

Looking backward, the advent of the medieval university as an institutional home for higher learning must have exerted a powerful appeal to scholars chaffing under the restrictions and prohibitions of established orthodoxy. The *universitas,* some imagined, would become an enclave of intellectual freedom and a haven for unfettered inquiry, wholly unlike the monastic community or cathedral chapter-house of the past. Instead, with the passage of time, universities evolved more narrowly into professional training schools for clerics, and subsequently, finishing schools for the sons of the gentry classes or vocational schools for civil bureaucrats.

The hope and promise of the Renaissance was that the recovery of antique learning would usher in a new millennium, that there would dawn a new age informed by the lofty ideals and cultural brilliance of the classical era. New schools would emerge to nurture the development of wise and virtuous statesmen, elegant courtiers, and other persons of exceptional taste and refinement. Instead, humanism led all too often straight back to the cloister, to pedantry and formalism in literary exegesis and analysis, to a debased neoclassicism slavishly imitative of the past and strictly derivative from it.

The Reformation in turn brought with it the prospect of religious purification and renewal, an end to papish idolatry, and in schools, colleges, and universities, a merging of the best of Greco-Roman thought with Christian truth to form a new kind of lettered piety. The tyranny of Rome would be overthrown, and the Western world would once again achieve peace and harmony in a common *imitatio Christi,* an authentic, revivified imitation of Christ. On the Catholic side, hope ran strong for a time that the tide of dissension and division could be turned back, that if reforms whose necessity was widely acknowledged could be effected, and heresy suppressed once and for all, the Church's imperium could be re-created anew. Learning in schools would buttress the one true faith, not undermine or destroy it. Instead there ensued only mutual intolerance, repression, and almost two centuries of constant warfare and bloodshed, during which time the work of maintaining schools of any sort became nearly impossible.

Scientific inquiry promised an enlargement of the human spirit, enhanced control over the circumstances of life and the world, and a vastly improved understanding of humanity's pivotal role in the universe. Academies and colleges would be enlisted to nurture scientific discovery and advance the ever-expanding bounds of human knowledge. The actual results, however, in some quarters at least, appeared to be only growing disillusionment, skepticism, and corrosive doubt. As for established institutions of learning, as it became obvious, they would remain largely unaffected and untouched by the excitement of scientific discovery for over a century to come.

In sum, the history of European higher learning from the close of the medieval era to the threshold of the modern age in the eighteenth century was fraught with irony, paradox, and ambiguity. In no sense is it possible to read the historical record as an account of incremental growth, expansion, and an evolving commitment to increased educational opportunities. However much modern sensibilities might encourage some such interpretation of unbroken progress and development, the historical particulars of higher education and its agencies suggest otherwise. In point of fact, what one finds instead over the passage of centuries are fluctuations and alternations, advances and declines, institutional openings and closings, periodic curricular reforms followed by intervals of degeneration and decay, expansions and constrictions. The story of higher education in Europe after the mid-1700s, in any event, becomes increasingly allied with the development of national systems of public education, including colleges and universities, beginning in the closing years of the eighteenth century and extending well into the nineteenth.

Meanwhile, however, in the New World, educational experimentation and innovation were destined to yield quite different types of higher educational institutions. Although the American colonial college at its inception was very much the offspring of European parentage, it was destined to evolve in a form uniquely its own.

PART 2

AMERICAN HIGHER EDUCATION: THE FORMATIVE PERIOD

4

The American Colonial and Antebellum College

A CITY UPON A HILL

Preaching to the future leaders of the Massachusetts Bay Colony aboard the ship *Arbella* in the late spring of 1630, John Winthrop prophesied, "Men shall say of succeeding plantations: the Lord make it like that of New England: for we must consider that we shall be as a city upon a hill, [and] the eyes of all people are upon us." Bolstered by absolute faith in a divine blessing upon their venture, the intrepid Puritans thus set out to create in the forbidding and oftentimes hostile wilderness of the New World a new order of things, a "city upon a hill."[1] As Francis Higginson was to explain in *New-Englands Plantation,* "That which is our greatest comfort, and means of defense above all others, is, that we have here the true religion and holy ordinances of Almighty God taught among us . . ." He asked rhetorically, "Thus, we doubt not but God will be with us, and if God be with us, who can be against us?"

Early on it was apparent that a desire to found an institution of higher learning ran strong among the first settlers of English America. "After God had carried us safe to New England, reported *New England's First Fruits,* a pamphlet first printed in 1643, "and we had builded [*sic*] our houses, provided necessaries for our livelihood, reared convenient places for God's worship, and settled the civil government: one of the next things we longed for, and looked after was to advance learning and perpetuate it to posterity."[2] Accordingly, in October of 1636 the general court of Massachusetts—then only in its eighth year of operations—appropriated funds for the establishment of a college at Newtown (later renamed Cambridge).[3] Instruction probably began in the summer of 1638, two years later. The untimely death of a benefactor some months later decided the question of a name for the fledgling college. A certain Edward Johnson recounted the story as follows: "This year, although the estates of these pilgrim people were much wasted, yet seeing the benefit that would accrue to the churches of Christ and civil government, by the Lord's blessing, upon learning, they began to erect a college, the Lord by his provident hand giving his approbation to the work, in sending over a faithful and godly servant of his, the Reverend Mr. John Harvard, who joining with the people of Christ . . . suddenly departed this life; wherefore the government thought it meet to call it Harvard College in remembrance of him."[4]

Harvard's earliest published rules announced the chief aim of the institution: "Every one shall consider the main end of his life and studies to know God and Jesus Christ, which is eternal life . . . and therefore to lay Christ in the bottom, as the only foundation of all sound knowledge and learning"; each scholar was to read the scriptures twice daily so that he "shall be ready to give such an account of his proficiency therein, both in theoretical observations of the language, and logic, and in practical and spiritual truths, as his tutor shall require, according to his ability"; every student was to attend diligently all lectures and tutorials, obey unfailingly the college's statutes and regulations, and eschew profanity and association with dissolute company; and no one was to "go abroad to other towns" without official consent.[5] Just as Emmanuel College at Cambridge had been founded in 1584 to educate clergy "at once learned and zealous, instructed in all that scholars should know," likewise Harvard, established according to its charter *pro modo Academiarum in Anglia* ("according to the manner of universities in England"), was to raise up a literate and pious clergy.[6]

To the new school was entrusted also the task of preparing men of refinement and culture, those destined to positions of responsibility and leadership in society.[7] Harvard's first president took special pains to emphasize to entering fellows what was expected of them: "You shall take care to advance in all learning, divine and humane, each and every student who is or will be entrusted to your tutelage, according to their several abilities; and especially to take care that their conduct and manners be honorable and without blame."[8] A commencement orator in the 1670s left no doubt that the college's civic function was as important as its religious purpose. Had the first Puritan settlers not founded Harvard, he avowed, "the ruling class would have been subjected to mechanics, cobblers, and tailors, the gentry would have been overwhelmed by lewd fellows of the baser sort, the sewage of Rome, the dregs [of society] which judgeth much from emotion, little from truth. . . . Nor would we have rights, honors or magisterial ordinance worthy of preservation, but plebiscites, appeals to base passions, and revolutionary rumblings."[9] Upon the success with which Harvard continued to discharge its duties depended the fate of both religion and the established social order.

HIGHER LEARNING IN ENGLISH AMERICA

Each of the eight other colleges founded prior to the American Revolution shared the same broad sense of dual purpose as that enunciated by Harvard, namely, educating civic leaders and preparing a learned clergy: the College of William and Mary (founded in 1693); the Collegiate School at New Haven (chartered in 1701 and later renamed Yale College); the College of Philadelphia (founded in 1740 and later renamed the University of Pennsylvania); the College of New Jersey, 1746 (renamed Princeton College); King's College, 1754 (renamed Columbia University); the College of Rhode Island, 1764 (renamed Brown University); Queen's College, 1766 (renamed Rutger's College); and Dartmouth College, founded in 1769.[10] As the founders of the College of New Jersey phrased it, "Though our great intention was to erect a seminary for educating ministers of the gospel, yet we hope it will be a means of raising up men that will be useful in other learned professions— ornaments of the state as well as the church."[11]

Whatever the particular circumstances of their origins, all of the first nine English colonial colleges in America subscribed to the goal, as expressed at the founding of William and Mary, of ensuring "that the youth . . . [be] piously educated in good letters and manners." As early as 1619 the Crown had appropriated acreage in the Virginia colony for a proposed institution of higher learning, only to have most of the project's supporters wiped out three years later in an Indian massacre.[12] When the king acceded to renewed pleas for a college charter, the royal attorney general, unimpressed by the argument that a college would be helpful for the saving of souls, reportedly exploded, "Souls! Damn your souls! Raise tobacco!"[13] Nonetheless, despite several false starts, in the closing years of the seventeenth century Virginia's first college was well under way.

The founding of the Collegiate School in Connecticut in 1701 was attended by much controversy over a proposed site. Beginnings had been made at both Saybrook and Killingsworth by Harvard graduates who, alarmed over the decline in their alma mater's Puritan orthodoxy, were resolved to start over. New Haven eventually captured the college as its own, however, with an endowment secured by a patron from Boston who had made his fortune with the East India Company at Madras. When a donation of assorted dry goods tendered by Elihu Yale raised a munificent endowment of 500 pounds, the college's overseers quickly assented to the suggestion that the new institution should be renamed after its chief benefactor.[14] Similarly, the chartering of the College of New Jersey in 1746 occurred as the result of doctrinal tensions among Presbyterians. Just as the founders of Connecticut's Collegiate School were fired by a desire to revive in a new seat of learning the Puritanism then allegedly in decline at Harvard, so-called "New Light" Presbyterians sought to discredit charges of their indifference to learning by creating an institution of higher education they could call their own. The outcome was the establishment of the college later called Princeton.[15]

The College of New Jersey was not the only higher school founded as a result of the "Great Awakening," a pan-Protestant arousal of enthusiastic religiosity that swept across the colonies in the mid-1700s.[16] Imbued with the same evangelical fervor and missionary zeal that had seized liberal Presbyterians, New England Congregationalists were upset over the religious complacency into which they felt the colleges at Cambridge and New Haven had fallen. Their solution was to throw their support to the Reverend Eleazor Wheelock in the founding of a new college, called Dartmouth.[17] Meanwhile Baptists had founded the College of Rhode Island at Providence in 1765 to advance their own sectarian ends.[18] Not to be outdone, the Dutch Reformed Church the next year took measures to secure a founding charter also. Its first institution of higher learning was named Queen's College.[19]

Yet even as a rising tide of denominationalism engulfed America's colonial colleges in the eighteenth century and traditional patterns of shared collegiate governance between established church and secular state were being challenged, agencies of higher education lost little of their sense of broad purpose and function. When the College of Rhode Island was chartered in 1764, its founders stressed the point that "institutions for liberal education are highly beneficial to society by forming the rising generation to virtue, knowledge and useful literature and thus preserving in the community a succession of men duly qualified for discharging the offices of life with usefulness and reputation."[20] However much sectarian passions contributed to the founding of any given college, its custodians never lost sight of a larger aim. As Provost William Smith of the College of Philadelphia expressed it, "Thinking, writing and acting well . . . is the grand aim of a liberal education."[21] Similar declarations that the secular purpose of colleges was to "guard against ignorance" and "to instruct in branches of useful knowledge" and thereby "advance learning" were commonplace.

At a very early date it was apparent that the Reformation principle of *cuius regio, eius religio,* by which a ruler's religious allegiance determined that of the sovereign's subjects as well, was poorly adapted for application to colonial America. In the same way, religious diversity throughout the colonies precluded the possibility that any one sect or denomination could long exercise exclusive control over whatever college it might establish. Hence, toleration was essential. Even as Anglicans, Presbyterians, and Congregationalists vied with one another to found institutions of higher learning, followed closely by Baptists, then Methodists, Quakers, Catholics, and Universalists, no college found it possible to impose a religious test for admission or doctrinal requirements for graduation; and members of minority congregations invariably were assured freedom of religious belief while attending the school of the dominant faith. William and Mary for a time did require that its teachers be Anglicans, but its proviso was an exception. No sectarian affiliation was insisted upon at the College of Philadelphia. At King's College in New York, the official persuasion was Episcopalian, but rival Protestants were free to attend without hindrance. (In the latter instance, rival sectarian pressures forced the issue of Anglican dominance to the point where the college was forced to relinquish half the proceeds from funds raised in a public lottery to support a city jail and "a proper pest-house for the reception of such persons as may be infected with contagious distempers.")[22]

Even at Yale and Harvard, tight sectarian control was soon loosened by the adoption of more liberal policies.[23] It was widely acknowledged, for example, that the creation of the Collegiate School at New Haven had not helped Harvard's cause, and the former in turn had been seriously weakened by the founding of a college in New Jersey. Nor was the latter institution in any condition to handle competition from Queen's College at New Brunswick. Forever desperate for patrons and tuition-paying students, colleges found it expedient even in matters of basic governance to provide for minority sectarian representation on their respective boards of trustees or overseers. The practice amounted to a tacit recognition among schoolmen everywhere that within a pluralistic society, there were no realistic alternatives to policies of conciliation and accommodation.[24]

A practical consequence of religious tolerance within and among collegiate institutions throughout the eighteenth century was a certain blurring between their "public" and "private" status.[25] (The distinction between the two would not become important until much later in the century following.) Puritan Harvard in its infancy was supported by the General Court through a combination of bank taxes and revenues generated by a toll on the ferry across the Charles River, then by a toll on the bridge that later replaced it. The 1693 charter for Anglican

William and Mary reserved a tobacco tax to help defray its cost; and the school was assigned further revenues returned by export duties on furs and skins, not to mention a tax on peddlers. The Collegiate School likewise was the beneficiary of state subsidies; after 1712 its students also were granted immunity from taxes and military service. Public subsidies notwithstanding, however, none of the colonial colleges was a state institution in the modern sense, even when secular authorities were represented alongside ecclesiastic representatives on a college's governing body.

Paradoxically perhaps, although shaped by aristocratic traditions of scholarship and learning, colonial colleges in the seventeenth century were never the monopoly of a single exclusive caste.[26] Unlike class-bound Europe, in the environment of the New World where privilege was suspect and individual striving for self-improvement strongly encouraged, opportunities for a poor but ambitious youth to attend college and thereby advance himself remained open. At Harvard between 1677 and 1703, for instance, surviving records attest to the fact that sons of clergymen comprised a majority of those admitted, followed by the sons of merchants, shopkeepers, master mariners, magistrates and attorneys, militia officers, and wealthy farmers. But included on the rosters also were the sons of artisans, ordinary seamen, servants, and poor farmers. It was not until well into the eighteenth century that colleges assumed an elitist, patrician cast as rising costs began to restrict attendance at college to the well-to-do. Even then, however, so-called "charity" scholarships supplied a degree of access for the nonaffluent; and schedules were devised that allowed some poor students to work their way through college by teaching school on a part-time basis.

Schoolmen often gave the appearance of wanting it both ways. On the one hand, they saw themselves as custodians of—and they remained unswerving in their devotion to—an educational tradition that in the final analysis held scant popular appeal. On the other, they excoriated men of practical affairs for their perceived failure to value learning and adequately support institutions devoted to its diffusion and dissemination. An early Harvard president, for example, complained that the many enterprising self-made men of the times had "waxed fat" in their pursuit of material abundance, but "kicked at supporting education."[27] More than a few academics undoubtedly subscribed to the point of view expressed by a South Carolina newspaper editorialist in 1770 that the colony ought not to support another college because "learning would become cheap and too common, and every man would be for giving his son an education."[28] Nevertheless, schoolmen repeatedly returned to the theme that the great unwashed masses were uncouth, overbearing, and indifferent to the fruits of erudition. As a somewhat self-pitying Harvard commencement orator lamented in 1677, "Mad nobodies, haranguers at street-corners, have more influence with the populace than reverent men, filled with singular gifts of the divine spirit."[29] Indicative of one widely-held perception was the criticism voiced by sixteen-year-old Benjamin Franklin in his family's newspaper, the *New England Courant,* that Harvard had become a rich man's school, a place that wealthy parents sent their sons to, "where, for want of a suitable genius, they learn little more than to carry themselves handsomely, and enter a room genteely."[30]

At no time prior to the American revolution, at any rate, did the colonial college touch the lives of the majority of the people at first hand. During the whole of the seventeenth century, less than six hundred students attended tiny Harvard, of which no more than 465 were finally graduated. Yale's enrollment in 1710 was only 36; it reached a peak of 338 in the year 1770. Harvard had 123 students enrolled in 1710; the total had reached 413 in 1770; and the school's largest pre-revolutionary graduating class (1771) numbered no more than 63 matriculants. It is estimated that probably no more than one in every thousand colonists attended any of the colleges in existence before 1776, and fewer still completed a bachelor of arts degree.

The course of study offered by the typical colonial college very much reflected the earliest settlers' resolve to effect a *translatio studii*—a direct transfer of higher learning from ancient seats of learning at Queen's College in Oxford and Emmanuel College at Cambridge to the frontier outposts of the American wilderness.[31] The curriculum basically was a combination of medieval learning, devotional studies judged conducive to the preservation of confessional religious piety, and late Renaissance arts and literature. In seeking to achieve the ideal of a learned clergyman, gentleman, and scholar, the fundamental disciplines required were Greek and Latin, proficiency in which was demanded for collegiate admission. During the first year of study, Greek, Hebrew, logic, and rhetoric were curricular staples. In the second year to them were added logic and "natural philosophy." The third year brought moral philosophy (ethics) and Aristotelian metaphysics, followed in a fourth year by mathematics and advanced philological studies in classical languages, supplemented by a smattering of Syriac and Aramaic.[32] Taken as a whole, the course of studies was regarded less as an induction into various branches of learning and more as a fixed body of absolute, immutable truths. It was a corpus or repository of knowledge to be absorbed and committed to memory, not criticized or questioned.

Shared in common by all academicians, whatever their sectarian persuasion, was the presumption that classical learning was essential for success in the various learned professions of law, medicine, or theology.[33] A thorough grounding in the languages and literature of Greco-Roman antiquity was therefore not simply a badge of gentility or sign of class status—however much it might be held in high regard on that account alone. More fundamentally, classical erudition was believed to afford the only sure guide for those destined to conduct affairs of state and church.[34] Subsequent additions of new subjects to the colonial college curriculum in the later 1700s, including mathematics, modern languages and literature, and natural sciences (astronomy, physics, chemistry) did little to weaken that conviction. Yet secular learning of a decidedly nonclassical character had begun to make inroads well before the end of the eighteenth century.[35] As early as 1734 Yale expanded its course offerings to include navigation and surveying as well as specialized mathematical studies.[36] At King's College in 1754 it was announced that henceforth modern geography, history, navigation, surveying, and "the knowledge of every thing useful for the comfort, the convenience and elegance of life . . . and everything that can contribute to . . . true happiness" would be offered.[37] Two years later the College of Philadelphia under the leadership of William Smith followed with a three-year course of study emphasizing practical arts and scientific studies.

Unshakable confidence in the efficacy of classical liberal learning, leavened by personal piety and righteousness of character, was reflected directly in early statements of degree requirements. The official statutes of Harvard in its formative stage (1642–1650) provide a good example. "Every scholar that on proof is found able to read the original of the Old and New Testament into the Latin tongue," it was decreed, "and to resolve them logically, withal being of honest life and conversation and at any public act hath the approbation of the overseers, and master of the College, may be invested with his first degree." Three additional years of application were required before the bachelor of arts became eligible to receive the master of arts certificate. This second degree, Harvard's rules announced, would be awarded "to every scholar that giveth up in writing a synopsis or summa of logic, natural and moral philosophy, arithmetic, geometry, and astronomy, and is ready to defend his theses or positions, withal skilled in the originals as aforesaid and still continues honest and studious."[38]

Commencement exercises at Harvard and elsewhere in the early colonial period still retained all of the pomp and circumstance of the traditional medieval disputation. Upon completing his formal studies, each candidate, having been assigned either the affirmative or negative side to a controversy, was required to make a formal presentation of his forensic and logical skills before an examining board. Typical subjects or topics might treat such questions as "Death is to be undergone rather than any sin perpetuated"; "Prudence is the most difficult of virtues"; or "Human reason alone does not suffice to explain how the true religion was introduced and built up so firmly in the world."[39] Records of the College of New Jersey in the early eighteenth century yield a vivid picture of a colonial college commencement: "It was a public holiday and gala occasion not only for the College but for all the county around. Lines of booths and wagons where refreshments were sold made their appearance at that time, and the town took on the aspect of a fair. The 'Old Road' was a race-course; there were playing for pennies, and dancing and fiddling, and even bull-baiting."[40] The striking conjunction of homely American frontier diversions, on the one hand, and the solemn rituals and observances of European learning, on the other, appears not to have been remarked upon.

Consistent with the American colonial aspiration to follow English academic precedents as closely as possible, early colleges were mostly residential institutions.[41] Whereas no college enjoyed sufficient resources to reproduce elaborate quadrangular enclosures after the fashion of Oxford or Cambridge, the tendency was to house students together in a residential dormitory of one sort or another whenever possible. The aim was to foster among all students a common social, moral, and intellectual life. Early experiments met with decidedly mixed results. In the seventeenth century instances of student misconduct were relatively rare; and stern admonitions usually sufficed to bring those who violated the rules back into compliance. Only in exceptional cases involving theft, assault, or fornication were authorities forced to resort to flogging or expulsion. When incidents did occur, they characteristically erupted over complaints about such matters as the food served in the commons, as was reported at Harvard where the president's wife was once accused of serving mackerel "with guts in them," and "goat's dung in the hasty pudding."[42] Generally, colonial colleges enjoyed a reputation for strict discipline and order—so much so that English parents often elected to ship their wayward sons off to the colonies for their education instead of entrusting them to the more relaxed atmosphere then prevailing at Oxford or Cambridge. Sometimes the strategy backfired. Commenting on what had transpired at Harvard, one friend of the College mused, "This hath been a place certainly more free from temptations to lewdness than ordinary England hath been, yet if men shall presume upon this to send their most exorbitant children intending them more especially for God's service, the justice of God doth sometimes meet with them . . . for of late the godly governors of the college have been forced to expel some, for fear of corrupting the fountain."[43]

From the early 1700s onward, residential overcrowding and expanding enrollments began to spell more serious trouble. Incidents—some of them quite serious—grew more frequent.[44] Drunkenness was rampant, as were violent assaults, uncontrolled gambling, and debauchery of one sort or another.[45] At Harvard in 1728, twenty-two students were reprimanded for "nocturnal expeditions" and "entertainments" involving the stealing and consumption of stolen geese.

Several members of the class of 1767 were sent home to be cured of "the Itch," the outcome of "associating with, countenancing, [and] encouraging one or more lewd women." More than once commencement revelries, Guy Fawkes Day celebrations, and similar observances got out of hand, ending in shattered windows, cracked furniture, and broken bones. Lawlessness reached a crescendo during the worst of several periodic food riots, the infamous "Bad Butter Rebellion" of 1766. That particular incident had begun as a complaint about rancid butter served in the Harvard student commons but soon escalated into a major political confrontation between students and the board of overseers over a host of other unrelated issues.[46] Few observers of the collegiate scene on the eve of the Revolution, surveying the record of student turmoil and misconduct, could have predicted how abruptly the situation would change within the span of just a few decades—and yet at once remain the same.[47]

In retrospect, judged strictly on its own terms and according to the standards it publicly professed, the colonial college was probably considerably less effective than its more ardent defenders would have conceded, but more successful than its strongest detractors alleged. It did in fact uphold for more than a century and a half a received academic tradition based upon a uniform, fixed regimen of liberal learning. It took seriously its self-appointed mission to prepare a learned and pious clergy; and it did actively pursue the announced goal of raising up successive generations of political leaders committed to the common welfare. The colonial college as an institutional type thus emphasized character as much as it did learning, piety as well as erudition, and civic virtue over private advantage. To these basic policies and goals the college held firm, without substantial alteration, from its inception in the colonies of Virginia and Massachusetts in the early seventeenth century until the outbreak of the War for Independence in the late eighteenth, and beyond. Moreover, for all of its faults and shortcomings, because the humble colonial college was the prototype emulated by nearly all of the liberal-arts colleges that were to make their appearance over the course of the succeeding nineteenth century, its historical importance as an academic archetype would be difficult to overestimate.[48]

THE REVOLUTION AND REPUBLICAN IDEALS

American colleges were very much embroiled in the turmoil accompanying the outbreak of the Revolution.[49] Princeton's lofty Nassau Hall, as a case in point, suffered severe damage during the hostilities. It was occupied in December of 1776 by the British and the next month by the Continental Army, whereupon the hall was pressed into service as a barracks to house troops for the next half year. Vandalized and disfigured, it subsequently found use as a military hospital late in 1777, and then again in 1783 when the facility furnished a refuge for congressmen fleeing mutinous soldiers. Yale, fearing invasion and occupation, suspended operations in 1777 and sent its students and tutors inland when no food could be found for the commons. William and Mary provided shelter for American and French troops during the siege of Yorktown; a building designed by architect Christopher Wren was accidently set ablaze by French soldiers; and the school temporarily shut down. Everywhere enrollments plummeted dramatically and necessary endowments were cut off. At King's College, the first casualty of the war was the school's Tory president, Myles Cooper: In May of 1775, with Alexander Hamilton of the Class of 1774 holding an enraged mob at bay, President Cooper fled in scanty attire over his back fence, from where he was able to make his way down to the harbor to find refuge on an English sloop of war headed for home.[50]

At war's end, the fate of the colleges seemed uncertain. Noah Webster, writing in 1790, observed, "Our constitutions of civil government are not yet firmly established; our national character is not yet formed; and it is an object of vast magnitude that systems of education should be adopted and pursued, which . . . may implant in the minds of the American youth, the principles of virtue and of liberty; and inspire them with just and liberal ideas of government, and with an inviolable attachment to their own country."[51] Benjamin Rush, writing in 1786, sounded much the same theme. "The business of education," he observed, "has acquired a new complexion by the independence of our country. The form of government we have assumed, has created a new class of duties to every American. It becomes us, therefore, to examine our former habits . . . and in laying out the foundations for nurseries of wise and good men, to adapt our modes of teaching to the peculiar form of our government."[52] The question was whether schools of higher learning, heretofore adapted to life under a monarchy and wedded to essentially aristocratic notions of leadership, could be adjusted to serve the emerging American democratic order. Additionally, while most academics ardently embraced the republican cause, some harbored grave doubts about what the future might bring.

President Charles Nisbet of newly created Dickinson College in Pennsylvania, for one, was troubled by the populist swell of democracy. "In a republic," he complained, "the demagogue and rabble drivers are the only citizens that are represented or have any share in the government." He added, "Americans seem much more desirous that their affairs be managed by themselves than that they should be well managed."[53] Old habits of thought were not abandoned overnight. Philip Schuyler, father-in-law to Alexander Hamilton, upon hearing of a petition signed by a thousand common citizens for the founding of Union College in Schenectady exclaimed, "May indulgent heaven protect and cherish an institution calculated to promote virtue and the weal of the people!"[54]

THE DARTMOUTH CASE

Antebellum colleges, like their colonial forbears, tended to be both small and poor. Even a well-established school of the 1820s and 1830s typically enrolled no more than a few dozen students at a time. As late as 1846, New York City's two colleges together accounted for a total enrollment of less than 250 students; at Lafayette College during the same period members of the school's governing board of trustees actually outnumbered the entire student body. In Ohio's two dozen or so colleges in the late 1850s, the average enrollment was less than a hundred. Not until 1860 did Harvard graduate more than a hundred students from a single class.[55] Tuition accounted for the bulk of a college's revenues. But not all students paid in full: many were on stipends or scholarships reserved for the needy. In bad times colleges were forced to accept payment in kind instead of hard currency—cotton, sheep, pewter, and foodstuffs—or, worse yet, promissory notes. The inevitable result was that most colleges subsisted on the verge of insolvency. Supplementing tuition were charitable donations and an occasional endowment. The only remaining source of income was public grants. Colleges assiduously sought such state support, but never exchanged it for control over internal policy-making, except in the sense of allowing for limited public representation on their governing boards. It required a decision by the United States Supreme Court decision in 1819 to help lay the foundations for the legal distinction between a "public" and "private" college.[56]

Dartmouth College originally had been chartered by the English Crown, a deed of trust which provided for a self-perpetuating board of trustees and a president authorized to appoint his own successor. Upon the death of the first founding president, Eleazor Wheelock, his son John succeeded to the presidency. Rebuked by the board for allegedly heavy-handed and erratic administration, the new president challenged the right of absentee trustees to "meddle" in the college's internal affairs. A lively controversy ensued when the board responded with a vote for his dismissal. Professing concern for the "literary progress" of the people of the state and ostensibly angered by the board's usurpation of power, the state legislature moved to amend the institution's charter to provide for a reorganized Dartmouth University. New members were added to the board of trustees, all of them pledging to support Wheelock's administration. The original board balked at the change, at which point two rival entities, Dartmouth College and Dartmouth University, began operating in legal competition with one another. Matters came to a head when the question arose as to who was entitled to the institution's records and original seal.

In 1816 the original trustees took their case before New Hampshire's high court. The issue in contention basically was whether the college was a public corporation whose founding charter was liable to amendment by the legislature, or an inviolate private corporation with a charter immune to legislative fiat. On November 17, 1817, the state court held that Dartmouth was in fact a public corporation, that its governors were officers responsible to the people, and therefore that it fell under the legislature's authority. If the college lay outside public control, the court declared, trustees would be free to exercise their authority in ways inimical to the general welfare. Hence, or so it was argued, legislative oversight was essential.

The attorney who had argued his alma mater's brief submitted an appeal to the United States Supreme Court. As the date for trying the case drew near, several prominent citizens weighed in with their own opinions. Among them was Thomas Jefferson who wrote to the state governor arguing that "the idea that institutions established for the use of the nation cannot not be touched or modified even to make them answer their end, because of rights gratuitously supposed in those employed to manage them in trust for the public, may, perhaps, be a salutary provision against the abuses of a monarch, but it is most absurd against the nation itself." On the other side, Dartmouth College's supporters were prepared to hold that the school's charter was a contract and that New Hampshire's attempt to amend it was a unilateral impairment of contractual obligation, in direct violation of the Constitution. Technical legalities aside, the argument advanced was that public control carried with it a risk that the college would fall prey to narrow political partisanship and the vicissitudes of popular whim.

On March 10, 1818, Daniel Webster, a relatively obscure and still unknown lawyer, (Dartmouth Class of 1801) argued the trustees' position. The oratory for which he would later become famous reportedly lasted five full hours. Winding up and, according to legend, close to tears, Webster concluded his plea, "This, sir, is my case. It is the case, not merely of that humble institution, it is the case of every college in the land. It is more. It is the case of every eleemosynary institution throughout our country . . . the case of every man who has property of which he may be stripped—for the question is simply this: Shall our state legislature be allowed to take that which is not their own, to turn it from its original use, and apply it to such ends or purposes as they, in their discretion shall see fit? Sir, you may destroy this little institution . . . but if you do . . . you must extinguish, one after another, all those great lights of science, which, for more than a century, have thrown their radiance over the land! It is, sir, as I have said, a small college, and yet there are those that love it."[57]

On February 2, 1919, the Court handed down a 5-1 decision in Dartmouth's favor. Siding with Webster, Chief Justice Marshall agreed that the college was neither a civil institution nor its holdings public property. The New Hampshire legislature had indeed violated the contract implied by its founding charter. Hereafter, the state would be prohibited from exercising direct control over whatever academic institutions it authorized, except in cases where it was expressly stated that the institution in question was a public entity, supported by funds from the state's treasury.

The meaning, significance, and ultimate consequences of the Court's decision are still disputed by historians of American higher education. Some have held that the Dartmouth decision, in delineating or underscoring the distinction between public and private colleges, encouraged the development of private institutions by protecting them from state encroachment. Private donors were moved therefore to found colleges. Public institutions would have to be direct creations of the state, not state transformations of existing colleges. Proof of the encouraging influence of the Dartmouth Case, some have held, is found in the rapid proliferation of "private" schools that took place after 1819. On the other side, it has been argued that the distinction between public and private institutions was not nearly as clearly laid down or popularly accepted as has been supposed.[58] Thus, for example, not long after winning their case, Dartmouth's trustees petitioned the New Hampshire legislature to pay the legal fees incurred in fighting the state; and they continued to offer state representation on the board in exchange for public appropriations. In many instances throughout the decades following, state authorities continued to contribute to the support of what, to all intents and purposes, were purely private ventures, treating them more as philanthropic community agencies than as arms of the state. What is apparent, however, is that state subsidies fell off substantially throughout the next half century, as did efforts by state officials to intervene directly in the affairs of colleges not created under direct public auspices.

"A LAND OF COLLEGES"

Historians also differ in assessing the consequences of the overbuilding of institutions of higher learning in the antebellum period, both before and after the Dartmouth decision.[59] Some view the post-revolutionary period as an age in which anti-intellectual evangelicals displaced traditional academic educators, causing a serious debasement in the value of higher education.[60] Had funds expended on higher education been concentrated in a select few institutions, it has been argued, the United States soon would have developed a system of education unsurpassed by any other in the world. On the other side, it could be argued that what was lost in intellectual quality as colleges of all types proliferated in the late 1700s and throughout the first half of the nineteenth century was more than compensated for by popular support and interest in higher learning, an involvement that would otherwise have been lacking.[61] What is plain, at any rate, is that the rush to found new colleges in the early Republican era proceeded without restraint.[62] Between 1782 and 1802, nineteen colleges were established, more than twice as many as had been chartered in the preceding century and a half. Denominational loyalties, state rivalries, increasing affluence, and an expanding population, the westward march of the frontier—all figured as contributing factors in the proliferation of colleges.[63] North Carolina, Tennessee, Vermont, and Georgia each had a state-chartered, state-supported institution prior to the turn of the century. Columbia University (formerly King's College) was temporarily taken over by state government, as was Dartmouth and the University of Pennsylvania at Philadelphia. Harvard, Yale and William and Mary all accepted more state representation on their respective governing boards.[64]

In Maine, supporters of what would become Bowdoin College were offering an entire township to any contractor able and willing to build them a four-story building to house the institution.[65] In 1826 the citizens of Easton, Pennsylvania, were busily engaged laying down plans for Lafayette College. In 1829 out on the midwest prairie, Illinois College opened its doors to an enrollment of nine students. At Bloomington, Indiana, in 1830 the Reverend Andrew Wyle alighted to assume charge of the newly created Indiana College. In November of 1832, five Presbyterian ministers founded Wabash College near Crawfordsville, Indiana. Six years later, in 1838, Emory College in Georgia opened its door, its founders undeterred by the fact that the new venture lacked any funds whatsoever, only promises of future donations. In October of 1841, eight French-speaking clerics, brothers of the Congregation of the Holy Cross, rode into the northern wilds of Indiana to inaugurate the college later called Notre Dame. On August 6, 1845, the University of Michigan proudly held its first commencement—for eleven graduates.[66] At the time of the American Revolution there were nine colleges; the total had jumped to 250 on the eve of the Civil War. Not without reason did a certain Absolem Peters remark in 1851: "Our country is to be a land of colleges."[67]

Everywhere the mania for founding colleges raged on uncontrolled.[68] Whereas England with a population of 23 million had only four institutions of higher learning, the state of Ohio, with a total population of just 3 million, at one point was hosting thirty-seven.[69] Sometimes the major cause at work was state pride. In 1819 supporters of the proposed University of Vermont hit upon a winning argument when they pointed out that the state had lost an estimated $14 million to neighboring states because it lacked a public institution of higher learning. The same argument surfaced in an 1851 newspaper editorial in Minnesota that urged that "not a single youth of either sex should be permitted to leave the territory to acquire an education for want" of a suitable public university.[70] Previously, the president of Indiana College had argued successfully along identical lines. Hanover's president received his college charter in 1830 by arguing that other state legislatures had shown little restraint in granting authorization for the building of colleges, and Indiana ought not to be an exception.[71]

Sometimes, as was the case with the founding of Bowdoin College, colleges were founded because of the sheer difficulty of traveling long distances to attend an established institution.[72] In other instances, the chief motivating factor seems to have been regional pride or local pride as rural frontier towns sought to remake themselves over in the image of a New England community, complete with an academic institution. Carleton, Oberlin, Colorado, Whitman, and Pomona were all products of the desire of transplanted New Englanders to make the western expanse resemble the more settled East. More than a few times, also, colleges and universities were fought over as political prizes among rival communities, as proved to be the case in Boone County, Missouri, where local citizens outbid all competitors for the honor of hosting the state's first university.[73] In a few cases, legislatures awarded a college as a sort of consolation prize to a town that had lost out in the competition for a penal institution or insane asylum.[74]

Philip Lindsley of the University of Nashville addressed himself in 1837 to the question of whether America needed so many colleges. He concluded that "our busy, restless, speculating, money-making people" wanted academic centers as scattered and mobile as themselves. But he wondered aloud if many of them could be sustained.[75] General John Armstrong, a member of the governing board at Dickinson was another, one of many, who cautioned against the impetus to build colleges. His alternative suggestion was to begin by establishing small-scale academies in the rural back counties and charging them with the preparation of students for admission to existing higher schools. With the passage of time, he conjectured, it would be discovered where colleges were actually needed.[76] But voices such as those of Armstrong and Lindsley were ignored—or countered by an argument extolling the advantages of diffusing knowledge as widely as possible. College founding would continue unhindered, as historian Frederick Rudolph once noted, in the same entrepreneurial spirit as canal-building, cotton-ginning, farming, and goldmining.[77] "More" was "better," and the appearance of colleges dotting the landscape everywhere, it was widely accepted, was a sure sign of American progress in the field of arts and letters, as in all other things.[78]

When all else failed, invocations of classical antiquity sometimes prevailed. Appealing to the state legislature for financial assistance in 1795, the trustees of Princeton promised that if their request was granted, they would make New

Jersey "the Athens of America."[79] The same plea was forthcoming in 1847 from those who urged that the College of Charleston be supported, such that it might serve as "the Athens of the South." In Ohio, it was no coincidence that the state's two public colleges were located in towns bearing the names of Oxford and Athens. So too did the trustees of Williams College in Massachusetts propose to the state's general Court that their college in the Berkshires become the true "Athens of the New World." Others states, from Georgia to Arkansas, inevitably chose the name "Athens" for one of their own communities.[80]

Whenever possible, prospective college founders wrapped themselves in the loftiest rhetoric imaginable. The commitment of the president of the board of trustees for the College of California (1868) was "to make men more manly, and humanity more humane; to augment the discourse of reason, intelligence and faith, and to kindle the beacon fires of truth on all the summits of existence."[81] Others, among them the founders of South Carolina College in 1801, spoke at length of the need to help heal sectional rivalries that formed part of the legacy of the Revolutionary era. At the University of North Carolina in 1837, officials resolved to educate a new generation of wise and virtuous republican leaders. The 1835 charter of Oglethorpe University in Georgia sounded the theme of colleges working to end the supposed monopoly on learning by the rich and powerful; while the 1828 incorporation of Indiana College committed the institution to educating youths in all branches of knowledge, both ancient and modern.[82]

Typical in its sentiment was an address by President McKeen at Bowdoin in 1802. "It ought always to be remembered," he reminded his audience, "that literary institutions are founded and endowed for the common good, and not for the private advantage of those who resort to them for education. It is not that they may be able to pass through life in an easy or reputable manner, but that their mental powers may be cultivated and improved for the benefit of society. If it be true no man should live for himself alone, we may safely assert that every man who has been aided by a public institution to acquire an education and to qualify himself for usefulness, is under peculiar obligations to exert his talents for the public good."[83]

DENOMINATIONAL SCHOOLS

Far and away the most active founders of colleges throughout the first half of the nineteenth century were various religious denominations. It seemed to matter little that many sectarian colleges and academies were begun without sufficient resources to ensure their long-term survival, that more than a few floundered in short order, or that most of the new ventures were capable of offering little more than the rudiments of secondary-level instruction. In every state, churches were at work establishing what purported to be genuine colleges of higher learning.[84] In Ohio, Franklin and Muskingham were founded by Presbyterians; Marietta and Oberlin were sponsored by Congregationalists; Kenyon College was the creation of Episcopalians; Denison was a Baptist college at its inception; Methodists founded Mount Union, Ohio Wesleyan, and Baldwin College; Otterbein was sponsored by the United Brethern; Wittenberg was begun by Lutherans; Urbana was the inspiration of Swedenborgians; Hiram opened its doors under the auspices of the Disciples of Christ; Heidelberg was the product of the Reformed church; and St. Xavier was opened under Catholic control—each founded prior to 1850. Denominationalism likewise left its mark in Kentucky where almost a dozen sectarian academies were established; in Illinois where twenty-one different religious colleges had sprung into existence; in Indiana where four colleges—Vincennes, Hanover, Indiana, and Wabash—were products of the home missionary movement; and in Iowa where there were at least thirteen denominational schools struggling to survive prior to 1869. Presbyterians alone accounted for the founding of at least one-quarter of those religious colleges that endured throughout the nineteenth century.[85]

The founder of Oberlin College, the Reverend John H. Shepherd, was forthright in announcing that he had come out to the Western Reserve to save the people from "rum, brandy, gin and whiskey" and to rescue the church from "Romanists, atheists, Deists, Universalists, and all classes of God's enemies."[86] Naturally, those so branded disagreed vociferously—all the while redoubling their own efforts in founding colleges where the "true" gospel might be preserved.[87] Finally, when it became obvious to all parties concerned that direct and unrestricted competition would be ruinous to all, the custom arose of apportioning territory among contending sectarian factions. Appointed to oversee the task were such interdenominational Protestant agencies as the American Home Missionary Society (founded in 1826) and in New York the Society for the Promotion of Collegiate and Theological Education at the West (1843). Meanwhile, by 1860 Roman Catholics had opened scores of colleges of their own, only a dozen or so of which managed to survive into the next century.[88]

Even those most active in the spread of sectarian schools wondered sometimes about the wisdom of their efforts.[89] As a committee on education of the General Conference of the Methodist Church conceded in 1856, "We have, in many parts of the land, called into existence institutions that were not needed and could not be sustained."[90] More acerbic in tone was the declaration of Philip Lindsley in 1829: "I am aware," he observed, "that as soon as any sect succeeds in obtaining a charter for something called a college, they become, all of a sudden, wonderously liberal and catholic. They forthwith proclaim to the public that their college is the best in the world—and withal, perfectly free from the odious taint of sectarianism. . . . They hold out false colours to allure and deceive the incautious."[91]

In fairness to denominational schools, it should be noted that many of the so-called "booster" and "hilltop" colleges of the period, such as Williams and Amherst, did in fact offer educational opportunities for poor but pious young men (often inspired by a local parson) who sought to prepare themselves for the ministry in locales far distant from the environs of New Haven or Cambridge and other mainstream colleges.[92] At Williams, Nathaniel Hawthorne spoke with only a touch of condescension of the typical divinity student as a type: "country graduates—rough, brown featured, schoolmaster-looking, half-bumpkin, half-scholar, in black, ill-cut broadcloth . . . a rough-hewn, heavy set of fellows from the hills and woods in this neighborhood."[93] These were the people the Reverend John Todd, in an appeal on behalf of a missionary society seeking patrons, undoubtedly had in mind when he declared in 1847, "Our colleges are chiefly and mainly institutions designed for the poor and those in moderate circumstances, and not for the rich. . . . We have no institutions in the land more truly republican than our colleges."[94]

JACKSONIAN IDEALS AND THE COLLEGE MOVEMENT

So-called female seminaries and academies were new additions to the growing roster of collegiate institutions that appeared in the first half of the nineteenth century.[95] Most were inspired by Emma Willard's famous Troy Female Seminary, founded in New York in 1821, and Mary Lyon's Mount Holyoke Seminary, opened in 1837. In the South, the Wesleyan Female College of Macon, Georgia, was the first institution of its type to grant its graduates a formal academic degree (1836). Alabama's Judson College, founded in 1836, and the Mary Sharp College for Women in Tennessee in 1852 likewise offered women opportunities to obtain a collegiate education. Whether many qualified as true post-secondary institutions, however, remains doubtful. In a majority of cases, admission standards were low and required preparatory training was almost nonexistent. The age at which students were admitted also tended to be lower than at exclusively male colleges. Almost all lacked sufficient endowments to assure their permanent survival, reflective perhaps of popular skepticism about the value of higher education for women. Serious scholarship, it was widely believed, lay beyond female capabilities.[96] Moreover, women who did acquire a modicum of formal learning ran the risk of finding themselves educated above and beyond the domestic station in life for which most were destined. For much the same reasons, coeducation was virtually unheard of until 1833 when Oberlin opened its portals to women as well as men. It was also Oberlin that was the pioneer in awarding bachelor of arts degrees to three women in 1841, each having completed precisely the same course of studies as their nine male peers.[97]

Very few blacks were afforded opportunities to pursue higher learning in the antebellum period. Throughout the South, it was a statutory crime in most states to teach even the rudiments of reading and writing to anyone of African-American ancestry.[98] Hence it was not altogether surprising that it was 1826 before the first black college graduate was awarded an A.B. degree—and there were no more than twenty-seven others prior to the signing of the Emancipation Proclamation. Avery College, founded in Allegheny City, Pennsylvania, in 1849 was among the very first black colleges to begin operations, followed in 1851 by the Miner Academy in the nation's capital. The next year a college for "colored youth" was begun in Philadelphia. In 1856 Wilberforce was founded in Ohio under Methodist auspices; two years before Presbyterians had opened Lincoln University of Pennsylvania for blacks.[99] Oberlin College, meanwhile, freely admitted people of color of both sexes for instruction.

Among Jacksonian democrats in the early 1800s, however, demands for the expansion and reform of higher education did not speak to the aspirations of women, blacks, indigenous peoples, or other ethnic minorities. Rather, the target of concern of labor groups and workingmen's associations was the growth of monopoly in the world of trade and commerce. Herein lay a fundamental paradox in American social and political thought of the time. On the one hand, Americans professed to admire self-taught, self-made men, ambitious entrepreneurs who, by virtue of their own efforts, had attained positions of eminence or prominence at the top of the social hierarchy. Wealth, accordingly, was taken as a symbol of respectability and achievement. On the other hand, there coexisted a deep-seated distrust of privilege and social inequality, a notion uneasily wedded to the equally potent appeal of egalitarianism.[100] The "common man" of plain and homely virtues was likewise venerated, no less than the self-made millionaire; but in both cases it was widely accepted that little or no formal learning was needed to make one's way or to achieve success in the rough and tumble of social life. Institutions of higher learning found it difficult to navigate their way between these two polarities. By tradition they were pledged to the training of leaders, in an era now grown suspicious of anything resembling elitism. Furthermore, the notion of a "higher" learning bent to some tangible, useful end—the colleges' very stock-in-trade—was itself suspect. In the end, more than a few institutions succumbed to a genteel sort of "collegiate anti-intellectualism" (for want of a better expression), a kind of affected indifference to learning aimed at winning popular acceptance and respectability for themselves. Nothing else explains why in many instances scholastic achievement was not emphasized even within academe, and why young students were counseled not to work too hard or to seek to excel at their studies.

President Lindsley of the University of Nashville, always an astute social critic, posed the dilemma of the colleges somewhat differently in his 1829 baccalaureate address. "The levelling system," he observed, "which is so popular and captivating with the multitude, may be made to operate in two ways, with equal success. . . . Colleges and universities, as implying odious pre-eminence, may be prevented from growing up among us: or every petty village school may be dignified with the name and legal attribute of a college." The basic problem, as he saw it, was that populist sentiment tended to equate excellence of any sort with privilege, while radically egalitarian democrats mistook quantity for quality.[101] The result, he and other critics argued, was that the country was in the process of acquiring a multiplicity of schools of indifferent or mediocre standing, rather than a few academic citadels of exceptional quality.

Sensitive to allegations of elitism, some colleges responded by holding out the promise of social mobility to those willing to subject themselves to an academic regimen. In Ohio in 1830 Philander Chase promised to make of Oberlin a true "People's College" committed "to teach the children of the poor to become school-masters . . . [or] to rise by their wisdom and merits into stations hitherto occupied by the rich; to fill our pulpits, to sit in our state chambers, and on our seats of justice, and to secure in the best possible way the liberties of our country."[102] Still another stratagem adopted by some colleges in their bid for popular acceptance was an attempt to make collegiate attendance self-financing. Basically, the idea was that students would be instructed in such practical skills as farming or carpentry. They would then be employed in a useful trade while attending classes and thus pay their own way through to graduation. By all accounts, the experiment was an abysmal failure. Collegiate farms lost money; student malingering was commonplace, and the cost of providing equipment for mechanical shops proved prohibitive. At Ohio University, according to one report, students made so many wooden barrels that they eventually glutted the market.[103] By 1837 or thereabouts, virtually all work-study ventures had been abandoned.

COLLEGE MANAGEMENT AND CONTROL

Nineteenth-century colleges commonly employed two types of teachers. Tutors were the most numerous. A typical tutor was a young man in his early twenties who had himself only recently graduated from the institution where he was employed. His assignment was usually a temporary one, assumed while he awaited a more permanent position outside academe (usually as a minister). In the interim his chief duties were to hear student recitations and act as a disciplinarian and overseer of students under his charge. The regular professor, in contrast, had some post-baccalaureate training in one of the established professions (albeit not in any particular teaching specialty), had served previously in an extended tutorship, or, as was more likely, had received an appointment from his alma mater following years of service in some nonacademic occupation—again, usually having served in some pastorate. Ordinarily, conditions precluded a professor from specializing: it was not at all unusual to find the same person teaching geography, mathematics, and natural philosophy; or Latin and Greek literature, plus history, ethics, and moral philosophy.[104]

Like the tutor, each professor or teaching master was expected to help enforce the college's many stringent policies and rules. It was a practice calculated to generate an adversarial relationship between faculty and students. Students who attempted to cultivate any sort of association with "the enemy," for example, were ostracized by their fellow classmates or were viewed with suspicion. Faculty, for their part, were inclined to resent being cast as disciplinarians and felt frustrated when their efforts to maintain order failed. (At South Carolina College, legend has it that on one occasion an immigrant political economist by the name of Francis Lieber had set out in hot pursuit of a student bearing a stolen turkey. He stumbled over a pile of bricks, injuring himself in his fall. Rubbing his shins as he lay sprawled on the ground, he was heard to exclaim aloud, "Mein Gott! All dis for two t'ousand dollars!")[105]

Presiding over the whole was the president. Answerable only to a nonresident board of trustees or governors in most cases, the college's chief executive tended to function—depending upon the individual institution involved—as an authority unto himself.[106] If the institution was still in its formative stage, his responsibilities encompassed the full range of duties later assigned to such subordinate functionaries as deans, registrar, bursar, treasurer, and so on. Whether his title was "rector," as at Yale; or "provost," as was customary at the University of Pennsylvania; or "chancellor," the title used at the University of Nashville; or even "principal," as custom dictated at Dickinson, the antebellum president was more than "first among equals" after the fashion of the English academic guild. On the contrary, his authority in all matters pertaining to his school's management was nearly absolute. College faculty members, of course, did not always readily acquiesce to the authority of political appointees, clergymen, or wealthy benefactors whose claims to academic legitimacy they questioned. Nor did they accede easily to the autocratic rule of a strong president. But from the outset, power struggles, such as they were, were conducted on uneven ground; and when a president was directly threatened, he could usually depend upon the college's statutory governors for backing.[107]

The accommodation or compromise that proved most enduring was to allow decisions regarding student admissions, academic standards, and curricular specifics to be controlled by faculty, while in all other matters the board and its president held sway. Thus, in those few colleges where traditions of faculty authority remained strong, some limits to presidential authority and power were at least tacitly observed. Elsewhere, however, in the majority of cases, there was little to prevent a strong-willed executive officer from ruling day to day with an iron hand.

Increasingly too, a president's position was strengthened by growing acceptance of the notion that college administrators and academics were two different breeds entirely. Samuel Eliot, a historian at Harvard, supplied a near-classic rationale for vesting power with trustees, and through them, to the president. Writing in 1848, Eliot observed, "Gentlemen almost exclusively engaged in the instruction and discipline of youth are not, usually, in the best condition to acquire that experience in affairs, and acquaintance with men, which, to say the least, are extremely desirable in the management of the exterior concerns of a large literary institution." Extending his theme, Eliot argued, "Arrangements for instruction must be adapted to the state of the times, and to that of the world around, as well as of that within, the college walls; and of this state men engaged in the active business of life are likely to be better judges than the literary man."[108] By implication, then, if ivory-tower academics were unsuited by temperament and lack of experience to deal with matters of academic governance and management, it was incumbent upon busy practical men to do so, delegating power as necessary to their surrogate in the person of the president.

With so many duties and responsibilities—teaching, fund-raising, maintaining student discipline, record-keeping, collecting and disbursing funds—vested in a single person, the president's position was apt to be both burdensome and time-consuming. A candidate for the presidency at Illinois College in 1844 agonized over whether or not he was up to the task. "May the Lord give me wisdom," he wrote to a friend. "If I am to be placed at the head of this College, may he pour out upon [me] his spirit till I am fully qualified for the holy and responsible work—to be wise, to be firm, to be humble, to shed over this College the holy influence of piety and to lead the successive generations of students. . . . How can I ever be sufficient for these things? Pray for me."[109] President Martin Brewer Anderson of the University of Rochester disclosed in 1868 that his biggest problem was safeguarding the welfare of the students entrusted to his tutelage. "No class passes through my hands which does not contain more or less young men who are on the eve of ruin from wayward natures, bad habits, or hereditary tendencies to evil," he claimed. "These men must be watched, borne with, and if possible saved to the world and to their families. . . . This work must mainly be done by the president."[110]

More than a few of the early colleges were fortunate enough to attract effective leaders. Not all college presidents were adequate to the task, however, nor did they always measure up to the high standards demanded of them. The Reverend Samuel Locke of Harvard, for example, was forced to resign his position when it was revealed in 1773 that he had something to do with his housemaid's pregnancy. Eliphalet Nott at Union College steadfastly refused to resign as president until he had occupied the post for sixty-two years. Illustrating the extreme pettiness to which some presidents descended was the case of the Reverend William M. Blackburn, an early president of the University of North Dakota, who appeared before the state board of regents with repeated complaints about a certain Mrs. E. S. Mott, who was employed as a preceptress and instructor in English. Among them, he recounted to the board, was her steadfast refusal to defer eating until he had finished the blessing. Mrs. Mott retorted that the food served was equally bad before and after his prayers. In the end, the board voted to remove them both from their positions.[111]

ACADEMIC SUPERVISION AND COLLEGIATE LIFE

Colleges and academies of the antebellum period, unlike their predecessors in the colonial era, tended to be located not in cities but in or near small rural towns. Agrarian mythology held that a bucolic setting far removed from the contaminating influence of the metropolis was better adapted for academic pursuits, more conducive to character-building, more protective of moral virtue.[112] President Wayland of Brown spoke for a minority when he declared in 1842, "It matters really but little whether an institution be situated in a town or in the country. Place it where you will, in a few years there will cluster around it all the opportunities of idle and vicious expenditure. Under such circumstances, it is obvious that no physical means can be devised which shall furnish such supervision as will present an impassable barrier to unlawful inclination." Furthermore, he argued, an enforced residential pattern encouraged the spread of disease, fostered unsanitary habits, reinforced the disinclination of students to exercise regularly, isolated young men from community life and the world's affairs, diverted funds needed for building up libraries and classrooms, imposed supervisory responsibilities the college lacked the means to discharge effectively, and actually served to expose impressionable young scholars to the vices and evil habits dormitories were intended to eliminate.[113]

But most college authorities were determined to attempt control over student life in all of its particulars. Student dormitories were viewed as a means admirably suited to accomplishing that end. Whenever possible, efforts were made—as in colonial times—to create residence halls on the model of the English college. Manasseh Cutler, who helped found Ohio University, in 1800 advised strongly against the attempt, viewing elaborate residence halls as a needless extravagance and an impediment to the very purpose for which they were intended, namely, protecting students from themselves. "Chambers in colleges," as he put it, "are too often made the nurseries of every vice and cages of unclean birds."[114] Nonetheless, even when students did not live "on campus" but in boarding houses nearby, most school officials spared no effort in regulating where students could live, how they should dress, what they were allowed to eat, and what use they made of the little free time that institutional routine—which usually began with compulsory chapel at dawn and lasted until evening prayers—allowed them.

At Dartmouth, the day commenced as soon as there was sufficient light for the president to read the Bible at morning chapel. One class was scheduled before the morning meal. More classes and study periods followed until the noon hour, when lunch was served. In the afternoon there were more classes and recitations, concluded by supper. Ever vigilant against the prospect of idle minds falling into devilish mischief, college tutors made regular rounds to ensure that students were occupied with their studies in the evening hours until they retired.[115] At Oglethorpe University in Georgia, much the same pattern prevailed. The routine opened at 6:30 with compulsory morning prayers and extended until the end of classes at 5:00 in the afternoon. Students were then obliged to return to chapel, where prayers were offered up begging God's forgiveness for whatever sins had been committed since daybreak.

Students deeply resented the regimen, judging by frequent reports of absenteeism, of obscene graffiti scribbled by students on the flyleaves of their hymnals, of spitting in the chapel aisle, and general inattentiveness. William G. Hammond, a student at Amherst in the 1840s questioned whether official religiosity served any useful purpose whatsoever. "I do really think," he remarked, "these public prayers do more harm than good to the religious feeling of a majority of students: they are regarded as an idle bore, and only tend to do away with that feeling of reverence with which everyone naturally regards an address to the Deity."[116]

Antebellum collegiate instruction was organized strictly according to classes. That is, all students accepted for admission in a given year were considered members of a single class, which was kept intact over the four-year period until its members graduated together. The course of studies was the same for all at most colleges, at least until the second quarter of the nineteenth century. Entering freshman were subjected to the English-school custom of "fagging," whereby lowerclassmen were expected to run errands upon demand

and otherwise serve as unpaid servants to upperclassmen. Fagging eventually disappeared, only to be replaced by a briefer but no less severe series of initiation rites or trials—"hazing"—by which first-year students supposedly proved themselves worthy of the company of their student superiors. Despite official disapproval, canings and other forms of physical punishment were freely administered by upperclassmen when their demands went unsatisfied.

College classrooms of the 1800s were bare and unadorned, stuffy and poorly ventilated during the warmer months, ill-heated in winter. Lectures and recitations were the two chief methods of instruction. Gifted speakers such as Charles Nisbet of Dickinson, Samuel Johnson at Columbia University, and Timothy Dwight at Yale were renowned in the early 1800s for their classroom eloquence, and did much to keep alive the medieval lecture tradition. (Mark Hopkins, president of Williams College, was especially well known for his skill in sustaining lively exchanges among his students, prompting an often-misquoted remark attributed to President Garfield that the ideal college was one with Mark Hopkins at one end of a bench—not a log—and a student at the other.) Elsewhere, at less prestigious institutions, according to surviving accounts, students were more likely to encounter uninspired pedants whose classroom presentations as a whole were considered a colossal waste of time. More typical still was the treadmill of constant recitations. Customarily the tutor drew names at random from a hat to determine which student would be summoned before the class and examined over how thoroughly he had committed particular texts to memory. Faced with the prospect of learning long passages by rote, students often resorted to "ponies," or "crib sheets." It was a practice that inspired the wry observation, "The keeping of same doth tend to produce stable scholarship."[117]

Isolated in a small town offering few diversions or amusements, obliged to memorize a seemingly endless and meaningless succession of materials, under constant faculty supervision, and allowed little release from the daily routine of collegiate life, students doubtless considered higher learning a tedious business. Discontent occasionally erupted into open rebellion. Commenting on a succession of incidents that had wracked Princeton between 1800 and 1830, President Ashbel Green attributed "the true causes of all these enormities" to "the fixed, irreconcilable and deadly hostility [of students] . . . to the whole system of diligent study, of guarded moral conduct and of reasonable attention to religious duty." A more practical assessment of the riots that broke out from time to time—at Amherst, Brown, Yale, Harvard, Dartmouth, Lafayette, Bowdoin, DePauw, Dickinson, the University of South Carolina, Miami University, at the City College of New York, and at countless other schools—might have taken into consideration the enforced seclusion, the isolation, the sheer boredom students experienced. In a small, closed environment where rumors abounded and tempers flared easily, it was almost inevitable there would be fights, duels, and stabbings. Even minor irritants could assume major proportions and foment rebellion. Poor food in the student commons, as always, was a frequent source of complaints. At South Carolina College in 1811, for example, students learned that the steward had purchased a tough old bull and intended it for slaughter. Enraged, the students took their revenge by driving the animal into the river where it was drowned. Elsewhere, wormy salt pork or leftovers offered up once too often drove students to riot. A young Harvard student, Augustus Torrey, recorded in his diary in 1822: "Goose for dinner, said to have migrated to this country with our ancestors."[118]

EXTRACURRICULAR PURSUITS

One of the few diversions approved by college authorities in the antebellum period were activities sponsored by religious societies. In the 1790s, Enlightenment ideals had enjoyed enormous if brief popularity among college students. Inspired by the French Revolution and the writings of such *philosophes* as Diderot, Voltaire, Condorcet and others, it became fashionable for a time to embrace Deism, to denounce the work of churches, and to otherwise espouse antireligious rationalism. But after the turn of the century, the pendulum of opinion swung back far to the right once again, now encouraging a return to theological orthodoxy and evangelical religiosity. On campuses across the country throughout the first half of the nineteenth century there were periodic religious revivals strongly reminiscent of those stimulated by the Great Awakening half a century earlier.[119] At Yale, the Moral Society required its members to adhere strictly to Biblical precepts, to "suppress vice and improve the interests of morality" and to refrain from profanity, gambling, cardplaying, and the consumption of alcoholic beverages. It was the same at Williams, Wofford, Amherst, North Carolina, Wake Forest, Wabash, Trinity, Emory, and the University of Georgia. At Dartmouth, moved by "an imperious sense of duty," members of the Theological Society, founded in 1813, ceremoniously dismissed one of their colleagues who had been found drinking. At Harvard, students devoted much of their free time debating such weighty questions as whether any sin was absolutely unpardonable or whether sexual intercourse after a formal marital engagement qualified as fornication. As late as the 1860s at Yale it was held, "If any student shall profess or endeavor to propagate a disbelief in the divine authority of the Holy Scriptures, and shall persist therein after admonition, he shall no longer be a member of the College."

The diary of William Otis Carr, a student at Amherst in the 1850s, recounts how the college president's sermonizing inspired a revival in March of 1855 and how it spread when a passing evangelist came to preach at the college. "One young man," Carr wrote, "who gloried in his wicked ways and seemed the first in any forbidden scheme, was stopped in his maddened course and, blessed be to God, made a new creature. And what a change! His first act was to banish from his room the servants of sin. He threw into the fire his cards ... and upon this he poured the contents of his brandy bottle. Many are giving up their foul feasts on tobacco, and instead of the curse, from almost every room may now be heard the voice of prayer. It is wonderful to perceive the holy calm that reigns around us."[120]

Literary societies and debating clubs of a more secular cast also were immensely popular among students of the early nineteenth century, sometimes commanding the fierce loyalties and rivalries later associated only with inter-collegiate athletics.[121] In stark contrast with the sterility of classroom exercises, the oratorical and declamatory "exhibitions" sponsored by literary societies were intellectually robust exercises greatly prized by students. Their enter-tainment value apart, forensic displays and oratorical contests were regarded as good practice for the sermonizing, teaching, and legal pleading for which stu-dents were preparing themselves in their future careers. Typical topics debated included questions about whether or not legitimate theater was prejudicial to public morals, and whether wealth or physical attributes "tended more to relieve a female of celibacy."[122] As the century progressed, other activities came to play an important role in the extracurricular life of students: amateur theater and orchestras, dancing (denounced from some quarters as satanic), hunting, foot races, bowling, skating, shooting marbles, and early free-for-all versions of football or soccer.[123] In the 1820s organized gymnastics came into vogue, prompting an official pronouncement at Rensselaer Polytechnic Institute that "such exercises as running, jumping, climbing, scuffling, and the like are cal-culated to detract from that dignity of deportment which becomes a man." Earlier, Princeton officials had judged that "shinny," a type of field hockey, should be forbidden on the basis that it was "in itself low and unbecoming gen-tlemen and scholars, and is attended with great danger to the health." Undeterred by official pronouncements of disapproval, the gymnastic move-ment in particular continued to enjoy great popularity among students.[124]

Greek-letter societies made their first appearance on college campuses in the early 1800s. Beginning at Union and Hamilton in the 1820s and 1830s, frater-nity chapters were founded within a very short span of time: Kappa Alpha in 1825, Sigma Phi and Delta Phi in 1827, Theta Delta Chi in 1847, followed soon thereafter by Psi Upsilon, Chi Psi, and Alpha Delta Phi. By the 1830s there already were local chapters of national fraternities flourishing at Amherst, Bowdoin, Brown, Columbia, Harvard, Yale, Princeton, Miami, Kentucky,

Wabash, and elsewhere. In the same period, local Greek associations had sprung up at the University of Vermont, Dartmouth, and Wesleyan.[125] Mark Hopkins, for one, was unalterably persuaded that college officials everywhere should act promptly to banish all fraternities while there was still time. "Their influences have been evil," he insisted. "They create class and factions, and put men socially in regard to each other into an artificial and false position."[126] Reuben A. Gould, a librarian at Brown, heartily agreed. "Secret societies," he declared flatly in 1852, "originate with the Devil, all of them."[127] Opposition tended to become muted in later years, after efforts at suppression had failed. By the 1850s the first Greek societies for women were also beginning to appear.

THE YALE REPORT

Allegations that the typical antebellum college was unresponsive to popular demands for curricular reform throughout the first half of the nineteenth century do a serious injustice to the historical record.[128] In point of fact, the American college's course of study was never rigid, and it evolved continuously over time in both form and content. Confronted with demands that new scientific knowledge be admitted within the academic cloister, Princeton between 1796 and 1806 experimented with the elimination of Latin and Greek requirements, substituting in their stead an array of scientifically oriented subjects.[129] Union College between 1802 and 1827 moved in much the same direction. At the University of Pennsylvania in 1816, trustees appointed a four-person faculty of physical science and "rural economy." Modern languages, applied mathematics, and courses in political economy were allowed to substitute for classical studies in several institutions, including Ohio University, Lafayette College, Union, Hobart, Wesleyan in Connecticut, and Columbia in New York throughout the 1820s and 1830s. Sometimes so-called "parallel" courses of studies were inaugurated which allowed students to choose between a classical and a literary-scientific progression of studies. More often, the approach taken was to supplement the required plan of ancient subjects with modern languages, mathematics, and various scientific specializations. Again, efforts were undertaken to merge both scientific and classical subjects within a single curricular sequence.[130]

At the University of Virginia, Thomas Jefferson's 1824 experiment in allowing students to choose from among different courses offered through eight specialized units or schools—ancient languages, modern languages, mathematics, natural philosophy, history, anatomy and medicine, moral philosophy, and law—excited much attention and was watched closely. Elsewhere, when such critics as Francis Hopkins, Jonathan Trumbell, Benjamin Rush, William Smith, and Benjamin Franklin complained that students should

be allowed to select from among several alternatives, schoolmen did not necessarily turn a deaf ear. President Horace Holley at Transylvania University
in Kentucky, James Perkins Marsh at the University of Vermont, Eliphalet Nott
at Union, and George Ticknor at Harvard were only a few of the scores of leading educators who experimented with enlarging the curriculum and expanding choices through parallel or "partial" courses of study.[131]

Clearly dominating the educational scene were controversies over the proper
course to be pursued. In an era increasingly shaped by science and technology,
some argued, it was incumbent upon colleges to go even further. "We have listened too long to the courtly muses of Europe," declared Ralph Waldo Emerson
in his famous 1837 "American Scholar" Address at Harvard.[132] Francis
Wayland of Brown concurred. "In a free country like our own," he asked,
"unembarrassed by precedents, and yet not entangled by the vested rights of
bygone ages, ought we not to originate a system of education which shall raise
to high intellectual culture the whole mass of our people?"[133] But anything
resembling a consensus of opinion on what was to be done proved impossible
to achieve. Some, like Henry Tappan of Michigan, held that efforts to crowd
both old and new subjects into the collegiate curriculum were impractical.
"With the vast extension of science," he reflected, "it came to pass that the
course of study was vastly enlarged. . . . We have only pressed in our four years'
course a greater number of studies. The effect has been disastrous."[134] Many
agreed with Tappan's diagnosis, even as they continued to disagree on a cure.

In September of 1827 President Jeremiah Day of Yale resolved to meet the
issues head-on. A select committee of college fellows was appointed to draw
up a position paper, specifically to deal with a proposal to eliminate "dead languages" from the school's required course of studies. The document that
ensued the next year, in 1828, ended up addressing a much broader range of
questions. Following its 1829 publication in the prestigious *American Journal
of Science and Arts,* the Yale Report quickly became the most widely read and
influential pronouncement on education of the time. It was, in essence, a spirited, closely reasoned defense of traditional classical education.[135]

Day's paper opened with the admission that Yale's existing educational system was not perfect and should remain open to improvements. It further
pointed out that new studies in chemistry, mineralogy, geology, political economy, and other subjects had been added to older courses. But it rejected outright the criticism that colleges were "not adapted to the spirit and wants of
the age," and discounted dire predictions that colleges soon would be deserted
unless drastically revamped and "better accommodated to the business character of the nation." Invoking the venerable theory of the mind as a receptacle
and a muscle capable of being strengthened through proper mental exercise,

the Report declared, "The two great points to be gained in intellectual culture, are the *discipline* and the *furniture* of the mind; expanding its powers, and storing it with knowledge." Hence the aim of a collegiate course should be to call the mind's "faculties" or potentialities into "daily and vigorous exercise." Branches of study therefore should be prescribed that were "best calculated to teach the art of fixing the attention, directing the train of thought, analyzing a subject . . . for investigation; following . . . the course of argument; balancing . . . evidence presented to the judgment; awakening, elevating and controlling the imagination . . . [and] rousing and guiding the powers of genius."[136] Appropriate subjects inherently adapted to these ends, the committee held, included mathematics, ancient and modern English literature, logic, rhetoric, oratory, written composition, and the physical sciences.

Undergraduate education, the argument continued, should *not* attempt to include professional studies: "Our object is not to teach that which is peculiar to any one of the professions; but to lay the foundation which is common to them all." Against the claim that a student should not be required to waste time on studies lacking any direct connection with his future profession, the committee responded, "The great object of a collegiate education, preparatory to the study of a profession, is to give that expansion and balance . . . those liberal and comprehensive views, and those fine proportions of character, which are not to be found in him whose ideas are always confined to one particular channel." Furthermore, the purpose of an education should not be confined to preparing one to make a living. Rather, learning should be directed to the larger task of acquiring the arts of living. Nor should preprofessional education "include all the minute details of mercantile, mechanical, or agricultural concerns." What one needs to know is best learned in the specific settings where such learning is applied: "The young merchant must be trained in the counting room, the mechanic, in the workshop, the farmer, in the field."[137]

To the objection that students should not be required to complete a uniform course of studies, the Yale Report held that "thorough education" should consist of those elements common to the needs of everyone, "those branches of knowledge of which no one destined to the higher walks of life ought to be ignorant." Personal preference or natural inclination, it was added, should not be allowed to dictate the shape of anyone's studies. Assessing the argument that educational opportunities should be opened to everyone, the Report agreed wholeheartedly. But by the same token it denied that the college of itself should attempt to supply all needs or attempt to be all things to all people. Further, study of the classics should be acknowledged and appreciated both as the foundation of good taste and judgment, and as the basis for precisely the sort of training most needed by future "merchants, manufacturers, and agriculturists." They too, no less than clergymen and academics, would profit from "high intellectual culture." It should be obvious "to the most cursory observer," avowed the Yale Report's authors, "that the classics afford materials to exercise talents of every degree, from the first opening of the youthful intellect to the period of its highest maturity." Classical discipline, they asserted, "forms the best preparation for professional study." The Report concluded, "Is it not desirable" that men of wealth and influence "should be men of superior education, of large and liberal views, of those solid and elegant attainments, which will raise them to a higher distinction than the mere possession of property; which will not allow them to hoard their treasures, or waste them in senseless extravagance; which will enable them to adorn society by their learning, to move in the more intelligent circles with dignity, and to make such an application of their wealth, as will be more honorable to themselves and most beneficial to their country?"[138]

Conservatives were greatly heartened by so forthright a defense of traditional learning. President Lord of Dartmouth went even further in declaring that a college education was not intended for people who planned to "engage in mercantile, mechanical or agricultural operations."[139] Classicists felt vindicated in opposing demands for more popular and practical learning. As South Carolina President James H. Thornwell urged defiantly, "While others are veering to the popular pressure . . . let it be our aim to make scholars and not sappers or miners—apothecaries—doctors or farmers."[140] Many hailed the Yale Report as a definitive statement on the nature and purpose of education offered by the liberal-arts college. They appealed to it repeatedly in attempting to counter demands that colleges turn themselves into preparatory training sites for the trades and professions. The true mission of the college, it was avowed repeatedly, was to serve as a custodian of high culture; to nurture and preserve the legacy of the past; to foster a *paideia,* or "common learning," capable of enlarging and enriching people's lives; and to impart the knowledge, skills, and sensibilities foundational to the arts of living themselves. But if traditionalists expected that the Yale Report would put an end to academic controversy, they were destined for disappointment. If anything, debate over collegiate priorities and purposes was to continue unchecked throughout the nineteenth century and beyond.

THE AFTERMATH: IN RETROSPECT

For all the brave talk among academic traditionalists about holding the line and not succumbing to cultural philistines, not even the most hidebound among them was able to avoid making some place in the college curriculum for utilitarian studies. By the 1850s if not before, to botany, chemistry, and zoology had been added a host of other applied scientific and technological arts in many institutions. At Yale in 1846 a professorship of "agricultural chemistry and animal and vegetable physiology" was established, not to mention a chair of "chemistry and the kindred sciences as applied to the arts."[141] Harvard meanwhile in 1851 had awarded its first bachelor of science degree and was contemplating the prospect of opening up a graduate school of arts and sciences. Other colleges and universities soon followed. John William Draper at an address before an audience assembled in 1835 at New York University announced, "Mere literary acumen is becoming utterly powerless against profound scientific attainment." He then posed two questions: "To what are the great advances of civilization for the last fifty years due—to literature or science? Which of the two is it that is shaping the thought of the world?"[142]

Some academics welcomed the advent of scientific studies, not on the grounds of practicality but as allies of religion. Long before, President Walter Minto of Princeton had hailed "natural philosophy" for having led "in a satisfactory manner to the knowledge of one almighty, all-wise and all-good Being, who created, preserves and governs the universe. . . . Indeed," he stressed, "I consider a student of that branch of science as engaged in a continued act of devotion."[143] Albert Hopkins at Williams returned a half century later, in 1838, to the same theme. Defending a proposal to open an astronomical observatory on campus, he bolstered pragmatic arguments with a religious rationale. The facility would be beneficial, he declared, because it would inspire students to direct their thoughts "toward that fathomless fountain and author of being, who has constituted matter and all its accidents as lively emblems of the immaterial kingdom."[144]

Critics nonetheless continued with a barrage of attacks upon those colleges slow to adjust their programs. In California in 1858, the state's superintendent of public instruction demanded to know, "For what useful occupation are the graduates of most of our old colleges fit?"[145] In Georgia the year before, a newspaper editorial criticized the professorate for its alleged intransigence in the face of social change and wondered aloud why its members deserved access to public funds. "We are now living in a different age, an age of practical utility," the paper announced, "one in which the State University does not, and cannot supply the demands of the state. The times require practical men, civil engineers, to take charge of public roads, railroads, mines, scientific agriculture." Rejecting claims that institutions of higher learning were never intended to supply the technical skills needed for the practice of any occupation whatsoever, the writer went on to argue that "practicality" and "utility" should become the watchwords of any public academic agency.[146] Henry Tappan, future president of the University of Michigan, interpreted the situation as he saw it in 1851 somewhat differently. "The commercial spirit of our country, and the many avenues of wealth which are opened before enterprise, create a distaste for study deeply inimical to education," as he put it. "The manufacturer, the merchant, and the gold-digger, will not pause in their career to gain intellectual accomplishments. While gaining knowledge, they are losing the opportunities to gain money."[147] By implication, the question was whether and for how long traditional colleges could manage to survive and about who they would serve.

For all the harsh criticisms to which they were subjected, it seems important to note that on the eve of the Civil War, colleges both public and private, sectarian and nondenominational, classical or otherwise, were still flourishing enterprises throughout America. By their own lights, collegiate leaders grappled honestly with significant social and intellectual questions of the day. Not all colleges were victims of a debilitating and narrow brand of sectarianism; nor were all necessarily bastions of suffocating paternalism. And the fact that vocal detractors viewed colleges as something of a luxury, even in an expanding economy, tends to obscure the point that a disproportionate number of leaders in all of the major professions from the 1820s onward *were* college graduates—notwithstanding that lack of formal academic credentials did not necessarily preclude professional attainment.

While the response of many educators to outside pressures for change may have been purely reactive and often clumsy, the seeming inadequacy of their responses falls far short of demonstrating that colleges somehow *should* have tailored their curricula to the demands of certain utilitarians. The truth of the matter was that academicians of the day genuinely disagreed even among themselves over whether liberal-arts schools could better serve society by converting themselves into professional trade schools or by resisting vocationalist appeals. Matters of principle and conviction were involved on all sides. Finally, some accounting must be made of the local pride that kept so many colleges alive through hard times. As President William Tyler of Amherst told the Society for the Promotion of Theological and Collegiate Education at the West in 1856, the genius of the American institution of higher learning was that close ties between college and community could be mutually beneficial. "While the college redeems the community from the curse of ignorance," as he put it, "the community preserves the college from an undue tendency to monkish corruption and scholastic unprofitableness."[148]

Brown's Francis Wayland was only one of many conflicting voices delivering pronouncements on the condition of the colleges at the century's halfway point. To him at least it was clear that the colleges had to change, that they stood in need of "a radical change" that would permit them to offer courses of study "for the benefit of all classes." "What," he asked, "could . . . Horace and Homer and Demosthenes, with a little mathematics and natural philosophy, do towards developing the untold resources of this continent?"[149] Others were less sure of the need for drastic measures, and more uncertain still of the direction urged upon them by President Wayland. But Brown's reform-minded president had posed a question not easily answered by defenders of the *ancien régime*. Assessing American academe as it appeared to him in 1850, he declared, "We have produced an article for which the demand is diminishing. We sell it at less than cost, and the deficiency is made up by charity. We give it away, and still the demand diminishes. Is it not time to inquire whether we cannot furnish an article for which the demand will be, at least, somewhat more remunerative?"[150] To that query no authoritative or widely accepted answer was immediately forthcoming.

5

The Evolving
American University

A NEW ERA

Michigan president James B. Angell, speaking on the occasion of his
1871 inaugural address, was moved to observe, "The public mind is
now in a plastic, impressionable state, and every vigorous college, nay,
every capable worker, may help to shape its decisions upon education." Surveying the collegiate scene of his time, Angell concluded, "In this
day of unparalleled activity in college life, the institution which is not steadily
advancing is certainly falling behind."[1] A more quintessential encapsulation
of the situation in American higher education in the post–Civil War period
is difficult to imagine. The "unparalleled activity" he spoke of was both real
and palpable. It was an era in which, as never before, institutions of higher
learning were scrutinizing themselves and reexamining their basic purposes
and goals. Although prognostications of the future of higher education differed greatly, the prospect of major change ahead was widely commented
upon. Ralph Waldo Emerson, among others, was keenly aware that institutions of higher learning in the latter half of the nineteenth century would
likely bear little resemblance to their antebellum predecessors. "The treatises
that are written on University reform may be acute or not," he recorded in his
journal in 1867, "but their chief value to the observer is the showing that a

cleavage is occurring in the hitherto granite of the past, and a new era is nearly arrived."[2]

Noah Porter, in his 1871 inaugural address as president of Yale, undoubtedly had something similar in mind when he commented, "Never, perhaps, did this subject [of higher education reform] occupy the thoughts of so many persons and occupy them so earnestly. It certainly never excited more active controversy, or provoked more various . . . criticism, or was subjected to a greater variety of experiments than with us in these passing years." He spoke eloquently about how "sharp" was "the criticism of real or imagined defects in the old methods and studies" and the determined demand for "sweeping and fundamental changes."[3] Ironically, Porter had yet to discover for himself just how potent and irresistible were those reform demands. The "new era" sensed by Emerson was indeed at hand.

Ultimately, the outcome of decades of ferment and turmoil, extending from the century's midpoint to the turn of the next, would be the supplanting of the quaint "old-time" college as a dominant institutional model by that of the modern university. New centers of scholarship and learning would be built from the ground up. Existing colleges—some of them at least—would be transformed in succeeding years into entirely different kinds of academic institutions. To them were to be added courses of preparatory instruction for a range of technical occupations and professions undreamt of by traditional schoolmen a scant generation or two previously. In the process of development, the meaning of post-secondary education itself would undergo profound alteration. The rise of the American university, marked though it was by false starts and much trial and error, was to prove itself a momentous phenomenon of almost revolutionary proportions. American higher learning would never be the same again.[4]

POSTWAR REBUILDING

Despite high levels of public indebtedness and inflation, the economy of the North had emerged from the Civil War relatively unscathed, bolstered as it was by the cementing of the industrial East with the rich agricultural Middle West. Colleges throughout the northeast and mid-Atlantic regions still appeared in reasonably robust health; and enrollments after the mid-1870s increased fivefold in the decades following, a proportional increase far in excess of the overall growth in the nation's population for the same period. Nationally, there were an estimated 62,000 students enrolled in some type of collegiate institution in 1870; only twenty years later their numbers had swollen to 157,000; and by 1910 the total would surpass 355,000.[5]

Yet in the aftermath of the nation's greatest internal conflagration, if the North had emerged intact, most of the South still lay in ruins. The entire region's economic infrastructure had been virtually destroyed, the dreams of its plantation aristocracy ground into dust. Not surprisingly, southern states were to share little in the tremendous expansion of higher education that took place elsewhere throughout the Union.[6] Unlike their northern counterparts, many southern colleges were left utterly destitute by the war. Lacking students, resources, and buildings, most had all they could do simply to survive. The University of Alabama's campus had been burned to the ground.[7] In Oxford, Mississippi, where the state's university was reopened under Reconstructionist control, officials wrestled with debilitating financial problems. The situation at Chapel Hill in North Carolina, where Union troops had occupied the campus, was much the same.[8] South Carolina's state college had lost its entire endowment, and had only debts and worthless securities to show for it.[9] The identical problem faced Wake Forest.[10] Everywhere, colleges bereft of assets confronted the herculean task of rebuilding for the future.

The crisis into which the University of Missouri, located in a border state, was thrown at war's end was especially acute.[11] There the school had virtually ceased operations between early 1861 and late 1862 as bloody struggles between the Union and the Confederacy raged on all sides. It was a hiatus marked by federal troops garrisoned on campus; a time when allegations of a "wanton and brutal" soldiery circulated widely; and local authorities were busily engaged rounding up suspected secessionists and administering loyalty oaths. Recalling the grim years of the immediate postwar period, Daniel Read, the institution's beleaguered president who assumed office in 1868, reported he had found the place in grave disarray. The school, he wrote, was "largely involved in debt, its officers paid in University warrants, unconvertible, at a large discount for cash, the payment of the income of the endowment suspended . . . the University building greatly defaced and injured in consequence of its occupation by the United States troops, and some of the rooms unfit for use; the roof leaky and the plastering fallen from the ceiling of many of the rooms."

According to Read's vivid account, "The fences around the campus were in a dilapidated condition. The chimneys of the President's house and portions of the walls stood mournful mementos of the conflagration which had destroyed the house." An attempt to reopen classes was made toward the end of the year 1862. However, as the president's report explained, "Upon the first week of the opening of the session, not a single student appeared to matriculate, there being a county fair in the neighborhood; and on the second, less than forty came forward for that purpose." The institution's future seemed in doubt. State legislators voiced misgivings over the advisability of attempting to rebuild the school at all. Some urged that it be relocated elsewhere. Others urged that what remained be left to its own devices to survive however it could, albeit stripped of its designation as a state university.[12]

Much the same story was repeated over and over again in other states to the south. In the end, some institutions managed to arise from the ashes and rebuild. A few closed their doors. Others were able to continue, although only at the price of becoming little more than insular little enclaves, consigned to isolated backwaters far removed from the mainstream of American cultural and intellectual life. Reconstruction in the South, it was plain, would hardly touch academic institutions at all, at least not until toward the end of the century.[13]

IMPERATIVES FOR CHANGE

The restructuring of American higher education elsewhere in the post–Civil War period was driven by a potent combination of social, political, cultural, and economic factors. Accelerating industrialization and urbanization, combined with the impetus to complete the settlement of a fast-disappearing western frontier, were contributing forces. The development of new scientific and technological knowledge upon which business and industry increasingly relied counted heavily in the equation. The allure of German universities, with their interest in scholarly research and inquiry, was another important consideration.[14] The gradual emergence of a more secular society and a consequent erosion of religious influence served in the view of some critics to make institutions that were chiefly preoccupied with the training of clergymen seem atavistic and outmoded. Most important of all perhaps was the growth in surplus capital potentially available for institution-building from the accumulated fortunes of industrial entrepreneurs, railroad tycoons and business magnates. Popular identification of education with material success and progress (a perception assiduously cultivated by reform-minded academic leaders) represented yet another part of the dynamic working to encourage change. Finally, indicative of the great divide between old and new, representing the fundamental cleavage that existed between the seemingly archaic antebellum collegiate era and that of the postwar university, was the passing of an entire generation of prominent college presidents.[15]

Aging leaders such as Mark Hopkins at Williams or Theodore Dwight Woolsey at Yale either had opposed change outright or at best were tepid in their endorsement of proposed reforms. Faced with declining enrollments and indications of unrest, their basic reaction had been to hold the line, to offer only minimal adjustments and accommodations, to rationalize away the need for fundamental alterations, to hope somehow that academe could weather the storm substantially unchanged.[16] Now in the postwar years a new generation of academic reformers was coming to power: men such as Andrew D. White of Cornell, John Howard Raymond of Vassar, William Watts Folwell and Cyrus Northrup at Minnesota, William B. Rogers of the Massachusetts Institute of Technology, Walter B. Hill at Georgia, James H. Kirkland at Vanderbilt, William Pepper at Pennsylvania, Daniel Coit Gilman of Hopkins, and Charles W. Eliot at Harvard.[17] Impatient, aggressive, sensing opportunities to be seized, they represented a new breed of innovators not easily deterred from their chosen course. Their shared goal, sometimes inchoate in its formulation and with details as-yet poorly defined, was nothing less than the refashioning of American higher education in a new mold: that of the university.[18]

Even proponents of the old order conceded that academe was changing. As Charles Kendall Adams of Michigan admitted, "In all parts of the country, the sad fact stares us in the face that the training which has long been considered essential to finished scholarship has been losing ground from year to year in the favor of the people."[19] Part of the reason in an increasingly urban society was that those who in an earlier day might have contented themselves with positions as village pastors or schoolmasters were now seeking new career opportunities in the cities. T. H. Safford, a professor at Williams, acknowledged as much in 1888 when he observed, "The varied attractions of city life restrain intellectual tendencies in the minds of many boys, and the variety of careers which they see opening before their older schoolmates leads to a strong tendency to follow business rather than classical courses."[20] The trustees of the University of Vermont in 1871 enunciated much the same view, noting that declining enrollments in rural academic enclaves could be accounted for by "our close connection by railroad and telegraph with our great cities."[21] And if students willing to subject themselves to the traditional regimen of memorized recitations and strict supervision offered by the typical small-town college were increasingly hard to come by, so too were academically respectable teachers. As Harvard's Eliot accurately remarked at his inaugural address of 1869, "It is very hard to find competent professors. . . . Very few Americans of eminent ability are attracted to this profession. The pay has been too low, and there has been no gradual rise out of drudgery, such as may reasonably be expected in other learned callings."[22]

Unless the old rural colleges revived themselves, it was argued, they stood in danger of slipping into oblivion. By 1894 matters had reached a point where John W. Burgess, a professor at Columbia, was prepared to sound the final death knell of the traditional college. "I confess that I am unable to divine what is to be ultimately the position of Colleges which cannot become Universities and which will not be Gymnasia," he declared. "I cannot see what reason they will have to exist. It will be largely a waste of capital to maintain them, and largely a waste of time to attend them. It is so now."[23]

Yet another problem in carrying forward major academic reforms throughout the sixties and seventies was vagueness surrounding the much-used term "university." Whereas many small colleges had long claimed university status for themselves, the label itself still lacked clear definition.[24] According to one commentator in 1860, the appelation meant nothing more specific that an institution of great size offering advanced instruction in a broad range of disciplines. Or it might simply connote a college boasting large library holdings. President John Hiram Lathrop of Missouri in 1864 captured part of the emerging pattern in claiming that a "true" university was distinguished by a department of arts and sciences as its nucleus or core, surrounded by other units offering more specialized instruction in practical arts and various applied sciences.[25] At Johns Hopkins in Baltimore, the position was being developed that a university, as distinct from a college, was primarily a post-collegiate institution whose main purpose was the advancement of learning, to which the diffusion of knowledge through undergraduate instruction was strictly subsidiary.[26] Comparable in tone was the 1872 pronouncement of Daniel Gilman at the University of California, who averred, "The university is the most comprehensive term that can be applied to indicate a foundation for the promotion and diffusion of knowledge—a group of agencies organized to advance the arts and sciences of every sort, and to train young men as scholars for all the intellectual callings of life."[27] Philosopher-logician Charles S. Peirce went so far in 1891 as to claim that a university had nothing whatsoever to do with instruction.[28]

Early on, a major theme surrounding discussions of the university was that of the practicality or utility of knowledge and the importance of linking academic learning with professional practice. "The college years are no longer conceived of as a period set apart from life," observed F. H. Stoddard, a professor at New York University. "The college," as he phrased it, "has ceased to be a cloister and has become a workshop."[29] F. W. Kelsey, a Latinist at the University of Michigan in 1883, concurred: "The throbbing life of to-day," he wrote, "demands from our colleges something besides learning and culture. It cares not for pedants steeped in useless lore. It calls for true men, who are earnest, and practical, who know something of the problems of real life and are fitted to grapple with them." Formal learning, Kelsey stressed, must help in "the fitting for real life in something besides discipline and culture of the mind."[30]

Industrial and business leaders, many of them prone to issuing scathing diatribes against academe, could not have agreed more heartily. As Andrew Carnegie himself put it in 1889 in an acidic attack upon classical learning, "While the college student has been learning a little about the barbarous and petty squabbles of a far-distant past, or trying to master languages which are dead, such knowledge as seems adapted for life upon another planet than this as far as business affairs are concerned, the future captain of industry is hotly engaged in the school of experience, obtaining the very knowledge required for his future triumphs." Carnegie's summary judgment: "College education as it exists is fatal to success in that domain."[31]

Both Eliot of Harvard and Andrew White of Cornell were vigorous in their support for more practical professional training. "There is no danger in any part of the university that too much attention will be paid to the sciences ordinarily supposed to have useful application," President Eliot declared. "The problem is to get enough attention made to them."[32] Andrew White, Cornell's first president, outlined his position with equal clarity in his inaugural address of 1868. "I would found an institution," he announced, "where any person can find instruction in any study." White poked fun at what he termed the "pedants" and "gerund grinders" who, he claimed, would substitute "dates for history, gerund-grinding for literature, and formulas for science." Then in an obvious gibe at the sort of arguments advanced by Carnegie and others of like persuasion, he made it clear he was equally unhappy with "Philistines," who saw no use for any education "beyond that which enables a man to live by his wits and to prey upon his neighbor." A broader vision was needed, White asserted, an ideal of the university as a place offering instruction in both humane and scientific disciplines in preparation for a wide variety of specialized occupations.[33]

The concept of "democracy" was often invoked in support of demands for academic reform.[34] To some critics, the democratic imperative was to acknowledge the fundamental equality of all branches of knowledge, no matter how nontraditional. For others, democracy in academe meant easing admissions standards and otherwise enhancing access to higher learning, so that all interested students, of whatever background or economic circumstances, might have the opportunity to pursue higher learning. Again, democracy was appealed to by proponents of the idea that collegiate institutions should expand their "service" role to the public at large. Finally, democratic ideals were invoked to support the theme that colleges should submit to the will of the common masses—not to a closed guild of academics—in deciding what should be taught, and to whom. E. E. Brown, a professor of pedagogy at Michigan, writing in 1892, gave support to the latter view with his assertion, "There is a wisdom residing in the people—the 'common sense of most.'"[35] Accordingly, he avowed, universities ought to take their direction from popular or "commonsensical" notions of what was wanted and needed.

Opposed from certain quarters, welcomed in others, the clear tendency in American higher education throughout the last quarter of the nineteenth century, more than anything else, was one of concessions to the demand for more utilitarian learning.[36] Some reformers, as noted, felt it would be sufficient if institutions of higher education simply broadened the scope of their curricula to incorporate more science, technology, nonclassical languages and other modern subjects. Some urged wholesale modernization, to the virtual exclusion of traditional subjects. Others urged that the concept of a "learned profession," once confined to medicine, law, and the ministry, be enlarged to encompass commerce, manufacturing, and any number of other practical occupations.[37] In an 1855 report as president of the University of Alabama, Frederick A. P. Barnard had confidently predicted, "While time lasts, the farmer will be made in the field, the manufacturer in the shop, the merchant in the counting room, the civil engineer in the midst of the actual operation of his science."[38] A decade or two later, people were not so sure. Perhaps the number of careers for which formal preparatory instruction was both possible and useful should be expanded. Possibly, also, the age-old distinction made between an unlearned occupation or vocation for which an apprenticeship was sufficient and a learned profession demanding collegiate training was indefensible and could no longer be sustained. Whatever the truth of the matter, it was plain that more and more critics, particularly those outside academe, were now demanding that colleges and universities offer direct training in support of any trade whatsoever, including carpentry, blacksmithing, or machining.

STATE UNIVERSITIES AND LAND-GRANT COLLEGES

Nowhere was the trend toward occupational utility more apparent or more widely illustrated than in the development of land-grant colleges.[39] Efforts to found nonsectarian state agencies of higher learning had begun well before the Civil War. Among the earliest were public institutions in Georgia, Ohio, Tennessee, North Carolina, Maryland, South Carolina, and Kentucky. Very few, if any, offered courses of study of sufficient stature to qualify them as universities in the modern sense of the term. Virginia, which opened in 1825, probably must be counted as the first true state university, if its original incorporation as a public enterprise, its secular and nondenominational orientation, and the provision made under Thomas Jefferson's plan to allow students to elect from among alternative courses of study are all taken into consideration. Leaving aside the disputed question of its primacy, Virginia's example was soon followed by Transylvania University in Lexington, Kentucky; by the University of Nashville in Tennessee; and by the founders of state institutions in both North and South Carolina. As the century wore on, several institutions in the South began claiming the status for themselves, Alabama in particular. But, again, virtually all lacked the characteristics later associated with full-fledged universities. Outside the South, most state academic institutions operating prior to the

Civil War were located in the Middle West. Among them, Minnesota's state school, established under the patronage of John S. Pillsbury, and the first public college chartered in Indiana, were perhaps the most important.[40]

Federal land grants, the precedent for which went back as early as the Northwest Ordinance of 1787, proved to be the major stimulus for the founding of state colleges.[41] After 1804, every new state west of the Appalachians joining the union was granted two entire townships for a "seminary of learning"; and by the mid-1850s or thereabouts, the central government already had donated nearly four million acres of public lands, in 15 different states, to provide the necessary endowments.[42] Miami University in Oxford, Ohio, and Ohio University in Athens were prototypical state-supported, land-grant institutions of this sort. Altogether, on the eve of the Civil War there were over a dozen such schools admitting students.

Unfortunately, as events were to make clear, land grants alone did not generate permanent revenues to keep public colleges or universities solvent and in business.[43] At the century's midpoint it would have been difficult to distinguish most of them from purely private ventures; and, in fact, many had since fallen under sectarian control for lack of support from the public sector. Long viewed with suspicion by denominational educators who resented their competition, denounced by religious evangelicals as "godless," and neglected by state legislatures unpersuaded of their need or relevance to the public's immediate concerns, most of the early western universities remained little more than small colleges. Characteristically, their enrollments were limited, their academic reputations mediocre. However much they sought to imitate the forms and customs of the better-established, more prestigious colleges of the East, or to reproduce the revivalistic architecture of their campuses, they continued to languish. Lyman Bagg of Yale, writing in *Four Years at Yale* (1871), contended that if would have been a blessing if all but a half dozen or so of the universities founded after 1800 had been "blotted from existence, or turned into preparatory schools for the other ones." Charles Eliot Norton, speaking to the same issue a quarter century later (1895), clearly had state colleges and universities in mind when he cited "the lamentable waste involved in the needless duplication of . . . instruments of study, of buildings, libraries, and laboratories."[44]

What saved the cause of public, state institutions of higher learning, even as it greatly complicated the question of their identity and purpose, was the enactment of the Morrill Acts of 1862 and 1890.[45] As early as 1848 Congressman Justin Smith Morrill of Vermont had suggested that American colleges should "lop off a portion of the studies established centuries ago as the mark of European scholarship and replace the vacancy . . . by those of a less antique and more practical value." He noted with approval the work of various agricultural societies in chartering such institutions as the Farmer's High School of Pennsylvania, founded in 1854, and New York State's Agricultural College. Comparable efforts were underway in Georgia, Kentucky, and Virginia. What Morrill wanted (possibly after the model of the Michigan State College of Agriculture in East Lansing, which first opened in 1857) was "to promote the liberal and practical education of the industrial classes in the several pursuits and professions of life."[46] That same year he introduced a bill calling for the donation of public lands equal to 30,000 acres for each state senator and representative. Proceeds from the sale of a specified portion of such lands would go to support in each state at least one college "where the leading object shall be, without excluding other scientific or classical studies, to teach such branches of learning as are related to agriculture and the mechanic arts." Morrill's legislative submission was not unopposed.[47] Typical was the fulmination of a senator from Minnesota: "We want no fancy farmers; we want no fancy mechanics."[48] President Buchanan showed little enthusiasm for the initiative; and support from congressional leaders was no better than lukewarm.

Despite initial apathy, the Land Grant College Act finally passed with substantial margins in both houses. Five years after it was first introduced, the bill was signed into law by President Lincoln in July of 1862.[49] Few took note of its passage at the time or ascribed to it much importance. The bill's long-term consequences, however, were far-reaching, although individual state actions varied.[50] Michigan, Pennsylvania, Maryland, and Iowa all converted existing agricultural schools into land-grant "A & M" universities. Connecticut, Rhode Island, Kentucky, Delaware, Indiana, and New York assumed control over private colleges and turned them into state institutions. Federal largesse sometimes was turned over to an existing state university, as occurred in Minnesota, Georgia, Missouri, Wisconsin, and North Carolina. In such cases, the result more often than not was to revitalize those previously established state universities; and for some the appropriations spelled the real difference between survival and extinction. Arkansas and West Virginia founded new state universities and added "agricultural and mechanical" elements. In other states, as in Kansas, Iowa, Oregon, Texas, South Dakota, and Washington, land-grant revenues were used to create a separate institution which more or less duplicated the work of an existing state university. The effect—repeated in no less than twenty different states—was to create fierce and unending competition between rival institutions, each lobbying for its share of state appropriations.

Traditional accounts of the development of land-grant colleges paint a roseate picture of populist institutions immediately responding to the swelling demand for utilitarian learning, of business and industry prospering from the ensuing diffusion of academic expertise, of rustics crowding into classrooms to learn how to boost agricultural productivity and increase their acreage yields. The actual historical record is at once more complex and more ambiguous. Until the second Morrill Act of 1890 provided for regular annual appropriations, for example, state support for land-grant colleges was rarely better than marginal. Colleges, after all, represented a loss of potential tax revenue; worse yet, they made burdensome claims on the public treasury. Hence, it was almost inevitable that for years financially pressed state legislatures temporized, reneged on promises and otherwise tried to evade the requirement to support an school authorized under the Morrill Act. Much effort went into the search for ways to make the colleges self-supporting: tuition surcharges, sales of produce for a college's farms, even work-study programs once again. Nothing worked. The University of Arkansas was one of several institutions forced to undergo a veritable paroxysm of salary cuts and faculty contract terminations as officials scrambled to make ends meet. Professors by the scores were forced to resign, then immediately rehired—but only at a fraction of their former salaries.[51]

Contrary to expectations, land-grant colleges in their formative period had a difficult time attracting students.[52] In New Hampshire, when the state's first land-grant institution opened its doors, not a single individual applied for admission. Pennsylvania was able to garner less than two dozen matriculants; neighboring Connecticut had half as many. Illinois anticipated an entering class numbering in the hundreds—only fifty showed up. North Carolina offered anyone a month's free board if he brought in another paying student. Missouri dispatched its faculty to tour the countryside and tout the advantages of its program among local farmers. Student demand in Kansas and Michigan where overcrowding had been expected was equally anemic; elsewhere university officials resorted to offering special awards and scholarships to attract prospective students. Sometimes there were more prizes than applicants. In 1892 at the University of Arkansas, after having been legislatively mandated seven years previously to lower admission requirements, officials abandoned them altogether. A prize of twenty-five dollars was offered to the agriculture student who made the best five pounds of butter.[53]

The basic disparity that existed between the presumption underlying reformers' rhetoric and the actual aims of their intended beneficiaries explained part of the problem. Jonathan Baldwin Turner, an early advocate for an agricultural and mechanical college in Illinois, had confidently declared in 1853: "The industrial classes . . . want, and they ought to have, the same facilities for understanding the true philosophy, the science, and the art of *their* several pursuits . . . and of efficiently applying existing knowledge thereto and widening its domain, which the professional classes have long enjoyed in *their* pursuits."[54] In theory, rural youth would welcome the opportunity to become scientifically trained agriculturalists. Armed with knowledge gained from the state's land-grant institution, they would then return to their farms where, presumably, they would be engaged in applying the expertise they had acquired in the laboratory and classroom and so contribute to the ultimate transformation and improvement of American agriculture.

In fact, what reformers underestimated was the extent to which those entering college were seeking to *leave* the farm. For many farmers' sons and daughters, attending college was a means of escaping the poverty, boredom, and drudgery of wresting a living from the soil. Even when college-attending was not regarded as a means of escape, farmers were not easily persuaded that classroom studies could be helpful. In an era when land was still abundant and crops could be raised without intensive cultivation, academic theory of any sort was highly suspect. A South Carolina legislator was heard to say in 1879, "[I have never] seen a man who could write a nice essay or make a good agricultural speech who could make corn enough to feed himself and a bob-tailed mule."[55]

Suspicions were sometimes more than amply justified. George C. Swallow, the first professor of agriculture appointed at the University of Missouri, was a botanist whose specialties were landscape gardening and viticulture. His self-appointed mission, as he saw it, was the beautification of the state's farms. It was Swallow who was responsible for inserting his favorite epigram into the university's official catalogue: "He can work better and sleep better, who has well kept lawns and beautiful perspectives."[56] If that was what passed for agricultural education, skeptical farmers must have concluded, little purpose would be served by sending their sons off to college.

Overlooked in traditional assessments of the land-grant college movement is the degree to which nonacademic considerations helped shape results. Conventional wisdom has it that the colleges exerted a major influence on American agriculture, serving to increase worker efficiency and boost crop yields. (Only toward the end of the century is there at least some partial evidence for the claim.) Actually, careful economic analysis suggests that the greatest increase in agricultural productivity per worker occurred well *before* land-grant colleges were firmly established; and, further, that federal and state land-use policies, natural conditions, market developments, canals and railroads, and a host of other factors were mainly responsible for whatever gains occurred. Whereas land-grant colleges certainly may have been important for other reasons prior to the 1890s, their contributions to the nation's economic development during the third quarter of the nineteenth century were apt to be more indirect or fortuitous than has been commonly supposed.[57]

Lack of agreement throughout the 1870s and 1880s on what an institution catering to the supposed needs of farmers and mechanics ought to be continued to thwart reformers' best efforts. One fundamental question at issue, as noted previously, had to do with the character or level of instruction appropriate to a land-grant college. Strong disagreements surfaced between those who envisioned the production of trained scientists, on the one hand, and those who wanted relatively low-level technical training suitable for farm laborers and mechanics, on the other.[58] If the former approach was to be pursued, "mechanic arts" posed no major problem—systematic bodies of knowledge in physics, chemistry, and metallurgy were already sufficiently well developed to serve as objects of formal collegiate study. But the same could not necessarily be said of "agriculture." If the latter approach was to be followed, then the issue was whether there was any real difference between an ordinary secondary technical institute and a true university of higher learning.[59] Confusing the situation still further was the chronic disagreement that existed over the proper balance to be struck within a land-grant institution between traditional classical studies and technical specialties. Land-grant schools typically tended to emphasize the practical over the ornamental. But it was an issue of bitter contention that often divided faculties and trustees.[60] In the end, with the federal government offering little or no guidance about how to proceed, each institution found itself free to experiment and to seek its own solutions.[61]

Isaac Newton, the U.S. Commissioner of Agriculture, suggested in 1863 that land-grant colleges might end up differing but little from more traditional institutions. "These colleges are not to be agricultural only," he emphasized. "The sons of our farmers are not less ambitious of distinction than others, and an education that regards them as farmers only cannot meet their approbation." Because the purpose of education was to teach critical thought and reflection, Newton felt, all pursuits might have "a common course of instruction."[62] A comparable outlook was expressed in 1871 by a trustee of the University of Missouri who predicted that "too much in practical education should not be expected, as the main purpose is to develop the social and mental nature of the students." (Reportedly a member of the state's board of agriculture retorted, "That is good, but what are they going to do about hog cholera?")[63]

Edward Orton, first president at Ohio State University, pledged in his 1874 inaugural address that the university would attend to "the education of a man as man, rather than that which equips him for a particular post of duty."[64] Reflecting the contrary point of view was a Philadelphia newspaper editorial of 1864: "Instead of introducing the student of agriculture to a laboratory and chemical and philosophical apparatus," the paper urged, "we would introduce him to a pair of heavy . . . leather boots and corduroy pants, and learn him how to load manure."[65] Possibly the same spirit lay behind graduation addresses delivered at the Connecticut Agricultural College in 1884 which bore such titles as "Irrigation and Drainage" and "The Feet of the Horse and Ox, and their Diseases."[66] The contrast with the spirit and character of the antebellum college of a half century earlier could hardly have been more pronounced.

In an age when the high school as an institution was either nonexistent or as yet still undeveloped, state colleges and universities played a vital role in helping to articulate secondary and higher education.[67] Faced with the prospect of admitting students woefully unequipped for academic success, the traditional approach taken by many colleges and universities had long been to append a preparatory department to their respective collegiate programs. Basically, these units served to bridge the yawning chasm that usually existed between elementary/secondary common schools and universities. In 1870 the University of Michigan began identifying those select few schools capable of graduating students whose academic achievements entitled them to university admission without further training. Gradually a system of certification or licensure evolved for those lower schools willing and able to supply adequate college preparatory programs of their own. Similar systems soon developed elsewhere: in the states of Minnesota, Iowa, and Wisconsin in 1872; followed by Indiana and Illinois the next year; then by Ohio in 1874.[68]

Over the next two decades, still other states adopted certification requirements of their own, including California, Texas, and Missouri. By the turn of the century, no fewer than forty-two state universities and land-grant colleges and an additional number of private colleges had established licensure linkages with secondary schools. By 1900 collegiate preparatory departments were fast becoming a thing of the past.[69] As Nebraska's chancellor had once advised those in attendance at a state teachers' convention, "I see the common school stuck in the mud and the university suspended in the air. If we are to have a [true] system of education, the word is 'Close up.'" Colleges and universities took him at his word.

Agricultural and mechanical land-grant colleges and state universities, it might be said, over time came to represent the fullest expression possible of Jacksonian egalitarian and democratic ideals applied to higher education. As historian Frederick Rudolph notes, there was a comfortable, homely ring to the phrase "state college," one invoking images of wholesome young yeomen of ingrained common sense gone off to school to prepare themselves for a life of honest toil. Its associations were those typical of rural America: the state fair, the Fourth of July picnic, church socials, and the Saturday-night barn dance.[70] Conventional wisdom of the time thus extolled the public college as a symbol of liberation from the elitist, hidebound collegiate traditions of the past. In the eyes of plain, hard-working farmers, the chief value of the state college was that it did not traffic overmuch in "fancy book larnin'." And when it did—or was perceived to do so—popular support for the institution was relatively unenthusiastic. But either way, the public college was a source of civic pride, a symbol of progress, of refinement and accomplishment that could not be discounted altogether by even the harshest critics.

Reflecting back from the perspective of 1890, a House Committee on Education judged that land-grant schools had "turned out a body of men who, as teachers, investigators, and leaders of industry, rank well up with the same class of men everywhere in the world." Their further contribution, the Committee's report held, was that they had served to bring older institutions "more closely into harmony with the spirit and purpose of the age."[71] Less effusive and more critical in tone was the judgment passed in 1903 by a foreign observer, who felt that burgeoning state colleges and universities had enthroned the practical almost wholly at the expense of other, equally important studies. They were, a certain Lord Bryce observed, "true universities rather in aspiration than in fact." Still, as he grudgingly conceded, they were probably "better than nothing."[72]

MUNICIPAL COLLEGES AND UNIVERSITIES

What land-grant and other state collegiate institutions were to small-town America, municipal colleges and universities were to the cities. Even as rural public colleges gained their foothold, momentum was building for the establishment of free, public post-secondary education in urban centers also.[73] Well before the Civil War, New York's state legislature had chartered (in 1847) the Free Academy of New York City, the embryonic beginning of what would later evolve into that city's vast, far-flung college system. In 1837, Charleston, South Carolina, had likewise assumed support of a formerly private college established several years before. That same year the city of Louisville in Kentucky took steps to found its own municipal university.

The pace of institution-building accelerated in the postwar period when Cincinnati (1873), followed by Toledo, created new city universities. The founding of Hunter College in New York and Wayne University in Detroit were initiatives undertaken by the two cities' respective boards of education. Akron, Wichita, and Omaha all moved to convert existing private schools into municipal colleges or universities. Privately endowed universities began to appear within or near the precincts of major urban municipalities during the same period: Boston University, the University of Buffalo, Temple University in Philadelphia, the University of Rochester, the University of Pittsburgh, Western Reserve in Cleveland, George Washington University and American

University in the nation's capital, and Fairleigh Dickinson University in Rutherford, New Jersey, foremost among them.[74]

Municipal schools differed greatly in size, scope of operations, and breadth and level of curricula. What they shared in common was a dedication to meeting the needs of urban students.[75] Some were pioneers in offering advanced industrial technical training. Others specialized in offering preparatory instruction for business careers in addition to more traditional liberal-arts courses. Many (albeit at a somewhat later date) pioneered the scheduling of evening classes and other measures designed to enhance accessibility to part-time students. Yet long before the term "nontraditional" came to be applied to certain collegians, city colleges were organizing themselves to meet their special needs and demands, including, for example, those who had resumed their studies after dropping out, mature students with spouses and families, and those seeking retraining for second careers. Many who lacked the financial means to attend a residential college full-time found enrollment at a municipal college catering expressly to commuting students a more viable alternative. Overall, in terms of accessibility and low cost, city colleges quickly established an important niche for themselves in American higher education. Their importance was to increase significantly after the turn of the century.

WOMEN'S COLLEGES AND COEDUCATION

Women's struggles to gain access to higher learning in nineteenth-century America were waged on two fronts. The first was represented by the founding or expansion of what had been called "academies" in the late 1700s, then "seminaries" in the early 1800s, and finally, true post-secondary colleges in the latter half of the nineteenth century.[76] The second was defined by experiments with coeducation.[77] Antebellum institutions for women had been far and few between: the Troy Female Seminary, founded in 1821; the Hartford Female Seminary (founded in 1823); the Ipswich Female Seminary in Massachusetts; Mt. Holyoke Female Seminary in New York; and the Georgia Female College of Macon, Georgia, first chartered in 1836 and opened in 1839.[78] Each had begun as little more than "finishing schools" designed to produce young women who would be suitable companions for their husbands.[79] This they remained for many years thereafter, scrupulously avoiding any appearance of striving to educate their students "beyond their natural sphere."[80] Referring to these institutions as they existed in 1851, Catherine Beecher's comment was still substantially accurate: "Those female institutions in our land which are assuming the ambitious name of colleges, have, not one of them, as yet, secured the real features which constitute the chief advantage of such institutions. They are merely high schools."[81]

The founding of Elmira Female College, which began issuing its own academic degrees in 1859, pointed the way (if only indirectly) for the eventual maturation of Mt. Holyoke and Bryn Mawr as full-fledged collegiate institutions.[82] Elmira's opening also anticipated the founding in the 1870s of such new womens' colleges as Wellesley, Smith, and Vassar. Each in its own fashion offered young women significant educational opportunities denied them in exclusively male colleges and universities.[83] Similarly, the establishment of so-called "coordinate" colleges, separate but affiliated with established colleges, marked an important step in enhancing women's access to higher education: Radcliffe at Harvard, Barnard at Columbia, Newcomb at Tulane, Pembroke at Brown, Jackson at Tufts, and Flora Stone Mather at Western Reserve.[84]

Equally important, if not more so, was the movement to allow women admission to colleges and universities that heretofore had been exclusively male in their student composition.[85] Received opinion had long held that women neither required nor were fit for serious academic pursuits. Given the vast intellectual and emotional differences separating the sexes, many Victorians held, comingling of the two in a collegiate environment amounted to creating a "powder keg" liable to explode at any time. Typical of prevailing opinion were the misgivings expressed by a certain Reverend John Todd in the early 1870s, who objected, "Must we crowd education on our daughters, and for the sake of having them 'intellectual,' make them puny, nervous, and their whole earthly existence a struggle between life and death?"[86] Forced to compete in a man's world, traditionalists were convinced, women would suffer nervous breakdowns and their pure and benevolent natures would be corrupted. Worse yet, or so it was believed, a woman's reproductive system might suffer irreparable harm under the rigors and stress of academic pursuits. Too much learning would render her unfit for her preordained destiny as wife and mother. Coeducation meant a violation of the natural division of complementary spheres of competence and influence between the sexes: it could serve only to "coarsen" or "masculinize" young women, even as it made men more effeminate and less aggressive. A fear repeatedly expressed was that the constant association of men and women in colleges would inevitably lessen the social distance between the two and render them less attractive to one another.[87]

Educated women threatened familial harmony and stability, ran another common argument. As a student at Vanderbilt was quoted as declaring, "No man wants to come home at night and find his wife testing some new process for manufacturing oleomargarine, or in the observatory sweeping the heavens for a comet." A foreign visitor to Wellesley shortly after its opening was impressed by the studious demeanor of the school's students. "This is all very fine," he commented, "but . . . how does it affect their chances [of marriage]?"[88] Nonetheless, the movement toward coeducation was irresistible. A declaration issued by Wisconsin's governing board in 1872 aptly illustrated how attitudes were changing: "It is too late, amid the noontime splendours of the nineteenth century, to ignore the claims of women to higher education," the board avowed. ". . . Whatever shall make her wiser and better, that she may learn; whatever knowledge she may be able to use, either in adding to her own happiness, or in promoting the happiness of others—that knowledge she may rightfully acquire."[89]

The earliest advances in coeducation were registered in land-grant colleges and state universities of the Middle West, beginning with Iowa in 1855 and Wisconsin in 1863, followed by Indiana, Missouri, Michigan, and California throughout the next decade. By the mid-1870s, most collegiate institutions in the West had accepted the practice.[90] There were an estimated seventeen southern colleges that admitted women and eight in the Middle Atlantic states. In the East—where the notion that women required little more than a secondary education hung on longer—no more than half a dozen or so collegiate institutions allowed admission to women. Wesleyan introduced coeducation in 1872; and Middlebury followed in 1883. Oberlin, of course, had long endorsed comingling of the sexes; and fledgling Cornell was equally willing to admit women. By 1880 upwards of a third of America's colleges and universities had adopted some limited form of coeducation. By the end of the century the percentage had risen to almost three-quarters of all collegiate institutions of higher learning throughout the country. Yet if the absolute numbers of women enrolled in colleges were increasing, as percentages of the total female population between the ages of eighteen and twenty-one, figures stayed low. In 1870, for example, it has been estimated that less than 1 percent of the nation's young women were attending college; twenty years later the total was still no more than 2.5 percent.[91]

Partially obscured by the growth in female enrollments registered between 1860 and 1900 is the extreme caution and hesitancy with which college experiments with coeducation were conducted. Progress tended to be a fitful and halting affair.[92] At the University of Wisconsin, custom obliged women to stand in the classroom until all male members were seated. Elsewhere, females were kept strictly segregated from males. It followed that women customarily were not allowed to participate in extracurricular activities. Rarely if ever, for example, were women allowed to join musical groups, debating societies, amateur photography clubs, or academic and social honoraries.

Indicative of the seclusion imposed upon women students was the situation reported at the University of Missouri at the opening of the 1868–1869 academic session, when twenty-two women were first admitted as students in the Normal College. President Daniel Read later recounted that at the time, the move was regarded as "a very bold and hazardous measure." At first, "the ladies" were not permitted to attend chapel services. Male students were barred from the special classes to which the new arrivals were assigned. Women students were prohibited from using the library except during special hours when men were not present. "Finding, however, that the young women . . . did no matter of harm," the president's report recalled, "we very cautiously admitted them to some of the recitations and lectures in the University building itself . . . providing always, they were to be marched in good order, with at least two teachers, one in the front and the other in the rear of the column as guards."

Other innovations followed. "The young women were permitted and invited to come into the chapel," President Read's account continued, "and, after the novelty of their presence was worn off, even to join their voices in prayer and praise in the morning worship." One of the first group of women admitted later wrote of the experience of attending chapel for the first time. "We were formed into a line at the Normal Building, with Prof. Ripley at the head and Mrs. Ripley forming the rear guard," she recalled. "We passed under the great columns and into the august building, not to be seated, however, on the same floor as the men, but given a place in the gallery above. There, with becoming modesty we sat with downcast eyes—upon the student body below—while the prayers and scripture lessons went on to the edification of our souls." Before long, University officials had become positively adventuresome: "By degrees, and carefully feeling our way, as though explosive material was all around us," President Read concluded, "we have come to admit them to all the classes . . . just as young men are admitted."[93]

William C. Russell, an academic vice-president at Cornell, was not quite so sanguine. On one occasion he learned "of a lady student calling one young man into the room, shutting the door, kissing him," he confessed in 1879. The experience, Russell testified, "produced stress which has embittered months of existence."[94] But by 1897 the president of Ohio State University, for one, was prepared to acknowledge that all of the dire predictions of calamity when young men and women were instructed together had proven unfounded. Moreover, he detected certain benefits having come from coeducation. "This inter-training and equal training," he observed, "takes the simper out of the young women and the roughness out of the young men."[95]

Changes in popular attitudes toward the place of women in academe lagged well behind growing confidence in the practicality of coeducation as an institutional arrangement. An ode to "Tender Delores" in the 1892 student yearbook at the University of California, for example, affords a fitting illustration. No matter how attractive a newly arrived female student might be, the ode warned, if she applied herself too strenuously to her studies, she would make "her pretty little nose very red," her "rosy cheeks would become jaundiced, and her hair thinned." Upon graduation, the only suitable career open to her would be that of the schoolmarm.[96] The same *Blue and Gold* yearbook contained a farewell address from the seniors to the coeds of 1892: "In your future careers as schoolmistresses, when, after a wearisome day, you push your spectacles upon your brow and dream of the past, think on us, your admirers and brothers."[97] President Benjamin Wheeler in a 1904 speech warned women students, "You are not like men and you must recognize the fact. . . . You may have the same studies as the men, but you must put them to different use." He emphasized, "You are . . . here for the preparation of marriage and motherhood." If women were diligent in applying themselves, Wheeler promised, the education they gained would make them "more serviceable as wives and mothers."[98]

Marion Talbot, dean of women at Chicago and author of *The Education of Women* (1910) disagreed. She firmly believed that the record of women's academic achievements over the preceding half century had amply demonstrated the folly of restricting higher learning to males alone. Women, she wrote, "have proved their ability to enter every realm of knowledge. They must have the right to do it. No province of the mind should be peculiarly man's. Unhampered by traditions of sex," Talbot predicted, "women will naturally and without comment seek the intellectual goal which they think good and fit. The logical outcome of the present status of women's education will be intellectual freedom on an individual basis."[99]

BLACK COLLEGES

Women's struggle for access to higher education roughly coincided in time with the first stirrings of a movement to expand educational opportunity among blacks. It is recorded that a certain Edward Jones and John Russwurm were the first two African Americans to earn bachelor's degrees from white institutions, each having graduated within weeks of one another from Amherst and Bowdoin, respectively, in 1826.[100] People of color attending college were nevertheless a rarity in the antebellum period, as indicated by the fact that no more than twenty-seven others were listed in the roster of all black graduates prior to the Emancipation Proclamation.[101] The first black colleges to come into existence were founded in the North. An Institute for Colored Youth was first created by Quakers in Philadelphia in 1842, ancestor to the institution later called Cheyney State College. Avery College in Allegheny City, Pennsylvania, chartered in 1849, was also among the first; followed by the Miner Academy, begun in Washington, D.C., in 1851; and then by Lincoln University (originally the Ashmun Institute), founded by Presbyterians in Pennsylvania in 1854. Wilberforce was established a year or so later by Ohio Methodists who in 1862 transferred the institution's control over to the African Methodist Episcopal Church. Later on, joining the ranks of northern black colleges was Central State University in Ohio, chartered in 1887 as the "Combined Normal and Industrial Department" of Wilberforce. It subsequently seceded in effect from its parent institution and became a four-year school in its own right. Of all the northern black colleges established in the nineteenth century, only four—Lincoln, Wilberforce, Cheyney, and Central State—survived into the twentieth century.[102]

In the South, in the years following General Lee's surrender at Appomattox, popular opposition to the notion that blacks should be educated at all, much less be afforded an opportunity to attend college, died hard. Prevailing opinion held that blacks were inherently inferior to whites, that the obvious differences favoring whites over blacks were innate and unalterable, and hence no good purpose was served by attempting to pretend otherwise. Perhaps not untypical in its expression of such widely held views was a diatribe launched by a Virginian by the name of Bebbet Puryear who, writing in *The Southern Planter and Farmer* under the pseudonym "Civis" in 1877, denounced proposals for any public support of black education whatsoever. Assailing what he characterized as the "hideous doctrine of negro equality," the author explained, "I oppose [education for blacks] because its policy is cruelty in the extreme to the negro himself. It instills in his mind that he is competent to share in the higher walks of life, prompts him to despise those menial pursuits to which his race has been doomed, and invites him to enter into competition with the white man for those tempting prizes that can be won only by a quicker and profounder sagacity, by a greater energy and self-denial, and a higher order of administrative talent than the negro has ever developed."[103] So far as many unreconstructed southerners were concerned, the prospect that childlike, indolent former slaves reared to be dependent and subservient could be educated as the social equals of whites was not simply wrongheaded and foredoomed to failure—it was ludicrous.

Intransigent opposition gradually abated in the postbellum period, thanks in part to pressure from civil-rights reformers, though strong reservations (in the North no less than in the South) still remained as to the character and extent of the education most appropriate for blacks.[104] In time, even as barriers of caste were raised and southern white rule was restored, the idea that blacks might be educated, even at nominal public expense, began to receive grudging acquiescence. Southerners on the whole were willing to accede to demands that educational opportunity be extended to blacks, but only so long as it was not viewed as posing a frontal challenge to white supremacy or otherwise encouraging the black to abandon his preordained "place" in the social order.[105]

Throughout the debate, it might be observed, white champions of the rights of African Americans, northern and southern alike, often betrayed a certain paternal condescension in their pronouncements about what blacks wanted or needed, but no one could deny them their sincerity or high-mindedness of purpose.

Under Reconstruction and for several decades thereafter, black higher education in the South developed chiefly as the product of work undertaken by northern white benevolent societies, denominational missionary bodies, and private black charitable organizations.[106] Later, corporate philanthropic foundations and wealthy individuals lent support to the establishment and spread of black private colleges. The federal government gave scant aid until late in the century; and support from southern state governments for black normal schools and colleges was similarly limited.[107] The Freedman's Bureau (1862–1872), acting on behalf of the War Department, was the first to take up the work of founding black schools. To its efforts were added those of civic and religious groups who cooperated with the Bureau and then developed special ventures of their own. Among the earliest was the Boston Educational Commission, later known as the New England Freedmen's Aid Society. In the same year of its founding, 1862, the National Freedmen's Relief Commission of Philadelphia and New York was organized. The two groups subsequently formed the United States Commission for Relief of National Freedmen, with headquarters in Washington, D.C. Three years later that consolidated body was replaced by the American Freedmen's Aid Union, which, after two more name changes, ceased operations in 1869. Other agencies engaged in setting up schools included the African Civilization Society and the Baltimore Association for the Moral and Educational Improvement of Negroes (a similar organization was established in Delaware.)[108]

Church bodies especially active in creating and supporting educational institutions for blacks included the American Missionary Association, the American Baptist Home Mission Society, the Friends Association for Aid to Freedmen, the Board of Freedmen's Missions of the United Presbyterian Church, and the Freedman's Aid Society of the Methodist Episcopal Church. Many former abolitionists assumed leadership roles in the various civic and religious organizations at work establishing schools and colleges, including Henry Ward Beecher, Salmon P. Chase, and Richard S. Rust. Some were prominent business or civic leaders, such as Mathias W. Baldwin, locomotive industrialist; Edward Atkinson, textile manufacturer; and William Claflin, former Governor of Massachusetts. Philanthropic agencies financing black schools through special trusts included the Peabody and Slater Funds, the Jeanes Fund, the Carnegie Fund, and the Rosenwald Fund.[109]

Supporters of black schools and colleges shared in common an ardent faith in the power of newly emancipated blacks to move into the mainstream of

American society if they were afforded opportunities to do so. Black Americans, they argued, should be free to do and become what they chose, limited only by the strength of their own endeavors. They were perfectly capable of transcending the evil legacy of the past, symbolized by the "peculiar" institution of slavery, and in time, with proper tutelage, it was believed as a matter of deep conviction that they would overcome all remaining barriers to full equality posed by postbellum discrimination and bias. Needed now were colleges where a new generation might be nurtured and inspired to uplift the black masses to their rightful place in the world.[110] As the Freedmen's Aid Society was to express it somewhat later, looking back on its efforts, "This society . . . has demonstrated to the South that the freedmen possess good intellectual abilities and are capable of becoming good scholars. Recognizing the brotherhood of mankind and knowing that intellect does not depend upon the color of the skin nor the curl of the hair, we [have] never doubted the Negro's ability to acquire knowledge and distinguish himself by scholarly attainments."[111]

In Alabama, the American Missionary Society sponsored and supported the establishment of what became Talladega College in 1867; Fisk (1866) in Nashville; Tougaloo (1869) in Mississippi; and Straight (later Dillard University). In 1872 a school in Pine Bluff, Arkansas, originally known as the "Branch Normal," became by a legislative act of 1872 the Arkansas Agricultural, Mechanical and Normal College. In Augusta, Georgia, the Augusta Institute was organized in 1867; it later became Morehouse College in Atlanta. The American Baptist Home Mission Society aided in the founding in 1865 of Virginia Union University, Saw University in North Carolina (1865), Benedict College (1871), and likewise helped found Bishop and Morehouse. In Mississippi the state legislature created Alcorn College in 1871. The Freedman's Aid Society of the Methodist Episcopal Church was instrumental in the founding of Shaw University in 1867; Bennett College, Clark University, Claflin College, Meharry Medical College, Morgan College, Philander Smith, Rust, and Wiley; while the Presbyterian Board of Missions for Freedmen set up Barber-Scotia College in North Carolina, and at Charlotte in 1867, Biddle University (later Johnson C. Smith).[112]

In Maryland, the Baltimore Conference of the Methodist Episcopal Church established the school later named Morgan State College. Meanwhile, the Congregationalist American Missionary Association, in cooperation with the Freedman's Bureau, played an important role in 1868 in the creation of Howard University and the Hampton Institute. Independent boards of northern missionaries cooperated in the continued support of these two institutions, as well as lending aid to Leland University and Atlanta University. The African Methodist Episcopal Church maintained Allen University, Morris

Brown College, and Wilberforce. Other African Methodist Episcopal institutions included Paul Quinn College, Edward Waters, Kittrell, and Shorter College. Still other black schools receiving northern missionary aid came to include Livingstone College, Lane, Paine, Miles Memorial, Arkansas Baptist, Selma University, and the Virginia College and Seminary.[113]

All told, possibly as many as two-hundred private and denominational colleges for African Americans were begun throughout the seventies and eighties. Unhappily, the overwhelming majority were actually little more than secondary schools, offering virtually nothing in the way of defensible college-level instruction. Most died out almost immediately for lack of endowments and support. Several, however, gradually developed normal departments for teachers, and some added full-fledged collegiate programs later on. It has been estimated that less than half of the forty or so private black colleges and seventeen public institutions founded in the immediate postwar era were still in existence by the year 1900.

The original intent of most of the founders of black colleges was to provide for their clientele an education indistinguishable from that commonly pursued by whites.[114] In the 1860s and 1870s, that presumption meant liberal learning: Latin, Greek, and mathematics, supplemented by science, philosophy, history, astronomy, English composition and literature, and other curricular staples of the New England liberal-arts college. Black leaders concurred that tomorrow's African American clergymen, lawyers, physicians, statesmen and businessmen, no less than their white peers, needed to acquire learning in the academic traditions of the past; and they stoutly resisted suggestions that rudimentary industrial and agricultural training was a more realistic alternative. If black leaders were to be sent forth to regenerate their own people, it was avowed, they required the best and "highest" education possible. White supremacists poked fun at black pretensions and lost no opportunity to invoke images of black sharecroppers dragging pianos into their shacks, of field hands discoursing in Latin, and house servants competing for jobs with unemployed black college graduates. But as President James G. Merrill of Fisk retorted in 1901, when the day arrived that white students who aspired to become teachers, professors, ministers, and doctors "should learn to hoe and plow and lay bricks rather than go to literary and classical schools," then, he observed, "it will be the right policy to shut off all our literary and classical schools for negroes in the South."[115]

Underlying reformers' bold rhetoric lay a harsher reality. However vociferously white missionaries and even black leaders themselves defended the wisdom of providing classical learning for a talented black elite, circumstances forced them to admit their efforts were falling woefully short. Lacking a supportive infrastructure of public elementary and secondary schools for blacks throughout the South, African American collegiate enrollments remained minuscule. In the last quarter of the nineteenth century, candor would have compelled even the most vigorous supporters of black higher education to acknowledge how few black institutions, chronically underfunded and impoverished, were true "colleges" in anything but name and aspiration. Most—the overwhelming majority in fact—offered little above secondary-level training, and some were at best engaged in teaching the rudiments of literacy at the elementary level. Only Howard University and Fisk, it was later noted, offered anything remotely approaching the collegiate-level liberal-arts training most black institutions promised but could not deliver. Tuskegee trustee William H. Baldwin, Jr., in 1899 gave voice to the disappointment surrounding missionary colleges. "We began at the wrong end," he alleged. "Instead of educating the negro in the lines which were open to him, he was educated out of his natural environment and the opportunities which lay immediately about him."[116]

Meanwhile, throughout the 1880s, the tendency among industrial philanthropists was to emphasize practical job training over classical learning for blacks. Attracted to an industrial and agricultural orientation or focus, trustees for the Peabody and Slater Funds, for example, were more inclined to lend support to the likes of Hampton Institute and Tuskegee, where utilitarian training was favored, than to liberal-arts colleges. Former Civil War general Samuel C. Armstrong, who headed the Hampton Institute, was persuaded that black youths should "go out and teach and lead their people, first by example, by getting land and homes; to give them not a dollar they could earn for themselves; to teach respect for labor; to replace stupid drudgery with skilled hands; and to these ends to build up an industrial system, for the sake not only of self support and intelligent labor, but also for the sake of character."[117] Black educator Booker T. Washington, who founded Tuskegee in 1881, essentially agreed with Armstrong. Keenly aware of white efforts to keep blacks politically inarticulate and as disenfranchised as they had been in the antebellum period but equally cognizant of black aspirations to achieve full and complete social equality, Washington offered trade training as a compromise.[118]

In a memorable speech delivered at the Atlanta Cotton States and International Exposition in 1895, Washington professed to sanction racial subordination, terming questions of social equality "extremist folly." If blacks were ever to overcome problems of poverty and ignorance, he concluded, they must begin by supporting utilitarian education for business trades. His advice to black youths everywhere was to educate themselves through "the shop, the field, the skilled hand, habits of thrift, and economy, [and] by way of the industrial school and college."[119] Washington's "Atlanta Compromise" mollified critics' fears over black higher education of a more traditional type. But it positively enraged others who opposed Washington's stand as a craven retreat from the principle of education for blacks as equals and as free men in a democracy. Insisting that blacks were entitled to the same rights and privileges as white Americans, New England black educator W. E. B. DuBois of Atlanta University, for one, denounced Washington's stand as an appeasement to racial prejudice and established doctrines of social inequality.[120]

Between 1870 and 1890 nine federal land-grant colleges were established in the South; that total was to increase to sixteen by 1915. Mississippi was the first southern state to allocate federal land-grant monies to a black institution. Virginia became the second the year following. Passage of the second Morrill Act in 1890 gave renewed impetus to the founding of black land-grant colleges.[121] In its original form the legislation had been designed to prevent the expenditure of land-grant funds in any state where "a distinction of race or color" was made. In its final form, the second Morrill Act served as a compromise to a bill that would have required that blacks be admitted to colleges supported under the original 1862 appropriation. The second Act, in its practical effect, offered an alternative to the much-dreaded prospect of racial integration in higher education. It now stipulated only that in those states where separate colleges were maintained, programs were to be of "like character" and funds distributed on a "just and equitable" basis. Thus, monies were now made available on condition that separate land-grant colleges for blacks be established and that funds be divided proportionately among these new institutions and those already established, which, with the exception of Alcorn Agricultural and Mechanical in Mississippi, were restricted to whites.

Several states moved quickly to designate existing black schools as recipients of land-grant funds. They included Alabama, Arkansas, Florida, Kentucky, Louisiana, Maryland, Missouri, Tennessee, and Texas.[122] New black schools were also created: Georgia Industrial College, the Agricultural and Technical College of North Carolina, and West Virginia State College among them. By 1900 state-supported black colleges had been founded in all of the southern and border states. Unfortunately, a federal governmental survey at the turn of the century revealed that most black colleges funded with land-grant monies were devoted primarily to general academic purposes and to teacher preparation. Most did not take agricultural and mechanic arts as the "leading object" required under the Morrill Act of 1862. It was further reported that black colleges not infrequently were offering instruction on a "grade as low as the 4th or 5th of the public schools."

In 1896 the U.S. Supreme Court handed down its historic decision in *Plessy v. Ferguson* affirming the constitutionality of the principle of "separate but equal."[123] For blacks, separation, not equality, was the reality so far as institutions of higher learning were concerned. With race relations having hardened significantly throughout the disenfranchisement campaigns of the 1890s in the South, no prospects for black entry into southern white colleges existed. By the same token, black institutions could expect to receive no more than the legally minimal level of support required under law for black colleges. Reflecting on the situation as he saw it shortly after the turn of the century, W. E. B. DuBois termed it "a day of cowardice and vacillation; of double-faced dallying with Truth and Right." The need to train leaders for a struggling people, he felt, was as great as ever, but that need was still unmet. His summation, writing in *The Negro Problem* (1903), assumed the shape of a challenge: "Men of America, the problem is plain before you. Here is a race transplanted through the criminal foolishness of your fathers. Whether you like it or not the millions are here, and here they will remain. If you do not lift them up, they will pull you down."[124] In the opening decade of the twentieth century, however, and for many decades thereafter, there were few signs that America's leadership was prepared to heed the message or to respond to DuBois's challenge.

ELECTIVE CURRICULA

Charles Eliot's famous inaugural address as president of Harvard in October of 1869 brought to the forefront a long-standing controversy within academic circles. In a sense, his remarks served as the opening salvo of a renewed struggle over the collegiate curriculum.[125] "This university recognizes no real antagonism between literature and science, and consents to no such narrow alternatives as mathematics or classics, science or metaphysics," he declared. "We would have them all, and at their best." Even as the trustee who had introduced Eliot to the podium sat glowering in the audience, the new president pressed his argument. "In education," Eliot asserted, "the individual traits of different minds have not been sufficiently attended to . . . [and] the young man of nineteen or twenty ought to know what he likes best and is most fit for. . . . When the revelation of his own peculiar taste and capacity comes to a young man, let him reverently give it welcome, thank God, and take courage. Thereafter, he knows his way to happy, enthusiastic work, and, God willing, to usefulness and success."[126]

With these words Eliot threw down a gauntlet before defenders of the old order.[127] Against traditionalists committed to the notion of a fixed, uniform course of studies required of everyone, Eliot announced that from now on under his regime, students would have more freedom to select from among different classes and courses of study. "The elective system," he alleged, "fosters scholarship, because it gives free play to natural preferences and inborn aptitudes, takes possible enthusiasm for a chosen work, [and] relieves the professor . . . of the presence of a body of students who are compelled to an unwelcome task." As if to dispel any remaining doubts about his intentions, President Eliot concluded, "The college therefore proposes to persevere in its efforts to establish, improve, and extend the elective system."[128]

Conservatives were appalled, branding the principle of curricular choice a "fraud" and a "monstrosity."[129] James McCosh of Princeton declared in 1885, "I cannot allow that it is an advance in scholarship. It is a bid for popularity." If broadly implemented, he feared, any such plan that encouraged or even permitted students a significant element of choice would lead them, say, to prefer duck-hunting to attending class, to idling about instead of concentrating on serious scholarly endeavors.[130] President Carey Thomas at Bryn Mawr sarcastically wondered aloud about the extremes to which student choice might lead. "In many colleges everything that is desirable for a human being to learn," she complained, "counts toward the bachelor's degree . . . [including] ladder work in the gymnasium (why not going upstairs?) . . . [or] swimming in the tank (why not one's morning bath?)."[131] In New Haven, Yale's president, Noah Porter, took a position diametrically opposed to Eliot's. Speaking to the question of whether students should be allowed curricular choices, he observed, "Their tastes are either unformed or capricious and prejudiced; if they are decided and strong, they often require correction. The study which is the farthest removed from that which strikes his fancy may be the study which is most needed for the student."[132]

Andrew F. West of Princeton took issue with the claim that acknowledging individual differences among students necessarily mandated multiple instructional patterns and courses. As he explained in 1886, "Minds resemble and differ from each other just as faces and complexions do. They are all different, but all human. It is nothing but fallacious, then, to argue that . . . colleges may not prescribe that students shall be trained in the great studies which demonstrably cultivate their essential characteristics before the colleges consent to call such minds liberally educated."[133]

And so the battle between proponents and opponents of the elective system in higher education was joined. Throughout the remainder of the century, the controversy would rage on, arousing strong passions on both sides.[134] Fundamentally, what was at stake was not simply a matter of curricular electives. More broadly, the clash was between two irreducibly different conceptions of what a college or university should aspire to become. "Modernists" like Eliot at Harvard and Andrew White at Cornell felt it was both necessary and desirable to encompass a full range of scientific and technical disciplines within a university's offerings, though not necessarily at the expense of the older, more established classical disciplines and humanistic belles-lettres. But to achieve this goal, they realized, it would no longer be possible to require everyone to complete exactly the same curricular regimen. Human knowledge had expanded to the point where no one was capable of comprehending the whole. Disciplinary specialization, to some extent, was therefore both inevitable and better adapted to the modern world. On the other side, "reactionaries"—which is to say, only, those who adhered to the traditional view enunciated in the famous Yale Report of 1828 and who accordingly opposed many late-nineteenth-century innovations—clung firmly to the notion of a single prescribed course of studies for all.

Chief spokesman for the traditional approach was Noah Porter. In his presidential inaugural address of 1871, delivered only two years after Eliot's, he opened with his own broadside. "Especially in matters of education should [higher learning] neither pander to popular prejudices nor take advantage of popular humors," he declared forthrightly. "If there is any sanctuary where well-grounded convictions should find refuge, and where these should be honored, it is in a place devoted to the higher education." Among his "well-grounded convictions," Porter counted the idea that the purpose of formal education was to discipline the mind's mental and moral faculties. Such a purpose could only be achieved, he felt, by prescribing a fixed, four-year course of collegiate study. As he phrased it in *The American Colleges and the American Public* (1878), "The college course is preëminently designed to give power to acquire and to think, rather than to impart special knowledge." Anything else, he believed, was tantamount to intellectual anarchy.[135]

Undergirding Porter's claim, of course, was the venerable theory of faculty psychology and "mental discipline"—that is, the belief that inhering within the vital force called the soul or the mind are specific potentialities or "faculties," such as will, emotion, and intellect. Certain disciplines or subjects, by their very nature, it was held, were uniquely adapted to the exercise and strengthening of mental faculties. Thus, the study of logic and mathematics enhance one's capacity for rigorous analysis; philosophy is intrinsically suited to the development of the mind's powers of rational reflection and critical judgment; rhetoric and dialectic as subjects of study most effectively encourage eloquence and powers of self-expression or persuasion; and so on. Centuries of experience, adherents of the argument claimed, had demonstrated that certain studies *are* superior to others in fostering mental discipline and development. Just as a muscle is strengthened through proper usage, and the body is nourished through proper diet, so likewise an elastic mind demands appropriate exercise.[136] As C. B. Hulbert, president of Middlebury College in Vermont, argued in *The Distinctive Idea in Education* (1890), "If you wish to develop physical power, put your physical organs to drill; if you seek to bring your mental powers up to a high degree of efficiency, put them to work, and upon studies that will tax them to the uttermost."[137]

Modern subjects, classicists were convinced, afforded no adequate substitute for the systematic study of Latin and Greek, ancient history and literature, metaphysics, philology, rhetoric, and other elements of the traditional collegiate curriculum. Utterly persuaded that classical studies were still essential in furnishing both the mind's "discipline" and "furniture," officials at Trinity College issued a reminder to students at the opening of the 1885–86 academic session that anyone deficient in the classics should not expect to receive the bachelor of arts degree. William T. Gannaway, a professor of Latin and French at Trinity, further averred that inasmuch as "it is believed that mental training and discipline can best be secured by a patient and thorough study of the Ancient Classics, the use of translations is strictly forbidden." To critics who objected that classical languages and literature bore little connection with the exigencies of modern life, Noah Porter inverted the argument for relevance. "The more urgent is this noisy tumult of life without," he declared, "and the stronger its pressure against the doors of the college, the greater need is there that certain studies which have little relation to life should be attended to." Hulbert's response to the claim that formal learning should be more practical, and less "academic" came with the wry comment, "Even now, in this day of practicality, a little wider sprinkling of theorists, book worms, pedants, even, would do our land no harm."[138]

Academic reactionaries stood for piety and morality as the chief ends to which colleges should devote themselves. An Iowa educator by the name of G. F. Magoun in 1891 spoke for many when he avowed that religiosity should pervade "the tenor, implications, and connections of . . . teaching" in every college classroom, and dominate the "very atmosphere" of the institution as a whole.[139] W. W. Strong, the president of Carleton College in 1887 weighed in with a comparable sentiment: "The grand aim of every great teacher, from Socrates to Hopkins, has been the building of character."[140] Coupled with the desire to build character and instill morality was the fervent resolve of traditionalists to preserve the paternalistic spirit so long infused in American higher education.

Unnerved by the "benign neglect" of students in their extracurricular activities outside the classroom, and the seemingly desultory fashion in which university officials superintended student life, conservatives argued vigorously on behalf of the pattern of minute student surveillance and regulation of conduct typical of the past. As the faculty at Princeton explained in a resolution adopted in 1885, "To hold the student to minute fidelity in little things is an enforcement of one of the most significant maxims of the Gospel."

(Possibly the ultimate in attempted student supervision was contained in a proviso of the same Princeton faculty resolution: "That should any students continue to have their washing done in town as heretofore, it must be done under the supervision of the College Office.")[141]

On the matter of curricular choice, no matter how earnest and sincere were the arguments put forth by academic conservatives, they were finding it increasingly difficult to persuade others to their cause. C. B. Dabney, president of the University of Tennessee, writing in *The Old College and the New* (1896), ventured what was fast becoming the majority opinion: "The harmonious and equitable evolution of man does not mean that every man must be educated just like his fellow," he claimed. "The harmony is within each individual. That community is most highly educated in which each individual has attained the maximum of his possibilities in the direction of his peculiar talents and opportunities. This produces not a Procrustean sameness, but an infinite diversity in purpose and potentiality."[142] Thomas Walsh, president of Notre Dame, offered a more pragmatic perspective in conceding that students and their parents, after all, possessed a certain right to determine what course of studies would be followed.[143] In 1893 the president of Illinois College remarked that so far as he was concerned, "the object of elective studies is not so much to permit a student to choose those branches which bear upon his future work as to enable him to select such as will interest him and thus lead his mind to act with greatest vigor."[144] Many were impressed by the argument that electives were necessary in an era when more and more students were appearing on campuses neither highly motivated to study nor certain of their eventual career plans.

Nicely summing up the crux of the debate was an observation offered by the president of DePauw in 1890. "The Old Education," he explained, "ascribed the virtue to the subject, the New Education ascribes it to the process. If the virtue be chiefly in the process rather than in the subject, then, within proper limits, and under proper advice, the choice of that subject should depend largely on the tastes and probable future vocation of the student."[145] Moreover, as though to seal the argument, there were already indications the fledgling discipline of experimental psychology would yield scant support for a belief in discrete mental faculties or, for that matter, the entire doctrine of mental discipline and transfer of training.

Rebuffed in their attempts to retain a fixed curriculum, their insistence upon strict discipline challenged on all sides, conservative proponents of mental discipline were thrown into retreat. In the South, despite some enrollment losses, the enforced study of classics, together with traditions stressing the importance of piety, character, and morality, hung on the longest.

Elsewhere traditional orthodoxy continued to prevail only in a diminishing number of private sectarian schools and liberal-arts colleges. The larger state universities of the Midwest and West were the most enthusiastic in embracing the principle of electives, followed by large universities with private endowments. Least receptive were the colleges of New England. In those collegiate centers where the elective principle won acceptance, expanded choice led step by step over time to the practice of instituting academic "majors" and "minor" study concentrations, the development of academic departments devoted exclusively to one or another specific discipline, and a marked specialization of scholarship within academe.[146] By the 1890s Wisconsin and Michigan ranked among the few major institutions that still maintained required freshman and sophomore courses. By 1896 Cornell was allowing an almost totally unrestricted system of electives. The next year even Yale, then Wisconsin, permitted unlimited electives after a student's first year.

Meanwhile, as required courses were dropped and elective courses of study became even more directly tied to occupational interests, the idea of acquaintance with a fixed body of knowledge, classical or otherwise, as the mark of an educated person began to disappear. Still left unanswered was the old question as to whether all subjects of study should be weighted equal in value—bookkeeping no less than physics; civil engineering together with Greek poetry; theology and accountancy; domestic economics and metaphysics. Increasingly, the tacit presumption was that no one discipline or field of study could be said to be more or less important than any other within academe. Each was entitled to its place. And if all careers were equal, it was incumbent upon the university to offer preparatory training for future teachers, journalists, musicians, pharmacists, and machinists, admitting each on an equal basis with students of law, medicine, or theology. David Starr Jordan, writing in *The Voice of the Scholar* (1889) made the argument explicit. "It is not for the university to decide on the relative merits of knowledge," he asserted. "Each man makes his own market, controlled by his own standards. It is for the university to see [only] that all standards are honest, that all work is genuine."[147] The age of radical curricular egalitarianism was at hand.

GRADUATE PROFESSIONAL STUDIES: THE ALLURE OF THE GERMANIC IDEAL

Throughout the last third of the nineteenth century, considerable confusion still surrounded the question of what distinguished an authentic "university" from a "college." Notwithstanding, a broad consensus of opinion was beginning to form. A university attracted larger student enrollments. It offered a broader array of subjects and more specialized courses of study than the typical collegiate institution. Its orientation was more professional, more utilitarian, more closely tied to matters of occupational preparation than that of a liberal-arts college.[148] Further, a true university offered post-baccalaureate or graduate instruction. And most importantly, whereas teaching had always been the primary, if not exclusive role of a college, in a university—or so many argued—the focus now was to be upon disinterested scholarship and research.[149]

Heretofore systematic post-baccalaureate study had rarely been offered— a state of affairs prompting more than a few foreign observers throughout the 1800s to conclude that American colleges more nearly resembled preparatory *gymnasia* than true centers of higher learning in their own right. At Harvard, for instance, the *master artium* had long been conferred "in course" to a student in residence three years after receiving the bachelor's degree. Because no formal program of study was required, it was said of the master's degree that anyone could qualify for it upon payment of a five-dollar graduation fee, provided only that the student could prove he had managed to stay out of jail in the interim. As for the doctorate, it was not until 1860 that Yale became the first to offer an earned Ph.D. degree upon a student's successful completion of a prescribed course of study in its Department of Philosophy and the Arts. Previously, and for some time thereafter, the doctoral degree tended to be a purely honorary designation, awarded in those special cases where it seemed expedient or advantageous for an institution to do so. By 1876, however, some two dozen or so other institutions had begun conferring doctorates, forty-four in all; and by 1918 there were over five hundred being awarded annually.[150] Increasingly, in stark contrast with the past, possession of a bona fide earned doctorate was a prerequisite for university employment as a faculty member.

What had changed was the rise to administrative power of men such as G. Stanley Hall, William Watts Folwell, James B. Angell, Andrew White, Daniel Gilman, and Charles W. Eliot, among many others, all of whom had first-hand experience with German universities. Most who returned after studying or visiting Heidelberg, Berlin, Tübingen, or Leipzig had come back with glowing reports of great academic institutions in Germany where specialized graduate seminars and lectures were offered in abundance to advanced students, and in an astonishing variety of specialized disciplines. American observers were quick to extoll the virtues of universities where such great academic celebrities as Leopold von Ranke, Hermann von Helmholtz, and Wilhelm Wundt were engaged in "pure" research wholly unconstrained by narrow utilitarian considerations.[151] With considerable understatement, G. Stanley Hall, writing in 1879, observed, "The influence of German modes of thought in America is very great and is probably increasing."[152]

Especially impressive to American observers was the Germanic emphasis upon the disinterested pursuit of truth through original scholarly investigation. German academic traditions, it was noted, were based on two fundamental ideas. The first, *Lernfreiheit,* or "freedom to learn," meant university students were allowed to choose whatever courses they preferred, with no formal attendance requirements or tests whatsoever, preliminary to their applying for a final degree examination. The second, *Lehrfreiheit,* or "freedom to teach," signified the scholar's right to pursue his investigations wherever they might lead, to draw from his research whatever conclusions were warranted, and to disseminate the results through teaching or publication without hindrance or interference from external authorities.[153]

Writing in the 1870s, President Frederick A. P. Barnard of Columbia University challenged American institutions of higher learning to provide "the attractions which are so abundantly offered in foreign lands." What was needed, he declared, was the development of true universities in America, places with adequate facilities for professional training and advanced graduate training in all of the arts and sciences.[154] Barnard's challenge was met in several ways. In some instances, the response was to establish separate, independent graduate institutions, as was the case with Johns Hopkins University, Clark University, and the University of Chicago. Elsewhere, a German-style university structure—designed to emphasize scholarly research and advanced preparation for the learned professions—was superimposed upon an existing English-type undergraduate college—which stressed more disinterested liberal learning—as occurred at Harvard, Princeton and Yale.

The first approach was best illustrated by the founding of Johns Hopkins University in Baltimore, Maryland, under the leadership of Daniel Gilman. In his inaugural address of 1876, Gilman announced that scholarly research would be the "guide and inspirer of fellows and pupils" in the university, just as it was reportedly in German schools of higher learning. Johns Hopkins henceforth would make "the acquisition, conservation, refinement and distribution of knowledge" its main goal. The president's hope, as he expressed it, was that the university as an institution dedicated to both pure and applied research would fulfill an important obligation to society, and that the results would make "for less misery among the poor, less ignorance in schools, less bigotry in the temple, less suffering in the hospital, less fraud in business, less folly in politics."[155] Writing in *The Benefits Which Society Derives from Universities* (1885), Gilman renewed his commitment to safeguard traditions of academic freedom. "It is the universities which edit, interpret, translate and reiterate the acquisitions of former generations, both of literature and science," he claimed. "Their revelation of error is sometimes welcomed but it is generally opposed; nevertheless the process goes on, indifferent to plaudits or reproaches." He then went on to point out that such "wonderful inventions" as the telegraph, the telephone, photography, the steam locomotive, and electric lighting had been "the direct fruits of universities studies," that they were "the creation not of industrial fabrics, not of mercantile corporations, not even of private enterprise, but of universities and . . . the motive which inspired their founders and directors was not the acquisition of wealth, but the ascertainment of fundamental law."[156]

Gilman's aim from the outset was to attract the best faculty and students possible. Student fellowships were offered to "men of mark, who show that they are likely to advance the sciences they profess." Chairs in mathematics, modern languages, ethics, mathematics, history, and the sciences were incorporated into a single undergraduate department, to which were subsequently added specialized graduate and professional courses. By the time Gilman resigned from the presidency in 1901, Johns Hopkins had achieved enormous influence and prestige.[157] Included among the ranks of its faculty were some of the country's most distinguished scholars; there were thirteen different academic departments organized for advanced work; and the school's medical school was fast attaining world-class status. Interestingly, perhaps imitating European precedent, Gilman made little effort to encourage any major investment in capital expenditures such as buildings. So unassuming was the university's outward appearance in its early days that passersby were apt not to notice it at all. Locals, it was said, sometimes mistook Johns Hopkins for a nearby piano factory.[158]

Many institutions aspiring to become major research centers looked to Johns Hopkins as a model, including Harvard, Columbia, Chicago, Clark, Catholic University, Michigan, Nebraska, Kansas, and Vanderbilt. Harvard's Charles Eliot frankly acknowledged the indebtedness in one of his later public addresses. "I want to testify," he said, "that the Graduate School of Harvard University, started feebly in 1870 and 1871, did not thrive, until the example of Johns Hopkins forced our faculty to put their strength into the development of our instruction for graduates." And what was true of Harvard, he added, "was true of every other university in the land which aspired to create an advanced school of arts and sciences."[159]

When William Rainey Harper opened the University of Chicago in 1892, he made it abundantly clear that the new institution's focus would be upon scholarship and research. "It is proposed in this institution," he announced, "to make the work of investigation primary, the work of giving instruction secondary."[160] G. Stanley Hall, as the first president of Clark University in Worcester, Massachusetts, which opened in 1889, made the case even stronger with his assertion that the university "should be financially and morally able to disregard practical application as well as numbers of students . . . and the increase of knowledge and its diffusion among the few should be its ideal."[161] Faculty, Hall claimed, should be "absorbed in and living only for pure science and high scholarship." Bishop John J. Keane of Catholic University had studied Gilman's example at close hand; he too was determined that advanced graduate instruction and scholarship would be paramount.[162] At Vanderbilt in 1875, Andrew Lipscomb announced his allegiance to the university ideal, particularly its commitment to freedom of scholarly inquiry and curricular comprehensiveness. "The University," he stressed, "is bound to recognize every department of true thought, every branch of human knowledge, every mode of thorough culture. . . . What is best in the University is the catholicity of its views. . . . It must have an open-minded hospitality to all truth and must draw men together in the unity of a scholarly temper."[163]

Writing in 1904, a geologist at the University of Michigan by the name of Israel C. Russell reiterated much the same theme, but with the emphasis upon active inquiry. Research, he argued, was "the highest function of the university, not only because it encourages her best students to strive to attain the higher walks of intellectual life, but because in the process of discovering the man or woman of exceptional ability, all her sons and daughters are encouraged to advance to the highest plane their mental endowments permit them to reach."[164]

The reorganization of an older liberal-arts college into a university proceeded more unevenly. In 1877 President James McCosh of Princeton took the first steps to create a graduate department at his institution.[165] By 1900, thanks to powerful faculty pressure, a full-fledged graduate school had been created. At Yale, until the retirement of Noah Porter in 1886, little headway was registered in establishing specialized graduate courses of study. Shortly thereafter, however, graduate and professional instruction began to flourish and expand. In other parts of the country, the attempt to import Germanic ideals of research, scholarship, and specialized graduate study fared less well. At the University of Arkansas in 1884, for example, the institution's president complained that two faculty members newly arrived from the University of Virginia had brought with them two extremely harmful tendencies: lack of concern for supervising students outside the classroom and excessive devotion to high standards of scholarship.[166]

THE WISCONSIN IDEA

The metamorphosis of the American college into the university as a predominant model in American higher education was marked by several highly visible changes: the introduction of electives and a greater element of undergraduate curricular choice; marked reluctance on the part of a growing number of schools to serve *in loco parentis,* that is, as parental surrogates for students; the addition of undergraduate and graduate preparatory training for careers formerly excluded from academe; the emergence of large graduate institutions whose professed loyalties were to pure research and *Wissenschaft,* or investigation and writing in the broadest sense (as distinct from the diffusion of knowledge through teaching); allegiance to academic freedom; and increasingly specialized scholarship, together with the institutional reorganization of faculties within separate, discipline-based academic departments. On the eve of the progressive era there appeared another theme: that of social service. It was an idea to which academic leaders were to return time and time again. One of its earliest manifestations had been the rural land-grant commitment to extension work, to the offering of short courses for agriculturalists and the development of experimental farms. By the late 1880s, universities were being urged—and were encouraging themselves—to address themselves to a much broader array of societal issues and problems.[167]

The university service ideal coincided nicely with the first stirrings of progressivist reform. In the waning years of the nineteenth century, many Americans had grown alarmed over the vast concentrations of power, wealth, and privilege that unregulated laissez-faire capitalism had seemingly encouraged. Special interests, reformers believed, now posed a major threat to democratic ideals, especially to the principle of equality of opportunity. Monopolies and trusts were chiefly responsible for rampant political corruption, for the political machine, for the spread of urban slums and the shameless exploitation of immigrant labor. The cure for the nation's ills, progressives announced, was still more democracy: the preferential party primary, universal suffrage, the secret ballot, the initiative, and the referendum. Tighter legislative control over working conditions and better regulation of industries were called for. Improved schools, honesty in government, more social responsibility in the commercial sphere, a reversal of declining standards of public and private morality were all important elements comprising the progressive agenda. In the battle for renewal and reform, academic institutions were called upon to play their part.

Nowhere else perhaps did the spirit of social service find more complete expression toward the close of the 1800s than at the University of Wisconsin. The so-called "Wisconsin Idea," which was widely imitated by other universities, was to engage the institution's resources and energies directly in the search for solutions to public problems.[168] Wisconsin's fifth president, John Bascom, in his baccalaureate address of 1877 lamented what he characterized as the "rambling, halting voluntaryism" upon which society appeared to depend for social and moral reform. Improvements would come, he predicted, only when all of society's institutions worked in concert, mounting together a systematic attack upon the nation's ills. The University of Wisconsin, he pledged, would contribute to the work of societal advancement by encouraging a more organic connection between its activities and community needs. Invigorated extension programs, the start-up of popular agricultural short courses, the development of expanded research projects devoted to solving specific problems plaguing the state's dairy industry, and a broadening of training programs in the physical and social sciences were only some of the initiatives launched. With the appointment of Richard T. Ely in 1892 as director of the newly established School of Economics, Political Science, and History, Wisconsin took the lead in preparing its students for posts in the state's civil administrative apparatus and in providing faculty advisory service to governmental leaders.[169]

Other states took up the call.[170] At Michigan, President Angell remarked how the old-time college had been little more than a "home of useless and harmless recluses" far removed and well isolated from the community at large.[171] Now, he said, the challenge of the modern age was to bring higher learning into the mainstream of social life, to extend the benefits of applied scholarship and research to the real needs of the people, to enshrine the ideal of public service as the organizing center of academic life. President Edmund J. James of Illinois in 1905 envisioned the state's university as "a great civil service academy, preparing the young men and women of the state for the civil service of the state, the county, the municipality, and the township."[172] Inspired by the progressive vision of social renewal, students at Harvard, Northwestern, Michigan, Chicago, and Butler in Indianapolis fanned out into the cities, descending upon urban tenement slums to assist with programs of hygiene, dietetics, and improved child care. Similar reformist measures in other cities across the country were signs that the notion of universities fulfilling their destiny as instruments of social service was gaining widespread acceptance and approval.

GRIDIRON LOYALTIES

Late-nineteenth-century reminiscences of collegiate life unquestionably idealized the college of an earlier day. Featured prominently in popular remembrances of college life was the image of yesteryear's professor. He might be recalled as a colorful eccentric, or perhaps as a stern and remote classroom tyrant. For some, he was a kindly, benevolent father-figure. However one's years spent at college were remembered, they tended to invoke nostalgic memories of friendships past, of dealings with one's former professors, and faded recollections of the academic trials and tribulations the alumnus had once experienced. The incorporation of football as yet another defining feature of the university transformed the nature of the loyalty and sense of institutional affiliation retained by alumni long after graduation. In effect, the growth of intercollegiate athletics generally (and of football in particular) at once increased public interest in, and support for, institutions of higher learning. But the basis of that sense of kinship and allegiance had less and less to do with academics, and more to do with an institution's ability to field a winning team.[173]

Historically, athletic activities had neither received much attention from college officials nor had any great significance been assigned to them. Ball games of one sort or another had always exerted an appeal among college students, going back at least as far as the 900s in medieval England, when it was customary for young men seeking sport to kick a skull or cow's bladder around an open pasture.[174] But apart from injunctions to their charges not to overexert themselves or criticism that sports were unbecoming for gentlemen, academic authorities tended to ignore students' improvised athletic contests. So far as can be determined, intercollegiate competitions were not held in the United States until the 1850s, when boat racing briefly gained a measure of popularity.[175] During the Civil War, baseball was in vogue, followed by an upsurge of interest in track and field events.[176] In 1869 the first organized football game was held between students from Rutgers and Princeton. It was reportedly an extremely informal and impromptu affair played by rules loosely adapted from soccer. Nevertheless, it presaged a demand for many more games like it in the years ahead. Few innovations so captured colleges and universities. Within an astonishingly short period, college students had popularized a running version of football which in its essentials closely resembled that of English rugby.[177] Students at first paid their own way to visit a rival college for a match. The equipment required was exceedingly simple. All games were organized by the undergraduates themselves. When President Andrew White of Cornell was approached by collegians in 1873 with a request that the school help defray their travel expenses for a game, he firmly declined, explaining he was unprepared to underwrite the cost of having students "agitate a bag of wind."[178]

Eight years later, in 1881, a team from Michigan ventured east to play Harvard, Princeton, and Yale within the span of a single week.[179] Football matches soon became a regular weekend diversion at scores of colleges and universities throughout the country. The game continued to prosper as the public began to take note and crowds of alumni from competing schools took to returning to their respective alma maters to cheer the home team. New York City in 1883 was caught up in the throes of excitement surrounding what by now had evolved into an annual Thanksgiving game between Yale and Princeton. Hotels were thronged with visitors. On Fifth Avenue, the stately mansions of the Whitneys and Vanderbilts were gaily decorated with gigantic blue and white banners. The Sloans, the Alexanders, and the Scribners, on their side, proudly put up Princeton's colors. Local pastors cut short their sermons in order to get to the game on time, much to the relief of their sports-minded congregations. Newspaper reporters descended in droves to report the outcome for an avid public. Unquestionably, the age of big-time football had arrived.[180]

The lesson was not lost upon university administrators. Aware that football offered valuable publicity and that alumni and the public alike often seemed to care more about athletic victories than academics, officials responded with alacrity in lending their support.[181] President Eliot of Harvard in 1892 already was bemoaning as "repulsive" what he termed "foolish and pernicious expenditures on sports"—but to no avail.[182] President Harry Garfield of Williams warned in 1908, "Here, as generally in American colleges, there is grave danger of departure from the essential idea of a college as distinguished from an institute of physical culture."[183] Few were listening. If parsimonious state legislatures were willing to open the public treasury to support athletic contests, academic leaders concluded, why dissuade them? Besides, as many argued (with great fervor and scant evidence), playing football built character; it prepared young men for success in the rough-and-tumble world of business; it instilled determination, cunning, and team spirit. Tomorrow's leaders in government, business and the professions were being honed on today's gridirons.[184] Football was good for democracy; as President Hadley of Yale reported, the game had seized "hold of the emotions of the student body in such a way as to make class distinctions relatively unimportant" and had made "the students get together in the old-fashioned democratic way."[185]

Here was something connected with higher education that people cared about passionately: not academics, but athletics. Football games inspired the most enthusiasm from potential donors; they kept alumni in touch with their schools; they brought public support and visibility. All the while, refinements were being introduced, the most important of which was the provision made for the forward pass. Individually numbered shirts personalized the game and further added to its excitement by allowing spectators to better keep track of individual players. A special mystique began to surround the campus football hero. In over four hundred paperback novels and no less than 986 consecutive installments in the *Tip-Top Weekly* between 1896 and 1915, for example, football enthusiasts thrilled to the exploits (on and off the field) of the fictional "Frank Merriwell of Yale." From its lowly beginnings as simple diversion, the football contest thus came to be elevated to the lofty status of a symbol for success, achievement, and gentlemanly masculinity. Ironically, institutions of higher learning had become genuinely "popular," but not because of the academic endeavors that purportedly represented their very raison d'être. On the contrary, and to an extent some were unwilling to acknowledge, popular support for higher education drew its strength from the entertainment value of activities formerly consigned to academe's outermost periphery.

MISGIVINGS AND DEMURRALS

Developing universities of the late 1800s revealed a passion for growth, an appetite for almost unlimited expansion. It was a phenomenon that did not go unnoticed by those already deeply troubled over the course and direction of American higher education. The professorate itself was changing. Growing specialization of scholarship meant the virtual disappearance of the master-of-all-disciplines, the traditional polymath who could be relied upon to teach many different subjects and teach them well. In his place surfaced the expert schooled in a single discipline, or more characteristically, a minuscule subspecialty thereof. His command of a subject was apt to be more thorough and more systematic perhaps, but depth of scholarship, so far as critics were concerned, had been purchased at the price of a certain parochialism, a decided narrowing of intellectual outlook or perspective.[186] For the catholicity of interest that supposedly had been characteristic of the old-time college, the sense of acquaintance with a common body of knowledge and ideals shared by all, had been substituted a discordant array of specialists, each bent on refining and extending his own disciplinary interests.[187] Dean Andrew West of Princeton said it best in 1906 when he warned, "Many of our scholars seem to be subjects of some petty principality rather than free men in the commonwealth of knowledge."[188]

During the same period, many universities began experimenting with elaborate hierarchical systems of academic rank, starting at the bottom with instructors, and ascending to assistant professors, then associate professors, and, finally, full professors.[189] At the University of Chicago under President Harper distinctions among faculty members were drawn out even further. Readers, lecturers, docents, assistants, associates, instructors, and assistant professors all were classifications denoting those with temporary or short-term appointments.[190] Above them were associate professors, followed by professors, then head professors, who were to enjoy indefinite tenure in permanent appointments. To this "vertical" arrangement of rankings was added the "horizontal" dimension of departmentalization. As an administrative expedient for organizing an otherwise unwieldy number of academic specialists within a single governance framework, the institution of an academic department was both necessary and probably inevitable. But as experience made abundantly obvious, the proliferation of quasi-independent bureaucratic structures tended to divide an already-fragmented academic community. Their chief effect, it seemed to many observers, was to release petty jealousies, to foster competition for favor and resources, to increase the importance of attention to public relations, and to set in motion an unseemly scrambling for students among rival satrapies. "Turf" battles and "empire-building" became the norm, not the exception.

Specialized scholarship had still other consequences, among them a proliferation of learned societies, each with its own professional and academic journal. Additionally, to those drawn into academe for the opportunities it afforded to conduct research, teaching was now coming to be regarded more and more as something of an irritating distraction. The new specialists in their own way tended to be as reclusive and inaccessible as the pedants of an earlier day. More than a few, at any rate, locked off in their laboratories and libraries, made no secret of the fact that if they had to teach at all, they preferred tutoring advanced graduate students in their respective specialties. Any obligation to teach young, immature undergraduates was to be fervently avoided if at all possible.

Cornell President Jacob Schurman was among the first to comment on what was happening. As he remarked with some understatement in 1906, "It must, I think, be admitted that most university teachers . . . have chosen their profession not so much from the love of teaching as from the desire to continue the study of their specialty. While the number of those who have a positive distaste for teaching is small, there are many whose interest in teaching is secondary to their interest in investigation."[191] In institutions where greatest importance was assigned to research, the situation could only worsen in years to come. Neglect of teaching and the "publish or perish" syndrome that would plague higher education throughout the next century were already manifest in many universities. A bitter complaint from one college graduate in the 1890s was typical in describing the new breed of professors as "self deceiving dreamers who solace themselves with the idea that they are doing for the world a service by their books, while their class work goes unheeded."

For better or worse, older traditions were dying out in larger universities (if not always in smaller colleges). Preoccupied with their research and writing, professors balked at taking class attendance, at sharing responsibility for monitoring student conduct outside the classroom, or otherwise helping to sustain the old paternalistic system of student supervision. In a very real sense, the attitude of turn-of-the-century professors toward students was more consistent with that of their German colleagues and, more generally, with long-standing European traditions of indifference to students' discipline or welfare outside the prescribed limits of the academic sphere. By the same token, the primary loyalty of a professor was more likely to be to a discipline and to a set of professional standards than to an institution.[192] Academic itinerants took full advantage of the situation, selling their services to the highest bidder, by and large indifferent to the particular institution in which they were, presumably, only temporarily employed.

At a more basic or fundamental level, according to certain critics, the real crisis in higher education that had been prompted by the growth of the university ideal was one of blurred or ambiguous purpose. From a practical viewpoint, grafting the Germanic university research pattern onto the English collegiate structure made sense because it allowed undergraduate programs to serve as "feeders" to more advanced, specialized professional programs offered at the graduate level. Even so research-oriented an institution as Johns Hopkins, after all, had found it impossible to dispense with undergraduate education entirely. But which was more important, some asked, teaching or research, undergraduate education or professional graduate training? Was it truly the case, as piously alleged from some quarters, that scholarly research enlivened and enriched teaching? Or did the two activities bear little connection with one another? To what extent did undergraduates in beginning courses benefit from the specialized research in which their professors were engaged, research whose results and significance oftentimes were comprehensible only to other advanced specialists within a given discipline? And where was the emphasis in higher learning to be placed, upon professional training, or upon the cultivation and development of the individual learner in his or her complexity as a full human being?

Charles Eliot Norton of Harvard in 1895 offered one view. "The highest end of the highest education," he declared, "is not anything which can be directly taught, but is the consummation of all studies. It is the final result of intellectual culture in the development of the breadth, serenity, and solidity of mind, and in the attainment of that complete self-possession which finds expression in character." Charles F. Thwing of Western Reserve weighed in with a supporting comment: "If I were a student," he offered, "I would seek less for knowledge and more for the significance of knowledge. I would care less to be a scholar and more to be a thinker." Yet another characteristic expression of the same perspective was forthcoming from Robert MacDougall, a professor of psychology at New York University in 1904, who asserted that "breadth of knowledge and catholicity of sympathy" were outcomes of a liberal education whose importance should not be underestimated or ignored. Students should be encouraged to acquire "discernment and rationality of judgment," he believed; they should become "sensitive to intellectual sincerity and consistency"; and come to possess "an appreciative acquaintance with . . . permanent expressions of human thought" at its best, in all of its varied manifestations. Knowledge of the achievements of generations past, a certain developing breadth of character, and a "lively sympathy with the true, the good and the beautiful," as W. A. Merrill of Miami University described them, were all educational aims still worth pursuing.[193]

More limited in scope than universities, less able to compete for the resources required to mount the elaborate professional preparatory programs of larger institutions, private colleges groped for an independent mission of their own. If the preoccupations of public and private universities were with research and professional training, many college leaders decided, for their part they would take on an altogether different task. Smaller enrollments could be converted into a strategic advantage, allowing colleges to offer the individualized attention to students now increasingly denied them in an impersonal university environment. Situated, as many of them were, away from the distractions of the city, colleges would dedicate themselves anew to providing an intimate, supportive academic climate where morality and good character might be nurtured to best advantage. Above all, colleges would become places where "liberal culture" would be enshrined as the basis of collegiate study. William DeWitt Hyde of Bowdoin College in 1904 most clearly expressed the new ideal: "The function of the college is liberal education," he announced. "[It is directed to] the opening of the mind to the great departments of human interest; the opening of the heart to the great spiritual motives of unselfishness and social service; the opening of the will to opportunity for wise and righteous self-control."[194]

Equally eloquent in its reaffirmation of the humanistic perspective in higher education was a ringing declaration offered by Alexander Meiklejohn of Brown in 1908. "The American college," he affirmed, "is not primarily to teach the forms of living, not primarily to give practice in the art of living, but rather to broaden and deepen . . . insight into life itself, to open up the riches of human experience, of literature, of nature, of art, of religion, of philosophy, of human relations, social, economic, political, to arouse an understanding and appreciation of these, so that life may be fuller and richer in content; in a word, the primary function of the American college is the arousing of interests."[195] But whether some such noble goal would suffice, whether "the arousing of interests" could be sustained as a viable and self-sufficient aim in academe, whether liberal-arts colleges could compete and survive in the shadow of university behemoths—in the opening years of the twentieth century the answers to such questions still remained unclear.

PART 3

AMERICAN HIGHER EDUCATION: MATURATION AND DEVELOPMENT

6

American Academe in the Early Twentieth Century

PARADIGMS OLD AND NEW

Reflecting back upon American higher education as he had experienced it in the early years of the 1900s, Henry Seidel Canby (*Alma Mater*, 1936) recalled it as a period of relative calm and tranquility underlain by a certain ambiguity of purpose. "Particularly in the first decade of the new century," he reported, "they were trying in our college to combine various incompatibles. . . . A young instructor on the faculty in, say 1905, could look upon this unheard of combination of sporting resort, beer garden, political convention, laboratory, and factory for research with a mind as confused as a Spanish omelet."[1] But Canby's sense of incompatibility seems not to have been widely shared, judging from the tone of the many writings on higher learning that appeared in scholarly and popular journals of the day. As compared with the deep divisions of opinion and sharply contrasting views vented in books and journals in the 1870s and 1880s, the overall climate was more nearly one of consensus and accommodation.[2]

Discussions of academic ideals and goals at the turn of the century seemed markedly less polemical, more restrained, more inclined to point to areas of agreement than formerly. Statements of academic purpose became hazier, less distinct, more temperate in their expression. The mood now seemed to be one of incorporating every desirable goal within a common institutional framework. Thus, commentators tended to speak in generalities about the value of a college education: about how it afforded contact with a cultural legacy, fostered exemplary habits of self-discipline and restraint, and promoted professional skill and competency.[3] The social prestige and financial worth of holding a college degree now came in for more attention than the actual content of the learning associated with it.

It is difficult not to detect in early-twentieth-century literature on higher learning a desire on the part of the larger universities to be all things to all people, to offer everyone something of advantage. "I do not believe," observed President Harry Pratt Judson of the University of Chicago in 1907, "that the college should aim at any one kind of product. There should be diversity of results as there is a diversity of natural traits. No college should aim to put its hallmark upon all men in such a sense as to expect that all will be substantially alike."[4] As a professor of Greek at Columbia interpreted them in 1907, the basic purposes of a university were multiple: to preserve and transmit liberal culture; to share useful knowledge with the populace at large; to serve as an agent of beneficial social change in a burgeoning industrial and commercial order; and to serve as a center for disinterested inquiry and the production of new knowledge through research and scholarly writing. "We may seek at times . . . to separate these notions," he observed, "but they are really so interwoven in the complete idea of a university that no clear boundary lines can be drawn between them. Least of all should the thought of opposition between them enter our minds."[5]

That apparent felt lack of tension among dissimilar academic goals, it might be argued, reflected the emergent hegemony of the research university as an ideal institutional type in American higher education. What seemed abundantly clear was that the model or paradigm prevailing at the opening of the twentieth century differed markedly from the old ideal that had held sway approximately a half century before. If the old-time college typically was defined by teaching and a fixed curriculum still dominated by classical languages and literature, the new university defined itself in terms of research and a bewildering array of modern utilitarian programs of study. If the old college tended to be paternalistic and intimately involved in the lives of its students, the new university was inclined to be more impersonal, more permissive, less directly engaged in student supervision. Above all, as the old college was small, the university was large. So predominant had the modern university model become, sanctioning as it did a monolithic set of institutional standards and priorities, it seemingly left little room for alternatives. The primacy of the university was such that other types of institutions could only seek to imitate its essential features or risk being left hopelessly behind.[6] In effect, higher education in America formed a pyramid, with the values of research universities dominating the structure at its pinnacle.

Most private liberal-arts colleges lacked the resources needed to transform themselves into institutions dedicated more to generating knowledge than simply to transmitting it. Unable or unwilling to compete directly with universities in offering specialized professional training, many colleges set about the task of redefining themselves exclusively as teaching institutions. Their basic role would be to serve as purveyors of liberal culture.[7] Faced with the choice of emulating universities or remaining something quite different, even if it meant a certain loss of popular support, colleges ultimately opted for the latter. Special-purpose or regional institutions, in contrast, rather quickly succumbed to the research-dominated model and sought to acquire the trappings of a full-fledged university as quickly as possible.[8]

The development of the normal school as an institution dedicated to teacher preparation affords a prime example.[9] Teaching seminaries and normal schools had long concentrated their efforts on the training of classroom practitioners for the lower schools. Successive name changes over time pointed to their evolution in an entirely new direction, however.[10] Thus, the "normal school" of the 1890s, which up until then had been little more than a glorified high school, became the "state teachers' college" of the teens and twenties. A few decades later, it had become the "state college." Eventually, much expanded, it took pride in being the "state university."[11] Directly reflective of the premium placed upon "doing research" associated with large universities, teachers' institutions shifted their values and priorities—usually by minimizing or de-emphasizing their role in teacher education. The goal always, it seemed, was to become a comprehensive, research-oriented university.[12]

MAMMON AND THE MONOLITHS

The transformation of relatively simple colleges into university organizations of great scope and structural complexity was not achieved without some stress and strain. The expanded role of the university president illustrated the process.[13] What academic governing bodies were searching for in a president was once described by Rutherford B. Hayes, a member of Ohio State's board in the early 1890s: "We are looking for a man of fine appearance, of commanding presence, one who will impress the public; he must be a fine speaker at public assemblies; he must be a great scholar and a great teacher; he must be a preacher also, as some think; he must be a man of winning manners; he must have tact so that he can get along with and govern the faculty; he must be popular with the students; he must also be a man of business training, a man of affairs; he must be a great administrator." Hayes was undoubtedly correct when he pointed out, "Gentlemen, there is no such man."[14]

The need, as Thorstein Veblen described it in *The Higher Learning in America* (1918), was for "captains of erudition"—which is to say, men who somehow miraculously combined the sagacity of a Mark Hopkins with the business acumen of a Rockefeller or a Carnegie.[15] Wanted were individuals who could perform for academe the functions served elsewhere in American society by captains of corporate business and industry. Gone were the kindly old presidents of yesteryear who knew everyone by name, greeted new arrivals in person, and took a personal interest in the academic progress of each student entrusted to their care.[16] They would be supplanted by a new breed of academic executive officers well versed in the intricacies of finance and administration, executive managers whose duties would inevitably remove them not only from faculty and students but increasingly from academics as well.[17]

One of the more obvious changes when it came to selecting a university's administrative leader was the preference for laymen over clergymen.[18] Whereas 90 percent of all college presidents serving in 1860 had trained for the ministry, by 1933 no more than 12 percent had theological preparation. The stereotypical minister was perceived to be lacking in worldly skills and ways. He was associated in the minds of many with a classical curriculum instead of the more practical or utilitarian learning favored by trustees.[19] And because institutions themselves were becoming more secular and less subject to religious influences, one by one various private and public colleges departed from precedent and elected laypersons to their presidencies: Denison in 1889, Illinois College in 1892, Yale in 1899, Princeton in 1902, Marietta in 1913, Bowdoin in 1918, Wabash in 1926. Replacing yesterday's clerics were lawyers, former military leaders, politicians and businessmen with experience or money.[20]

Despite laments over the passing of the old-time college president, increasing enrollments and greatly enlarged endowments seemed to render him something of an anachronism. The modern imperative, as trustees saw it, was to secure someone capable of supplying strong, directive leadership to all of a university's far-flung endeavors. His challenge was to hold the institution together, reconciling as much as possible each of the disparate elements and interests—students, faculty, alumni, external constituents—while simultaneously imparting to all a sense of shared mission and purpose. Upon the president depended the success with which the university transcended its internal differences and moved forward in accord. Hence, while it had once been customary to regard the college president as *primus inter pares,* first among his faculty equals, the clear and distinct trend in the early 1900s was toward thinking of him simply as *primus.* Whereas once the president had served *non dominus sed dux* (as "a leader, not a master"), now it was becoming ever more difficult to separate the two roles.[21]

Because an institution of higher learning needed a continuous flow of funds for its support, raising money became the president's most urgent task. Finding prospective donors and wooing them was likely to occupy most of his energies. It was a task that could only draw him even further away from campus affairs.[22] Responding to complaints that presidents were being turned into financial drummers for their institutions to the virtual exclusion of all else, Langdon Stewardson of Hobart College replied, "Disagreeable as the job of money-raising actually is, the President clearly recognizes that it is for him a plain and imperative duty."[23] To the president fell the job of persuading wealthy corporate donors—the McCormicks, the Havemeyers, the Goulds, the Rockefellers, the Vanderbilts—to bestow their largesse. If he was successful, millions poured in for new buildings, new departments, new professional schools.[24]

On the other hand, corporate philanthropy could be a mixed blessing, particularly to the degree to which donations came with strings attached. It was often the case, for example, that a recipient was obliged to match or even double the amount of some prospective contribution as a precondition for its bestowal. Second, many benefactors sought to influence institutional policy or to earmark funds for some specialized purpose. It then fell to the president to negotiate the terms of a gift, protecting the university's academic independence as best he could. Third, benefactors began seeking places on collegiate governing boards. The outcome was boards of trustees dominated not by scholars, but by businessmen whose priorities and loyalties were not always aligned with, or especially responsive to, academic considerations.[25]

Philanthropic organizations such as the Carnegie Foundation, established in 1906, and the Rockefeller Foundation, begun in 1913, began to take on a life of their own within academe, holding out the promise of gifts only if universities met certain conditions. University leaders found it difficult to resist demands for the elimination of duplication and waste, for consolidation, for nonsectarianism, or whatever else was mandated. More than a few institutions—Drake, Coe, Hanover, Rochester, and perhaps a score of others—rather promptly shed their denominational affiliations, for example, in exchange for foundation support. Academic leaders grew troubled by the expanding power of external bodies. President Jacob Gould Schurman of Cornell expressed his misgivings in 1909 when he declared that "the very ambition of such corporations to reform educational abuses is itself a source of danger. Men are not constituted educational reformers by having a million dollars to spend."[26] Corporate donors believed otherwise. Rockefeller's General Education Board in its 1914 report, for instance, defended its efforts to bring a greater measure of rationality and standardization to educational reform. "The states have not generally shown themselves competent to deal with higher education on a nonpartisan, impersonal, and comprehensive basis," the report alleged. "Rival religious bodies have invaded fields fully— or more than fully—occupied already; misguided individuals have founded a new college instead of strengthening an old one."[27] Foundations were resolved to put an end to all such abuses and bring more efficient business management to academe. Philanthropic corporations were fast becoming a power to be reckoned with by academic leaders.

Other external bodies besides foundations were beginning to exercise a formative influence of their own. In 1892 the National Education Association's famous Committee of Ten had taken on the task of trying to standardize secondary curricular requirements for admission to college. A later Committee of Twelve went further in outlining a common set of collegiate admission standards.[28] Finally, at the urging of Columbia's Nicholas Murray Butler, those attending an 1899 meeting of the Association of Colleges and Secondary Schools of the Middle Atlantic States and Maryland took under consideration a proposal to create an independent board of examiners responsible for administering academic achievement tests to college applicants.[29]

President Ethelbert D. Warfield of Lafayette College led the opposition. "Lafayette College does not intend to be told by any Board whom to admit and whom not to admit," he informed the assembled delegates. "If we wish to admit the son of a benefactor, or of a Trustee, or of a member of the Faculty, and such action will benefit the institution we are not going to be prevented from taking it." Harvard's Charles Eliot rose to issue a rejoinder. "The President of Lafayette College has misunderstood," he declared. "It will be perfectly practicable under this plan for Lafayette College to say, if it chooses, that it will admit only such students as cannot pass these examinations." Amid laughter from the audience, Eliot added, "No one proposes to deprive Lafayette College of that privilege."[30] Opposition now effectively silenced, the first College Board examinations were held in June of 1901. Ten years later, at least two dozen leading eastern colleges and universities were making use of test scores in deciding who to admit.

Yet another factor in the changing power equation was the growing influence of university alumni. American higher education in the early twentieth century had reached a point in its development where large numbers of college graduates had achieved positions of wealth. They qualified as potential supporters of colleges and universities alongside corporate foundations. Academic leaders thus began turning to alumni for financial help. But not unlike corporate givers, donors had a tendency to exhibit a certain proprietary attitude of their own.

Organized into increasingly powerful associations largely outside or beyond the direct control of the very institutions to which they gave allegiance, alumni groups began to exert more and more influence. In exchange for their generosity, they too expected their elected representatives to be granted positions on governing boards. Rare was the college administration capable of ignoring the wishes of alums when it came to policies affecting those aspects of collegiate life that most interested them.[31] Typically, their support was for stadia, not *studia,* for athletic gymnasia, not laboratories or libraries, for extracurricular matters rather than activities lying at the very core of the academic enterprise.[32] Hence a certain distortion of institutional purpose was introduced at the expense of scholarship and instruction. Yet it was a tendency most hard-pressed college presidents were unable—or possibly unwilling—to resist.

BUREAUCRATIZATION AND THE BUSINESS ETHOS

The development of universities as bureaucratic organizations was the result of increased size, expanding student enrollments, and demands for new services. Bureaucratization represented also a logical if unplanned response to the need to keep teachers and researchers free from the detailed but essential duties required in managing a complex organization.[33] Formerly, a small college had been able to make do with a president, a bursar or treasurer, and perhaps a part-time librarian. Now, given universities' enlarged functions and scope, administrative duties necessarily grew more specialized and divided. The result was a hierarchical arrangement long familiar in business though new to academia. At the top reposed the board of trustees and the president. To the president's office was appended a registrar, then vice-presidents and associate vice-presidents, a chief business officer, then in succession, deans, an admissions director, and, in time, an array of secretaries and subordinate administrative assistants. Full-time administrators were placed in charge of student affairs, faculty relations, institutional development, athletics, facilities management, custodial functions, and other operations. The actual exercise of power downward through the graduated ranks of the administrative hierarchy might vary, but within each rank specific roles began to develop. Roughly paralleling the administrative structure, of course, was the graduated system of faculty rankings: department heads, full professors, associate and assistant professors, instructors, and several classes of graduate students.

The new generation of professors just embarking upon their careers in the early years of the twentieth century probably accepted the university's administrative structure with a certain degree of equanimity. But to some faculty, schooled in the traditions of academe as a closely-knit, somewhat insular community of scholars, the "Administration" seemed an alien virus introduced into the corporate body. Administration in a very real sense connoted not simply a style of management but a state of mind, a form of consciousness; and it differed greatly in its values and priorities from the academic mind. It valued orderliness, efficiency, accountability, and quantification. Later on it symbolized regimentation, and ubiquitous standardization throughout the institution. Faculty were willing to concede that rules and regulations were useful, indispensable even. If nothing else, explicit policies and procedures served to protect professors from the vagaries of administrative dictate. Students for their part welcomed codifications of requirements because they served to clarify what was expected of them. The alternative to a certain minimal level of regimentation, most observers realized, was institutional drift or autocracy or chaos.[34]

The acknowledged need for bureaucracy notwithstanding, critics were quick to point out its obvious affinity with the corporate business mentality as a whole. John Jay Chapman, writing in 1909, was among the first to complain about how thoroughly businesslike attitudes and methods already had infiltrated academic life. "The men who stand for education and scholarship have the ideals of business men," he declared. "They are, in truth, business men. The men who control [universities] to-day are very little else than business men, running a large department store which dispenses education to the millions."[35] John Dewey deplored what he called "the atmosphere of money-getting and money-spending" prevailing in academe, which, he claimed, "hides from view the interests for the sake of which money alone has a place."[36] Thorstein Veblen's *The Higher Learning in America,* written mostly before 1910, detected the hand of business control dominating practically every aspect of the modern university. The tendency to expend large sums on impressive buildings; the growth of bureaucracy; the prominence given intercollegiate athletics; the preponderance of vocational courses of instruction offered; the undignified scramble for prestige, competitive advantage, and power among institutions— all, so far as Veblen was concerned, were symptoms of the corrupting influence of the business ethos.[37] Upton Sinclair, writing in *The Goose-step: A Study of American Education* (1923) concurred. Love of power and money, he judged, had irremediably undermined the academic integrity of most institutions of higher learning in America, and with it their leadership. As for the typical university president, Sinclair dismissed him as "the most universal faker and the most variegated prevaricator that has yet appeared in the civilized world."[38]

The university, observed one commentator, writing in a 1900 issue of the *Nation,* "cannot follow the definite, precise methods employed by the manufacturer . . . from the very obvious fact that [students] are not precisely alike, and are not, moreover, mere passive blocks of raw material." Andrew S.

Draper of the University of Illinois agreed, noting in an *Atlantic Monthly* article in 1906, "Of course the university cannot become a business corporation, with a business corporation's ordinary implications. . . . The distinguishing ear-marks of an American university are its moral purpose, its scientific aim, its unselfish public service, its inspirations to all men in all noble things, and its incorruptibility by commercialism." Draper then went on to add a vital qualification: "Sane and essential business methods should . . . be applied to the management of its business affairs. It is a business concern as well as a moral and intellectual instrumentality, and if business methods are not applied to its management it will break down."[39]

There was a certain inexorable logic to the growth of academic administration and bureaucracy, a seeming inevitability about it all that made criticism ineffectual, and outright resistance nearly impossible. Much of the growth and complexity had come about unplanned. As President Angell of Michigan, writing in 1904, observed almost ruefully, "Our rather multifarious usages . . . have grown up without much system under peculiar exigencies."[40] More than a few critics went on at length about what was being lost, about the erosion of academic community and collegiality in an age increasingly enamored of Taylorite efficiency and operational rationality. But protests were to little avail. To oppose growth seemed vaguely quixotic, carrying with it (to mix the metaphor) the risk of being branded as the latter-day equivalent of a Luddite attempting to thwart progress.

In any case, not even the most ardent critics of business influence were prepared to advocate the elimination of bureaucracy entirely. To do so, faculty would have had to collect tuition payment themselves, pay for buildings and equipment, raise endowments, compile and file reports, keep accounts, supervise student admissions and course registrations, and otherwise attend to the myriad tasks since assumed by administrative functionaries. They agreed with Draper's position that any other alternative was unthinkable, that without the organizational infrastructure that was fast becoming a distinguishing characteristic of the modern university, the entire system would indeed "break down." Still, many worried about the monolithic character of the institution, its growing impersonality, its tendency to dehumanize collegiate life. And more than anything else perhaps, faculty worried about their own place within the power structure.[41]

Faculty participation in governance, professors argued, amounted to little more than a symbolic gesture extended by those who held real power. To be sure, there existed the rudiments of faculty consultation. But in the main it was more a matter of administrators sounding out opinion within the professorial ranks so as to deflect it, to isolate faculty discontent, and to disarm whatever dissension threatened to weaken the university's official posture of unity and solidarity. An anonymous contributor to *Scribner's Magazine* in 1907 compared the professor's lot to that of a lowly seaman: "There is set up within the university an 'administration' to which I am held closely accountable," he complained. "They steer the vessel, and I am one of the crew. I am not allowed on the bridge except when summoned; and the councils in which I participate uniformly begin at the point at which policy is already determined. I am not part *of* the 'administration,' but am used *by* the 'administration.' . . . In authority, in dignity, in salary, the 'administration' are over me, and I am under them." The writer then went on to compare his standing with that of "the humblest clerk in a department store," who was allowed to remain on the sufferance "of a single despot."[42] The issue then, reduced to its most elemental level, was whether faculty exercised any substantial control over the circumstances of their own work. Many suspected, with John Jay Chapman, that "as the boss has been the tool of business men in politics, so the college president has been his agent in education."[43] Still unclear was what professors could do, individually or collectively, to avoid becoming victims of the process.

ACADEMIC FREEDOM

Job security had always been a tenuous affair among the nineteenth-century American professorate. Any teacher held his post at the president's pleasure, or that of his board. He could be readily dismissed if those above him so desired.[44] When a professor was fired for expressing an unpopular point of view (within the classroom or without) it was usually a matter of his having taken a stand contrary to prevailing religious orthodoxy. Toward the end of the nineteenth century, the grounds upon which a professor was liable to get into trouble shifted to the political and economic sphere. Over and over again the same pattern repeated itself: an academic publicly urged reforms or criticized the existing social order and was then summarily dismissed for his trouble.[45] In 1892, it was George M. Steele, president of Lawrence College, who was fired for his leanings "toward free trade and greenbacks"; the next year, the president of North Dakota Agricultural College was fired for unspecified "political" reasons; in 1894 Richard T. Ely, a professor of economics at Wisconsin, was charged with fomenting public unrest for his views on labor relations and corporate abuse; I. A. Hourwich of the University of Chicago was dismissed the same year for participating in a Populist convention; in 1895 Edward W. Bemis, an economist at Chicago, was dismissed for imprudently criticizing monopolies and the railroad industry; in 1896 John R. Commons, an economist from Indiana University, lost his job for promulgating controversial political views; in 1897 Allen Smith, a political scientist employed at Marietta College, was severed from his post over "antimonopoly teaching"; and in 1897 E. Benjamin Andrews of Brown was forced to resign for having advanced views favorable to free silver.[46] To Thomas Elmer Will of Kansas State, writing in 1901, the lesson to be drawn from the long chronicle of professors who had lost their positions for presuming to speak out on social issues was a simple one. "With the arrogance equalling that of the slave power," he claimed, "our plutocracy has issued its edict that the colleges and universities must fall into line."[47]

Of all the academic freedom cases that attracted public attention, the dismissal of Edward A. Ross from Stanford University in November of 1900 aroused the most controversy.[48] The previous May, Ross had given a speech opposing Asian immigration. He followed it up with another speech shortly thereafter in which he failed to oppose municipal ownership of public utilities. Jane Lathrop Stanford, wife of Leland Stanford, the university's founder, who served as sole trustee (and considered the institution her personal possession with which she could do whatever she liked) directed President David Starr Jordan to dismiss Ross forthwith. Jordan was something of an autocrat in his own right, having been hired because he reportedly could manage university affairs "like the president of a railroad." It was reported of him by a friend, for example, that Jordan avoided convening his faculty because "the holding of faculty meetings inevitably led to differences of opinion in the faculty, and . . . the best way to avoid the forming of parties in the faculty was never to get the faculty together except perhaps for a yearly meeting."[49] Despite a personal friendship with Ross, Jordan felt he was in no position to oppose Mrs. Sanford's repeated demands. In November he demanded Ross's resignation. A major controversy ensued.[50] Several faculty members resigned in protest. In the end, however, Ross failed to recover his position.

The Ross case renewed a debate about freedom of teaching and research, an issue that had been raised only intermittently during previous decades and then usually involving expressions of belief connected with the controversy between science and religion, evolution and fundamentalist creationism. Ross's defenders argued that so-called "extramural" utterances, that is, pronouncements issued by a professor outside of the classroom, were as deserving of academic protection as what was taught inside the classroom or written for publication. The hallowed tradition of *Lehrfreiheit*, of freedom to teach and research without outside interference, was an absolute right and should be considered sacrosanct. If corporate business interests or their agents were allowed to dictate what a professor might profess, so it was argued, the integrity of all scholarship within a college or university was directly threatened.

Those who supported President Jordan's action in firing Edward Ross, on the other hand, tended to respond in one of three ways: denying there was any vital principle of academic freedom at stake; denouncing academic freedom as an archaic and outmoded concept lacking current application; or affirming freedom in the abstract while insisting that professorial prerogatives should always be kept subordinate to an institution's legitimate concern for its own reputation.[51]

Andrew S. Draper of Illinois summed up his own thinking with the simple declaration that "fool talk" should never be allowed within a university.[52] Historian Frederick Jackson Turner in 1902 recalled comparable sentiments expressed "when the members of the Board of Regents of Wisconsin used to sit with a red lead pencil in consultation over the lists of books submitted by their professors, and strike out those that failed to please their fancy, with irreverent comments on 'fool professors.'" For President W. H. P. Faunce of Brown University in 1901, the issue was about the extent to which "incendiary enthusiasm" for unorthodox views should be protected, and the degree to which free speech should be balanced against responsible speech. As he put it, "If to this principle of freedom of speech we add the equally important principle of responsibility for speech, responsibility to the institutions we represent, and to the public whose confidence we value, we have a sound and sensible basis for our academic future." According to President W. O. Thompson of Ohio State, writing in 1910, any professor contemplating the airing of an unpopular viewpoint needed to be reminded of his responsibility to behave like a "gentleman." "If we regard the institution as a conservator of society's best interest and at the same time a leader in the search for the truth," he felt confident, "reasonable people will at once agree that the orderly progress of research and scholarship does not demand unnecessary offenses."[53]

Alton B. Parker, a former judge of the New York Court of Appeals and later a presidential candidate for the Democrats, in 1904 gave expression to the typical conservative view of propertied interests: "When in opposition to the wishes or without the consent of the supporters of the institution [a professor] persists in a course that must tend to impress upon the tender minds of the young under his charge theories deemed to be false by a vast majority of the most intelligent minds of the age, it seems to me that he has abused his privilege of expression of opinion to such an extent as to justify the governing board in terminating his engagement." Professors, in other words, should refrain from voicing positions opposed by a majority, or, as Parker and others were agreed, when the utterance in question was likely to "inflame public sentiment."[54] Therein lay the crux of the matter. For faculty defenders of academic freedom, issues of high principle were at stake. To their opponents, however, the dispute was not about ideas, and still less about truth. Rather, questions of academic freedom were about public relations, about the consequences of having one of a school's members voicing sentiments calculated to arouse the ire of those upon whom the university necessarily depended for support.

A professor by the name of Ira W. Howerth, writing in 1900, summed up the issue of academic freedom from the professorial side. "It is contended by the authorities that there is complete liberty, and the claim is logical, for they make a careful distinction between liberty and license," he observed. "Thought is free so long as it is sound, and the authorities have their own convictions in regard to what constitutes sound thinking. While freedom of thought is doubtless increasing in all our higher institutions of learning . . . yet it is probably true to-day that there is not a college or university in the country that would long tolerate an active and formidable advocate of serious changes in the present social order. He would be required to go, and the occasion of his removal would not be avowed as opposition to intellectual liberty, but to his capacity as evidenced by his vagarious opinions."[55]

Coupled with professors' demands for academic freedom was a plea for greater job security. As Henry Seidel Canby recalled, "Our strongest desire was to be made safe, to stay where we were on a living wage, to be secure while we worked. . . . No scrimping, no outside earning, could safeguard us. We were dependent upon the college, which itself was always pressed for money, and could not be counted upon to be either judicious or just."[56] (During the period to which Canby was referring, the average faculty salary was extremely low, about the same as a skilled industrial worker.) The problem was that in the opening years of the twentieth century there was still no legal recourse for redressing grievances. Courts, disinclined to interfere in the internal affairs of academic institutions, had not yet taken cognizance of the principle of academic freedom. Consequently, no matter how reasoned were the arguments advanced on professors' behalf, demands for a living wage, for job security, and for freedom to teach and publish without fear of hindrance, they were virtually unenforceable. So far as many university trustees were concerned, an errant professor was an employee of the institution, no more, no less. If his conduct was displeasing to management, officials were entitled to give him his walking papers as readily as business executives might fire any factory hireling. In short, claims to special status or autonomy for professors were rejected out of hand.[57]

The beginnings of a response came in 1915 with the formation of the American Association of University Professors (AAUP), an outgrowth of a series of discussions and planning efforts jointly conducted by the American Economic Association, the American Sociological Society, and the American Political Science Association. By no means did the new organization win immediate acceptance or broad support, even within the professorate. To some, the idea of a general academic association of college and university teachers too closely resembled unionism.[58] The New York Times, reporting on the group's inception, let loose with a broadside against "organized dons" and ridiculed academic freedom as "the unalienable right of every college instructor to make a fool of himself and the college by . . . intemperate, sensational prattle about every subject under the sun, to his classes and the public, and still keep on the payroll or be reft therefrom only by elaborate process."[59] In spite of such criticism, the AAUP's leadership moved ahead with the preparation of a draft Statement of Principles outlining the importance of safeguarding academic freedom and tenure in the nation's colleges and universities.[60] The document emphasized that professors should be allowed to speak on their own authority and not be made to serve merely as "echoes of the opinions of the lay public or of the individuals who endow or manage universities." In the years that followed, even while instances of alleged abridgements and violations continued unabated, the AAUP became the single most influential and important defender of professorial tenure and academic freedom.[61]

No sooner had the American Association of University Professors established itself as a voice of the professorate and enunciated a statement of principles than it was faced with a succession of crises brought about with the advent of World War I. Even as the fighting in Europe raged on, Americans at home found themselves deeply divided in their opinions about the conflict. Some professors in their public declarations assumed a posture of militant pacifism. The United States, they warned, should lend aid to its allies, but at all costs should avoid allowing itself to be drawn into the conflagration. At the opposite extreme, a few academics adopted a pro-German position, up to and including urgings that America take up Germany's cause in the war. Unpopular views expressed during the war years inflamed popular passions.[62] What during calmer times might have been overlooked as merely objectionable was now regarded as outright sedition and treason.[63] Several professors were forced out of jobs at the University of Minnesota; at Harvard a German sympathizer kept his position only when President Lowell intervened on his behalf. So far as academic freedom was concerned, most controversies turned on the paradoxical question as to whether freedom of speech could be legitimately curtailed or constrained under extraordinary wartime circumstances in order to protect the principle of free speech itself.

In the 1930s, academic freedom cases hinged on the propriety of teacher-oath statutes. As the nation sank into the greatest economic depression it had yet experienced, tolerance disappeared for views questioning whether existing American social institutions were adequate to deal with collapse or, possibly, had even contributed to the general malaise. Accordingly, state after state passed legislation requiring teachers at all levels to affirm their loyalty to the state and federal constitutions. A special AAUP committee was assembled to consider whether the imposition of involuntary loyalty oaths represented a threat to academic freedom. It concluded that if the intent of such oaths was to prevent criticism of the existing social order or to preclude anyone from offering suggestions for reform, then they did in fact pose a limitation on academic freedom. In almost all of the major cases of the day that arose over loyalty oaths, the AAUP found itself in the midst of the struggle.[64]

Meanwhile, following a succession of joint conferences between the AAUP and the Association of American Colleges, which had begun meeting in 1934, leaders of the two organizations came together in 1940 in agreement upon a restatement of principles as set forth in a 1925 Conference Statement on Academic Freedom and Tenure. In style and tone, the document gave the appearance of attempting to mollify critics of alleged professorial abuses. At the same time, it stoutly reaffirmed professors' rights to freedom of expression. "Institutions of higher education are conducted for the common good and not to further the interest of either the individual teacher or the institution as a whole," the 1940 Statement proclaimed. "The common good depends upon the free search for truth and its free exposition." Therefore, "academic freedom is essential to these purposes and applies to both teaching and research. Freedom in research is fundamental to the advancement of truth. Academic freedom in its teaching aspect is fundamental for the protection of the rights of the teacher in teaching and of the student to freedom in learning."

The Statement continued, "[Academic freedom] carries with it duties correlative with rights. Freedom and economic security, hence, tenure, are indispensable to the success of an institution in fulfilling its obligations to its students and to society." After affirming due process and tenure rights, the AAUP paper went on to endorse a teacher's classroom freedom, though it cautioned, "he should be careful not to introduce into his teaching controversial matter which has no relation to his subject." Similarly, it affirmed the right of the professor as a citizen to be free from institutional censorship and discipline, but counseled him to "remember that the public may judge his profession and his institution by his utterances." Hence, it was said, "he should at all times be accurate, should exercise appropriate restraint, should show respect for the opinions of others, and should make every effort to indicate that he is not an institutional spokesman."[65]

In all probability, no other single document in twentieth-century American higher education was so widely read, appealed to, discussed, or criticized as the AAUP's 1940 Statement of Principles. As an effort to codify and clarify what meaning academic freedom should have for colleges and universities, its force was moral rather than legal; and it lacked provision for enforcement in particular cases. Nevertheless, what it did offer was a set of general standards to which aggrieved parties could appeal when controversies erupted. In time, most colleges and universities accepted its broad outlines, and were reluctant to be found in noncompliance with its strictures.

COLLEGE STUDENTS AND CAMPUS LIFE

To a growing number of American undergraduates in the first third of the twentieth century, attending college marked a pleasant interlude between the end of adolescence and the assumption of adult responsibilities. The college years in some cases amounted to little more than a prolonged childhood: a time to develop friendships, to socialize, to indulge in good fun.[66] Students generally did not expect to work hard; they rarely studied any more than was minimally necessary; and regular attendance in class was the exception rather than the rule. Professors who held students to high standards were deeply resented— even while lenient professors were regarded with a certain measure of ridicule and contempt. Intense study was frowned upon as excessive; and it was thought "poor form" to earn anything better than the "gentleman's C" in one's courses.[67] When professors first introduced unannounced examinations as a way to keep students in line, collegians arose in protest. When formal course papers were required, a black market in student themes quickly sprang up. There were many authentic accounts of the period reporting instances in which students earned passing grades without ever having attended classes; and of cases where students hired "widows," or private tutors, to help them prepare for an examination in a last-minute "cram session." Books were not often checked out of the library. It was said of some students that they had contrived never to purchase a textbook throughout the course of their entire undergraduate careers.[68]

Freed from pecuniary concerns, students of the early 1900s preferred to devote themselves to good times. Most felt secure in the knowledge that while the college degree still carried with it a measure of prestige and social standing, its acquisition no longer demanded the sort of expenditure of time and effort formerly required. In 1897 an observer had commented that "if it is at all noteworthy that many of the very rich men of the United States, who have made their riches by their own energy and foresight, are not college-bred, it is certainly most significant that the sons of these men are receiving a college education."[69] Writer Calvin Thomas judged the situation in 1905 in precisely the same way: "Notwithstanding all the attacks that are made upon college, notwithstanding all the satiric questionings of its utility, its popularity steady increases. Men decry it, crack jokes about it, and—send their sons to college."[70] The credential itself, not the academic achievement it supposedly represented, was the main interest.

The collegiate atmosphere at the turn of the century and for a decade or so thereafter was one distinctly marked—for want of a better term—by a species of student infantilism.[71] It was a play world in which young middle-class men occupied themselves with hoops and marbles, with nonsensical slang and pig Latin.[72] Much time was given over to childish pranks. Sometimes it was a matter of disrupting a class with rhythmic foot-stomping in unison, or issuing collective groans of feigned anguish when an assignment was handed out. Elsewhere, as at Princeton in the 1890s, there was an outbreak of incidents in which students brought alarm clocks to class set to ring at frequent intervals throughout the lecture. Psychologically, the gulf between students and their teachers had never been wider. Professors, with their remote, humorless demeanor and icy formality, were considered the "enemy." In the attitude they displayed toward students, it must be said, many professors all too frequently reciprocated in kind. Sometimes attempts were made to bridge the gap between the two: rounds of faculty teas, which students dutifully attended as a matter of social obligation, or the creation of a system of mentorships and advisement, which all too often degenerated into little more than perfunctory interviews conducted as infrequently as possible.[73]

Students were not easily distracted from their preoccupation with extracurricular pursuits.[74] President Woodrow Wilson of Princeton acknowledged as much in 1909 when he observed, "The work of the college, the work of its classrooms and laboratories, has become the merely formal and compulsory side of its life, and . . . a score of other things, lumped under the term 'undergraduate activities,' have become the vital, spontaneous, absorbing realities for nine out of every ten men who go to college." He worried that in their indifference to academic pursuits, students were missing important benefits. As he phrased it, "If young gentlemen get from their years at college only manliness, esprit de corps, a release of their social gifts, a training in give and take, a catholic taste . . . and the standards of true sportsmen, they have gained much but they have not gained what a college should give them."[75] Wilson returned to the same theme in a 1910 baccalaureate address, when he compared college students with trade unionists. Students, he declared, typically assumed "the attitude of employees [who] give as little as possible for what they get."[76] Writer Randolph Bourne registered the same point in 1911. "Most of these young men," he lamented, "come . . . from homes of conventional religion, cheap literature, and lack of intellectual atmosphere, bring few intellectual acquisitions with them [to college], and, since most of them are going into business . . . contrive to carry a minimum away with them."[77]

The situation was little changed in the 1920s—the age of flappers and bootleggers, coonskin coats and bathtub gin, hot jazz and new dance crazes. On college campuses across the country, academics took a decided back seat to the electing of beauty queens, popularity contests, and adulation of football heroes. Some time earlier, psychologist G. Stanley Hall had defined a college as a place "where picked youth and maidens are protected from the necessities of self-support, exempted from competition, business and to some extent from social restraint, and within the largest practicable limits left free to follow their own will." His characterization was as apt in the twenties as it had been two decades earlier. And if students seemed to be living off in a world of their own, well protected from the realities of life outside academe, much the same could be said of the professorate also. An especially acerbic critique was forthcoming from Upton Sinclair in his 1923 publication *The Goose-step: A Study of American Education.* "Slaves in Boston's great department store, in which Harvard University owns twenty-five hundred shares of stock, be reconciled to your long hours and low wages and sentence to die of tuberculosis," he sarcastically advised, "because upon the wealth which you produce some learned person has prepared for mankind full data on 'The Strong Verb in Chaucer.' . . . Men who slave twelve hours a day in front of blazing white furnaces of Bethlehem, Midvale and Illinois Steel, cheer up and take a fresh grip on your shovels—you are making it possible for mankind to acquire exact knowledge concerning 'The Beginnings of the Epistolary Novel in the Romance Languages.' . . ."[78] Sinclair's attack may not have been representative of public opinion as a whole, but it did accurately reflect a current of popular resentment and ambivalence toward collegiate life within American society at large.

College life in the late 1920s and through the 1930s presented a somewhat more complex picture than in preceding decades.[79] The Depression era was a shattering experience for most Americans, a time of massive economic dislocations and widespread financial hardship. In the aftermath of the stock market crash of 1929, as banks collapsed like so many dominoes, people saw their life savings wiped out practically overnight. Unemployment skyrocketed. With hard times came great uncertainty and doubt—about the viability of democracy and the staying power of its social institutions in a world seemingly marching toward totalitarianism, about the capacity of laissez-faire capitalism to sustain affluence and material abundance, about the proper role of government vis-à-vis a marketplace fallen into chaos. Virtually no one was immune from the effects of the worst economic debacle in the nation's history, collegians least of all.

The scene on college campuses in the thirties was thus a study in contrasts. Between 1935 and 1943, the government poured over $93 million into emergency assistance for students.[80] Many, lacking prospects for employment, tended to remain in school any way they could. Yet coincident with the popular impact of the automobile, movies, and radio, popular interest in collegiate athletics, for example, reached new heights; and attendance at football games across the country broke all records. Campus fads and fashions were as outrageous and varied as ever. College life (as depicted in the popular press at least) was as replete with fraternity and sorority dances, parties and lighthearted high jinks as it had ever been.[81]

Nevertheless, partially concealed behind the usual frivolity was a more serious aspect. Shocked, confused, sometimes angered by events of the times, students showed far more social awareness and a sense of political involvement than had their predecessors a decade or so before. Collegians now joined picket lines and protest marches, they circulated petitions, they demonstrated for an astonishing array of causes.[82] Some—perhaps no more than a tiny minority—flirted with communism, hoping Marxist ideology pointed the way to a better future. Others—again, always a small minority—wondered aloud whether America had something to learn from Hitler's Germany and Mussolini's Italy. And as war clouds began to gather on the political horizon, campus peace demonstrations attracted large crowds. Students lined up by the hundreds to sign solemn pledges vowing they would never go to war. If there existed any common denominator at all, it was poverty. At Marietta College, where economic circumstances had forced the school to cut teachers' salaries in half, the campus newspaper observed sardonically that faculty had "come a lot nearer to a common feeling with the students. Now everyone on the campus can admit quite freely that he is broke."[83]

Among the more important changes to occur on college campuses nationwide throughout the first half of the twentieth century (and most especially in the twenties and thirties) was the increasing attention paid to students' extracurricular life. By the time of World War I, academic leaders were becoming persuaded that athletics, social clubs, Greek-letter societies, theater groups, campus newspapers, and student magazines—all the features of college life that seemed to occupy an increasing share of collegians' interests and time—were evolving without benefit of adequate coordination and supervision. Nonacademic activities, it was argued, carried with them a potential for substantial benefits. In terms of making students more well-rounded, forming character, encouraging socialization, and so forth, such activities could be a good thing if guided and directed into constructive channels. Perhaps it was time to revive the old-time collegiate attention to the nonintellectual side of a student's development. Besides intellectual training, colleges and universities needed to give more attention to students' social, emotional, and physical development. Closer supervision of students' off-campus housing, including rooming houses and fraternity or sorority chapter houses, was required. On-campus student housing facilities needed to be expanded, refurbished, and placed under closer surveillance. Dormitories needed to be made more attractive. It seemed important to ensure students' physical health by making certain they were afforded access to essential medical services. Taking into account the indecision of many collegians regarding their future careers, better academic counseling was also considered essential.[84]

From such concerns originated the student personnel movement.[85] Deans of students began to appear, followed rather quickly by cadres of administrative support staff charged with overseeing dormitories, academic and career counseling centers, extracurricular activities, social events, admissions counseling, scholarships and financial aid, and so on.[86] Campus chaplains became an established feature of college life, as did fraternity and sorority advisors and chaperones. By the twenties and thirties, full-time professional advisors were well on the way toward filling the gap left by professors who were unwilling or unable to take the time for mentoring and advising students. By the late 1930s and early 1940s, academic advisors had assumed extensive authority in granting waivers, helping students select courses and majors, and otherwise assisting them with decisions outside the classroom.[87] Practically all observers were agreed, given the increasing size and diversity of the undergraduate population, the emergence of an elaborate extra-academic support structure was both necessary and probably inevitable.

FROM MARGINALITY TOWARD THE MAINSTREAM: NEW STUDENTS

Of the five hundred or so institutions of higher education in existence in the United States around the turn of the century, it has been estimated that perhaps no more than one fifth deserved to be considered genuine colleges or universities. Faculty teaching loads were heavy—as high as twenty-two weekly teaching hours at some schools—a figure somewhat closer to that of secondary schools than to what came to be the collegiate norm of twelve to fifteen hours in later years. Admission standards tended to remain low. Mere completion of a high-school course of study was sufficient in many cases to win entrance into a college. Inevitably, the presence of large numbers of ill-prepared collegians kept academic standards relatively depressed at all but a handful of the more prestigious universities and liberal-arts colleges. In 1870, about 52,000 students were enrolled in four-year post-secondary education, or less than 2 percent of the population aged 18 to 21. In the 1890s the figure had risen to 3 percent; and by 1900 it hovered around 4 percent, representing a total of around 238,000 undergraduates and an additional 5,700 graduate students. By the 1920s, the percentage doubled; and it was to reach 12 percent in the next decade. On the eve of World War II the figure stood at 18 percent.[88]

Indicative of the growing democratization of American higher education, much of the student influx responsible for college enrollment increases in the early twentieth century came from the admission of groups heretofore effectively excluded. Jewish students, as an example, were first admitted in large numbers in the second decade of the new century.[89] Their arrival occasioned considerable controversy at some institutions; and in the wake of nativist prejudice that swept the country immediately after World War I, anti-Semitism became a conspicuous feature of the collegiate landscape.[90] Many schools imposed special admission tests or quotas for Jews, fearful that their presence would alter the character of the schools involved, and for the worse. Typical in its expression of the general apprehension was a comment from Harvard president Abbott Lawrence Lowell in 1922. "Where Jews become numerous they drive off other people and then leave themselves," he claimed. Lowell was undecided as to whether gentile prejudice or Semitic "clannishness" was chiefly responsible for the tendency of Jewish students to "form a distinct body, and cling . . . together, apart from the great mass of undergraduates." A better explanation was provided by Vincent Sheean, a noted journalist of the day, who recounted (*Personal History,* 1936) how a former girlfriend of his at the University of Chicago had explained the student caste system to him. "The Jews," she confided, "could not possibly go to the 'nice' parties in the college. They could not be elected to any class office, or to office in any club, or to any fraternity except the two that they themselves had organized; they could not dance with whom they pleased or go out with the girls they wanted to go out with; they could not even walk across the quadrangles with a 'nice' girl if she could possibly escape."[91]

Women students were not always welcome either. Even as coeducation was being adopted by many schools throughout the latter half of the nineteenth century, there were several instances where male students stoutly resisted the expanding presence of female collegians on campus. An alumnus of the University of Wisconsin in 1877 reported that among males, "the feeling of hostility was exceedingly intense and bitter." He reported, "As I now recollect, the entire body of students were without exception opposed to the admission of the young ladies, and the anathemas heaped upon the regents were loud and deep."[92] Practical experience had dispelled fears about women's purported frailty and mental unfitness for academic life. Possibly male resistance proceeded from the opposite fear that women would outperform them scholastically. Or, again, much of the opposition might have traced back to prevailing nineteenth-century notions of the cardinal womanly virtues—purity, piety, submissiveness, and domesticity—and the expectation that attending college would corrode or undermine coeds' feminine attributes. In any case, despite occasional opposition, the percentage of women undergraduates continued to rise, increasing from about 21 percent in 1870 to 32 percent by 1880, to almost 40 percent by 1910, and then to over 47 percent by 1920.[93] Fears grew that women were arriving on campus in such numbers as to pose a real threat to male students. So massive an increase in female enrollment, it was predicted, might ultimately drive men out entirely.

More than a few colleges in the late 1920s began to reevaluate their commitment to coeducation. Suggestions were advanced that certain restrictive measures might be necessary. A few all-male schools that had formerly contemplated admitting women now deferred their plans indefinitely. Only fear of tuition loss and of competitive advantage with nearby institutions prevented other colleges from limiting female enrollments or otherwise imposing quotas. Several universities considered single-gender registration for certain classes once it was discovered that when women constituted the majority of those enrolled in a course, men tended to shun it. Similarly, when male enrollments predominated, women avoided the course. At the University of Chicago, a brief experiment with separate lower-level colleges for men and women was launched, then abandoned.[94]

The decade of the twenties proved critical for educated women.[95] During that specific ten-year span, women achieved their highest proportion of the undergraduate population, of doctoral recipients, and of faculty members. By 1930, almost a third of all college presidents and professors were women. In other professions as well, women more than held their own. In the mid-twenties, women constituted almost 45 percent of the professional work force, a share that began to decline in 1930 and reached its lowest point in 1960, after which it began climbing again. Moreover, between 1870 and 1930 the proportion of women in the various professions was nearly twice as high as that in the work force as a whole. By the end of the 1930s, the proportion of all undergraduate women had entered upon a slight decline (though the proportion of women awarded bachelor's degrees was still increasing), and the number of women as a proportion of all those awarded doctoral degrees was dropping. Writing in 1938, Marjorie Nicolson, who was born in 1894 and received her bachelor of arts degree from the University of Michigan in 1914, described the unique situation in which many women professionals of her generation found themselves: "We came late enough," she mused, "to escape the self-consciousness and belligerence of the pioneers, to take education and training for granted. We came early enough to take equally for granted professional positions in which we could make full use of our training. This was our double glory. Positions were everywhere open to us."[96]

By no means, however, were opportunities anywhere near equal between the sexes. In academe, women were hired in record numbers in the years preceding the Depression, but invariably at lower salaries than their male peers. They were granted tenure less often; and promotions in rank came more slowly than for males. When a certain Alice Hamilton was accepted as an assistant professor on the Harvard Medical School faculty in 1919, for example, a formal provision of her appointment precluded her marching in the commencement procession. Similar instances of discrimination against women and blatantly unequal treatment were documented in colleges and universities throughout the nation.[97] By the late 1930s the tide of opinion had shifted and fewer women than before were embarking upon professional careers. Conventional opinion reasserted once again the woman's obligation to appear youthful, to seek to be physically attractive and submissive, to find her fulfillment not in some professional career but in the joys of domesticity.

African Americans of course had long occupied a position of marginality so far as higher education was concerned, as in all other aspects of social life. In 1899–1900, no more than eighty-eight blacks were awarded degrees from white colleges (most of them from Oberlin); and there were an estimated 475 graduated from predominantly black colleges. These new graduates, added to a pool of about 3,000 who had previously graduated (almost all of them from small, unaccredited black colleges), represented an infinitesimally small fraction of a total black population of nearly 10 million. As the twentieth century opened, there were approximately 3,900 blacks enrolled in nearly a hundred different black schools and colleges, perhaps less than two-thirds of which offered real collegiate-level courses of instruction.[98]

According to a 1917 survey of black higher education, only one of sixteen black federal land-grant schools in the former slave states offered college-level work. Of the 2,500 or so black students enrolled in colleges in the southern states, only 12 attended land-grant and state institutions. The remainder was enrolled in private black schools. Black collegiate enrollments in southern state institutions rose to 12,600 by 1935, while black enrollments in black private colleges nationwide increased to almost 17,000—still representing only a small proportion of the country's total black population. In 1917 only 33 out of almost a hundred private black colleges were identified as teaching at anything remotely approaching the college level, and nearly all lacked significant endowments. As late as the 1930s, precollegiate enrollments represented 40 percent of the total combined student enrollment in all black institutions of higher learning. At a time when at least 5 percent of all whites aged 18 to 21 were attending college, the figure for blacks stood at less than one-third of 1 percent. A 1928 survey revealed there were less than 14,000 black students receiving collegiate-level instruction, three-quarters of whom were attending private black institutions. By the mid-1930s, the number of black students attending college had grown to

19,000, the vast majority of whom were now enrolled in public black colleges, fewer in private black colleges, and only a very small percentage attending predominantly white institutions. Perhaps the only bright spot in an otherwise dismal picture was the fact that by 1939, 119 doctoral degrees had been awarded to blacks by leading white colleges and universities. Most had previously attended black undergraduate schools, public or private.[99]

Lack of progress in the struggle for racial equality undoubtedly owed much to the indifference or antipathy demonstrated by the country's white majority. By 1900 many whites who in previous decades had lent strong leadership to the black cause had now withdrawn their support. Despite Jim Crow legislation throughout the South and widespread discrimination in the North, the tendency among many liberals was to believe that the worst was over, that all that could be done had in fact been accomplished. From now on, many believed, blacks themselves would have to exercise the initiative, that further progress would depend almost exclusively on the ambitions and abilities of African Americans working on their own.[100] More broadly, the tacit consensus seemed to be that a racially separate and unequal society was about all that could be hoped for once the more egregious symbols of a slave past had been eliminated. In vain, black leaders such as W. E. B. DuBois and others railed against the injustice of the system, protested against prejudice and bigotry, and appealed for assistance.

In a 1930 commencement address at Howard University, DuBois chastised black male students for their insularity and indifference. "Our [black] college man today is, on the average, a man untouched by real culture," he complained. "He deliberately surrenders to selfish and even silly ideals, swarming into semiprofessional athletics and Greek letter societies, and affecting to despise scholarship and the hard grind of study and research." DuBois urged his listeners to rouse themselves from complacency. "The greatest meetings of the Negro college year like those of the white college year," he noted disgustedly, "have become vulgar exhibitions of liquor, extravagance, and fur coats. We have in our colleges a growing mass of stupidity and indifference."[101] Historian and educator Carter G. Woodson argued in 1933 that the "miseducation" of black students had led to the emergence of a highly educated but reactionary bourgeoisie whose individual members had grown estranged from "the very people upon whom they must eventually count for carrying out a program of progress."

Many others sounded the same theme. In 1934 black poet Langston Hughes denounced what he characterized as the "cowards from the colleges" who had acceded to the general subjugation of their own people and failed to face up to the harsh realities of a racist society. Lafayette Harris, president of Philander

Smith College in Little Rock, Arkansas, castigated black students for their apathy and social irresponsibility. "Probably nothing gives one more concern than the frequently apparent fatalistic and nonchalant attitude of many a Negro college student and educated Negro," he alleged. "With him very little seems to matter except meals, sleep and folly. Community problems are never even recognized as existing." So far as he was concerned, the vast majority of black students he had observed knew "nothing of their less fortunate fellowmen."[102] If African Americans did not seize their own destiny in their own hands, black critics insisted, they would be implicated in consigning future generations of black youths to the same inequalities and injustices endured by generations past.

Black youths seeking a college education faced two unpalatable alternatives. If they chose to attend a black college, they were apt to find themselves in a small, struggling institution lacking the accreditation standing, status, resources, and support enjoyed by white schools. If admitted to a white school, they faced barriers built of fear and racial prejudice. They were outsiders. The proportion of black students on northern campuses rarely if ever reached more than 2 percent, and usually it never exceeded one half of 1 percent of a college's total enrollment. At Harvard in 1914 President Abbott Lawrence Lowell closed the freshmen dormitories to blacks, explaining later on that though the buildings originally had been built to reduce students' social segregation, he felt it was important not to offend whites by introducing a black within their midst. A rule was passed stipulating that no one was to be excluded "by reason of his color," but in the same breath it declared that "men of the white and colored races shall not be compelled to live and eat together."[103] The University of Chicago met the problem by allowing a majority of students in a dormitory to decide through formal vote whether a black would be allowed accommodations. Elsewhere, qualified blacks were freely admitted as students, but discouraged from interacting socially with their white peers.[104] At some integrated institutions, according to local newspaper accounts of the time, the specter of miscegenation loomed large in people's minds.

Edythe Hargrove, a black freshman enrolled at the University of Michigan in 1942, arrived knowing her social life would be practically nonexistent. "First of all," she later wrote, "being a Negro, I was exempt from all the sororities on the campus. I knew that I would never dress for a sorority 'rush' party, or become a pledge. I knew, also, that I would never dance at the [fraternity] houses." She recalled one occasion "when I was among three hundred girls at a social dance, and the instructor and one other girl ventured to drag me over the floor, when all of the other girls had run frantically clutching at each other to dance with everyone else but me, simply because I was a Negro, a brown conspicuous person. That was the time I went home and fell across the bed and cried, cried until I was exhausted. That was the time I hated a white college."[105]

Legal action was needed to tear down racial barriers. In 1934, to cite one instance, Donald Gaines Murray, a black graduate of Amherst College applied for admission to the University of Maryland's law school. Refused admission for reasons of color, he appealed through the courts and won the right to be admitted. Victory in the Murray case established the vital precedent for a similar suit filed shortly thereafter. Once again a black student, Lloyd Lionel Gaines, a graduate of Lincoln University in Jefferson City, Missouri, was denied admission to the law school at the University of Missouri in Columbia. The case ultimately made its way up to the United States Supreme Court. In December of 1938, the chief justices held that the state was bound to furnish "within its borders facilities for legal education substantially equal to those . . . afforded for persons of the white race." The Gaines decision fell far short of extending genuine equality of opportunity since, for all practical purposes, it still allowed separation at the expense of equality. Nevertheless, it marked an important advancement of sorts; and for blacks in the late 1930s, even small symbolic victories had to count for something.[106]

CURRICULAR INNOVATIONS AND EXPERIMENTS

The first four decades of the twentieth century witnessed a remarkable flurry of curricular reform and experimentation in American higher education. The supplanting of the more or less fixed, uniform classical curriculum of the mid-1800s with an elective system and the introduction of a vast array of utilitarian courses of study by century's end had marked an important shift in academic thought. Changes subsequently introduced between 1900 and 1940 or thereabouts in many colleges and universities, however, were equally notable. There was irony possibly in the fact that some were inspired by dissatisfaction over the results of just those innovations enacted in the period immediately preceding. In a sense, with the pendulum of academic opinion having swung far in one direction, it now began describing an arc leading in precisely the opposite direction. Specifically, the target of much criticism was the elective principle or system pioneered at Harvard under President Eliot.[107]

The original idea of allowing undergraduates to select their own patterns of study had been prompted by a desire to make academics more interesting and relevant. Instead of being compelled to submit to a single regimen of subjects selected for their supposed disciplinary value, students were allowed to pick and choose, based on their own individual interests, preferences, and career aspirations. But taken to its extreme, whatever gains had been registered by permitting unlimited personal choice were set off—or so it now seemed to many—by a concomitant loss of coherence and intellectual integration. The elective system, in a word, had borne bitter fruit. Its application had resulted in fragmentation, in courses taken in isolation from one another, the whole lacking any overall unity or design. Specialization of interest and professionalism, many warned, had advanced to the point where general education of a more liberal character was suffering neglect and might soon disappear entirely. The traditional concept of liberal learning had assumed a common humanity, a belief that despite differing abilities, interests, needs, and vocations, people should share in the accumulated wisdom of the past. Within society there were certain responsibilities—for example, those concerned with citizenship— which could be discharged only in the exercise of a type of understanding possessed by all. Perhaps the idea of a shared "culture" or *paideia* had been too narrowly circumscribed in the classical conception of liberal learning. Yet the social and personal needs it sought to satisfy were real. Some common learning, many argued, was indispensable. Or, alternatively, the problem now was to find a way to hold modern learning together.[108]

As reaction to the "smorgasbord" or "cafeteria" curricular approach set in, many former advocates of electives reversed themselves. It was time now, they claimed, to seek a better balance between elective anarchy and rigid curricular prescription.[109] Writing from retirement in 1908, Andrew D. White expressed his second thoughts on the matter. "There is certainly a widespread fear among many thinking men," he acknowledged, "that in our eagerness for . . . new things we have too much lost sight of certain valuable old things, the things in university education which used to be summed up under the word 'culture.'" Having come almost full circle in his own thinking, White urged, "I believe that, whatever else we do, we must [not only] make men and women skillful in the various professions and avocations of life, but . . . [also] cultivate and bring out the best in them as men and women."[110]

Even as academicians continued to make vague rhetorical obeisance to the demand for social utility, they returned to the theme of liberal culture as the proper aim of higher learning. At an alumni dinner in 1904 Princeton's Woodrow Wilson declared the university should be "not a place of special but of general education, not a place where a lad finds his profession, but a place *where he finds himself.*"[111] Wilson resolutely opposed the creeping vocationalism of academe. "If the chief end of man is to make a living, why, make a living any way you can," he advised. "But if ever has been shown to him in some quiet place where he has been withdrawn from the interests of the world, that the chief end of man is to keep his soul untouched from corrupt influences, and to see to it that his fellow-men hear the truth from his lips, he will never get that out of consciousness again."[112]

Defenders of liberal culture repeatedly returned to the same themes. Vocationalism had superseded liberal learning. Professionalism was rampant. Technocracy and amorality reigned supreme. Appreciation had been lost for that generous, broad learning that "liberated" the learner from ignorance, provincialism, and philistinism—perhaps almost in the biblical sense of "You shall know the truth, and the truth shall make you free." Institutions of higher learning stood in danger of losing their moorings, their guiding sense of identity. Higher education had surrendered to a trade-school mentality, and in process had substituted ignoble ends for those higher values that had once given it intellectual purpose and dignity. A. Lawrence Lowell was insistent on the point. Not all subjects are equally useful or liberal, he argued. "Any man who is to touch the world on many sides, or touch it strongly," he observed, "must have at his command as large a stock as possible of the world's store of knowledge and experience; and . . . bookkeeping does not furnish this in the same measure as literature, history, and science."[113]

The question, of course, was how to balance out professional and liberal aims. One practical expedient that eventually suggested itself was a "concentration and distribution" requirement. That is, as a sort of compromise, students would "concentrate" their studies in a given discipline or an assemblage of closely related disciplines (i.e, select an academic "major"). At the same time they were to "distribute" or spread their other choices across a range of subjects in the sciences, arts, and humanities. The academic major would afford "depth" of content; the distribution would safeguard "scope" or breadth of coverage. The former was the antidote to intellectual shallowness or dilettantism. The latter would serve as the corrective to narrow overspecialization. The chief virtue of such a balancing act, supporters argued, was that it mandated valuable exposure to fields of knowledge a student might otherwise seek to avoid. It promoted balance among many disciplines and different forms of knowledge. At the same time it allowed—and required—a student to acquire more than a passing acquaintance with one particular specialization. Admitting of almost endless variations, some such system of concentration and distribution ultimately came to be adopted at dozens, then hundreds of colleges and universities throughout the country.[114]

An alternative approach that placed still greater emphasis upon synoptic integration focused upon what came to be called "general education," "general studies," or "general culture." As early as 1902, John Dewey, among others, was suggesting that overcrowded courses of study lacked much internal logic or cohesion. They were, he claimed, deficient in terms of organizing structure or some larger architectonic frame of reference. He argued that a way was needed to integrate the parts, to pull them together holistically so that interrelations among their constituent elements would become more apparent.[115] No one seemed clear about what would suffice for the purpose, but Dewey's partial suggestion was for "a survey, at least, of the universe in its manifold phases from which a student can get an 'orientation' to the larger world."

Among the earliest to try out the idea was Alexander Meiklejohn, who while serving as dean and professor of philosophy at Brown in the years before World War I, developed an undergraduate survey course in 1914 entitled "Social and Economic Institutions." Ten years later he was advocating two different types of general survey courses, one for first-year students and another as a "capstone" experience for fourth-year students.[116] The latter served as the prototype for senior symposia introduced in 1924 at Reed College in Oregon. Their stated purpose, it was announced, was to assist students in achieving a synthesis of the multiple historical, literary, and scientific forces shaping contemporary society. Earlier, Reed had been among the first to require a qualifying examination prior to the senior year as well as the preparation and oral defense of a senior thesis. Symbolizing Reed's commitment to academics was its virtual elimination of all extracurricular activities.

In 1928 Alexander Meiklejohn moved to the University of Wisconsin where he was instrumental in establishing a new, experimental two-year college. Briefly, its underlying theme was that students enrolled would devote their entire first year to the study of Greek and Roman civilization, utilizing a variety of disciplinary perspectives—historical, literary, economic, social, and cultural. Classes were to be kept small and informal. In the second year, students would turn their attention to an intensive analysis of modern civilization, once again as illuminated from an interdisciplinary vantage point. Throughout, the effort would be to trace connections and relationships among many different disciplinary prisms. In practice what ensued amounted to a return to a prescribed course of study, with few variations or options to accommodate students' individual interests.

By far the most celebrated approach to general education was that begun by John Erskine at Columbia University in 1919 when his popular "war issues" course, now reworked and revised as "Introduction to Contemporary Civilization," was required of all entering freshmen.[117] The Columbia course was the first of several offered that emphasized historical social development through the reading and discussion of primary sources. "There is a certain minimum of . . . [the Western] intellectual and spiritual tradition that a man must experience and understand if he is to be called educated," a faculty prospectus explained. By 1936 Columbia was also offering an integrative humanities sequence, then a survey of the sciences. Before long, the Columbia and Reed prototypes were being tried out on scores of other campuses. Extensive experimentation followed as colleges and universities attempted to provide their students with the broad outlines of human knowledge through various synoptic surveys and introductory overviews of the disciplines.[118] Especially noteworthy were survey courses developed at Dartmouth in the 1920s, and a social ethics course started at the University of Utah around 1930 treating "the ethical foundations of private and public action in human relations."

Even as general survey courses came into vogue, however, they too were severely criticized. Charges of shallowness, of superficiality, and lack of depth were frequent. A common complaint was that introductory courses treated those enrolled in them as prospective majors in the disciplines represented, thereby frustrating the original intent of providing a broad intellectual perspective. Others faulted surveys for their apparent lack of structure. Alexander Meiklejohn himself, in criticizing the typical survey course, described it as "a little music, a taste of philosophy, a glimpse into history, some practice in the technique of the laboratory, a thrill or two in the appreciation of poetry."[119] Quite obviously, the discovery or invention of a way of bringing knowledge into some kind of unity was a difficult task, one not easily achieved by any single method. Much of the curricular history of higher learning in America between the 1920s and the 1940s in fact turned on the issue of how colleges and universities attempted to avoid the intellectual anarchy of excessive specialization. Gradually, however, it became established policy to give over most or all of the first two years of the collegiate experience to general education. The most striking feature of the various schemes devised was their diversity of approach. Breadth of intellectual experience was a common theme, but otherwise no uniform patterns emerged.

Some institutions retained the emphasis upon "survey" or "orientation" courses. Others, like Princeton, tried out a preceptorial plan of instruction, taking the approach that academic integration was best achieved by having students work closely with supervisory preceptors in highly individualized study programs. At Harvard under President Lowell the emphasis was upon general examinations and the distinction introduced between "honors" and "pass" courses. At Swarthmore in the early 1920s under Frank Aydelotte, experiments were begun with special colloquia, honors instruction separate from the regular course of instruction, and general final examinations conducted entirely by external examiners. At Yale and elsewhere, efforts were made to revive the sense of intimacy and individualized attention supplied by special "houses" or student "colleges." At Hiram College in Ohio, beginning in 1934, a pattern of intensive study of one subject at a time, to the exclusion of all others, was inaugurated. Arthur E. Morgan at Antioch College in 1921 inspired a revival of the work-study idea, this time as a five-year program combining liberal education, social training, and real-life work aimed at bringing students face to face with "practical realities in all their stubborn complexity." Experimental progressive colleges, such as Black Mountain in North Carolina and women's schools such as Sarah Lawrence and

Bennington, mounted Deweyan programs emphasizing extramural work requirements, interdisciplinary courses, individualized studies aimed at addressing current social issues and problems, and independent study.[120]

If concern for meeting the needs of exceptionally talented learners was the preoccupation of northeastern Ivy League schools, at the University of Minnesota in 1930 Dean J. B. Johnston was claiming that "one of the functions of the freshman and sophomore years is to bring to a graceful end the habit of going to school on the part of those who can learn lessons fairly well and can never do anything more." His notion that a democratic college should provide for "graceful failure" contributed to the planning of a General College, which opened in 1932 for lower-quality or unmotivated students judged unlikely to complete a full four-year program.[121] The first year, over a thousand students of doubtful academic potential were enrolled. They were set to work in courses bearing such titles as How to Study, Home Furnishings, Earth and Man, and Foods and Nutrition. No foreign languages were taught, no laboratory courses, no advanced technical specializations. Attesting to the lower-middle-class orientation of the College was the fact that by 1939 fully one-fifth of all students enrolled were listed as the offspring of working-class immigrants. The controlling theme in all respects was one of social adjustment and practical living skills for nontraditional students. Rigorous academic study, by design and intent, had no place in Minnesota's General College.

GREAT BOOKS AND THE CHICAGO PLAN

Surely one of the most remarkable and controversial curricular experiments undertaken by a major university was that launched in 1930 at the University of Chicago under the leadership of Chancellor Robert Maynard Hutchins.[122] Running counter to all prevailing trends, his was a bold initiative aimed at nothing less than a revival of the "classical" liberal-arts tradition. Accompanying faculty approval for the creation of an autonomous undergraduate college unit was its endorsement of a new required curriculum. It was intended to avoid the atomization of an elective system while at the same time promoting general learning on a scale impossible to attain through survey courses alone. The course of study was built up around the reading and discussion of original sources, the so-called "Great Books" of Western civilization. Henceforth, it was announced, general education at Chicago would mean the study "of the greatest books of the Western world and the arts of reading, writing, thinking, and speaking, together with mathematics." The hope expressed was that a curriculum had been framed that would address all of the elements of humanity's common nature.

The course of study prescribed was both uniform and demanding. It assumed the form of a series of one-year tightly packed, interdisciplinary survey courses taught through lectures and supplemented by frequent small-group discussions. Course credits and tests were dispensed with altogether. Course attendance was voluntary, though students were required to prepare themselves for comprehensive examinations in English composition, humanities, social sciences, and the physical and biological sciences. Minimal proficiency in a foreign language also was required. Overall, the curriculum purported to include all subject matter indispensable to every educated person, regardless of his or her eventual calling or future professional specialization. Applicants could submit themselves for testing whenever they felt prepared. Only when all examinations had been passed successfully were students permitted to extend their studies at an upper-divisional level or in another college of the University. Under Hutchins's energetic leadership, the so-called Chicago Plan became the most talked-about innovation in American higher education yet undertaken in the twentieth century.[123]

In a series of essays, articles, and books, Hutchins spelled out the educational philosophy inspiring what he was attempting to accomplish at Chicago. Most widely read among his many works was a collection of manifesto-like addresses delivered at the Storr Lectures at Yale and published in 1936 as *The Higher Learning in America*. There he gave trenchant expression to a point of view aptly characterized much later on by historian Frederick Rudolph (*The American College and University*, 1962) as "a kind of strange and wonderful throwback to Jeremiah Day and the Yale Report of 1828."[124]

Looking out over the rest of American higher education, Hutchins professed to find only rampant confusion, capitulation to materialism and consumerism, and craven institutions distinguished chiefly for their unabashed vocationalism and unprincipled opportunism. "Love of money," he alleged, had had the practical effect of creating a "service-station" university. Scrambling to be all things to all people, he claimed, the typical university had bent its energies to flattering the spirit of the age and accommodating to popular demands of the basest sort. He excoriated the university's tendency to attempt to frame responses to each and every exigency in the name of social utility. In its headlong rush to meet miscellaneous, immediate low-level needs of every sort and kind, Hutchins judged, curricula had proliferated mindlessly. Worse yet, the university had shown itself willing to offer instruction to practically any clientele whatsoever. Once begun, the process of social accommodation promised to continue with no end in sight. More and more, the service-station university was framing its policies to suit those who paid the bills—students, private donors, and state legislatures. The typical academic institution, Hutchins insisted, was neither free nor independent, for it was always obliged to pursue money to support its multitudinous tasks.[125]

Confusion over the meaning of democracy, Hutchins went on to say, had given rise to the mistaken notion that everyone was entitled to the same amount of education. In fact, he argued, the democratic imperative, rightly understood, mandated only that everyone be extended an opportunity to profit from higher learning. Higher education *should* be elitist, in the meritocratic sense of being reserved exclusively for those best able to profit from it, for those of sufficient interest and ability to be capable of sustaining serious intellectual endeavor. As for the peculiar American passion for credentials, the factor mainly responsible for so many students flocking to campuses, Hutchins felt it might be alleviated by conferring a baccalaureate degree upon every citizen at birth. Only then would colleges and universities be left free to educate those few people genuinely interested in learning.

Contemporary society, Hutchins felt, was confused in its assumption that education should serve a vocational purpose. The true aim of the university, he argued at some length, should be the disinterested pursuit of truth for its own sake. "Every group in the community that is well enough organized to have an audible voice wants the university to spare it the necessity of training its own recruits," he observed. "They want to get from the university a product as nearly finished as possible." The problem as he saw it was that universities had freely acceded to that pressure. The consequence, he announced prophetically, would be that soon everyone would be clamoring for admission to academe "for the purpose of being trained for something."[126]

Hutchins conceded the need for job training. Nevertheless, he felt the university was a poor place to attempt direct instruction for employment. "Turning professional schools into vocational schools degrades the universities and does not elevate the professions," he insisted. The inherent ambiguity in any training program is how to secure immediate technical proficiency, and at the same time some larger understanding of general principles underlying a craft or profession. As he put it, "My contention is that the tricks of the trade cannot be learned in a university, and that if they can be they should not be. They cannot be learned in a university because they get out of date and new tricks take their place, because the teachers get out of date and cannot keep up with current tricks, and because tricks can be learned only in the actual situation in which they can be employed."[127] What the university should concentrate on, as Hutchins saw it, was promoting the broad understanding that constitutes the basis or foundation for specific skills and places their application in some intelligible context.

Hutchins's decidedly unfashionable prescription was for a forthright return to "a common intellectual training." Without it, he asserted, a university would remain a series of disparate academic units lacking any common understanding, language, or shared sense of purpose. More specifically, what was needed, in his view, was a "common stock of fundamental ideas" to overcome the "disunity, discord, and disorder" he believed had overtaken the educational system. In apparent defiance of a hundred years of experience, he asserted: "Education implies teaching. Teaching implies knowledge. Knowledge is truth. The truth is everywhere the same. Hence education should be everywhere the same." Education rightly understood should therefore address "the cultivation of the intellect" and devote itself to the single-minded pursuit of intellectual virtues: "The heart of any course of study designed for the whole people will be . . . the same at any time, in any place, under any political, social, or economic conditions."[128]

For Hutchins, as for Mortimer Adler, Mark Van Doren, Jacques Barzun, Irving Babbitt, Gilbert Highet, and many others, the "permanent studies" that best reflected a common human nature were those furnished through the Great Books—those works which through the centuries had attained the status of "classics" in all major fields of knowledge. A truly great book, Hutchins explained, is one that has survived the test of time, that is always contemporary and not merely of antiquarian interest, for its fundamental appeal is timeless and independent of any particular set of economic, social, or political circumstances. It endures long after lesser works have been forgotten. A great book is readable by almost everyone. It speaks to universal themes that always occupy thinking persons. Most important, a great book, as Hutchins described it, is one capable of helping to develop standards of taste and criticism conducive to rational thought and reflective action.

Hutchins did not foresee any great inclination on the part of the American public to embrace his ideas. Quite the contrary, he felt they would be exceedingly unpopular though no less valid. A quarter century later, long after he had departed from the University of Chicago, his views remained unchanged. In the preface to a later reissue of his *Higher Learning,* he saw the same tendencies at work he had warned against in 1936. "One of the easiest things in the world," he remarked acidly, "is to assemble a list of hilarious courses offered in the colleges and universities of the United States. Such courses reflect the total lack of coherent, rational purpose in these institutions."[129] In his judgment, if institutions of higher learning had ever given the nation intellectual leadership, any claim of their continuing to do so had long since lost credibility. Educational standards had collapsed entirely. The triumph of specialization, vocationalism and triviality, as he assessed the situation, was well-nigh complete.

At least some of the elements of the Chicago Plan were replicated in experimental colleges and the honors programs of other institutions throughout the country in the late 1930s. The creation of Monteil College at Wayne State University, for example, was one of the first of several attempts to adapt Hutchins's ideas. Better known was the program built up by Stringfellow Barr and Scott Buchanan at St. John's College in Annapolis, Maryland, and later at a sister campus in Santa Fe, New Mexico. Critics assailed all such initiatives as undemocratic, outmoded, and utterly out of touch with modern needs. Defenders, for their part, continued to assert the worth and utility of an education based on a fixed system of sources. Although approaches to general learning and liberal culture organized around Great Books would always represent a minor motif in American higher education, they too found a place within the array of curricular experiments undertaken by colleges and universities.[130]

TWO-YEAR COLLEGES

Early in the century, echoing an often-repeated assertion, David Starr Jordan in 1903 predicted that "as time goes on the college will disappear, in fact, if not in name. The best will become universities, the others will return to their place as academies."[131] One of several factors seeming to confirm Jordan's judgment was the frequency with which many collegiate institutions were striving to turn themselves into universities by expanding their graduate courses of instruction. For a time it appeared that any college that did not aspire to university status or was not taking steps to become one was somehow lacking in ambition and self respect. Another factor at work was the expectation that secondary high schools would steadily improve, to the point ultimately where they would be more comparable to German *gymnasia* in feeding students directly into university-level professional preparatory programs. In fact, it had long been customary for graduates of the better private secondary academies and a few exemplary public high schools to be admitted as college sophomores, thus allowing them to complete the undergraduate program in three years. With secondary schools pushing up from below and university professional schools above demanding earlier specialized training, colleges felt squeezed between the two. Many wondered whether the four-year college would have any role at all to play in the future if contemporary trends continued. More than once suggestions were advanced that undergraduate education, if it survived at all, should be compressed into three or possibly only two years. Among those urging abolition of the collegiate four-year tradition was Chicago's William Rainey Harper, who spoke scornfully of the "four-year fetish" associated with undergraduate colleges.[132]

Some academic leaders felt the need for a better compromise.[133] As a professor at Brown expressed it in 1908, "The problem that lies before all the stronger institutions is to mingle, in due proportion, the best from the old

English-American college with the best from the modern German university."
Free-standing private colleges that elected not to try to become universities
were resolved to go their own way. They would concentrate on liberal learning and culture, or trust to a mix of traditional liberal-arts and a limited number of undergraduate pre-professional preparatory programs to attract
students. Having steeped themselves in general learning first, their graduates
would then be free to apply to larger universities for whatever additional professional training they needed. Less clear was the status of undergraduate colleges *within* universities. In principle, the idea of having a graduate school
perched upon an undergraduate college was widely supported. The more
immediate question as the century wore on was whether it was possible to sustain and nurture liberal studies within a larger environment aggressively dedicated to professional specialization. Some institutions experimented with a
complete separation of undergraduate and graduate education. More common
by far were efforts to organize undergraduate and graduate faculties as a single
body, exercising unified control over all degree programs from the baccalaureate to the doctorate. Taking a supposed "middle" route were schools
where the undergraduate college was partitioned into lower and upper divisions. In still other cases, undergraduate programs were simply appended
beneath the graduate programs offered through the university's constituent
professional schools.

Meanwhile, pressed in the name of democratic opportunity to relax admission requirements and to accept students in ever increasing numbers, by the
early 1920s some public institutions were beginning to experience severe
problems of overcrowding. Professor Norman Foerster of North Carolina
spoke for many in protesting what he felt was the resultant decline in academic standards. "If higher education is to deserve the name," he wrote, "it cannot be brought within the reach of the ineducable and the passively educable."
Similarly, a call to allow any high school graduate admission to the state university was dismissed by one professor at Ohio State as "arrant sentimental-
ity."[134] Gradually the lines of disagreement hardened. On one side were those
who supported the impulse toward almost unlimited growth, even if it meant
a certain compromising of academic standards. On the other were those who
felt a need to preserve some greater measure of elitism and academic excellence in public higher education, even if it meant turning students away.

An alternative to four-year public education came with the emergence of the
so-called junior college.[135] In 1918 there already were 85 such institutions in
existence, with a combined enrollment of 4,500 students, representing slightly
less than 2 percent of all undergraduates. Of the 85, located in nineteen different states, well over half were concentrated in the five states of California,

Missouri, Virginia, Texas, and Illinois. (There were none located east of Michigan or north of Kentucky and North Carolina.)[136] By the mid-1920s their number had increased to 196, with a tenfold increase in enrollment. By 1938, junior-college enrollments had tripled again, accounting for an even larger share of the 18 percent of all college students enrolled nationwide. Catering to the needs of lower-class students who lacked the means or desire to embark upon a four-year curriculum directly from high school, or to those who sought relatively inexpensive instruction within commuting distance, public two-year institutions had obviously found their own special niche within American higher education. Without them, American higher education could scarcely have accommodated the phenomenal increase in college enrollments registered between 1920 and 1940.[137]

Initially, many two-year schools saw themselves preeminently as "feeders" to the more academically demanding and more prestigious four-year colleges and universities. The junior college curriculum, under this view, simply represented the first half of the total course of study students completed before transferring to a four-year institution to complete the bachelor's degree. Many continued long afterwards to view the junior college as a preparatory step to university life and a professional career. That perception was not lost upon leaders of liberal-arts colleges, some of whom professed to find in the two-year newcomers a substantial threat to the existence of their own four-year institutions. But by the late 1920s and early 1930s the trend was for public junior colleges to begin thinking of themselves more as terminal institutions where students of limited means (and allegedly more limited abilities or aspirations) might prepare themselves for the skilled trades and semiprofessions. President A. Lawrence Lowell of Harvard professed satisfaction with the proliferation of two-year schools because, as he admitted quite frankly, "One of the merits of these new institutions will be [the] keeping out of college, rather than leading into it, [of] young people who have no taste for higher education."[138] Lauded as instruments of social utility and efficiency, praised for giving concrete expression to the democratic impulse to offer learning for everyone, junior colleges continued to flourish throughout the Depression years, even when larger public universities languished for lack of adequate funding from state legislatures.[139]

With the wisdom of historical hindsight, it is easier to see the somewhat ambiguous and paradoxical role two-year institutions came to play in higher education. Their contribution was to satisfy the precept that in a democracy everyone is entitled to access to higher education. Two-year schools were perceived to be useful not only because they contributed to the diffusion of higher learning within society, but also because they promised to satisfy the needs of those of lesser means and ability. Insofar as the door was left open for deserving two-year graduates to move onward into a four-year institution, junior colleges gave the appearance of enhancing rather than limiting social mobility. To the extent they became terminal institutions, they helped satisfy the equally important need to educate a trained work force, while simultaneously leaving to four-year institutions the opportunity to supply credentials for tomorrow's professionals and leaders in society.[140]

7

Postwar Higher Learning in America

ACADEMIC WITCH HUNTS

On the eve of World War II, when popular fear of "subversives" and "nonconformists" of all stripes was running strong, the mood of depression-era America was definitely not one congenial to academic freedom. Illustrative of the climate of the times was the formation in 1940 of the Rapp-Coudert Committee of the New York State legislature, whose self-appointed task it was to seek out and expose suspected "subversives" within the municipal college system of New York City (now the City University of New York, CUNY).[1] It was, to say the least, an inopportune moment for the College of the City of New York to extend an offer of a professorship to the distinguished but controversial British mathematician and logician Bertrand Russell, then on temporary assignment at UCLA.

No sooner had Russell accepted the post than a public outcry promptly broke out, beginning with a suit brought by one student's mother against the municipality for having offered employment to someone described as "lecherous, libidinous, lustful . . . erotomaniac [sic], aphrodisiac, irreverent, narrow-minded, untruthful, and bereft of moral fibre."[2] Episcopalian Bishop William T. Manning joined in with a denunciation of Russell as a "recognized propagandist against both religion and morality" who allegedly defended adultery.[3]

Other prominent church leaders and politicians echoed their horror at the appointment of an atheist advocate of skepticism and free love. Only the student body and some faculty members spoke out on Russell's behalf. One was Albert Einstein, who, with tongue only partly in cheek, wrote that "great spirits always face violent opposition from authorities."

John E. McGeehan, presiding judge of the New York Supreme Court, in ruling against Russell's appointment, avowed that he was unprepared to allow a man like Russell to occupy a "chair of indecency." Someone whose books promulgated "immoral and salacious doctrines," the justice declared, was wholly unqualified for an academic post.[4] As a sort of codicil to the entire unhappy incident, a subsequent edition of Russell's *An Inquiry into Meaning and Truth* included a new title page listing his various honors and teaching positions. It concluded: "Judiciously pronounced unworthy to be Professor of Philosophy at the College of the City of New York (1940)." No one could have been more pleased, Russell reportedly told friends.

If there was something tragicomic and farcical about Russell's dismissal, the same could not be said of the more than forty other professors who were fired or whose contracts were not renewed in the year 1940, either because they were alleged to be communists, or because they refused to divulge their political beliefs. Red-baiting subsided briefly during the war years, in no small measure because the United States and the Soviet Union were officially allied in the struggle to defeat the Nazi menace. But in the immediate postwar period, as superpower rivalries intensified and the wartime alliance gave way to global confrontation and animosity, political witch hunts for assorted domestic communists, "statists," "collectivists," "socialists," "fellow travelers" and "pinks" resumed nationwide with renewed vigor and enthusiasm.[5] The infamous House Committee on Un-American Activities, set up in 1938 as an ad-hoc investigative body under the chairmanship of Martin Dies, was now reconstituted in 1945 as a standing body and set loose to wage a campaign of intimidation and harassment of anyone whose political sympathies were pronounced suspect.

The committee's blatant disregard for judicial procedures, its publicizing of charges without adducing proof of their veracity, its presumption of guilt until innocence was proven, and the group's tendency to resort to the principle of guilt by association set a notorious example that other propagandist organizations were all too ready to emulate. As Robert Maynard Hutchins observed, testifying in 1949 before the Illinois Seditious Activities Investigation Committee, "The miasma of thought control that is now spreading over this country is the greatest menace to the United States since Hitler."

As cold war hysteria deepened, apprehension over the supposedly monolithic, worldwide communist menace only increased. Even as the Soviet state proceeded to swallow up eastern Europe and turn its nations into client states, while China fell under Maoist control, the fear at home was that communist agents and their sympathizers were busy burrowing into the very foundations of American life itself, insinuating themselves into government, business and industry, and the schools. Because conventional wisdom held that any kind of nonconformism or liberalism was dangerously akin to communism, it followed, according to the conservative line of thought, that any attack on proponents of such ideas registered a blow against communism itself. Protestations that essential constitutional guarantees of freedom were being trampled upon in the process typically met with official expressions of derision and scorn. Throughout the late 1940s and into the 1950s, purges continued: libraries were searched for subversive texts; suppressive controls were enacted by municipal and state authorities; loyalty oaths enjoyed tremendous popular support; and successive waves of intolerance swept the land.

Academics especially were scrutinized for leftist tendencies.[6] Estimates from some quarters of the numbers of "subversives," broadly defined, lurking within academe ran as high as 20 and 30 percent of the professorate; and institutions of higher learning were accordingly singled out for close surveillance. The Senate's Judiciary Committee on Internal Security (the McCarren Committee) made national headlines when it announced it would spare no effort to root out leftist influences in higher education and expose the "nests of communists" presumably at work subverting the nation's innocent, unsuspecting youth.[7] McCarren's report to the Senate Judiciary Committee on January 2, 1952, as a case in point, charged with great fervor but no supporting evidence, "The Communist Party of the United States has put forth every effort to infiltrate the teaching profession of this country. In this endeavor to corrupt the teachers of youth, the agents of the Kremlin have been remarkably successful, especially among the professors in our colleges and universities." Senator McCarren continued, "In these few years the Communist Party has enlisted the support of at least 3,500 professors—many of them as dues-paying members, many others as fellow travelers, some as out-and-out espionage agents, some as adherents of the party line in varying degrees, and some as the unwitting dupes of subversion."[8]

Senator Joseph McCarthy of Wisconsin, chair of the Senate Committee on Government Operations, proposed that the government redouble its efforts not just to clear the groves of academe of all "communists" but of suspected "communist thinkers" as well. He predicted that this undertaking would prove to be "the most unpopular, the most unpleasant task anyone can do . . . because the minute you do that all hell breaks loose. From coast to coast you hear the screaming of interference with academic freedom." Challenged to defend his committee from charges that it was running roughshod over academic liberties, he responded contemptuously, "Academic freedom means their right to force you [the American citizen] to hire them to teach your children philosophy in which you do not believe." The National Council on American Education, a rightist organization headed by Allen Zoll, went even further. Dedicated to "the eradication of Marxism and collectivism from . . . colleges," the Council charged that "academic freedom is the major Communist party line for American higher education." Comparable sentiments were voiced by conservative columnist William F. Buckley who joined in with criticisms of what he called "the superstitions of academic freedom."[9]

Not all of the attacks upon academic freedom came from without. A 1949 National Education Association resolution drawn up by Harvard President James Bryant Conant, for example, enunciated the principle that membership in the Communist party "and the accompanying surrender of intellectual integrity, render an individual unfit to discharge the duties of a teacher in this country."[10] Considerations of academic freedom were not to be allowed to thwart efforts to get rid of subversives. The Reverend Hunter Guthrie, S.J., in his inaugural address as president of Georgetown University, was quoted in the *Georgetown Journal* of October 1950 as deriding "the sacred fetish of academic freedom" for much the same reasons. "This," he declared, "is the soft underbelly of our American way of life, and the sooner it is armor-plated by some sensible limitation, the sooner will the future of this nation be secured from fatal consequences."

The AAUP had taken as its position that "so long as the Communist party in the United States is a legal political party, affiliation with that party in and of itself should not be regarded as a justifiable reason for exclusion from the academic profession."[11] The opposing view, one shared widely both within academe and without, however, was that anyone who was a communist was, of necessity, an intellectual automaton—that is, the individual had renounced his or her own intellectual liberty and was no longer qualified to seek out or to impart knowledge in an unbiased manner. Few believed that communist teachers openly propagandized in their classes or were successfully indoctrinating students in any overt way. But, so the argument proceeded, if someone was ideologically subservient to the party line, and committed to a movement that would extinguish all freedom if allowed to do so, the communist could not be said to be a free individual.[12] Therefore he or she should be barred from teaching. (The possibility that one might join the Communist party because he or she held certain beliefs, rather than that one hewed to an ideology because Communist party discipline demanded it does not appear to have been given much credence.)

By the early 1950s, so prevalent and entrenched was the belief within the academic community that a Marxist could not perform any role other than that of party hack that even when professors were fired for suspected but unproven communist sympathies, the resulting outcry was often muted. Faced with overwhelming pressures to "clean house," many colleges and universities responded with alacrity. State colleges and universities tended to be the most repressive, firing anyone found guilty of lack of candor about his or her political loyalties and convictions.[13] At Princeton, Michigan, Rutgers, Washington, and scores of other institutions, more than a few professors lost their jobs.

Many academics, when brought before some investigative body to be grilled over their political loyalties, as a matter of principle had invoked their fifth-amendment right of protection against self-incrimination. Senator McCarthy seized upon their actions as confirming evidence of guilt, declaring confidently that "a witness's refusal to answer whether or not he is or is not communist on the ground that his answer would tend to incriminate him is the most positive proof obtainable that the witness is a communist." University officials tended to agree. Hence, either membership in an unpopular but nonetheless legal political organization or refusal to confirm or deny the affiliation came to be viewed as adequate grounds for dismissal.

Not until well into the decade of the fifties, when Senator McCarthy's sweeping allegations of subversion began to lose credibility, did pressures start to subside. But in the aftermath of the red-baiting of the postwar period, literally hundreds of academic reputations had been tarnished, with many careers sidetracked or utterly destroyed. It was by any accounting an unhappy and tragic opening chapter in the history of American higher education at the midpoint of the twentieth century.[14]

CHANGING GROWTH PATTERNS

Colleges and universities had showed remarkable growth throughout the first half of the 1900s, with enrollments expanding exponentially well beyond the increase in the nation's population for the same fifty-year period.[15] At the end of the 1899–1900 academic year, for example, institutions of higher education collectively awarded a total of about 29,000 degrees; for the 1949–50 academic year, the comparable figure had risen to nearly half a million. Numbers of students enrolled in postsecondary education doubled about every fifteen years or so, as did the number of faculty employed in colleges and universities. Graduate education grew even faster, with the number of earned Ph.D.'s doubling every eleven years. Over two-thirds of those awarded doctorates entered academe.[16]

Postsecondary education continued to expand throughout the second half of the century.[17] By 1947, two years after the end of World War II, some 2.3

million students were enrolled in over 1,800 four-year and two-year institutions; and enrollments were almost evenly divided between public and private colleges or universities.[18] Rapid and constant growth in the nation's higher-education system continued for more than a decade thereafter, from 1947 to around 1962. Much of the growth was a function of rising levels of educational persistence at all levels: a steady increase in the proportion of the population completing high school; the expanding proportion of high-school graduates entering college; and a rise in the percentage of college graduates who continued their studies at the post-baccalaureate level.

The same trends held in succeeding decades, though at slightly reduced rates, with the partial exception of figures showing the percentage of high-school graduates entering college going up steadily.[19] In 1960, for example, about 40 percent of all secondary seniors were being accepted into college; by 1970 the percentage rose to 52 percent; a slight decline to 51 percent was registered in 1980; and the percentage resumed its upward march, reaching 61 percent by 1991. Nevertheless, other enrollment trends had begun to flatten out slightly, and with slower rates of increase, indications appeared to point to the possibility that a "saturation point" was being approached. Thus, the *rate* of the proportional increase of graduating seniors admitted to college appeared to be stabilizing; and the percentage increase (though not the absolute total) of bachelor's-degree holders seeking admission to graduate school failed to keep pace with earlier annual increases common prior to the early sixties.

College enrollments mounted steadily throughout the fifties. In the sixties, expansion continued as before, reflecting the changing demographic characteristics of the college-attending segment of the national population. Specifically, much of the enrollment increase of the period reflected a rise in the absolute numbers of the college-age cohort of the population, those between the ages of 18 and 21, resulting from the "baby boom" of the immediate postwar period. Those born in the latter half of the forties were now of college age in the sixties and had begun to flood the nation's college campuses. A second population surge in the late fifties and early sixties would produce yet another burst of enrollments in the late seventies, peaking in the early eighties.

Much of the enrollment growth that occurred between the seventies and the nineties was absorbed by public institutions at the expense of comparable increases in private enrollments. In 1970, student collegiate registrations stood at 8.5 million, 6.2 million of which were in four-year institutions and 2.3 million in two-year colleges. Whereas 2.1 million were attending private schools, fully 6.4 million out of the 8.5 million total were registered in public colleges and universities. In 1980, 7.5 million were enrolled in four-year schools and 4.5 million in two-year colleges. The greatest increase occurred in public institutions, which had reached 3 million since 1970, with much slower growth apparent in private-school enrollments, amounting to no more than half a million. Out of an estimated 12.5 to 12.6 million students enrolled in higher education in 1990, fully 10.5 million were in public institutions, together with about 3 million in private colleges, a net increase of about 400,000 since 1980. In terms of enrollment percentages and rates of increase, public colleges and universities expanded faster than did private institutions between 1970 and 1990.

There was an appreciable increase also in the number of postsecondary institutions between 1970 and 1990. In 1970 there were 2,556 colleges and universities operating (1,665 four-year and 891 two-year schools); in 1980, out of a total of 3,231 postsecondary institutions, 1,957 were four-year schools and 1,274 were two-year institutions. By 1982 there were an estimated 7.7 million students enrolled in four-year colleges and universities, and another 4.5 million in two-year colleges; over a million graduate students; and 5.1 million part-time students scattered among various categories of institutions of higher learning. Two-year colleges numbered 1,311; and there were 2,029 four-year institutions; together they employed some 865,000 instructors of various ranks. Total expenditures for higher education were calculated at around $95 billion annually. About 75 percent or more of all undergraduate students were attending large public universities or state colleges, which collectively represented less than one-quarter of the number of institutions enrolling undergraduate students. A substantial portion of that same 75 percent was concentrated in some 280 state-supported colleges or universities.

By 1986, enrollments in roughly 3,200 institutions were running around 12.3 million, with fully 77 percent of all students to be found in public institutions. All colleges combined were awarding annually about three and a half times the numbers of degrees conferred in the late 1940s. By 1990 there were over 2,100 public colleges or universities in existence in the United States, including some 900 public community colleges. The remainder, about 1,400, were private colleges.

The mix of factors responsible for student enrollment increases changed over time. From the mid-seventies onward, an increase in the number of women attending college contributed materially to growth, as did the increasing percentage of blacks and other minorities seeking post-secondary education. The balance between undergraduate and graduate education shifted. More significant still was a marked rise in numbers of part-time students. Most dramatic of all was the change in the age composition of the college student population, with ever increasing numbers of older, so-called "nontraditional" collegians attending.

According to figures released in 1992 by the National Center for Educational Statistics, U.S. Department of Education, there were an estimated 14.2 million students enrolled in American colleges the year previously. Between 1978 and 1983 the figure had risen from around 11.5 million to 12.4 million, an increase of 11 percent over the five-year period. In 1984 and 1985, higher education enrollments actually dropped slightly, then increased from an estimated 12.3 to 12.4 million to the 1991 total, representing an increase of about 13 percent since 1986. Enrollments in public institutions had grown from around 8.8 million in 1978 to an estimated 11 million in 1991, an increase of 26 percent.

Public enrollments were expected to increase to between 11.8 and 13 million by the year 2003, with the most probable percentage increase projected to be about 14 percent. Similarly, enrollments in private colleges reportedly grew from around 2.5 million in 1978 to 3.1 million in 1991, also representing an increase of 26 percent. Expectations were that the figures would range between 3.3 to 3.7 million shortly after the turn of the next century, amounting in all likelihood to a 14 percent increase. Total combined student enrollments in public and private institutions were expected to have reached between 15.1 and 16.7 million by the year 2003.

Graduate enrollments since 1978 had gone up at a faster rate than that for undergraduate enrollments; and some signs pointed to a continuation of the trend into the twenty-first century. Undergraduate enrollments went from 9.7 million in the late seventies to an estimated 12.2 million by 1991, an increase of 26 percent. Government projections foresaw a rise to almost 14 million within the first three years of the 2000s, a projected increment of 14 percent. Graduate enrollments between 1978 and 1991 had risen from 1.3 million to 1.7 million, a 30 percent increase; and projections called for a probable increase by at least 10 percent, to around 1.9 million by 2003. Other independent projections held that graduate enrollments might increase much faster.

There were reportedly 4.6 million part-time students attending college in 1978, according to the U.S. Department of Education. Owing to higher costs, among other factors, the percentage of those attending on a part-time basis rose to 6.1 million in 1991, an annual increase of 2.3 percent, making for a 34 percent increase overall between 1978 and 1991. Among those attending two-year community colleges especially, undergraduate enrollments were dominated by part-time students. Whereas the percentage of all part-time undergraduates went up significantly, including those registered at both two-year and four-year schools, expanding numbers of part-time graduate students fueled an even greater share of the increases in graduate enrollments typical of the eighties and early nineties, especially at four-year public institutions.

Continuing a trend that had begun long before 1950, women began to out-number men among those attending American colleges and universities.[20] There were an estimated 5.6 million women on campuses in 1978; by 1991 their numbers had increased to an estimated 7.8 million, growing at a yearly rate of 2.5 percent, or by 38 percent over the five-year period. Between 1970 and 1991, the number of women in college had actually more than doubled, with the largest increases in attendance registered by white females (followed by the next highest percentage increase among blacks of both sexes). Under-graduate women in 1989, for example, received almost 53 percent of all the baccalaureate degrees awarded that year. In 1973, according to figures compiled by the National Research Council, women were awarded around 18 per-cent of all doctorates conferred. A decade later the total had increased to around 21 percent; ten years later it stood at 23 percent. The projected enroll-ment increase for women was between 8.3 and 9.1 million by the year 2003, a rise of around 13 percent.

Virtually all assessments in the early 1990s foresaw major shifts in the age distribution of college students continuing into the next century. Students 18 to 24 years of age had increased from 7.2 million in 1983 to an estimated 7.8 mil-lion in 1991, an increase of 8 percent. That number was expected to ascend to 9.2 million by the year 2003, up 19 percent. Consequently, the proportion of stu-dents age 18 to 24, which fell from 57.4 percent in 1983 to 54.8 percent in 1991 was expected to rise once again to about 57.2 percent after the century's end. On the other hand, students 25 years of age and older had increased from 5.1 million in 1983 to an estimated 6.2 million in 1991, an increase of 23 percent. The number was expected to attain 6.7 million by 2002, an increase of about 7 percent. The percentage of females age 35 or older between 1972 and 1991 had grown from 3.4 to 6.3 percent; and indicators suggested that ever increasing numbers of older women would be joining the ranks of students on campuses.

Minority enrollments were expected to expand, in both absolute and rela-tive terms, faster than for any other segment of the college population.[21] In the late eighties and mid-nineties, confirmation was forthcoming from reports that at some specialized local and regional colleges, "minority" students actually accounted for the majority of entering students.[22] The biggest gains, rela-tively speaking, were achieved by Hispanics, occurring both in majority-culture colleges and universities such as New Mexico Highlands University and East Los Angeles College; and in such predominantly minority-culture institutions as the Colegio Jacino Trevino in Texas, the Universidad de Astlan in California, the Escuela y Colegio Tlatelolco in Colorado, and Oregon's Colegio César Chávez. Enrollment patterns among Native Americans were more mixed. However, it was noted that what had formerly been designated

"Indian colleges" such as the Oglala Sioux Community College in South Dakota and New Mexico's Southwestern Polytechnic Institute were continuing to attract students in increasing numbers.

GOVERNMENTAL AND BUSINESS INVOLVEMENT

No mind-numbing litany of statistics, however extensive and important, could do justice of itself to the growth of American higher education in the postwar period. The greatly expanded role of the federal government in academe represented just one of several formative influences at work, albeit one that decisively shaped both the character and the direction or thrust of much of that growth.[23] During the war years, confronting a precipitous drop in enrollments and higher operating costs under wartime conditions, many colleges became almost entirely dependent upon government subsidies for their very survival. Aid usually assumed the form of contracts for specialized military training programs. Utilizing existing faculty and facilities, literally hundreds of colleges and universities undertook to provide war-related technical training and research under federal auspices.

By 1945, upwards of half of the income supporting certain academic institutions came from the national government. Governmental policy was to continue and extend research grants and training contracts in the postwar period; and much of the increasing attention paid to scientific and technical studies within the universities, not to mention support for an expanding array of cooperative research projects, derived exclusively from federal funding. In the late 1940s, for example, it was estimated that upwards of 80 percent or more of the nation's total expenditures for research in the physical and biological sciences was underwritten by the federal government. An ever-increasing percentage of research funds found its way onto college campuses.[24]

Equally important, if not more so, were provisions of the Servicemen's Readjustment Act of 1944 (popularly known as the G.I. Bill) and Public Law 550 of 1952, which released literally billions of dollars to help underwrite the cost of a college education for millions of returning war veterans. Colleges and universities were inundated with students. Makeshift dormitories and classrooms sprang up on campuses everywhere to accommodate their swelling enrollments.[25] Toward the close of the war, the Surplus Property Act of 1944 and subsequent legislation led to the donation or sale at reduced discount prices of millions of dollars' worth of surplus military supplies and buildings for use by hard-pressed academic institutions. Again during the Korean War, federal largess helped underwrite the cost of new construction. (At some schools "temporary" facilities thrown up in the immediate postwar period were still in use and had not been replaced by the early 1960s, fully a decade and a half after the end of the war. To them had been added many more built with governmental loans authorized by Congress in the early 1950s.)

At the century's midpoint, a dozen or more federal agencies, not counting each branch of the armed services, was spending well in excess of $150 million annually for contract research with colleges and universities. Federal subsidies continued into the 1960s, in some years exceeding $45 million for various specialized programs and research contracts.[26] In 1962 $2 billion was allocated in loans for the construction of student residence halls and other revenue-generating facilities at schools across the country. The year following, in 1963, the Higher Education Facilities Act expanded support for the building of new classrooms, laboratories, and libraries, in addition to loans and grants. In-service training of federal personnel on campuses continued; and total federal expenditures for university-sited research alone annually exceeded $750 million. The federal government's overall investment in higher education for 1947 was $2.4 billion; that total had jumped dramatically by the late 1950s; and it increased still further over the next four decades, though it was accompanied over time by major shifts in spending categories.[27] In 1958, additional federal dollars were forthcoming in the form of direct and indirect aid to students under programs inaugurated through the National Science Foundation, the National Institutes of Health, and the National Defense Education Act.

Increased federal funding for higher education in the fifties and early sixties, at the height of the cold war, was usually defended by the argument that in strengthening colleges and universities, the government was bolstering the nation's defenses and helping to advance vital national policy objectives. The President's Committee on Education Beyond the High School, in its report of 1957, for example, took an unequivocal stand: "America would be heedless if she closed her eyes to the dramatic strides being taken by the Soviet Union in post-high education, particularly in the development of scientists, engineers and technicians," the report's authors declared. "She would be inexcusably blind if she failed to see that the challenge of the next 20 years will require leaders not only in science and engineering and in business and industry, but in government and politics, in foreign affairs and diplomacy, in education and civic affairs. A responsible exercise of our nation's role in world leadership also requires a broadened citizen interest in and understanding of foreign relations and world affairs."[28]

Not everyone regarded federal aid as an unalloyed benefit to higher education. Skeptics harbored misgivings over federal support for university research at the expense of instructional support and needed capital improvements. Even when construction costs for buildings were paid for by the government, it was noted, increased operating cost and overhead returns were rarely adequate. Thus, while it was apparent that a marked increase in the availability of federal funds was fast becoming a prevailing pattern in the post-war period, critics wondered whether federal support would entail federal dictation or direction, with some consequent loss of autonomy for colleges and universities. At the very least, it seemed a question worth posing.

The response of many student dissidents as well as of many outside critics of academe in the turbulent 1960s was strongly in the affirmative—that federal support *did* in fact pose a major threat to the ostensible independence and autonomy of colleges and universities. Defenders of the federal connection, on the other side, could point to the Higher Education Act of 1965 authorizing federal financing to enable academic institutions to assist in solving community problems of public health, poverty, housing by means of research, extension, or continuing education. Such legislation and other acts like it, it was pointed out, were helping to expand libraries, construct capital facilities, and otherwise keeping academic efforts in the forefront of the struggle for social improvement.[29] Furthermore, without federally funded national teaching fellowships, and low-interest loans or outright grants, as provided in the Higher Education Act of 1972, to cite but one of several instances, hundreds of thousands of students who otherwise lacked the necessary resources were afforded the means to attend college and pursue an education. The connection between federal and state governmental agencies and the groves of academe, it became fashionable to claim in the decade of the eighties, was more akin to a working partnership, a collaboration, than a dependency relationship. Increasingly, federal policy was to channel funds to students in the form of low-interest loans and outright grants rather than directly to the institutions themselves. Hence, presumably, the potential for undue governmental influence upon colleges and universities was somewhat mitigated.

Henry Rosovsky, former dean of the faculty of arts and sciences at Harvard, was more candid than most in his assessment of the situation. Writing in *The University, An Owner's Manual* (1990), Rosovsky openly conceded that federal, state, and local government in part "owned" the university. Government, he observed, had become the "financier of research, banker to students and universities, regulator, judge and jury of many academic activities." He avowed, "Virtually no university in this country can function without federal support and in many cases without state support. That means being owned in some fashion by government."[30] UCLA historian Page Smith (*Killing the Spirit: Higher Education in America,* 1990) judged that universities were tied to the military-industrial complex by financial bonds that he suspected could "never be broken." But he drew out a rather different implication from Rosovsky's. "Today," Smith wrote, "90 percent of all federal research funds come from the Nuclear Regulatory Commission, NASA, and the Department of Defense." He then asked rhetorically, "Can we really speak of the independence of the university in the face of that statistic? The best we can say is that so far the federal government has been relatively restrained in using its power as the dispenser of enormous sums of money to bend universities to its will." "Perhaps," he hypothesized, "that is because the universities are so compliant rather than because the government is so restrained." The desire to tap into federal grants and contracts, Smith alleged, was playing a large role in determining the composition and character of university faculties. Disciplines or fields well supported by government contracts were apt to wax prosperous, while less favored fields or academic specialties withered. Professors in ever growing numbers were building their professional careers on "grantsmanship," the ability to attract lucrative grants and contracts.[31]

Equally troubling to some was the question whether anything was left of the vaunted independence of universities in light of their alliances with corporate business and industry. Having allegedly sold their souls when they began accepting enormous federal grants to do work for the military-industrial complex, critics claimed, universities were now engaged in building a parallel corporate connection as well. In common with federal funds, corporate contributions were observed to descend disproportionately on academic institutions. That is, they tended to enrich certain academic departments and disciplines while serving indirectly to impoverish other, less favored specialties. According to some detractors, the growing involvement of business and industrial corporations with universities, in which university research was funded by corporations that marketed the results and divided the profits with the funded universities, should have raised serious ethical questions. It rarely did. An editorial of September 19, 1988, in the *New York Times,* questioned the propriety of intimate corporate-academic ties: "Oscar Wilde could resist everything except temptation. University presidents, it seems, can resist everything except money."

Especially irksome to critics of corporate involvement was the blatant huckstering associated with universities' setting up of quasi-independent cooperatives devoted to marketing products or processes of commercial value generated from faculty research. Smith's reaction was not atypical: "Let us pray that we . . . will hear no more pious pronouncements about the universities' being engaged in the 'pursuit of truth.' What they are clearly pursuing with far more dedication than the truth is big bucks. . . . Any profession of exalted ideals by the university will have a hollow ring." The modern university, in his judgment, was "knee-deep in hypocrisy." By right of purchase, "capital" had purchased the modern research university and was well advanced in bending it to its own ends.[32]

The role of state-government control over public higher education similarly became a topic of concern and debate, beginning in the late sixties, intensifying in the seventies and eighties, and continuing with great fervor well into the 1990s. As academics saw it, state legislatures could best serve the cause of higher learning by providing adequate funding for public colleges and universities, while otherwise leaving matters of internal governance to individual institutions' governing boards and administrative leaders. In California and New York, followed by other states, however, legislative planners working in concert with some academic administrators began drawing up elaborate plans for more centralized coordination and control.[33] The product of their labors, from the fifties onward, in certain states at least, were huge multicampus institutions topped by central governing boards. Otherwise, in state after state, public postsecondary institutions were drawn into state "systems." (Sometimes the incorporation of individual, fiercely competitive regional colleges within a single governance system was secured in exchange for promises to make each constituent member a full-fledged university.) From an efficiency perspective, expectations were that a strong centralized governing board, directly answerable to the state governor or legislature, would work to eliminate waste, prevent unwarranted duplication of degree programs, and otherwise discourage expensive academic "empire-building."

More often than not, centralized governance failed to yield expected results. Overlooked in the planning process was the tendency of individual state legislators to become advocates or "boosters" for whichever public colleges or universities happened to be located in their respective local districts. Despite elaborate planning efforts, few state governing boards had enough political clout to counter demands from individual institutions to add programs or to expand existing ones. Regionalism and localism, in other words, proved to be extremely potent forces working against the ideal of coordinated management, budgeting, and programmatic development at the state level. The result, apparent to almost everyone in the eighties and nineties, was the academic equivalent of "pork barrel" politics. Additionally, more than a few states now found themselves saddled with cumbersome higher-education bureaucracies, too weak to impose meaningful constraints on unmanaged growth, yet strong and influential enough to prevent their "top-down" rules and regulations from being disregarded altogether.

Coordinating patterns and degrees of control varied by individual states. Florida, North Carolina, and Virginia empowered highly centralized governance structures. Indiana allowed its four major public institutions—Purdue, Indiana, Indiana State, and Ball State—considerable latitude and autonomy. Tennessee developed a two-tiered system, as did Pennsylvania. In the latter case, Pitt, Penn State, and Temple as major state-assisted institutions were more or less allowed to set policies for themselves. More coordination attended the operations of the state's other regional colleges or universities, most of them former normal schools or state teachers' colleges. Rural western states, such as Montana, Nevada, Wyoming, and North Dakota, were largely unaffected by the trend toward centralized control. Nor were tightly controlled systems common throughout the southern states. Elsewhere, the situation was quite different. Ohio's Board of Regents repeatedly sought to expand its policy role in higher education (though, it must be said, its efforts were often successfully resisted by the state's regional universities and sometimes were undermined by separate legislative initiatives). The power and authority of Missouri's Coordinating Board were precariously set off against local institutional prerogatives. Michigan retained its tradition of decentralized governance. Maryland experimented with some centralized planning in the eighties, then in the 1990s led a counter-trend toward more local independence for each of its public institutions.

The more general pattern in the eighties and nineties was one of state governing boards and legislatures seeking to exercise greater control over the internal workings of public colleges and universities. Admissions standards and procedures, faculty workloads, student-loan allocations, work-study programs, and other related matters came under closer legislative scrutiny and review than ever before. Faculty members and administrators alike found themselves occupied with drawing up strategic plans, mission statements, and detailed operational analyses mandated under state law. In sum, while private colleges were left largely to their own devices, the public sector in higher education by the mid-1990s was struggling to accommodate to a level and intensity of state surveillance and supervision unlike anything to which traditionally it had been accustomed.

CORPORATE ACADEME

The emergence of American higher education as a corporate enterprise perfectly congruent in all major respects with free-enterprise capitalism was a phenomenon that did not long go unnoticed or unremarked upon.[34] It stemmed, most observers were agreed, from the rapid expansion and proliferation of colleges and universities of all types in the immediate postwar period; the growing popularity of management strategies borrowed from business and industry in the sixties, and subsequent attempts at their application to the academic enterprise in the seventies and eighties; and the combined effects of burgeoning enrollments and diminishing resources characteristic of the last third of the century. The so-called corporate "revolution" or "transformation," as it was sometimes dubbed, was an extremely complex, multifaceted development. It reflected and combined many different yet interrelated strands: technocratic rationality, corporate industrialism, bureaucratization, demands for greater accountability, radical egalitarianism, a rough-and-ready brand of positivism (manifest, for example, in attempts to reduce qualitative measures and criteria to quantitative indices), an obsession with institutional efficiency, and, above all, the corporate ethic of free markets.

In their internal workings, many academic institutions of higher learning appeared to have taken on much of the trappings of large-scale business organizations: mission statements, strategic planning, elaborate budgeting systems, meticulous record-keeping, cost-effectiveness analyses, marketing research, public-relations efforts, total-quality-management, hierarchical governance structures and pyramidal bureaucracies, the mathematical calculation of units of learning (course credits and hours; grade point averages), division and specialization of labor, the use of professional "headhunters" to recruit administrators or well-known scholars, and so on *ad infinitum*.

The key to understanding what had occurred, as analysts saw it, was the degree to which academic institutions in many fundamental respects had come to differ but little from traditional business enterprises seeking to survive in the marketplace.[35] Schools of higher learning had evolved into entrepreneurial capitalist institutions, highly individualistic and intensely competitive with one another. Thus, the once-popular notion of colleges and universities as idyllic ivied enclaves, more or less isolated from worldly distractions and concerns, dedicated to disinterested learning, leisured contemplation, and the intellectual nurturing of youth, as critics were quick to point out, had become something of a caricature of academic realities in the late twentieth century. It was a popular image, but one no longer adequate to comprehend the state of modern academe in all of its operational complexity.[36]

Many observers of American higher education took particular note of the myriad ways in which free market forces had begun to exercise a deep and pervasive influence upon the workings and behavior of institutions of higher learning. Competition now was built into the system at every level. Among students, it had become a matter of competing for admission to their institutions of choice; then, once admitted, for grades, loans, and scholarship stipends; and upon graduation, for jobs or admission to graduate school. Among faculty, the competition was for tenure, salary increments, advancement in rank, for grants and contracts, preferred work assignments, sabbaticals and leaves of absence, for office and work space, for awards and honors, for prestige and professional "visibility." Likewise, individual departments, centers, schools, and colleges within the university were set to competing with one another as never before for space, funding, and administrative support. In boom times, colleges took on extra hands at piece-work rates: temporary, full-time or part-time adjunct faculty, consigned to the margins, often paid with so-called soft monies from grants and contracts, unlikely ever to secure tenure-track appointments.

Competition between or among institutions intensified greatly throughout the latter part of the century. Given overexpansion, it was now a buyer's market, forcing colleges and universities (both public and private) to vie actively with one another for students and their tuition. Because student fees represented a much higher proportion of operating revenues for private colleges than for those in the public sector, fluctuations in the student head count often could spell the difference between financial health and economic disaster. Hence, student recruitment had long been a matter of some urgency. On the other hand, publicly assisted universities with enrollment-driven budgets of their own, dominated by funding formulas that rewarded large enrollments, similarly were finding it necessary to redouble their efforts at maintaining or increasing the numbers of students admitted.

Academic institutions of differing types developed their own unique recruiting markets and submarkets. Ivy-League schools and prestigious private universities with highly selective admissions sought one particular kind of student clientele. Leading public research universities attracted a different though overlapping class of students. Traditional liberal-arts colleges and sectarian schools operated within their own submarkets. Four-year public state colleges and regional universities tended to recruit in yet another market. Two-year schools, public or private, serviced the needs of still others. A school's geographical location; whether it was situated in an urban, suburban or rural environment; its size; the types of degree programs and courses of studies it sponsored; its admissions policies; the level of student support it was capable of extending; the general academic reputation and prestige (or lack thereof) the college or university happened to enjoy—all figured now as major elements defining the markets within which any given institution could most successfully compete.

Not surprisingly, successful colleges and universities had become adept at marketing themselves by paying careful attention to image-building, public relations, and recruitment strategies. By differentiating their "products," packaging them with care, and adapting curricular offerings to changes or shifts in market demand, institutions of higher learning thus positioned themselves to best advantage. Sometimes they found it expedient to enter into partnerships with other producers so as to dominate a given market. Just as often, if at all possible, individual schools preferred to go it alone. But either way, in almost all respects, academic institutions most closely resembled other capitalistic enterprises engaged in the business of buying and selling.

If further evidence of competition within corporate academe was needed, observers had only to look at how intercollegiate athletics operated at some of the larger universities. Athletics had become big business in the fullest and most complete sense of the term, an important source of revenue and a major image-builder for many academic institutions. Coaches were under pressure to turn out winning teams. Schools competed feverishly for players. Ticket sales to major sporting events—basketball and football—received close scrutiny by accountants and athletic directors attentive to the "bottom line" in their ledgers. Paralleling corporate business scandals were investigations of rules violations, and chicanery and skullduggery in the recruitment and payment of favored stars by the athletic departments of major academic institutions. Hardly a year passed without some new revelation of illegal or questionable practices.[37]

To some observers in the 1990s, it appeared that academic "brand name" had become more important than "product quality" in higher education; and that institutions within the same broad category perhaps differed from one another in style but rarely in substance. Others pointed out that taken as a whole, the American system of higher education was by no means homogeneous; that, on the contrary, it had become incredibly diverse, incorporating a multitude of institutions of every possible sort, at every possible level of seriousness, representing quite divergent standards and degrees of academic rigor, offering study in practically any subject imaginable.[38] In fact, some alleged, it was misleading to refer to a "system" of higher education at all. But practically everyone was agreed, the uniqueness of American higher education in the waning years of the twentieth century was that it offered a high degree of access, to some part of the total system, to almost anyone expressing a desire to gain admittance, and in many cases without imposing any requirement that applicants demonstrate evidence of academic ability or talent in order to qualify for admission.

BLACK HIGHER EDUCATION

Nowhere were the changes that had taken place in American higher education more apparent than in the participation rate of African Americans.[39] Black postsecondary enrollments on the eve of World War II had been minuscule: there were probably no more than 5,000 black students in white colleges outside the South in 1939, representing five-tenths of 1 percent of total enrollments in the North, and about half of these students were concentrated in fewer than two dozen institutions, Similarly, only a handful of blacks were enrolled in southern colleges and universities; and of that handful, only about 1 in 10 was enrolled in a predominantly white college or university.[40] After the war, black enrollment in southern white institutions increased to a few hundred by the early 1950s, an estimated 453 students in twenty-two historically white institutions in the South for the 1952–53 academic year. During the period from 1940 to 1950, black enrollments in white colleges outside the South grew to 61,000, which was about 47 percent of all black enrollment but only 3 percent of the total enrollment in those colleges. Black enrollments nationwide in 1947, it was estimated, represented 6 percent of total college enrollments that year, a high point that was not surpassed again until the year 1967.[41]

Following the U.S. Supreme Court decision (*Brown v. Topeka Board of Education*) in May of 1954, desegregation of historically white institutions in the South began to accelerate. Sometimes it came about voluntarily or in response to social pressure. In other cases, protracted legal efforts were required.[42] In February of 1956, a black student by the name of Autherine Lucy registered for classes at the University of Alabama—only to be expelled immediately thereafter on the grounds she had conspired to aid in the rioting by white students accompanying the news of her admission. No African Americans were admitted to Alabama for the next seven years.[43] On June 11, 1963, three blacks appeared to register, only to find their entrance physically barred by Alabama governor George C. Wallace, who publicly announced that he would never accept desegregation. He stepped aside an hour later when the federalized Alabama National Guard arrived to enforce an order admitting black students.[44]

An even more bizarre turn of events accompanied an initial attempt to desegregate the University of Mississippi. In June of 1958, a black student named Clennon King sought admission to pursue his doctorate. He was promptly arrested on a charge of disturbing the peace and remanded to a state mental hospital for a lunacy hearing. Only when hospital officials reported they could find no evidence of mental disorder was King released. As it turned out, however, he still was not allowed to enroll at the university.[45]

Three years later, in June of 1961, James Meredith, a black student at Jackson State, sought to transfer to the University of Mississippi. As in the Clennon King case, university attorneys argued that he suffered from a psychiatric disorder and should be denied admission. On September 30, armed with an appeal court's decision, Meredith arrived on campus accompanied by a force of federal marshals. Riots broke out and troops were sent in. The next day Meredith was registered and proceeded to pursue his studies without further major incident.[46]

By late 1961 desegregation was ostensibly complete in most of the border states and in about a third of the states of the Deep South. In 1964, there were an estimated 15,000 blacks enrolled in predominantly white colleges in the South, representing a fourfold increase since 1957.[47] Meanwhile, black undergraduate enrollments in northern colleges had increased from around 45,000 in 1954 to almost 95,000 in 1967–68.[48] The number of blacks attending white colleges in the South during the first half of the decade of the sixties rose from 3,000 in 1960 to 24,000 in 1965, and to 98,000 by 1970. Between 1965 and 1970, black enrollment in white institutions more than tripled. Simultaneously, black enrollments in historically black colleges and universities had dropped from 82 percent of all college-attending blacks to 60 percent between 1965 and 1970; it declined to 40 percent by 1978.[49]

Black enrollment as a percentage of total students attending colleges and universities nationwide mounted steadily after the mid-sixties. By 1971, the figure stood at 8.4 percent; by 1977 it had risen to 10.8 percent of the total college enrollment. Between 1967 and 1974, for example, black enrollment in white institutions increased fully 160 percent, compared to a 34 percent increase in the black enrollment of traditionally black colleges and a 33 percent increase in total enrollment. The greatest numerical growth in black enrollment occurred in northern white colleges and universities. By 1987, for the first time in American history, black students were more likely to matriculate at predominantly white institutions than at traditionally black schools. Slightly less than 1 in every 5 black students was then enrolled at a black college.

Less well publicized at the time was the fact that black enrollments in both black and white institutions of higher education had actually *declined* from the high mark reached in 1979–80, despite having doubled overall between 1960 and 1980. Likewise, the numbers as percentages of the black age-cohort 18 to 21 continued to lag well behind the percentage of whites attending college. Analyses differed as to why white higher education institutions had begun experiencing a decline in the number of black students attending. Some of the fall-off, it was claimed, was the result of high attrition and non-completion rates registered by African-American students enrolled at predominantly white colleges and universities. Another factor was the increase in numbers of blacks who in the eighties elected to attend public black colleges. Their combined total enrollments had risen from 120,000 in 1987 to 140,000 by 1990. Many private black institutions were reporting similar or even more dramatic enrollment gains.[50] The lower cost of attending a black college may have been part of the reason. Some commentators alleged that black college enrollment growth also resulted from the desire by many African Americans to escape what was perceived to be a backlash, or a rising tide of racism, on white college campuses. More common still was the claim that black colleges and universities were better adapted than their competitors in meeting the special educational and developmental needs of African-American collegians.

By the early nineties, the nation's three dozen or so public black institutions were enrolling close to 20 percent of all blacks in higher education, and about 60 percent of those enrolled in all predominantly black institutions.[51] Advocates of black schools alleged that such institutions were granting a statistically disproportionate share—roughly 37 percent—of all the baccalaureate degrees awarded to blacks. On the other hand, it was pointed out that over 40 percent of all African-American students were enrolled in *two*-year institutions, whereas 90 percent of all black colleges were four-year institutions. The conclusion drawn by some, then, was that the seeming statistical difference between white and black schools was largely illusory. When the respective baccalaureate productivity records of all four-year institutions were compared, it could be shown that black colleges were enrolling only one-third of all black baccalaureate-degree candidates, while producing 34 percent of all black baccalaureate degrees—not a significant difference from the black baccalaureate-degree productivity of predominantly *white* colleges and universities.[52]

Defenders of historically black colleges advanced their case on other grounds beside numbers. Black schools, they argued, were educating a sizable number of African-American students who otherwise might not be willing or able to pursue a college degree at all. Unlike most of their majority-culture counterparts, the smaller black colleges had tended to concentrate on meeting the needs of those from extremely disadvantaged backgrounds. Thus, as compared with either black or white students attending predominantly white institutions, African Americans enrolled in black colleges were more likely to come from low-income families, to have undistinguished or poor high-school achievement records, and lower standardized test scores. Hence, they were considered to be "high-risk" students who would have been unlikely to qualify for acceptance at predominantly white colleges and universities. Black colleges, it was pointed out, prided themselves on their ability to accept the challenge posed by academically marginal students, to compensate for and correct their scholastic deficiencies, and to carry them forward to successful completion of a degree program.

The college experience for African Americans attending a black school was claimed to differ markedly from that characteristically supplied at a predominantly white institution. Despite society's protestations of support for equal opportunity, African-American students at white institutions allegedly fared poorly in comparison with white students in terms of persistence rates, academic achievement, and overall psychological and social adjustment. Black collegians reportedly experienced greater difficulty adjusting to college life;

they earned lower grade point averages; they felt more alienated; they were enrolling less frequently in postgraduate programs, they were dropping out sooner, and at a higher overall rate than were white students. In contrast, black students in black colleges reportedly did better in terms of adjustment to collegiate life, enjoyed greater cultural awareness, and retained higher career aspirations than their black peers attending white colleges and universities.

Their alleged superiority in meeting the needs of black students notwithstanding, by the nineties, all signs appeared to point to a crisis for most of the nation's black colleges and universities. Beset by unpredictable fluctuations in enrollment, ill-prepared faculty in many cases, insufficient financial resources, scanty alumni support, and woefully inadequate facilities, many were finding it a constant struggle just to survive. Despite their historic importance to the education of blacks in the past, some critics argued, black colleges by and large had outlived their usefulness in the modern world. Precisely because they allowed and even encouraged the segregation of their students from the larger society in which they ultimately would have to make their way, their continued existence was alleged to be doubtful. Even among some black leaders, black schools whose identity was based on race seemed to have become something of an embarrassment. Alan N. Whiting, former chancellor of North Carolina Central University, a predominantly black institution, expressed his misgivings in 1988 over the prospects that racially identifiable institutions would endure. "Social changes," he argued, "especially related to desegregation, have diminished what was once a 'categorical imperative' to almost a peripheral or interstitial role in the higher education community. And, as predominantly white schools perceive and internalize the demographic shifts toward a dramatically increasing minority . . . population in this country, they will exert greater and greater effort to adapt to the special learning needs of these populations." Whiting predicted that in the long run, "majority-group institutions will come more and more to displace institutions, heretofore labeled 'minority,' and pre-empt the special historic function they performed in the delivery of higher education in this country."[53]

Defenders of black colleges strongly disagreed. "We are not yet convinced that predominantly white institutions are ready to accept and take the risk with some of the black students . . . we accept," declared Ben E. Bailey, director of research at Tougaloo College in Mississippi, in 1991. "Further, we do not believe that white colleges are ready to accept black students and black faculty in numbers that allow them to wield power in shaping educational processes at those institutions. Society is constitutionally incapable of accepting black people and their culture on equal grounds."[54] Dr. Sock-Foon C. MacDougall of Bowie State University in Maryland concurred. "In view of the prevailing racial climate on campuses across the nation," he wrote in 1991, "the probability that 'multi-racial' institutions could successfully redouble their efforts to meet the needs of minority students is low. Racism is going to be with us for a long time." Niara Sudurkasa, president of Lincoln University of Pennsylvania, offered a similar perspective: "Mainstream academia is pulling in the welcome mats it only recently laid out for minority students," she warned. "It has only been a little more than two decades since America's majority colleges and universities began the 'experiment' of opening up to blacks and other minorities, Yet, in many quarters, this 'experiment' is already being pronounced a failure."

Roy Hudson, vice-president for administration at Mississippi Valley State College, spoke for many black college leaders in predicting the durability of black institutions of higher learning. "The future of black colleges is in the hands of black people," he insisted. "As long as black people see these colleges as enterprises that work to their advantage, the colleges will exist." Hudson added emphatically, "The biggest threat to black colleges are white people who instinctively feel that if white people are not running something, it should not exist; and black people who are not sure about who or where they want to be." Black college administrators returned repeatedly to the same themes. Their schools, they declared, would remain an important part of American higher education so long as their unique advantages remained unavailable elsewhere. In a society still tainted by racism and ethnic prejudice, blacks would need institutions they could call their own. If nothing else, they would serve as protective enclaves where minority students would be more likely to feel accepted, where feelings of ethnic identity and pride would always be nurtured, and where they would be afforded opportunities denied them elsewhere. Norfolk State University's Maxine Allen summed up prospects for the future with an optimistic note. "Black colleges have a bright future," she declared in 1991, "if they continue to provide students with a quality education . . . that will allow them to be productive citizens in this high technological society. The special function of black colleges," she avowed, "is to provide students with black experiences in an . . . environment which deals with information on the cutting edge in higher education."

CURRICULAR INCLUSION

Accompanying the emergence of a corporate structure within American higher education and the inclusion of new groups were major shifts in thinking about the college curriculum itself. From the perspective afforded toward the end of the century, major trends over the previous fifty years were not hard to discern.[55] There had been a marked shift away from an intellectualist basis for higher learning. The liberal arts had undergone successive definitions and rede-finitions. Courses of study had been more or less continuously broadened and diversified.[56] New disciplines (together with an apparently endless prolifera-tion of subdisciplines) had been introduced. A degree of democratization aimed at opening learning to a wider array of abilities and talents had occurred. The usual time frame for studies had been loosened. Courses of study more responsive to interests based on age, gender, and ethnicity had been incorpo-rated to an unprecedented extent.[57]

Illustrations of how curricula were broadened in the last third of the 1900s to incorporate new areas of study included the emergence and development of special programs in black studies, Hispanic studies, gay studies, and women's studies. In the latter case, women's studies first appeared in the last half of the 1960s, when women faculty, stronger in numbers than ever before, began to create new courses dealing with feminist experiences and aspirations. Their efforts at organization and course development were inspired partly by the civil-rights movement, which earlier had provided the model for black studies courses and programs. Among the pioneers, courses by and about women were believed to be essential for correcting the neglect and distortion of women in standard university courses and curricula. San Diego State ranked among the first to have a program structure in place. It was followed between 1970 and 1975 by the creation of 150 new women's studies programs, a feat that was repeated between 1975 and 1980 on campuses across the country.

Leading female scholars saw the emergence of women's studies basically as a third phase in American women's long historic struggle for educational opportunities. The first was the period in which, accepting early nineteenth-century assumptions about women's nature, demands were advanced for a higher education suited to women's unique and distinctive needs as then pop-ularly defined. The second phase in the later 1800s came when women began seeking access to the standard course of studies found in colleges and uni-versities. The third phase was marked by a challenge to the alleged "male hegemony" over the curricula, most conspicuously symbolized by the advent of women's studies programs themselves. The purpose of the earliest programs was thus twofold: to expose the fact of longstanding social, economic, and cul-tural oppression of women; and, secondly, to redress traditional neglect of women's contributions to culture and society through scholarship and instruc-tion. An enormous literature was spawned in the 1970s and 1980s, much of it drawn from nontraditional sources, documenting women's experience and consciousness. Yet despite the continuing proliferation of courses and the building-up of programs, in the 1980s women's studies as a field still tended to remain marginal, well outside the academic mainstream.[58]

Belatedly recognizing that women's studies courses had not reached a large or diverse audience and that many college students, including women, did not necessarily subscribe to early feminist principles and precepts, attention shifted in the late eighties and early nineties to "integrating" or "main-streaming" scholarship on women. The focus now became less a matter of building up separate academic programs and more one of changing courses outside the domain of women's studies. Myra Dinnerstein, director of women's studies at the University of Arizona, was quoted in the September 9, 1987, issue of the *Chronicle of Higher Education* as saying, "We were reaching a fairly small portion of students. Unless you took a women's-studies course, you could graduate and never hear the words 'women' or 'gender.'"

The changing complexion of the student population—women already made up slightly more than half of all undergraduate enrollments nationwide—added momentum to the campaign for integrated courses. Proponents of change sometimes met with powerful resistance. Some scholars disputed the academic legitimacy of women's studies as a discipline or field of inquiry. Others perhaps were uncomfortable with the new, disquieting questions raised by scholarship on women. Leading women's-studies scholars nevertheless continued their efforts to achieve a "feminine transformation" of the curriculum. The goal, as most commonly defined in the 1990s, had become one of total "gender inclusivity," that is, an approach to knowledge in which the presence of the heretofore "hidden half" of humankind would be taken for granted as an integral and unquestioned part of any study or inquiry.

GENERAL LEARNING AND LIBERAL STUDIES IN AN AGE OF SPECIALIZATION

The addition of programs and courses of study aimed at fostering better understanding and appreciation for women and minorities represented an important curricular innovation in American higher education in the last third of the twentieth century. Indeed, a major thematic movement defining curricular change within colleges and universities was that of inclusion, the curricular reification, so to speak, of minority interests and concerns. Yet more fundamentally, inclusivity was a subset of a still larger intellectual mosaic, one that transcended all others in terms of debates over how knowledge should be defined, systematized, and structured for purposes of collegiate instruction. That larger dominant pattern, arguably, was one of oscillation back and forth between the two poles of commonality and diversification, between efforts to bring unity and coherence to the undergraduate curriculum in the form of some type of learning shared in common by all, on the one side, and the logic of larger societal forces whose effects were to divide and fragment courses of study, on the other. In the final analysis, much of the enduring controversy over collegiate curricula in an age of increasing specialization related in some fashion to the perennial issue of how to define and preserve general education.

In 1939 the National Society for the Study of Education (NSSE) devoted its thirty-eighth yearbook to the topic of general learning in contemporary society.[59] A retrospective look back at the experiments of the preceding two decades, according to Stanford's Alvin C. Eurich, suggested apparent failure to reach consensus on the meaning of general education. "Each person who uses the term has some definite connotation in mind," he wrote. "Commonly it is thought of in contrast with specialization and as implying an emphasis upon living in a democratic society."[60] But different interpretations had led to considerable confusion about the means or methods of implementation.

Close to everyone's mind was Hutchins's attempt at Chicago to root general education in an intellectual tradition defined through the Great Books of the Western world. In their protest against the whole of contemporary culture with its corporate industrialism, science and technology, its controlling institutions, its ethical relativism and secularism, crusaders of the likes of Hutchins, Mortimer Adler, Mark Van Doren, Jacques Maritain, and Norman Foerster had thrown down a challenge. Modern society, they insisted, had misconstrued entirely what true education was all about. In the wisdom of the past—in its classic intellectual principles, enduring values, and fixed standards— humankind would find the best means for developing mental power and fostering humane self-development.[61] But the "historical presentism" of a viewpoint so obviously at odds with prevailing trends in the 1930s could hardly be expected to gain broad acceptance. And in fact it had not. It was but one approach to defining general education, and not a popular one at that.

John Dewey, by contrast, had emphasized the need for experience with present-day personal and social problems as an alternative way of providing students with a general (as opposed to specialized) education. Directly or indirectly, his views already had inspired at least a half dozen or so interesting experiments with progressive curricula, life-adjustment education, and other experimental courses of study; and they would continue to do so throughout the decade following the appearance of the NSSE's yearbook. For Eurich, writing at the end of the 1930s, the only commonality to be discerned in efforts to promote general learning was dissatisfaction with collegiate specialization and agreement on the need for more curricular "integration." General education, he felt, was "an expression of a quest for unity and a renewed emphasis upon the democratic ideal." It designated no fixed procedures or program. General education was "what one finds in American colleges that are seriously attempting to modify their programs in order to provide more unifying experience."[62]

John Dale Russell, a professor of education at the University of Chicago, in the same NSSE yearbook shared the results of his national survey of programs in liberal-arts colleges.[63] He too found in statements of purpose wide variations in how the term "general education" was understood. Some respondents viewed "liberal" and "general" education as synonymous. Others disagreed but felt the distinction between the two was unclear. A majority was agreed that general education excluded technical, vocational, and professional preparation—though others were less sure. Some believed general education did not need to exclude vocational or professional training so long as the subject matter pursued was integrative and interdisciplinary. Some thought general or liberal education could be defined in terms of its content. As many others disagreed, claiming that general education was distinguished more by the spirit and means of its instruction than by any specific subject matter.

Henry M. Wriston, president of Brown University, offered an especially provocative essay attacking the notion that traditional liberal education was ever "aristocratic." On historical grounds, he took issue with the familiar argument that general education was ill-adapted to meeting the needs of a mass population and that its chief beneficiaries had always been a select few. "The history of American higher education," he insisted, "is replete with examples of those who have come from environments that sociologist and psychologist alike would regard with horror, and yet these students have done brilliantly in intellectual work—and in the development of social graces." Nor were they isolated exceptions to some larger pattern. Cant about the need to vocationalize collegiate curricula, to accommodate "newcomers" to higher education, in his opinion, was just that—cant. Wriston's conclusion was worth noting. "The expression of dislike of liberal education because it was 'aristocratic,' is too often an expression of an innate anti-intellectualism—a suspicion that the higher learning and more refined aesthetic taste cannot be attained by all men, hence cannot be democratic," he commented. But there was nothing whatsoever in democratic theory, according to Wriston, that justified such a feeling. "The 'aristocracy' of intellectualism," as he phrased it, "is of a character wholly in harmony with both the theory and practice of democracy."[64]

The 1939 yearbook marked a dividing point between the first phase of activity on behalf of general education, extending from World War I to the end of the Depression, and a second general-education movement, which began in the 1940s. This second movement or phase followed a pattern similar to the first of the 1920s. Once again the revival came in the aftermath of a world war, when the country's mood closely resembled what it had been a quarter century before. Like its predecessor, the postwar rebirth of interest in general education was very much a product of the times. As in the 1920s, general education was once again called upon to counter vocationalism, overspecialization, and the elective curriculum. The familiar themes of educating citizens for public responsibility, of promoting a common cultural heritage, and promoting "self-realization" gained new currency. In an era when the United States found itself locked in cold-war conflict with world communism, an urgent need felt by many was for an education that would reaffirm the cardinal values of Western civilization and American democratic society.[65]

The best illustration of revived interest in general education was a 1945 Harvard faculty committee report entitled *General Education in a Free Society*. Bound in red, it was promptly dubbed the "Redbook."[66] It soon won acclaim as an articulate exploration of the meaning of general education in the modern era. The committee's analysis opened with the observation that education seeks to fulfill two objectives: first, to prepare people for their unique and personal functions in life; and, secondly, to fit them "so far as it can for those common spheres which, as citizens and heirs of a joint culture, they will share with others."[67] The challenge was not merely to foster skills and outlooks that differentiated individuals according to their talents and differing aspirations. It was also to develop the traits and understandings that people should share in common despite their differences. In an age marked by a "staggering" expansion of knowledge and consequent specialization, the report noted, the latter task had become increasingly difficult. What was needed, the committee argued, was an "over-all logic, some strong, not easily broken frame" within which academic institutions could simultaneously fulfill their diversifying and uniting tasks.[68]

The Harvard Redbook stopped short of specifying what might furnish an optimal framework for unifying undergraduate learning. It cautioned against assuming any single pattern was workable for all colleges and universities. For Harvard, the report urged the institution of a system whereby students would be required to complete at least one course each in the natural sciences, humanities, and social studies, and an additional three courses of a general nature prior to, or coincident with, advanced specialized training. A combination of survey courses and distribution requirements, it was proclaimed, would safeguard the more general or common aims of undergraduate education. The basic need, the report concluded, was for a balance between "general" and "special" (i.e., specialized) education. Distinguishing between the two, general education was said to denote "that part of a student's whole education which looks first of all to his life as a responsible human being and citizen; while the term special education indicates that part which looks to the student's competence in some occupation." The former is "an organism, whole and integrated," whereas the latter is "an organ; a member designed to fulfill a particular function within a whole." Both were held to be essential in a free society. Both were necessary for the development of the educated person—an individual capable of thinking effectively, communicating clearly, making relevant judgments, and discriminating with care among values.[69]

The Redbook's authors were concerned to emphasize the point that general education should not be thought of as having to do with "some airy education in knowledge in general." Nor should it be formless, the product of a person's taking one course after another. Neither should it be defined negatively, in the sense of whatever is left over apart from a field of concentration and specialization. Finally (in an obvious reference to Hutchins), the report claimed that general education should not be conceived of in terms of a specific set of books to be read or courses completed.

The challenge facing modern democracy in a social order where all are free to pursue private ends but everyone shares responsibility for the management of the community is to preserve the ancient ideal of liberal education and to extend it as far as possible to all members of society, the Redbook concluded. Whatever its shape or specific content, general education was held to be indispensable, because it speaks to the larger ends of personal development and social service. The most critical question, therefore, the committee asserted, was "How can general education be so adapted to different ages, and, above all, differing abilities and outlooks, that it can appeal to each, yet remain in goal and essential teaching the same for all?"[70] To that question, unfortunately, *General Education in a Free Society* offered no definite answer.

Ironically, Harvard's faculty ultimately rejected its own committee report. Elsewhere, however, support for the Harvard plan ran strong, and variations of its recommendations were adopted in dozens of colleges and universities. Two years later, a White House Commission on Higher Education for Democracy released a report enthusiastically endorsing general education along the lines sketched out in the Harvard Report. Around the same time, a flurry of reform activity marked collegiate curricula development. At Denison University in Ohio a core course entitled "Problems of Peace and Post-War Reconstruction," begun in 1942, continued to attract national attention. At Wesleyan, in Connecticut, and in a number of Ivy League schools, new general-education seminars were launched with much fanfare.

Horace M. Kallen, author of *The Education of Free Men* (1949), decried the identification of general education with a fixed historical content. Although he opposed particularistic vocational training, he was equally uncomfortable with pedagogic custodians of a traditional "body of knowledge" inherited from the past who urged schools to hand it on intact. "Any thought or thing, any vocation or technique momentous to a mind may become the base of its liberation," he asserted. "Any art or craft, any theme, datum or system of ideas, is an instrument of liberal education when it serves as a road and not as a wall for him who studies it. Whatever be the avowed field and purpose of the study—farming, engineering, business, law, medicine, the ministry, teaching, garbage collecting, archaeology—when it liberates, it is liberal."[71]

Kallen admitted that the curriculum of a traditional liberal education, properly mastered, could serve to free a student's mind from the provincialism of his or her place and time; the experience was "liberal" at least with respect to a world dead and gone. "To be liberated into the life more abundant of the actual world, however," he hastened to add, "has so obvious a priority over this other, that the recurrent debate over its dignity and worth argue an inexplicable blindness of spirit in those who deny it."[72] The past exalted by traditionalists, Kallen argued, is a living past only as people alive today cherish and study and use it to enrich their existence in the present. The criterion or standard of relevance for liberal studies and general education then, is whether it teaches people to learn about one another; to understand, respect, and appreciate differences among themselves, and to assist them in working together for common ends. Traditionalists, with their "mortuary cult" of a moribund past, Kallen claimed, were guilty of exalting one phase or aspect of human culture while denigrating all others. The practical implication of Kallen's view, of course, was that liberal or general education was undefinable in terms of any specific subject matter in particular.[73]

Interestingly, in the 1940s and 1950s, some writers attempted to introduce a sharp distinction between "liberal" and "general" education, the suggestion being that the former consisted of a fixed body of traditional liberal-arts disciplines, and the latter of any course of study exhibiting breadth or diversity. This usage was decidedly at odds with earlier practice in the 1920s and 1930s, when the two terms were used interchangeably and almost synonymously. As always, writers harbored great expectations about what liberal-general education might accomplish, but were forever in disagreement over structure and substance.[74]

Gresham Riley, a dean at the University of Richmond, writing from the perspective of 1980, judged that the mixture of required courses and limited choice within groupings of closely related disciplines exhibited by the general-education model of the 1950s had been "seriously flawed." Besides being restricted parochially to Western society and its dominant ethnic and socio-economic groups, the typical curriculum, he claimed in the Fall 1980 issue of *Liberal Education,* focused predominantly on the subject matter of various disciplines, with little or no thought having been given to relationships among bodies of knowledge. That model, Riley felt, encouraged student passivity and dependency instead of providing opportunities for learners to gain intellectual independence and to function as active learners.

Furthermore, according to Riley, the typical introductory course, which could satisfy distribution requirements, tended to stifle student interest rather than to stimulate intellectual excitement. "I find it appropriate," he observed, "that we frequently characterized those introductory courses as providing 'an exposure' to the various disciplines. As a matter of fact, they 'exposed' students to disciplines like a smallpox vaccination exposes a child to the disease: One is 'cured for life'—in the latter case of the disease and in the former case of any possible interest in the subject matter."[75]

As in the 1930s when the Depression prompted renewed concern for practical utility and vocational curricula, another dramatic crisis, this time symbolized by Sputnik, slowed the second revival of general education in the late fifties. With the launching of the first artificial satellite in 1957 by the Soviet Union, Americans fell into a state of near panic. The shift from preoccupation with individual to corporate values, from concern with personal attitudes to intellectual and social skills in the larger society, already in process earlier in the decade, was now greatly accentuated. As the decade of the fifties drew to a close, the trend was toward assessing schooling at all levels for its potential contribution to national requirements and policies, and less for individual needs. As concern mounted over the possibility that the United States lagged behind the Soviets in the "space race," the official standard for judging education was whether it could be made politically or militarily useful. To some critics, general education was a luxury the nation could no longer afford.

The Kennedy years of the early 1960s further reinforced a mood emphasizing technical proficiency and expertise.[76] The task ahead, declared John W. Gardner, author of the widely discussed *Excellence* (1961), was to draw upon the talents and abilities of each citizen and to educate people so that the country could retain its position of world leadership. "The difficult, puzzling, delicate and important business of toning up a whole society," he declared, framed the nation's most pressing educational challenge.[77] It was widely accepted that schooling should be bent to national ends if the country was to counter Soviet expansionism and safeguard its own security. In the push for specialized competence and professionalism, an earlier preoccupation with general education now seemed less urgent, less important, in an age fraught with new danger and uncertainty.

The cause of general education was further weakened by the subsequent social turmoil of the sixties, when a reaction *against* social efficiency and the use of education as an instrument of national policy set in. One of the few major attempts to reexamine the meaning of general education amidst the general confusion of the period was undertaken by Daniel Bell of Columbia

University, in a 1966 volume entitled *The Reforming of General Education*.[78] For him, the need was to focus on "modes of conceptualization, explanation, and verification of knowledge," while at the same time finding a way "of giving a student a conspectus of relevant knowledge as an intellectual whole."[79] Achieving this dual, sometimes paradoxical goal of "conceptualization" and "coherence," he felt, would require better understanding of how knowledge is acquired in different categories of disciplines. In mathematics and the sciences, the acquisition of knowledge is mainly sequential and proceeds to build in linear fashion. Knowledge in the humanities is "concentric," as a few major themes continually reappear and recycle themselves (the nature of tragedy, love, self-discovery, and so on). In the social sciences, knowledge or understanding is acquired by linking one kind of phenomenon to another in its appropriate setting or context.[80]

Based on these epistemological presuppositions, Bell recommended a college curriculum based on a "general background" of information, followed by "training in a discipline," and capped with "the application of this discipline to a number of relevant subjects."[81] The key to coherence, Bell believed, was a scheme that envisaged the first year of a student's undergraduate program given over to acquiring necessary historical and background knowledge, the second and third years devoted to training in a discipline, and the fourth year occupied with a combination of seminar work in the major discipline and synoptic courses—a "third-tier" level—that would give the student a sense of how his or her major subject might be applied to specific problems and how it related to other knowledge domains. Bell denied that he had in mind a set of survey or "interdisciplinary" courses, or courses of the type called "great issues." In his sequence, the concluding phase would set the fund of knowledge previously acquired into some larger appropriate context, showing its possible applications and connections.[82]

Some few others besides Bell wrestled with the question of what general education could mean in contemporary society. At a five-day Liberal Arts Conference sponsored in 1966 by the University of Chicago in observance of its seventy-fifth anniversary, a dozen or so conferees met to ponder the question first posed in the nineteenth century by Herbert Spencer: "What knowledge is of most worth?" Out of that meeting came a collection of papers published the following year under the title *The Knowledge Most Worth Having*.[83] During the course of the discussions, philosopher Richard McKeon offered four useful distinctions in the ways education might be considered "general." In his view, it could connote common learning shared by all—what the traditional prescribed curriculum had attempted to supply. Secondly, it could be construed as the search for principles or structures underlying all knowledge—what proponents of epistemic "unity" and curricular "integration" had once looked for in theology or metaphysics and now sought in their modern surrogates. Thirdly, according to McKeon, general education might be taken to mean the search for learning appropriate to all human experience— no matter how acquired, through books or practical experience. Finally, it could be understood as the search for learning derived from or applicable to all cultures.[84] McKeon's distinctions surfaced repeatedly throughout the conference. Although the meeting concluded with agreement as to the basic goals and outcomes of general education, agreement on how to organize a curriculum to achieve them proved as elusive as ever. In the meantime, however, other events on campuses had begun to overshadow academic discussions of how to preserve general learning in the modern world.

STUDENT ACTIVISM AND DISSENT

Observers of the American collegiate scene in the late 1950s and early 1960s had marveled over how quiet things seemed. There was little of the excitement or ferment of the Jazz Age or of the activism of the Depression era. Correspondingly, relative quietude prevailed on the nation's campuses, punctuated occasionally only by "panty raids" and other post-adolescent rituals of a similar character. One did not hear much discussion on campus, for, it was widely assumed, there was not very much to discuss. Professors found college students lethargic, passive, acquiescent, and apathetic. They seemed to lack "big ideas," ran a common complaint. It was—or so it was assumed—a time when academe had sunk into the cultural and intellectual doldrums.

Comparing the apathetic collegians of the fifties with college students of an earlier day, commentators recalled incidents in which nineteenth-century students had rioted over bad food, inadequate housing, and excessively strict rules. In the early twentieth century, as previously noted, students were marching in protest against rearmament and the nation's involvement in the First World War. In the 1920s and 1930s, students gave strong expression to their views about immigration, free speech or the World Court.[85] Yet after World War II, when returning veterans flooded campuses, the climate changed. These older and more mature students, intent upon pursuing their studies and obtaining employment, had little time for outside social involvements. Throughout the 1950s, the same trend continued. There was muted criticism of racial segregation; and sporadic protests took place against the escalating international arms race. Opposition to the atmospheric testing of nuclear weapons was another cause that inspired relatively small numbers of students to join in petition drives, marches, and rallies (until by international treaty all testing by the superpowers went underground, whereupon interest waned). The anti-Communist agitation of Senator McCarthy of Wisconsin and the nefarious witch hunts of the House Committee on Un-American Activities likewise aroused students' ire. But those in the main were exceptions that proved the rule. On the whole, it was noted at the time, college students typically remained quiet and relatively uninvolved with larger social concerns. They were, according to pundits, a "silent generation."

As the decade of the sixties opened, the nation's mood seemed almost euphoric. A new president had just been elected—young, bright, and charismatic. Heady idealism was in the air, a sense of commitment very different in spirit from the seeming apathy and conformism characteristic of the fifties. With a "New Frontier" at hand, Americans looked to the future with confidence and renewed optimism. A scant three years later, the staccato report of gunfire in Dallas abruptly brought the dream to an end. Energetic optimism suddenly turned into doubt. Before the decade was over, the general mood would become one of profound disenchantment. Few could have foreseen the series of traumas into which the country would be plunged over the next few years, shaking it to its very foundations.

The first seismic tremor came when leaders of the nation's 19 million blacks served notice they would endure no longer the humiliation and discrimination they had suffered since Emancipation. Deprived of the right to vote by poll taxes and trumped-up literacy tests, consigned to segregated housing, and isolated in schools that all too frequently prepared only for menial employment, blacks were now resolved to gain for themselves the basic civil rights to which they were entitled under the Constitution and which had been so long denied them. What ultimately evolved into a major crusade for social justice and equality of opportunity had its beginnings in early February, 1960, when four black students in Greensboro, North Carolina, were refused service at a segregated Woolworth lunch counter. They remained seated for the rest of the day. A sit-in began.[86] The confrontation touched off scores of similar incidents throughout the South, followed by sympathy picketing of stores owned by the same chain in the North. On February 17 the Congress for Racial Equality (CORE) weighed in with its support for the sit-ins. The movement continued, gaining strength from a successful economic boycott staged in Montgomery, Alabama. More protests followed. At first scores, then hundreds, and finally thousands joined in the marches and demonstrations that had begun to spread across the country.

In the North, college students circulated petitions, solicited funds, and joined picket lines. Hundreds, black and white alike, set out at considerable personal risk to themselves as "freedom riders" to lend their support to the work of civil-rights activists in the Deep South. There they faced assaults, fire hoses, police dogs, and jeering, angry mobs. Within a matter of months the civil-rights crusade was making itself felt on college campuses across the country. More rallies and fund-raisers and demonstrations were held. Once-silent students, many of them at least, had aroused themselves from indifference and taken up the cause of racial equality.

At the same time, the United States was gradually becoming embroiled in a bitter civil war half a world away. Starting as a small-scale effort to "contain" Communist aggression in southeast Asia, it now had expanded to the point where inconclusive military involvement threatened a major debacle. The American public grew disheartened and ever more confused as the nation's commitment escalated, each step inexorably drawing the country in deeper. Costs and casualties rose at an alarming rate. Scattered antiwar demonstrations broke out in various parts of the country. Still the conflict dragged on, seemingly without purpose or resolution. The prospect of defeat was unthinkable. Yet military victory remained as elusive as ever. Time and time again, officialdom offered bland assurances that the end was in sight. But skeptics believed otherwise, and their misgivings proved contagious. In 1965 U.S. forces began bombing North Vietnam, setting off another round of domestic protests. By the late 1960s, with peace still not achieved, antiwar sentiment had grown stronger still. Pacifist sit-ins, open resistance to the draft, and expanding youth dissent threatened to tear the nation apart.

One social cause interacted with another synergistically, building momentum; and in process many American youths were thoroughly radicalized. College campuses increasingly were scenes of feverish activity as students marched, staged protests, gathered for rallies, and prepared their demands. At Berkeley, the issue was free speech. On September 16, 1964, officials announced that a strip of land owned by the university which had long been used by off-campus political groups as a convenient site for soliciting support and distributing literature was now off-limits. Protests erupted. There were all-night vigils, marches, and picketing of the chancellor's office. University officials were unmoved. On October 1 a nonstudent was arrested for soliciting funds for the Congress of Racial Equality (CORE). Student demonstrations resumed with even greater vigor and militancy. Over the course of the next three months, university officials vacillated between offering concessions to students' demands and issuing their own. Draconian penalties were imposed, then rescinded; concessions were offered, and as quickly retracted. The mood on campus grew even uglier. Students were suspended, among them a young graduate student by the name of Mario Savio who had emerged as the de facto if unofficial leader of what was now dubbed the Berkeley Free Speech Movement. A student-faculty strike was called, and protesters began engaging in calculated acts of civil disobedience on an unprecedented scale.[87]

The protest at Berkeley gave rise to comparable confrontations and demonstrations over free speech as well as other issues at colleges and universities coast to coast.[88] A protest group, the Students for a Democratic Society, or SDS, quickly expanded into a powerful national organization offering its support and encouragement to student protesters everywhere.[89] Young people distrusted the political system and doubted whether change within a framework of law and politics-as-usual was possible. The assassination of black leader Malcolm X, the later assassinations of Martin Luther King, Jr., and Robert Kennedy, the Watts riots that broke out in greater Los Angeles, and the bombing of North Vietnam all sparked further anger, confirming in the eyes of many their conviction that the world had run amok. Simultaneously adding to the general chaos was the rise of a strong separatist movement among blacks. Black power was symbolized by the expulsion of white sympathizers from a civil-rights organization and movement led by Stokely Carmichael and by the rise to national prominence of such strident advocates of black pride and black power as Huey Newton and Bobby Seale.

In April of 1968, black students seized the administration building at Columbia University.[90] Their protest was directed in part against the university's proposed relocation of black residents from a ghetto area where it owned property near the edge of the campus. The intent was to clear the way for the construction of a new gymnasium. In the ensuing melee, several were injured and many more arrested. Classes were suspended. Violence broke out repeatedly between students and law enforcement officers called in to quell the disturbance. Not until February of 1969 did Columbia announce an indefinite suspension of its construction plan.[91]

The war in Vietnam overshadowed all else as student dissidents became ever more unruly and combative. As the decade wore on, violence on all sides increased in both scale and frequency. Terrorist acts occurred and threats of bombing became almost commonplace. Black separatists and antiwar protesters alike issued "non-negotiable" demands. Faculty suspected of not supporting students were subjected to acts of humiliation and intimidation. Administers were branded racists and traitors when they resisted. Nasty racial confrontations occurred at Northwestern, at Cornell, and at San Francisco State. Black separatists loudly demanded more black faculty and students, special admissions for blacks, and autonomous black studies programs.[92] Students' targets expanded, now encompassing not simply the war or conscription or racism, but also issues involving student governance, government defense contracts, and military recruiters on campus. Sometimes controversies flared over issues far beyond the control of academic institutions; other times debate fastened upon colleges and universities as the alleged instruments of what student protesters were now claiming was an unjust, irremediably corrupt Establishment.[93]

President Edward J. Bloustein of Rutgers in a speech delivered in May of 1968 (reprinted in *The University and the Counterculture*, 1972) attempted to make sense of the chaos. "Too many of our academic leaders have mistaken the true nature of the student revolt," he declared. "They are confused because at different times it appears to be addressed to one or another of different, relatively insignificant, or, even when not significant, relatively isolated, facets of college life. First it is free speech on campus, then it is visitation hours in student rooms, then admissions and scholarships for black students, then recruitment of students by war industries, then the building of a gymnasium in an urban slum, then the contract relationship between the university and a defense research corporation." Bloustein's analysis linked seemingly disparate phenomena together, tracing them back to a single theme. "The connection between these seemingly isolated forays is that they all represent a testing of the academic decision process; they all go to challenge the legitimacy of the constitutional apparatus of the college or university." He concluded, "Student activists have chosen to throw the gauntlet down . . . on issues which go to test the academic hierarchy."[94]

As the incidence and intensity of protests spread from a select few large, prestigious, highly selective institutions to other public and private colleges and universities, as the violence increased and disruptions grew more pronounced, as students' rhetoric became still more inflammatory, public alarm and hostility increased. Highly sensationalized accounts of each new incident appeared in newspapers, magazines, and on the nightly television news, further fanning the flames of discontent. A culmination of sorts took place in the summer of 1968 with a massive, bloody confrontation at the Chicago National Democratic Convention, where youthful, long-haired demonstrators fought pitched battles in the streets. Shouting antiwar slogans and hurling invectives at the police, self-styled revolutionaries assaulted the barricades at every turn. To onlookers, it seemed the world had gone mad. No longer was it possible to dismiss student dissent as the product of youthful high spirits—there was too much anger. No longer was it possible to blame unrest on a handful of wild-eyed radicals lacking any broad basis of support—the streets were mobbed. Nor could blame for much of the disruption and unrest be placed on a few black malcontents alone—dissidents numbered in the thousands and they came in all colors.

Especially bewildering to many was the emergence of a youth counterculture utterly contemptuous of traditional middle-class values. Most of the renegades, observers noted, were themselves products of the "middle America" they so despised or at least professed to reject, a world of economic security and social respectability. Yet for the first time in recent memory, college students—or a vocal segment of them, at any rate—were in open rebellion against the traditional ethic of hard work, social status, and competition for material success. They rejected with derision and scorn all the established verities of the past, opting instead for an ill-defined ethic of radical individualism and self-absorption. They were, some feared, anarchists and barbarians on the loose in the midst of what heretofore had been a well-ordered, technocratic social order.[95]

The contagion spread from campus to campus, from college to college, from university to university. Parents barely recognized their offspring. Young men wore their hair indecently long. Young women openly flaunted their sexuality, or just as conspicuously obscured it. Garbed in tattered fatigues, baggy pants, and ankle-length skirts, they adorned themselves with beads and luminous body paint. Some were resolutely apolitical. As many others were deeply involved in protest. And they were everywhere, not just as cultural dropouts in New York's East Village or the Haight-Ashbury section of San Francisco, long-time meccas for hippies and assorted flower children. They were to be found now in Madison and Bloomington, in New Haven and Cambridge, on campuses across the country.

What seemed incomprehensible to many was how young radicals seemed to have turned their backs deliberately on modern civilization. Equally troubling were the preachments of their gurus, with their strange credo of peace and protest, of harmony and confrontation, of love and hatred, of avowed toleration combined with the most egregious intolerance. The music of the counterculture was hard acid rock; its art was psychedelic; its diversions were sex and drugs; and its religion was conformity to nonconformity. Students—or, rather, the minority engaged in open rebellion—were an enigma, and a direct frontal challenge to almost everything traditionalists held dear.

President Bloustein, once again, captured to good effect the seeming contradictions of the new generation. "They profess individuality," he observed in a speech in Cleveland in August of 1971, "but exemplify conformity in their attachment to their own hair styles and dress codes. They profess humanism, but they tend to degrade reason, the very quality which makes us human. . . . They celebrate consciousness, but then paralyze it with drugs. They eschew our technology, but delight in motor bikes, electronic music, recordings, television and hi-fi. They thoroughly disdain wealth and property, but live . . . on parental allowances. They profess to the love of all mankind, but many of them steal and cheat from each other and from us. They seek universal peace, but often undertake or applaud violence in the service of their ends. They pretend to humility, but display arrogance and self-righteousness toward those with whom they disagree. They cherish the freedom to express themselves, but would often deny that right to those they violently oppose."[96] And finally, he reminded his audience, they were their own children.

On April 30, 1970, the Nixon administration announced a U.S. invasion of Cambodia. Within hours, sporadic protests and student strikes had broken out at a dozen or more colleges and universities, among them at Kent State University in Ohio. Ensuing events portended a major tragedy in the making. Up until then, the Kent State campus had been relatively free of major disturbances or upheavals. The president's announcement on Thursday was followed the next day by an orderly antiwar rally. That Friday evening and over the weekend, however, roving bands of students smashed local merchants' store windows and engaged in random acts of vandalism. On Saturday, the university's ROTC building was set afire. The city mayor declared a state of civil emergency; and on Sunday the state's governor responded by calling in contingents of the National Guard.

Shortly after noon on Monday, May 4, guardsmen found themselves the targets of jeers, obscenities, and rock-throwing by a large angry crowd of students assembled near an open field in the middle of the campus. Eyewitness reports and official accounts differed on what happened next. Apparently fearing for their safety, armed guardsmen let loose with a total of at least sixty-one shots. Four students were killed, another lay wounded. The nation was in shock.[97] Again, ten days later, at predominantly black Jackson State, roving crowds of students threw rocks, set trash fires, and angrily confronted law enforcement officers sent in to restore order. On the evening of May 14 a fusillade of some 150 shots sprayed across the facade of Alexander Hall, a women's dormitory. The result was two students dead and a dozen others wounded. Later that same summer, fatal violence erupted once again, this time on the campus of the University of Wisconsin, where a building alleged to house defense-related research was wrecked by a bomb explosion. One person was killed, four were injured.[98]

Groping for explanations of the violence, various commission and fact-finding panels began issuing reports. A national "Commission on the Causes and Prevention of Violence" devoted an entire chapter to the politics of student unrest and dissent. The president's 1970 Commission on Campus unrest, chaired by former governor William Scranton of Pennsylvania, weighed in with its own opinions and recommendations. Less conciliatory in attitude than that displayed by the Commission he had appointed to investigate, President Nixon dismissed campus radicals as "bums." His vice-president, Spiro Agnew, was even less charitable, deriding activist students as "an effete corps of impudent snobs." But if violence on campuses did not end soon, and if the response to it were either too lax or too harsh and indiscriminate, some editorialists averred, there was a danger that the vast moderate student majority might be forced into the arms of revolutionaries bent on destroying the fabric of higher education. As an editorial in the June 8, 1969, *New York Times* expressed the thought, "If lasting damage to the independence of the universities is to be avoided, if the society's attention is to be redirected to its larger, more serious problems, violence has to cease and tranquillity has to be returned to the campuses."

Apocalyptic predictions abounded. Some imagined that if campus unrest continued unchecked, faculty might be tempted to retreat into exile, abandoning colleges and universities for research institutes or other careers. Students would emulate their teachers and depart for student-run "free" or independent, improvisational "counter-universities." Alternatively, some critics cautioned against overreaction, warning that "police-state" tactics on the part of officialdom would serve only to inflame passions further. Everywhere confusion reigned.

From the radical left came demands for the wholesale dismantling of the "Establishment" and mainstream bourgeois culture. Radical rhetoric reached deluge proportions. Calls were sounded for new forms of education, for alternatives to traditional usages, for more socially relevant learning. Proponents of reform rather quickly won national prominence for their militant denunciation of universities as instruments of repression and alienation. The same themes cycled repeatedly. Protesting against American materialism, racism, social and economic injustice, inequalities, class favoritism, against dehumanization and cultural oppression, student critics of education and their faculty allies argued for more diversity, pluralism, and individual freedom. Liberal learning, when it was mentioned at all, was denounced as elitist, undemocratic, class-bound, and anti-egalitarian. Social "relevance" was now the sole criterion by which learning should be judged—that is, education capable of providing leverage against society's immediate pressing needs.

Disconcerted, troubled, sometimes angered, often traumatized by the emotion-ridden young, college and university officials felt unsure how to respond. Were these youthful revolutionaries harbingers of a new age to come? Or were they simply troubled students with no one else to taunt? Many observers were uncertain, especially when they sympathized with students' reformist aims without necessarily subscribing to their specific curricular demands. Official reactions reflected that ambivalence. More than a few commentators later ruefully concluded that the elimination of course and distribution requirements frequently effected was often mindless, and enacted without much thoughtful consideration of possible consequences. Robert Blackburn and his associates, in a Carnegie Council–sponsored survey of educational reforms between 1967 and 1974, cited the case of one institution where prolonged faculty tension (exacerbated by the discovery of an FBI agent agitating students to burn down the ROTC building) was relieved by an unplanned, spur-of-the-moment faculty meeting at which all curricular requirements were instantly eliminated. While this was an admittedly extreme instance, Blackburn and his colleagues concluded that major curricular change was seldom accompanied by extended faculty consideration of the larger aims of collegiate education or judgments about what knowledge was most worth having. All too frequently, rather, changes were framed by the exigencies of the moment and by immediate political expediency.[99]

Nightmarish visions of academic genocide, quite unexpectedly, began to recede as the 1970s progressed. In 1971 there had been an estimated one thousand incidents of varying magnitude on college campuses. Twelve months later, the frequency of campus disruptions and protests had dropped by half. By the middle of the decade, unrest had virtually ceased.[100] Some commentators found the sudden quiet nothing less than "eerie."[101] The winding-down of the war, an end to the draft, a severe economic downturn—each had probably contributed in its own way to the return to "normalcy." Whatever the factors responsible, compared with what had gone before, an almost funereal calm descended on campuses. Students behaved almost as though nothing had happened. Once again colleges and universities were thronged with collegians more interested in burning the midnight oil than draft cards, bras, or buildings. It was a new generation of collegians once again, a group whose members were more interested in grades than sit-ins, intent now on securing jobs after graduation or gaining admission to graduate school. For a time at least, the era of confrontation and protest, of student dissent and campus obstruction, was over. Peace had somehow inexplicably returned, and it would endure for some time to come.

PART 4

CONTEMPORARY CHALLENGES AND ISSUES

8

Another Season of
Discontent: The Critics

GENERAL EDUCATION RECONSIDERED

Once it became apparent that the era of collegiate turmoil in the sixties was over and relative tranquility had returned to the campuses of the nation's colleges and universities, there were signs in the early 1970s that the American academic community was now willing to take a fresh look at general education. Once again, official enthusiasm for liberal learning resurfaced. Once again there ensued a national debate, an outpouring of books and articles on the subject, a rash of curricular experiments, and a few new proposals which, in the public mind, came to epitomize the movement.

In the aftermath of the Vietnam war and the isolationism that swept the country, many pundits began calling for the development of curricula designed to foster a more global perspective, a larger world consciousness. New learning was called for at a time when it had grown obvious that the nation's destiny was linked inexorably with the fate of other peoples around the world. Others, in the wake of the Watergate scandal of the Nixon administration in Washington, urged more attention to moral training and ethics education. Environmental education took on new urgency. Above all, some sort of general education was argued for as an antidote to the narcissistic self-absorption allegedly characteristic of the college student generation of the 1970s. Liberal learning likewise was viewed as a palliative for rampant vocationalism and professionalism on campuses. Calls for common learning to counter the elimination of general requirements effected a decade or so earlier in the 1960s were repeatedly issued.[1]

"Contemporary liberal education," declared Willis D. Weatherford, chair of the 1971 Commission on Liberal Learning of the American Association of American Colleges, "seems irrelevant to much of the undergraduate population and, more especially, to middle America. The concept of intellect has not been democratized; the humanities are moribund, unrelated to student interest, and the liberal arts appear headed for stagnation. Narrow vocational education has captured the larger portion of political interest." Weatherford placed the blame equally on faculty, students, and public officials. "The liberal arts college," he alleged, "are captives of illiberally educated faculty members who barter with credit hours and pacts of nonaggression among their fiefs and baronies. Illiberally educated politicians, who want a bigger gross national product with scant regard for whether the mind and lives of the persons who produce it are or are not gross, make their own negative contribution, as do illiberally educated students."[2] As though to confirm Weatherford's indictment, half a dozen years later the Carnegie Council on Policy Studies in Higher Education reported that between 1967 and 1974 general-education requirements, as a percentage of undergraduate curricula, had dropped dramatically. "Today there is little consensus on what constitutes a liberal education," the Council found, "and, as if by default, the choices have been left to the student." General education, the report claimed, "is now a disaster area. It had been on the defensive and losing ground for more than 100 years."[3]

Attempts at analyzing causes for the "disaster" dominated an ever-growing body of literature. Between the mid-seventies and mid-eighties, the total number of published books and articles treating relevant topics registered a tremendous increase, more than doubling the number for the preceding ten-year period, from 1965 to 1975. The same trend continued into the mid-1990s. Throughout, however, there was remarkable unanimity of opinion on what forces threatened to gut the substance of liberal and general education, leaving perhaps only an empty rhetorical shell. Commentators were agreed that the professionalization of scholarship in higher education had been a major factor contributing to fragmentation and specialization. A second factor inimical to the cause of the liberal arts was the modern tendency to treat knowledge as a commodity, something to be "used" or "consumed." Finally, the structural organization of the university itself was identified as a culprit. Such allegations had been heard before, of course. But they were given new clarity and force in analyses of the apparent decline of liberal educational values.

Clark Kerr, former president of the University of California at Berkeley, had argued in the opening years of the 1960s that the American university had become a "multiversity" under pressure from its many publics.[4] Faced with an explosion of knowledge and rising demands that it serve the needs of business, government, the military, and other groups and causes, the character of the university had been transformed. Too harassed to lead, university administrators had become mediators among competing interests, trying to balance contradictory demands, treating students as consumers, knowledge as a factory product, and course offerings as supermarket wares. In the confusion, general learning was bound to be overlooked. For Kerr, the rise of the multiversity had come about as a result of the radical democratization of higher education and the colleges' inability to resist social, business, and governmental pressures.

Critic Robert Paul Wolff in *The Ideal of the University* (1969), Brand Blanchard in *The Uses of a Liberal Education* (1973), and Christopher Jencks and David Riesman in *The Academic Revolution* (1977) all tended to offer the same diagnoses. Universities, they alleged, had grown complacent, less reflective about their own practices.[5] Bereft of any guiding intellectual vision, most institutions of higher learning had settled for hodgepodge curricula, which thinking students rightly disdained as "required irrelevance." Corrupted by populism, professionalism, and assembly-line scholarship, universities had allegedly given themselves over to turning students to specialized professional careers as quickly as possible. Having abandoned their integrity to marketplace flux and flow, such institutions had lost the will to insist upon any intellectual coherence or unity in their vast offerings. Universities, many further argued, had become knowledge factories. They were the principal manufacturers and retailers of knowledge as a commodity. Their buyers included students seeking credentials to guarantee themselves prosperous futures, industries in search of the skills and products of research, and governmental agencies needing an array of specialized services. In their quest for competitive advantage and prestige, such critics lamented, academic institutions had "sold themselves out" to the highest bidders.[6]

In the absence of a scheme of values commanding broad assent within society, it was said, academic disciplines had sought to be value-free, each imitating the neutral discourse of the so-called "hard" sciences. The result, according to one anonymous wit, was the appearance of social sciences that were not terribly "social" and humanities that were not very "humane." The American university had committed itself to all that was objective, countable, precise, and verifiable. Its focus, once again, was upon knowledge as a commodity, packaged for consumption in tidy little bundles called credit units, hours, and courses.[7] Further, given the standing assumption that larger questions of human meaning, purpose, or significance are unanswerable, and hence not worth asking seriously, universities had acceded to the popular belief that ultimate questions are nonintellectual, subjective, and not amenable to reasoned analysis or dispute.[8] The proof, or so it was claimed, as Herbert I. London, dean at New York University, phrased it, was the degree to which a so-called cult of neutrality prevailed in academe. Combining behavioristic, reductionist, and positivist leanings, London alleged, it was a mentality or mind-set that had "created a Gresham's Law of curriculum design: That which is measurable will drive what is not measurable out of the curriculum." The "minimalists," he feared, if unopposed, would eventually destroy what was left of the liberal-arts tradition in higher education and make general learning impossible.[9]

Historian Page Smith, founding provost of the University of California at Santa Cruz, later referred to the same phenomenon as a species of mindless reductionism. It was, he alleged, a kind of "academic fundamentalism" at work in the marketplace of ideas, where all ideas are considered equal and no value judgments are admitted or considered worthy of examination. The result, as he analyzed it, was a profound impoverishment of the human spirit within academe, exacerbated by the general demoralization of all of the nonscientific disciplines and a fragmentation of knowledge to the point where it no longer made sense to speak of a "community of learning." What was left, Smith alleged, was an aggregation of specialists scarcely able to communicate with one another, much less with any outside public.[10]

Herbert London, writing in *Change* magazine in 1978, was not optimistic about prospects for liberal and general learning in the modern college or university. Efforts to find a shared view of appropriate undergraduate experiences, in his opinion, reflected compromise among faculty factions, not consensus. The issue of a possible "core curriculum," for example, had become particularly touchy at a time when many academic departments were more concerned with survival than principle. Behind the rhetoric of some holistic approach, specialists were pressing for a wider array of specialized courses. And in the intense competition for space, time, and resources, "a ballot to determine the complexion of the curriculum is very often simply a pork barrel bid." Anxious to preserve faculty jobs and bolster enrollments, one department votes for another's preferred course selection in exchange for support of its own required course in the general education program. "Of what value is debate about academic issues in this climate of academic backscratching?" London asked rhetorically.[11]

Critics of American higher education from the late 1970s through the 1990s sensed the malaise affecting colleges and universities across the country, though less often were they in agreement over its meaning or significance. It had been brought on, it was said, by an economic crunch, by changing student enrollments, by curricular disagreements, and, more broadly, public skepticism over the practicality of any general education whatsoever. Writing in 1978 in *Change* magazine, Barry O'Connell felt college students would not easily be disabused of the persistent notion that general learning had nothing to do with career preparation. But he was inclined to offer a more charitable interpretation of students' expectations and desires. Taking their cues from their elders, he said, students were pressured to elect courses most directly relevant to their chosen careers. Told of the oversupply of graduates competing for fewer desirable jobs, it was understandable that they should feel compelled to hold everything else in abeyance as they prepared themselves for employment. "This process does not conduce to much self-respect among the current student generation," O'Connell commented. "Having lost their faith, as it were, they must now endure the excoriations of their teachers and the media for being narrowly obsessed with careers, and, if one believes most of the curricular reports, inept at writing, incompetent in mathematics, and moral barbarians."[12] Students unquestionably needed a broad general education, he argued, but their disinclination to pursue it was entirely understandable.

Throughout the last two decades of the twentieth century, studies lamenting the state of general learning in collegiate curricula were issued with almost monotonous regularity.[13] In all cases, recurrent themes included pleas for more stringent academic standards, demands that ethical values be given more attention in learning, reiteration of the need to restore citizenship education to a place of primacy, and arguments in defense of a common learning capable of supplying a more coherent unifying purpose and structure to undergraduate curricula.[14]

MULTICULTURALISM AND THE "POLITICAL CORRECTNESS" CONTROVERSY

Were it not for the fact that the so-called PC controversy of the late 1980s and early 1990s received so much attention in the public press, it would be tempting to dismiss it as just another short-lived if curious episode in the history of American higher education. But campus debates over affirmative action, the attempted proscription of "hate speech," and curricular "canonicity" pointed beyond themselves to a host of quite fundamental issues having to do, among other things, with the sociology of knowledge, with academic politics and equity, free speech, multiculturalism, ethnic separatism and feminist activism, textual criticism in the humanities, the role of general education in higher learning, and, more broadly still, with the very nature of the role of colleges and universities within the social order. To some observers, the various controversies and debates over "political correctness" lacked much sense or substance, amounting to little more than an intellectual tempest in an academic teapot, an exercise in overblown rhetoric soon to be forgotten. To others, the furor symbolized a long overdue protest against subversive professorial radicalism; misplaced egalitarianism; and the moral bankruptcy of academic institutions allegedly brought about by a wholesale politicization of higher learning. To still others of different persuasion, the conflict represented nothing less than a needed effort to expose once and for all the enduring "mystification" of the university's role in the reproduction of social, economic, and cultural inequality and injustice in American society.[15]

National debate over political correctness began in the fall of 1990, with the appearance of a lengthy article in the *New York Review of Books* (December 6, 1990) authored by John Searle, a philosophy professor at Berkeley. A new postmodern generation of professors molded by the radicalism of the 1960s had finally come to power in American academe, he reported, and the results promised to be devastating to the world of conventional scholarship. The new breed of radicals, as he represented them, included radical feminists, gays and lesbians, Marxist ideologues, a diverse assortment of deconstructionists, structuralists, poststructuralists, reader-response theorists, new historicists, and a bewildering array of others. What they shared in common, Searle and others argued, was a desire to expose the facade of objectivity and critical detachment claimed by traditional bourgeois thought, and a programmatic disdain for all standards of judgment—intellectual, moral, and aesthetic—except their own ideologically-driven imperatives, which allegedly they held immune from criticism. Their precepts, according to the indictment, included the denial of any objective difference between truth and falsity, or between disinterested inquiry and partisan proselytizing. These new academic mandarins, or so it was claimed, were distinguished chiefly by a contempt for bourgeois rationality; and by their antipathy toward color-blind justice and advancement based on merit rather than according to gender, race, or ethnicity.[16]

Having come to positions of influence and authority in academe, Searle and others claimed, campus radicals were now engaged in promoting an ideology informed by a conviction that all of Western civilization was hopelessly oppressive and reactionary. Their conviction, it was said, was that general studies had been dominated exclusively by treatments of the accomplishments of "dead white European males" to the virtual exclusion of all others, that the entire historical, literary, and cultural "canon" was "Eurocentric" and "elitist." Because traditional general education courses were racist, sexist, and homophobic, study of the classic works of Western civilization needed to be replaced with courses devoted to Third-World cultures and victims of oppression. Multiculturalism as a curriculum reform initiative thus implied the retrieval of minority cultural capital from the marginality to which it had historically been consigned. But in process, or so it was alleged, postmodern radicals had generated an atmosphere of fear and repression. In the name of sensitivity to others, under pain of being denounced as a sexist or racist, radicals were forcing everyone to adhere to their own codes of politically correct speech and behavior.[17]

So arcane a controversy might have attracted little public attention beyond the precincts of the nation's ivory towers had it not been for the appearance in 1991 of a work entitled *Illiberal Education: The Politics of Race and Sex on Campus* by Dinesh D'Souza, former editor of a right-wing campus newspaper at Dartmouth, manager of a conservative public-policy quarterly, and a fellow at the American Enterprise Institute. His book, more than any other single work, served to focus and popularize the debate over political correctness in the first half of the decade of the 1990s.[18] At the root of divisive, often bitter controversies over race and gender simmering on college campuses across the country, D'Souza argued, lay conflicting standards of excellence and justice. The problem as he saw it began with preferential treatment for ethnic minorities. Although university administrators might try to disguise the truth about affirmative-action plans with evasive verbal gymnastics, according to D'Souza, the truth of the matter was that Orwellian "doublespeak" could not mask the inherent unfairness of racial quotas and double standards, no matter how laudable the desire to enhance minority opportunity or to redress historical inequities. Whereas people were entitled to their own opinions about tinkering with standards, he declared, they were not entitled to their own facts: "It is unequivocally the case that affirmative action involves displacing and lowering academic standards in order to promote proportional representation for racial groups."[19]

Precisely because affirmative action depended on unjust means to achieve its goal, he declared, it exacerbated racial tension and made authentic racial pluralism all the more unlikely. Only when measures that exalted group equality above individual justice were decisively repudiated, he judged, would interracial conflict abate. Administrative censorship of derogatory speech, mandated codes of discourse, and etiquette seminars would never suffice to eliminate campus racial tensions. Nor would acceding to the demands of special groups who sought to protect their own racial or ethnic identity on campus through separatist measures or institutions. "No community," he observed, "can be built on the basis of preferential treatment and double standards, and their existence belies university rhetoric about equality." He warned, "If the university model is replicated in the country at large, far from bringing ethnic harmony, it will reproduce and magnify the lurid bigotry, intolerance, and balkanization of campus life in the broader culture."[20]

D'Souza assailed what he felt was a chilling tendency on the part of campus radicals and some liberals to circumscribe debate about race and ethnicity, to insist upon a special lexicon of words in reference to women and minorities, and to insist that all others adhere to their code—in short, that everyone be "politically correct" in speech and conduct. Worse yet, D'Souza and other like-minded critics alleged, there was something terribly disingenuous about the way leftist radicals obfuscated or obscured their own motives by loudly denying that their intent was to harass or intimidate anyone, or that, indeed, any such thing as "political correctness" existed.

Those, in turn, who stood accused of intimidation from the left responded with criticisms of their own, scoffing at what they characterized as the "alarmist" posturing of a phalanx of dour political reactionaries and right-wing conservatives. The real problem, they argued, was that conservatives had willfully misrepresented their attempt to broaden or widen courses of study to reflect the differing needs and standards of marginalized groups formerly not adequately represented within the academy. To criticize the dominant curriculum as "Eurocentric," for example, was only to point out the obvious: that learning circumscribed by the culture and history of Europe and North America was limiting and no longer functional in a global community.[21] As Catharine R. Stimpson, dean of the graduate school at Rutgers University, expressed it in her 1990 presidential address before the Modern Languages Association, "Multiculturalism promises to bring dignity to the dispossessed and self-empowerment to the disempowered, to recuperate the texts and traditions of ignored groups, to broaden cultural history." She professed not to understand why any such movement would arouse such strident opposition. "I am baffled," she declared, "why we cannot be students of Western culture and of multiculturalism at the same time, why we cannot show the historical and present-day relations among many cultures."[22]

Dinesh D'Souza, for one, remained unconvinced. Multicultural courses, he charged in a television interview in June 1991, had "degenerated into a kind of ethnic cheerleading, a primitive romanticism about the Third World, combined with the systematic denunciation of the West."[23] Roger Kimball, author of a widely-read work entitled *Tenured Radicals: How Politics Has Corrupted Our Higher Education* (1990), took much the same position. Multiculturalist ideologues, he argued, were engaged in the "aggressive politicization" of academic studies. He deplored what he saw as "a pervasive animus against the achievements and values of Western culture" and the "subjugation" of teaching and scholarship to political imperatives. Celebrating "diversity" would be unobjectionable, Kimball averred, were it not for the fact that the concept or general theme had been converted into a rigid multiculturalist orthodoxy, any deviation from which by dissidents was likely to lead to social ostracism and expressions of contempt.[24]

Studying Western civilization as the appropriate core for general and common learning, defenders claimed, was justified, if by nothing else, by the ineluctable fact that contemporary American society *is* the product of the Western intellectual and cultural tradition, extending from classical antiquity down to modern times. If it was deemed too exclusionary, the remedy then was more inclusion—better representation of the achievements and works of non-European, non-male, non-white figures. Some opponents argued their objections had been misconstrued.[25] Defenders of the Western canon, they argued, were advocating a narrow and specific aggregation of cultural capital and holding it up as a normative referent for everyone. Opening the canon of itself was not enough, not so long as a small and powerful caste was able to claim it for its own. Nor was it a matter of proprietorship alone. The internal history of Western civilization, leftist critics charged, internally is a chronicle of the oppression of women and minorities. Externally, the story is one of imperialism and colonialism. Specific debate over what is or is not hegemonic, patriarchal, or exclusionary was therefore held by radicals to be fruitless. The solution to a closed, privileged club is not to open it to new members, but to abolish the "club" itself. Likewise, authentic cultural and curricular pluralism could not be achieved until old structures had been demolished and new learning configurations erected in their place. The answer to the problem of exclusion, as leftist critics saw it, was the development of an entirely different order of knowledge, a new construction quite unlike anything known before in American higher education.[26]

Curriculum theorist Michael Apple of the University of Wisconsin offered a leftist perspective on canonicity. Basically, his argument amounted to a categorical denial that there could be one textual authority, one definitive set of "facts" divorced from its context of power relations. A "common culture," he labored to show, could never be an extension to everyone of what a minority mean and believe. Rather, and crucially, an authentic shared culture would require not the stipulation and incorporation within textbooks of lists and concepts that make everyone "culturally literate," but the creation of "the conditions necessary for all people to participate in the creation and recreation of meanings and values." He concluded that a democratic process in which all people—not simply those who see themselves as the intellectual guardians of the "Western tradition"—nevertheless could be involved in the deliberation of what is important.[27]

Inevitably, increased visibility for leftist professorial voices and groups led to the spawning of rightist organizations as well, most notably the National Association of Scholars, a group dedicated to opposing what it characterized as the radical left-wing political agenda being advanced on campuses. By 1983 the eight-year-old organization had grown to nearly 3,000 members and claimed affiliated groups in 29 different states. William Pruitt, a literature professor from the City College of San Francisco, was quoted in the *Chronicle of Higher Education* (April 28, 1993), explaining the organization's rapid growth as a backlash to the criticism to which the NAS had been subjected. "A lot of these guys were hiding in carrels hoping the multicultural stuff would go away," he said. "Now they're coming out because they believe American democracy is at stake."[28]

In the 1990s, academe remained deeply polarized over affirmative action, speech codes, the movement toward a more multicultural curriculum, and the treatment of women and members of minority groups. Nevertheless, as the United States approached the end of the millennium, some observers detected a certain muting of inflammatory rhetoric, a greater willingness on both sides to offer concessions, a lessening of extremism. Activists on the left had grown more wary of policies aimed at restricting offensive speech. Scholars on the right appeared to be more open-minded about revising courses of study to include minority perspectives. Cautious experimentation was under way in many colleges and universities with devising new courses incorporating a more pluralistic cultural outlook.

Gerald Graff, an English professor at the University of Chicago and founder of Teachers for a Democratic Culture, a professional group formed to combat charges that campuses were dominated by political correctness, foresaw no immediate or dramatic resolution of issues raised by the PC controversy. But as quoted in the April 23, 1993, issue of the *Chronicle of Higher Education,* Graff anticipated greater civility in the discussions to come. "We still haven't constructed regular channels for conflict resolution," he remarked, "and we don't even recognize the need for them. I've been arguing that the place to do that is in the curriculum."[29] If nothing else, protagonists on all sides appeared more willing than formerly to explore the questions anew. In that respect, historically, they stood very much in the tradition of constant curricular revision that had characterized higher learning in America since its inception.

DIAGNOSING THE MALAISE

Despite its apparent robustness, some observers of American higher education in the last years of the twentieth century professed to detect a kind of pervasive "dis-ease" afflicting academe, what more than a few critics called a spiritual malaise, and others termed a peculiar "joylessness." George H. Douglas, a professor of English at the University of Illinois, writing in *Education Without Impact* (1992), agreed something was wrong with the nation's colleges and universities, though he dismissed claims they were in a state of "crisis." It seemed to him histrionic, alarmist even, to proclaim a crisis in higher education once again, for crisis had been the norm for decades on end.[30]

With the advent of Sputnik in 1957, when the country's technological leadership seemed jeopardized, alarms were sounded proclaiming a state of crisis in education at all levels, higher education included. Toward the end of the sixties, when colleges and universities were under siege by youthful student radicals and dissidents and all forms of authority were being attacked as illegitimate, pundits loudly proclaimed yet another campus crisis of major proportions. Ten years later, crisis loomed anew amidst claims that academic standards from kindergarten to graduate school had been seriously eroded, that the traditional curricular canon had disintegrated, and that compulsory multiculturalism and media-manufactured hysteria over "political correctness" had seemingly transformed each and every pedagogical debate into a life-or-death ideological conflict, a brouhaha threatening to tear asunder the fabric of American intellectual culture and, with it, academic institutions of higher learning.

But crisis by definition cannot be chronic, as Benjamin R. Barber, a professor of political science at Rutgers, observed in his *An Aristocracy of Everyone: The Politics of Education and the Future of America* (1992). As he phrased it, "On tenth hearing, the alarm bells inspire despair rather than action. Tired out by our repeated crises, we roll over in bed."[31] For Douglas, the condition afflicting American academe might have been better likened to a low-grade fever than to a terminal illness. America's colleges and universities, he judged, were suffering from "a kind of lethargy, a tediousness, a middle-age disease of some kind—something like arthritis, shall we say, or any disease that ebbs and flows."[32]

Interpretations of *what* precisely was wrong differed. Critics disagreed over the causes of academic malaise, and still more in their prescriptions for a cure. There was remarkable unanimity, nonetheless, about the more obvious symptoms. Historian Page Smith, in his 1990 work *Killing the Spirit: Higher Education in America* claimed the current academic scene resembled nothing so much as a vast metaphorical "desert." Sketching out historically what he perceived to have gone awry, he cited as major themes an alleged flight from teaching by the professorate, the egregious neglect of undergraduate education, the meretriciousness of most academic research, and the alliance of universities with corporate and governmental agencies. Each in its own way, he argued, had contributed to "killing the spirit" of American higher education, leaving behind something that to all outward appearances might appear as vibrant as ever, but within was hollow or dead.[33]

Comparable in its targets but far less temperate in tone was a diatribe unleashed by Charles J. Sykes, author of a widely read, muckraking work entitled *Profscam: Professors and the Demise of Higher Education* (1988) and a follow-up work, *The Hollow Men: Politics and Corruption in Higher Education* (1990). Professors, he claimed, were chiefly to blame for the ills afflicting academe; and in his opinion, they had a great deal to answer for. "Overpaid" and "grotesquely underworked," he alleged, they presided over a scandalous satrapy of inefficiency and waste. As a professional class, college and university teachers were typically neglectful of their teaching duties, "unapproachable, uncommunicative and unavailable" to the typical undergraduate, obsessed with research, and prone to turning over their classroom chores to an underpaid and overworked lumpen proletariat—graduate assistants—whenever expediency dictated.

Worse yet, as Sykes portrayed them, professors were guilty of inflicting thousands of useless articles and books upon the world, written in "stupefying and inscrutable jargon" that served only to mask the vacuous and trivial nature of their content. In their lust to fulfill their own professional careers, he claimed, professors were busily engaged filling up whole libraries with "masses of unread, unreadable and worthless pablum." American universities had degenerated to the point where they were now mere factories for "junk-think," their inhabitants devoted to woolly-headed, pettifogging theorizing of no conceivable value to anyone. The ubiquity of dull pedants raking over the dust heaps of learning, dispensers of tiny little packages of abstruse learning, Sykes declared, lay at the heart of almost everything wrong with American higher learning.[34]

CAREERISM AND THE ENTREPRENEURIAL UNIVERSITY

Often cited as a corrupting influence upon academe was its unholy alliance with business, industry, and government. Page Smith rehearsed the familiar story of the rise of the corporate university and its historic entanglement with business enterprise and the military-industrial establishment. "One must ask," he observed, "whether the university can, in the long run, preserve its freedom to carry on . . . in the face of . . . shameless huckstering. Who pays the piper calls the tune. There is no reason to believe that the university is immune to that law."[35] Benjamin Barber's *An Aristocracy of Everyone* went even further: "We may moralize about the virtues of education," its author wrote, "but higher education has come to mean education for hire: the university is increasingly for sale to those corporations and state agencies that want to buy its research facilities and, for appropriate funding, acquire the legitimacy of its professorate." He emphasized, "I do not mean the university in service to the public and private sectors; I mean the university in servitude to the public and private sectors. I mean not partnership but a 'corporate takeover' of the university."[36]

Barber judged that in the early 1990s the hegemony of markets in academe had grown virtually complete. Free inquiry in many fields had been subordinated to guided—which is to say, subsidized—research. Autonomous pedagogical standards had long since been displaced by market pressures from both immediate consumers (students) and long-term consumers (the private and public sectors). If established trends continued, he predicted, colleges and universities would end up becoming little more than pawns of the tastes, values, and goals of society at large, if they had not already become so.[37] Faculty who acceded to the system would continue to share in the spoils; those who did not would find themselves on second-class career tracks or even out of work. Research, publications, and external grants and contracts were what counted. And where commerce encroached upon higher education so blatantly, he judged, it was not to be wondered at that professors more and more were thinking like capitalists, or more modestly, like proletarians.

Barber's analysis of what was wrong with American higher education hinged in part on two contrasting models of the university, each allegedly a mirror image of the other, neither of them in his view fully adequate or satisfying. The first—the so-called purist model—as Barber depicted it, calls always for refurbishing the ivory tower and reinforcing its monastic isolation from the world. The other, the "vocational," apes the marketplace and urges that the tower be demolished, overcoming its isolation by embracing servitude to the market's whims and fashions, which—*mirabile dictu*—then pass as its purposes and aims. The purist model, essentially an embellishment on the medieval university as favored by nostalgic scholastics, seeks to insulate the university from society at large. Its primary concern is the abstract pursuit of speculative knowledge for its own sake. Learning is for learning's sake, not for power or happiness or career, but for itself as a self-contained, intrinsic good. To the purist, knowledge is "radically divorced from time and culture, from power and interest . . . [and] above all, it eschews utility."[38] The purist ideal of the university "knows a social context exists but believes the job of the university is to offer sanctuary from that context."

As Barber noted, the purist model in a sense was the old-fashioned liberal model of academe as a neutral domain in which free minds "engage in open discourse at a cosmic distance from power and interest and the other distractions of the real world." While he did not specifically allude to Robert Maynard Hutchins, the Chicago Plan of the 1930s might have come to mind as a prime example of some such model or ideal prominent in the history of twentieth-century American higher education.

The vocational model, in contrast, abjures tradition no less decisively than the purist model abjures relevance. Indeed, it is highly responsive to the demands of the larger society it believes education must serve. The vocationalist, according to Barber, wishes to see the university prostrate itself before the new gods of modernity. "Service to the market, training for its professions, research in the name of its products are the hallmarks of the new full-service university, which wants nothing so much as to be counted as a peer among the nation's great corporations, an equal opportunism producer of prosperity and material happiness." The vocationalist model looks with approval upon the image of the university forging alliances with research companies and with government, plying corporations for program funding and stalking the public sector in search of public "needs" it can profitably satisfy. "In each of these cases," Barber wrote, "it asks society to show the way and compliantly follows."[39]

Again, Barber adduced no specific historical precedents to illustrate his second model. Had he elected to do so, he would have found an ample supply of illustrations, for example, in the rhetoric of post–Civil War proponents of the modern research university throughout the late 1800s, and again in public pronouncements of the role and mission of the American university in the late 1950s and early 1960s.

If the purist model ignores issues of power and influence, the vocationalist model ignores how a focus upon research adapted to the needs of society corrupts, Barber believed. Advocates of the "Entrepreneurial University," he claimed, were impervious to the dangers. They were perfectly willing to subsume teaching to research, and research itself to product-oriented engineering. They showed little concern over careerism in academe. As he phrased it, "If it requires that education take on the aspect of vocational training, and that the university become a kindergarten for corporate society where in the name of economic competition the young are socialized, bullied, and brainwashed into market usefulness, then the curriculum must be recast in the language of opportunism, careerism, and professionalism—in a word, commerce. Every course is affixed with a 'pre' (as in premedical, prelaw, prebusiness, and pre-professional). Academic departments hem in students' intellectual lives with a bevy of technical requirements, which leave no room for liberal or general education and which assume that education for living is in fact education for making a living. . . . Where the philosopher once said that all of life is a preparation for death, the educational careerist now thinks that all of life is a preparation for business—or perhaps, more bluntly, that life *is* business."[40]

Many critiques of American higher education in the 1990s, like Barber's, were strikingly reminiscent of Thorstein Veblen's indictment in *The Higher Learning in America* (1918), which had appeared three-quarters of a century earlier. Veblen's complaint then, it will be recalled, was that captains of industry (among them Johns Hopkins, Daniel Drew, Leland Stanford and James B. Duke) had captured the nation's sleepy little colleges with promises of largesse and proceeded to turn them—some of them, at any rate—into stone, granite, and marble monuments to themselves. They had inflicted upon the academy, Veblen complained, a certain cast of mind, a crude utilitarianism, an expectation that universities would become more productive and more attentive to output, after the fashion of the businesses through which they as industrial magnates had built up their own fortunes. Under the model prescribed by a business ethos, the university was transformed into a place whose style or mode of operation was shaped by the spirit of business management, that is, by an insistence upon salesmanship, boosterism, bureaucracy, cost-control measures, and public relations, by a constant seeking of competitive advantage within the academic marketplace. The tone set was one of activity, bustle, and intrigue.

The institutional environment thereby created, Veblen labored to show, was one in which professors were reduced to mere hirelings, hemmed in by rigid professional practices and the dictates of the guild, and set to clawing their way up a ladder of career advancement not unlike that prevailing in business and industry. Veblen's somewhat overblown characterization of professors as prisoners of an inhumane and debilitating system, in the final analysis, fully anticipated Barber's equally sweeping claim in the early 1990s that "the vast apathetic mass of faculty . . . do not give a damn one way or another about what goes in [the classroom]."[41] Far too many professors on too many campuses, the latter alleged, "either do not care or cannot afford to. Certainly university administrators give them neither reason nor incentive. They have become 'employees' of corporate managers. . . . The demeaned status of teachers in the modern university gives scholars little reason to measure their career progress other than by how quickly they get tenure, how much they get paid, and how little time they have to spend in the classroom."[42]

SPECIALIZATION AND FRAGMENTATION

Robert Bellah, a professor of sociology at the University of California at Berkeley, who together with a number of associates authored a widely discussed analysis of American culture entitled *Habits of the Heart: Individualism and Commitment in American Life* (1985), linked the transformation of the nineteenth-century American college into the twentieth-century corporate university with a concomitant array of other social and cultural changes, none of them necessarily healthy for modern academe.[43] Before the Civil War, as he pointed out, liberal-arts colleges were too small to be divided into departments. (In 1872 the entering freshman class at Harvard had only 200 students; Yale had 131; Princeton, 110; Dartmouth, 74; and Williams, 49.) As late as 1869, there were no more than two dozen faculty members at Harvard, and they mostly taught the traditional subjects of classical languages and mathematics. The antebellum college was organized on the assumption that higher learning constituted a single unified culture; and literature, the arts, and sciences were viewed as branches of that whole. It was the task of moral philosophy, often a required course in the senior year, usually taught by the college president himself, not only to integrate the various fields of learning, including science and religion, but even more importantly to draw out the implications for the living of a good life individually and socially. The social sciences, Bellah noted, so far as they were taught at all, were subsumed under the heading of moral philosophy.

Throughout the latter half of the nineteenth century the research university began to supplant the college as the model for higher education—contemporaneously with the rise of the business corporation. The two institutions were manifestations of the same social forces. "Graduate education, research, and specialization, leading to largely autonomous departments, were the hallmarks of the new universities," Bellah and his colleagues noted. "The prestige of natural science as the model for all disciplined knowing and the belief that the progress of science would inevitably bring social amelioration in its wake partially obscured the fact that the unity and ethical meaning of higher education were being lost."[44]

On balance, Bellah felt there had been "great positive achievements" in that transformation of higher education. The new academic system was better adapted to preparing vast numbers of people for employment in an industrial society; and it included as students those who, because of class, sex, or race, had formerly been excluded. In an undeniable sense, the research university and its many spinoffs in the twentieth century brought democratization. Though the full promise did not begin to be fulfilled until after World War II, from the very beginning there was the idea of institutions open to a much wider spectrum of the society than the old colleges had ever been. And the new university, rather than providing the final polish to an already-established upper class, would itself be an avenue of advancement in the world. As Francis H. Snow of the University of Kansas, in his inaugural address of 1890 put it, "Let it be everywhere made known that the University of the State, every son and daughter of the state may receive the special training that makes chemists, naturalists, entomologists, electricians, engineers, lawyers, musicians, pharmacists and artists, or the broader and more symmetrical culture which prepares those who receive it for that general, well-rounded efficiency which makes the educated man a success in any line of intellectual activity."[45]

But there were costs also. Part of the price entailed by the rise of the modern research university and its attendant specialization and professionalism was, as Bellah put it, "the impoverishment of the public sphere." The new experts in science, in particular, exchanged general citizenship in society for membership within a smaller, more specialized community of experts. Within his field of expertise, the specialist's opinions would be judged henceforth not so much by the literate public at large as by his or her professional colleagues and peers. He was apt to become less intelligible to lay readers. Today's academic specialists, he observed, were writing within a set of assumptions and a vocabulary shared only by other experts. Specialization was inevitable. What was *not* inevitable, as Bellah judged it, was that discourse would tend to confine itself within the narrow limits of subcommunities of specialists without ever addressing any larger audience or informing public discussion beyond those subcommunities. Needless to add, in academe, any sense of integration, any moral dimension whatsoever, had disappeared.[46]

In a later work entitled *The Good Society* (1991), Bellah and his colleagues cited a still more troubling consequence flowing from the enthronement of scientific knowledge as a cultural paradigm for the modern research university. "Within less than two decades of its founding the effort to create an integrated, democratic higher education had degenerated into an early form of what we have come to know as the multiversity cafeteria," he and his associates remarked. "The research university, the cathedral of learning, rather than interpreting and integrating the larger society, came more and more to mirror it. Far from becoming a new community that would bring coherence out of chaos, it became instead congeries of faculty and students, each pursuing their own ends, integrated not by any shared vision but only by the bureaucratic procedures of the 'administration.'"[47] (As a university president was once heard to declare, "A university is an untidy constellation of academic and administrative units sharing in common little more than a heating plant.")

What Bellah referred to as the "multiversity cafeteria," and Barber the "full-service" university, George Douglas called the "giant bazaar" model of academe. "Since the end of the nineteenth century," he commented, "we Americans have gravitated toward the idea that the university is like a giant department store, an emporium, a bazaar of some kind, a place where people come to shop for things. People come to the university to purchase goods that are prepackaged or made to order. Students, for example, want to obtain degrees so that they can step out into a technologically complex world that requires specialized knowledge. They pay for those degrees and expect to receive them on time and at the right price, just like a person who buys a bolt of cloth in a dry goods store." Yet, as Douglas noted, just as buyers sometimes are shortchanged or cheated, today's students might not be receiving fair value for their investment. Further, there might be something quite fundamentally wrong with their being encouraged to think of knowledge as a consumable commodity, or education as something to be purchased off the shelf. Some such attitude, he felt, might be responsible for the tendency of many college students to consider their education as something simply to be endured, to be gotten over or gotten through, "as a cat shakes its paw to get rid of a few drops of water into which it has unfortunately been obliged to step."[48]

Part of the problem also, as many critics discussed it, was the extent to which "credentialism" had come to dominate students' attitudes toward higher education. The college degree, as Pierre Bourdieu and Jean-Claude Passeron noted (*Reproduction in Education, Society and Culture,* 1979), might not function directly as a guarantee or affidavit of job competency in a given field, but its acquisition signified the acquisition of a certain "cultural capital" recognized by employers and society at large as symbolizing a rite of occupational initiation, and hence required of those aspiring to a certain occupational status. The academic system, in other words, to the extent that it had replaced guild and apprenticeship training, had now become the means of controlling access to jobs.[49] It was not to be wondered at, therefore, that labor market considerations loomed large in students' interpretations of the meaning and purpose of their college education.

THE "PUBLISH OR PERISH" SYNDROME

Bellah's analysis did not explicitly treat university research or discuss it as a social phenomenon. If it had, it could easily have accounted for the importance accorded research in many institutions of higher learning; for how the model of cumulative extension of knowledge as a product of scientific investigation historically gained currency and came to generate separate imperatives for "doing research" in the social sciences and humanities as well as the physical and biological sciences or mathematics; for the ways in which the Germanic research ideal, as peculiarly adapted to the American cultural milieu, had the unintended outcome ultimately of encouraging a "publish or perish" mentality within the professorate; and for the weighty, sometimes mixed consequences of the research emphasis on undergraduate education.

In any case, many critics of American higher education in the 1980s and 1990s seized upon research as another part of the problem plaguing academe.

"If there is one thing that the general public has heard about college professors," observed Douglas, "it is that they are somehow burdened with the necessity of publishing the results of their research."[50] He went on to note that in many small colleges the emphasis on research was much less compulsive and in some places virtually nonexistent. Lack of pressure to publish in some smaller institutions, he further observed, was sometimes taken as a token of their mediocrity or inferiority by those holding appointments in the more prestigious institutions—which might or might not be true. But conversely, claims by those in liberal-arts colleges or other smaller institutions that they stressed good teaching rather than publication also might or might not be true. Either way, all observers were agreed that research productivity had become the *sine qua non* of the activist, corporate university. The issue at stake was how to assess the meaning and significance of that emphasis upon research and publication, both on its own terms and as a controlling consideration for academic advancement.

Economics professor Henry Rosovsky, a former dean at Harvard, offered a characteristic defense for university research.[51] University-level teaching is difficult without the new ideas and inspiration provided by research, he argued. Students are apt to interpret an interest in research as a symptom of lack of interest in teaching, and are encouraged to believe that teaching and research are a zero-sum game—that is, that more research leads to a neglect of teaching and vice versa. What they fail to understand, ran his argument, is that for faculty who find it congenial to work in research institutions, some combination of teaching and research is considered ideal. The university teacher is not a teacher who is expected to confine him- or herself to the transmission of received knowledge to generations of students, after the fashion perhaps of the old antebellum college teaching master. He or she is assumed to be a producer of new knowledge as well.

Rosovsky conceded that promotion, tenure, salary, and professional esteem were all closely associated with research and scholarship, and that pressures to publish in some cases could have adverse consequences. But he felt on balance that researchers tended to be "more interesting and better professors."[52] His argument, of course, was a familiar one: that the best teachers are obviously the leaders in any field of academic endeavor, that people who are on the "cutting edge" of inquiry are more likely to be creative teachers as well. Further, because published research is subject to peer scrutiny, it serves as a useful "quality-control" on the scholarship behind classroom instruction.

It was precisely that article of faith that increasingly came under attack in criticisms of higher education in the eighties and nineties. As Page Smith saw it, academic research had come to be viewed in a perverse sort of way as its own justification, without any real-world referent, producing a corpus of literature "as broad as the ocean and as shallow as a pond." The vast majority of research turned out in a modern university, he alleged, is essentially worthless, does not result in any measurable benefit to anything or anyone, does not push back the frontiers of knowledge so confidently and frequently invoked, and does not contribute much of significance to the general populace or any particular segment thereof—with the possible exception of those external agencies that sometimes subsidize its costs. So far as Smith was concerned, it was all "busywork on a vast, almost incomprehensible scale." The pity of it all was that so many professors had been forced into becoming unwilling accomplices to a system that forced them to write when, it was painfully obvious, they had nothing of significance to say.[53]

For Charles Sykes, research was an absurdly inflated boondoggle, an enterprise of doubtful worth carried on, often at public expense, without any real utility, cultural or otherwise. As for Rosovsky's argument and others like it that research and teaching are interdependent and mutually reinforcing, Barber remarked that the supposed synergy of the two amounted to a very dubious proposition lacking much supporting evidence. To talk about a "balance" between research and teaching, as he saw it, was an exercise in wishful thinking at best, and at worst, a lie. "The dirty little open secret of American higher education," he observed, "known to every faculty member who manages to gain tenure, is this: No one ever was tenured at a major college or university on the basis of great teaching alone; and no one with a great record of research and publication was ever denied tenure because of a poor teaching record. Teaching is the gravy, but research is the meat and potatoes."[54]

Much criticism of academic research fastened on the character or quality of what was being produced. Some alleged that the system forced professors to become even more specialized than the demands of their respective disciplines required, given the common academic expectation that "serious" scholarship confine itself to small problems, narrowly drawn topics or issues, and in-depth analysis of subjects of microscopic proportions and sharply delimited boundaries. Large sweeping theories had become suspect; straying beyond one's accredited field of expertise was now more and more frowned upon—in short, as one commentator expressed it, the message was that professors were safe only as they became intellectual and scholastic miniaturists. Other critics, like Bellah, assailed the withdrawal of much academic scholarship from issues of large public import, its seeming isolation from the cultural mainstream, its abdication of responsibility for forging linkages to society as a whole.

Still others criticized scholars for their alleged preoccupation with method and technique; and their deliberate penchant for writing in specialized, inaccessible languages intelligible only to other specialists. "They feast," claimed George Douglas, "on a weak gruel of dead abstractions occasionally seasoned with obscure pomposities."[55] Barber, for his part, felt that criticisms of academic scholarship were more than fully justified, and he felt they applied with special force to the new champions of democratic education no less than to others. The oddest feature about radical scholarship on race, ethnicity, and feminism, for example, he commented, "is how inaccessible it is to its purported constituencies. At least Marx's *Manifesto* was a good and popular read. . . . But a good deal of post-modernist criticism is intelligible only to insiders . . . and, trapped in its own metacritical jargon, is no less elitist than the canon it challenges."[56]

Detractors of academic research and scholarship apportioned blame in equal measure. Researchers in the natural sciences, they alleged, had shut themselves up within their respective specializations, each hermetically sealed and locked apart from one another. Social scientists had just as willfully erected fixed barricades around their own disciplines. Plagued by feelings of inferiority to their colleagues in the physical sciences, they allegedly had drawn a cloak of near-impenetrable technicality over their work and, in a vain attempt to ape the conventions of the "hard" sciences, were engaged in dressing up their investigations with ponderous argot and spurious quantification. Humanists—teachers of literature, language, history, and philosophy—according to Douglas, had indulged themselves in a new and deadly form of scholasticism distinguished chiefly by its obscurantism, bombastic prose, and introspective solipsism. The assorted "perversities" of structuralism, poststructuralism, deconstructionism, and other "murky impostures" in literary and historical analysis, he felt, held full sway. The scholasticism of the humanities, Barber agreed, was well illustrated by its tendency to take the very culture that is its putative object of study and to turn it into the study of the study of culture. Thus, he observed, one no longer reads and interprets books; one studies what it means to read books; one does not interpret theories, but develops theories of interpretation.[57] Overall, the constant refrain of a flood of books commenting on the state of American scholarship in the 1990s was that it appeared to have succumbed to a chilling form of "mandarism," that it had grown utterly remote and removed from the vital concerns with which academic inquiry had once been engaged. The ivory tower, it was said, had become a tower of babble.

LOSS OF COMMUNITY

Loss of a sense of community figured as a recurrent theme in several late-twentieth-century analyses of American higher education. Once again, although there were many other studies of the same genre which emphasized much the same motifs, George Douglas's *Education Without Impact* supplied an incisive case in point. Americans, he argued at length, had long demanded the "wrong" thing of colleges and universities, and institutions of higher learning had responded by developing an educational style well adapted to meeting the technical and commercial needs of society but not necessarily the needs of individuals as human beings, and certainly not the fundamental civic needs of the republic. Universities, he judged, were failing to provide the type of human setting in which education worthy of the term could thrive. They were too big, too full of activity, too busy to be places of authentic learning. Instead they had become merely factories for producing specialized expertise or for imparting information, in both cases doing so in a relatively routine and unimaginative fashion.[58]

For all of their primitivism, social isolation, stagnancy, and detachment, their limited curricula and autocratic paternalism, Douglas avowed, the old-style colleges that had their footing in colonial times were more authentic communities of learners. They offered little that was directly useful or practical; they prepared for an exceedingly narrow range of careers, and they were forced to make do with only a modicum of support, financial or otherwise. Nevertheless, for all their faults and shortcomings, at their best they provided an environment or an atmosphere in which genuine learning was possible. They afforded time and space for intellectual transactions between professors and students, opportunities for youthful learners to pose fundamental questions, chances to ponder and analyze and discuss issues of common interest. They took seriously the challenge to shape and inform character and to engage questions of normative judgment and standards. Their very smallness made for a type of cohesiveness and personal unity that was later lost. They were learning communities. Above all else, even when college authorities treated their charges as unruly schoolboys whose deportment had to be monitored and regulated in every particular possible, they did take them seriously as learners.[59]

Douglas and other like-minded critics might have invoked as an example of the guiding ideal of the old-style college William Johnson Cory's address (*Eton Reform,* 1861) to a group of young men about to embark upon the next phase of their academic careers. "You are not engaged so much in acquiring knowledge as in making mental efforts under criticism," he told them. "A certain amount of knowledge you can indeed with average faculties acquire so as to retain; nor need you regret the hours that you have spent on much that is forgotten, for the shadow of lost knowledge at least protects you from many illusions. But you go to a great school, not for knowledge so much as for arts and habits; for the habit of attention, for the art of expression, for the art of assuming at a moment's notice a new intellectual posture, for the art of entering quickly into another person's thoughts, for the habit of submitting to censure and refutation, for the art of indicating assent or dissent in graduated terms, for the habit of regarding minute points of accuracy, for the habit of working out what is possible in a given time, for taste, for discrimination, for mental courage and mental soberness." Cory concluded, "Above all, you go to a great school for self-knowledge."[60]

Something of that arcadian ambience of intimacy and leisured contemplation lingered on as formerly bucolic colleges and universities grew larger and were transformed into something else altogether. "Even when huge institutions grew up in the years just before the turn of our century," as Douglas phrased it, "persistent efforts were made to keep something of that essence of the small, ivy-covered college—otherwise we wouldn't have erected universities with Georgian or 'collegiate Gothic' buildings, with quadrangles and shaded paths. We would have stopped planting ivy."[61] (Interestingly, in another context altogether, historian Daniel Boorstin also discerned a special symbolic significance, albeit of a different sort, in collegiate architecture. If there was to be a new "religion of education," he observed, the universities would serve as its cathedrals, just as the high schools would become its parish churches. It was no accident, he felt, that American universities had adopted the architecture of the great age of European cathedral building. In short, for institutions that could afford it, "Collegiate Gothic" naturally became a standard.)[62]

On balance, critics of American higher education in the nineties did not appear overly optimistic about prospects for re-creating the spirit of a genuine learning community in academe. Gigantism—the sheer size and complexity of the modern university—seemed to militate against recapturing the closeness and intimacy said to be characteristic of higher learning in former times. The likelihood that mega-universities could be downsized to any appreciable extent (even if some such scaling-down was deemed desirable or necessary) seemed remote. Another factor at work, it was pointed out, was a dramatic increase in the percentage of students in colleges and universities attending on a part-time basis. Unable or unwilling to invest in full-time instruction, many students had long since abandoned the traditional four-year time frame for completing requirements for a bachelor's degree. Campuses were now thronged with older, returning students, both graduate and undergraduate, nontraditional collegians in their middle years, men and women whose career and familial responsibilities competed with academic pursuits for their time and energy. Even among the traditional 18- to 22-year-old cohort, economic pressures demanded that many hold down part-time or even full-time jobs while going to school. Under these circumstances, it was observed, chances of reviving the leisurely environment of the old-time college as a tightly knit community seemed nil.[63]

ACADEMIC STANDARDS

Allegations that academic standards had dropped precipitously was a familiar refrain among observers of the American collegiate scene in the eighties and nineties. Similar complaints had been voiced many times before, of course, and were hardly novel, but they appeared more frequently and seemingly with greater force than ever before. Part of the problem, according to one line of analysis, was that America as a democratic society had set for itself the goal of ensuring that as many of its youth as possible should graduate from high schools and continue on to college. Unlike pyramidal European models in which schools traditionally were called upon to perform a "winnowing-out" function, sorting and screening students and passing on only those of exceptional academic talent to the next higher echelon, the American approach was more radically egalitarian.

No effort was to be spared in seeing to it that everyone completed secondary education, and, further, that virtually anyone desiring access to higher education was afforded an opportunity to pursue a college degree. However, in the absence of national standards of academic achievement, not to mention the prevalence of open admissions policies, or so it was claimed, colleges and universities could take very little for granted in terms of ability or achievement among entering students. The presence on campuses of increasing numbers of students of indifferent or mediocre ability, many of them having graduated from the bottom half of their high-school classes, was bound to affect the rigor of collegiate education.

What was indisputable, in any event, was the trend toward nonselectivity in admissions. Whereas in 1955 over half of the nation's colleges and universities had some type of selective admissions policies in place, three decades later, in 1985, according to the New York Times' *Selective Guide to Colleges,* out of almost 3,000 institutions surveyed, fewer than 175 institutions were classified as "selective." What constituted "selectivity" was always open to debate, but at the extremes, the differences were obvious enough. In 1985, for example, Stanford University accepted no more than 15 percent of those applying; in the same year the University of Arkansas accepted fully 99 percent of all applicants.[64]

Considerable confusion continued to surround debates over the meaning and implications of egalitarian admission policies and practices. Some argued for an unabashedly "elitist" approach based on the concept of intellectual and academic meritocracy. Only the "best and brightest" ought to be admitted.

Sometimes a proviso was added that special efforts be made, in the sports jargon popular in the nineties, to "level the playing field"—that is, to equalize opportunities for anyone to demonstrate his or her potential to profit from higher learning, especially those from disadvantaged backgrounds. But the principle that higher learning was not for everyone was to be preserved. Others argued that opening the gates of academe to anyone seeking entrance was entirely unobjectionable and innocuous, so long as the principle was kept clear that "opportunity" did not mean "entitlement"—that is, that everyone deserved a chance to succeed, but they would be held accountable to certain institutional standards of academic achievement as a condition for retention.

In response, opponents argued it was a cruel hoax to hold out hope for success by admitting masses of students who, by any predictive standard, were unlikely to succeed. Accordingly, some commentators continued to claim that lack of stringent admission standards threatened to undermine the integrity of the entire academic enterprise. Finally, a few radical egalitarians, possibly a minuscule number, went so far as to urge the abandonment of any proficiency standards whatsoever—in which case, of course, concerns about possible failure would be rendered moot. Everyone would succeed in some way, at some performance level.

Misplaced egalitarianism had contributed to the problem of confusion over standards. Some conservative critics, however, felt that a more important cause of the apparent erosion or loss of academic rigor in colleges and universities was traceable back to the period of campus turmoil of the 1960s and early 1970s. In an era when authority was suspect, when all standards and constraints were under attack, and everything traditional was assailed as undemocratic and elitist, academic administrators and faculty were anxious to sidestep confrontations with angry students. In the face of unrelenting pressure to relax requirements, professors ultimately capitulated.[65] Because they lacked strong convictions of their own about which standards were defensible, professors surrendered by allowing students to decide. They acceded, in other words, to the substitution of easier, less demanding courses for more difficult ones. Additional choices and alternatives were created, even as expectations and workloads were lowered. Foreign language, mathematics, and science requirements were cut back or eliminated. Students were allowed greater freedom to shape their courses of study. The general curriculum became softer, more pliable. Withdrawing from courses became easier, and new pass/fail options were introduced to allow students to protect their academic grade-point averages.

Tacit acceptance of a "market model" for higher education exacerbated the tendency to relax standards. If students were "consumers" and education were a "commodity" available for purchase, ran the logic, then students were entitled to pick and choose as they saw fit. And if tuition-paying students were not to be denied good grades, more or less independently of their actual achievements, the inevitable result would be grade inflation—which, as critics hastened to point out, was precisely what happened in the 1970s. In the 1920s at Harvard, for example, no more than one student in five made the dean's list. By 1976, over three-quarters—76 percent—did so. In the 1950s the modal letter grade awarded undergraduates was a C. In the 1980s, three decades later, studies showed that among a national representative cross-section of public colleges and universities of varying sizes surveyed, the average grade awarded had risen to B.[66] Because students were the beneficiaries of the new dispensation, they were least likely to complain, even if inflation implied a certain devaluation in the worth of their credentials.

Revelations of lax grading standards continued with depressing regularity well into the 1990s.[67] At Harvard in 1992, for example, 91 percent of all undergraduate grades were B- or higher. At Stanford, no more than about 6 percent of all grades reported were C's. At Princeton, A's rose from 33 percent of all grades to 40 percent in four years.[68] Harvard instructor William Cole diagnosed the cause of the problem as a loss of nerve. "Relativism is the key word today," he avowed. "There's a general conception in the literary-academic world that holding things to high standards—like logic, argument, having an interesting thesis—is patriarchal, Eurocentric, and conservative. If you say, 'This paper is no good because you don't support your argument,' that's almost like being racist and sexist."[69] Similar in tone was the explanation offered in 1994 by Stephen Cahn, former provost and vice-provost at the Graduate Center of the City University of New York. The general reluctance of academics to award low grades, Cahn claimed, reflected the temper of the times in its wholesale rejection of the concept of comparative merit. The results, he concluded, were plain for all to see: lowered expectations, misguided egalitarianism, abandonment of standards of quality, and finally, what he characterized as an "eclipse of excellence."[70]

Meanwhile, students seemed unaffected by debates over the quality of their education. For most consumers of collegiate training, their sojourn on campus was considered an entitlement and a rite of passage, almost implacable in its inevitability, something practically everyone was both allowed and obliged to pass through en route to something else—graduate school perhaps, or a job, or another rung on the career ladder. By the 1990s, the suggestion that a college education ought to be appreciated as an intellectual adventure to be savored and enjoyed instead of being merely endured as a conduit to some further destination point might have seemed to many students, literally, incomprehensible.

NEGLECT OF UNDERGRADUATE EDUCATION

As some critics assessed the situation, the modern university, public or private, all too often had lost sight of the conditions needed for promoting genuine education. Traditionally, it was alleged, the task was conceived of by academic leaders as simply one of "imparting information," preferably in as expeditious a fashion as possible. But students entering college were not looking for, and did not need, yet another experience that only "imparted" data—they had had plenty of that in the lower schools. Whether they consciously realized it or not, they did not need some perfunctory or impersonal handing down of information, more often than not in large lecture classes, often taught by relatively inexperienced graduate teaching assistants or, often reluctantly and only under duress, by faculty members unlucky enough to be assigned responsibility for supervising lower-level courses. Nor was the cause of high-quality undergraduate education well served by framing introductory courses as intellectual antechambers to professional specialization, as devices for recruiting departmental majors to some particular discipline.

Students did not need to be talked "at," but conversed "with," preferably in small seminars and colloquia, recognizing that meaningful learning is inherently "labor intensive" and cannot be conducted on a large-scale, assembly-line basis. Undergraduates, some said, did not need competency testing, and outcomes assessments, and standardized computer-scored tests, or any of the other mechanistic appurtenances of corporate academe. They would not benefit from technological innovations employed in ways that made learning less meaningful and more impersonal. Students, critics asserted (perhaps unfairly), deserved something better than to be allowed by default to pass like stones through the intestinal tracts of the nation's colleges and universities, only to emerge as fundamentally unenlightened and illiterate as they were when they first entered.

What undergraduates allegedly needed in order to be truly educated, it was said, were opportunities to stretch their minds, to be provoked and challenged, to pose fundamental questions, to assess alternative answers, to integrate and synthesize and apply what they had learned. This they were unlikely to receive, unless or until undergraduate education was no longer neglected or devalued as an enterprise strictly ancillary to professional and graduate training. The real imperative for any self-respecting institution of higher learning, it was argued, was to enshrine undergraduate learning once again as the very raison d'être of the college or university. Left unclear in most of the discussions of the nineties were detailed analyses of what it would require in terms of altered priorities, changes in the professorial reward system, and the transformation of academic culture to effect that proposed restoration of undergraduate education to a position of centrality.

William D. Schaefer, a former vice-chancellor at the University of California at Los Angeles, ranked among those who attempted to offer a diagnosis of the problem.[71] In his view, institutions of higher learning for years had "mindlessly mixed vocational and academic courses without continuity or coherence or anything approaching a consensus as to what really should constitute an education." To him, this was the crux of the problem—one that would need to be addressed with thought and deliberation, not dollars. "I believe," he remarked, "that we should be . . . deeply concerned about this confusion of purpose—a confusion that has led colleges and universities to make fraudulent claims about their goals and missions as they package a hodgepodge of unrelated courses and incoherent requirements."[72]

Schaefer took note of the many national reports and studies on undergraduate education that had appeared throughout the eighties. Criticism of the baccalaureate degree had achieved the status of a national pastime amidst allegations that general education was a "disaster area," that colleges offered a smorgasbord of courses from which students were allowed to pick and choose their way to graduation, that the standards for a bachelor's degree had come to vary so greatly that no one could say what the degree was supposed to represent, that academe had sunk to the point where there was more confidence about the length of a college education than about its substance or purpose, and so on.[73] What, he asked, would be the *least* a college or university should expect its undergraduates to attain in the way of knowledge and analytic skills? His proposed minimum for ensuring that students received a meaningful general education included the following: (1) the expectation that students could read, write, and converse in English at a level sufficient for serious academic discourse; (2) the ability to read and converse in at least one foreign language, and to understand in general how language works; (3) a basic understanding of the studio and performing arts (origins, historical development, theory, and so on); (4) a similar understanding of the world of letters, including sufficient literary criticism to enable one to read literature, including major works in the fields of philosophy, religion, and the social sciences; (5) awareness of the historical development of humankind, its roots, traditions, and achievements, and its civilizations—both West and East; (6) a solid grasp of the scientific approach to knowledge, a more than superficial awareness of the physical sciences, and an understanding of mathematics; and, finally, (7) a similar understanding of the human body and the workings of the human mind. Acknowledging that one might argue for other goals and different priorities, Schaefer insisted nonetheless that "not until such goals are identified and agreed upon can we talk intelligently about required courses and general education programs."[74]

Schaefer concluded with a plea. "What is needed," he observed, "is a commitment on the part of each institution—without qualification, without reservation, without compromise—that through a carefully organized, coherent program of instruction it will share with its students what today it deems to be the best known and thought, through time and space, in this our world." A viable college education in the twenty-first century, he added, demanded a "complete rethinking" of what an educated person could and should know.[75]

INTEGRATING THE CURRICULUM

In 1959 the English scholar C. P. Snow published a lecture delivered at Cambridge entitled *The Two Cultures*.[76] His judgment at that time was that the university had divided into two camps, consisting of culturally illiterate scientists on the one side and scientifically-illiterate humanists on the other. Between the two, Snow alleged, there had grown up "a gulf of mutual comprehension . . . hostility and dislike, but most of all of lack of understanding." Scientists, as he portrayed them, showed little interest in the social, moral, or psychological dimensions of human existence, and tended to be indifferent to matters extending beyond the range of empirical science. Humanists, he felt, were even more indifferent to, and ignorant about, even the most basic scientific principles. But as regards general learning, Snow's judgment was that scientists and technologists bore the greater burden of responsibility for failing to address questions of how to integrate the college curriculum. Meanwhile, it was later observed, college students had since managed to bridge the "two-cultures" gap with indifference and universal shallowness. Equally ignorant of both, illiteracy and innumeracy had come together to create, as one wit put it, "a splendid egalitarianism of ignorance."

Thirty years after Snow's analysis, Allan Bloom, in *The Closing of the American Mind* (1989), returned to the same issues.[77] The professorate, he claimed, had abandoned liberal learning because it was too difficult to conceptualize or administer. Having trashed the traditional curriculum without having anything coherent to replace it, faculties everywhere had given themselves over to trendy intellectual fads or retreated inward to their specialties. The very idea of a shared general culture was forgotten, and undergraduates were left to their own devices. Universities, Bloom observed sarcastically, can do everything yet "cannot generate a modest program of general education for undergraduates."

Bloom's critique apparently hit some kind of nerve. Overshadowing practically all other issues in American higher education toward the end of the century was the search for an anchor or "center" for undergraduate liberal learning. Much of the national debate had begun a half dozen years earlier with the publication of a 1983 essay in the *American Scholar* entitled "Cultural Literacy" by E. D. Hirsch, Jr., a professor of English at the University of Virginia. In his essay and in a subsequent book bearing the same title, Hirsch argued that in the absence of a common curriculum, American society was drifting dangerously close to losing "its coherence as a culture."[78] "We need to connect more of our students to our history, our culture, and those ideas which hold us together," he argued. Similar in tone was the declaration by philosopher Mortimer Adler and his associates in a 1982 work entitled *The Paideia Proposal:* "For mutual understanding and responsible debate among the citizens of a democratic community, and for differences of opinion to be aired and resolved, citizens must be able to communicate with one another in a common language."[79]

Responding to the calumny heaped upon his suggestion that school curricula should share common elements, Hirsch took the offensive. Against those who claimed that celebrating multicultural diversity within American society was far more important than imposing "monoculturalism," and that the latter amounted to a form of "cultural imperialism," Hirsch declared, "American literate culture has itself assimilated many of the materials that those who favor multiculturalism wish to include." To those who accused him of ethnic elitism, he rejoined, writing in *NEA Today* in 1988, "It is true that many of the richest and best-educated Americans of the nineteenth and early twentieth centuries were white, Anglo-Saxon and Protestant, and it's true that the literate culture they possessed is still dominantly present in American literate culture. But to think that literate culture is Waspish and elitist just because the educated people who possessed it happened to be, is to reason *post hoc ergo propter hoc,* which an expert in critical thinking will quickly identify as a logical fallacy."[80]

Hirsch's focus was primarily upon the secondary-school curriculum. But the basic terms of the argument played themselves out at the college level also. It reached a crescendo of sorts in 1988 in a pitched battle between then-Secretary of Education William Bennett and his critics over a decision by the faculty of Stanford University to replace a required freshman course, "Western Culture," with a course entitled "Cultures, Ideas, and Values." In its revised edition, the course de-emphasized fifteen "classic" texts and required inclusion of writings by "women, minorities, and persons of color." Bennett's charge that the faculty's action would "trivialize" the university's course of studies set off a storm of protest in the nation's magazines and newspaper op-ed pages.

Critics of so-called "monoculturalism" ridiculed Hirsch's suggestion that one could identify a discrete set list of topics, names, and ideas everyone should share in common. Others argued that in attempting to preserve an exclusionary past, Bennett and his disciples appeared to have fallen prey to a certain mean-spiritedness that was at root both antidemocratic and intellectually elitist. Some theorists took special exception to the notion of a common curricular canon. There can never be a fixed content at the core of liberal learning, they argued; it must be constantly revised, reformulated, reinvented, and then reacquired by the learning community as a function of balanced interests and shifting social values, all of which are dynamic rather than static and always in a state of flux.

The practical problem, as most observers saw it in the 1990s, was finding new and more creative ways of reconciling legitimate demands for diversity with the equally urgent need to find a unifying center—if not a common core, then a fund of experiences that would breathe life once again into the ideal of general or liberal learning. "General education," as Howard Lee Nostrand characterized it a half century ago in his introduction to José Ortega y Gassett's *Mission of the University* (1946), "means the whole development of an individual, apart from his occupation training. It includes the civilizing of his life purposes, the refining of his emotional reactions, and the maturing of his understanding about the nature of things according to the best knowledge of our time." Toward the end of the twentieth century, there was little to indicate there was much consensus on how to achieve that venerable goal of holistic development. Some had abandoned the effort as impossible. Other colleges and universities were still engaged in experiments to preserve the spirit of general learning in an era of rampant specialization and intellectual fragmentation.

9

Epilogue:
In Historical Retrospect

DIALOGUES WITH THE PAST

As one reflects on the long and colorful history of higher education, the temptation runs strong to conclude by drawing parallels between past and present, between what once was yesterday and what is today. The impulse is to try to link events separated from one another in time, to draw out broadly defined thematic connections, to locate basic continuities and patterns in the flow of things. Admittedly problematic, the enterprise is hazardous if carried too far. Straining after precedents, for example, readily lends itself to distortion, as does didacticism of any sort in historical inquiry. The danger of succumbing to cheap historicism of the worst kind is quite real. Respecting the historical autonomy of past events, treating their unique, contingent identity on their own terms, so to speak, is an obligation that must always be borne in mind.

It has been rightly said, however, that in education there is only a single perdurable set of questions, a finite number of truly basic or fundamental issues: the educational institution's role in society, and whether its contribution is to serve society or to challenge it; the possibility of objectivity and impartiality in knowledge; the appropriate balance between curricular commonality or integration and diversification and specialization; issues of inclusion and exclusion;

and so on. Depending on the time and place in question, the ways in which both philosophical and practical policy issues have been framed and responded to admit almost endless permutations and variations in detail. Yet in some deep underlying sense, the queries themselves and the divergent responses they have provoked are perennial. Similarly, it may be the case that the range of possibilities open for the conduct of higher education is finite, in which case one would expect to discover that certain features of the academic enterprise are recurrent over time. It may be instructive for illustrative purposes therefore to touch if only briefly on the more obvious thematic and topical continuities, to note just some of the more interesting specific similarities and contrasts that seem to surface from the historical record of higher learning.

DISINTERESTED LEARNING

Contemplating the spectacle of careerism and narrow professionalism common among so many of today's collegians, some purists are apt to wax nostalgic, invoking some idyllic past when motivations were more exalted and students gathered in admiration at the feet of their professors to drink of the fountain of knowledge. Was there ever any such time or place? Was it ever the case that students, animated by an intrinsic love of learning and largely indifferent to considerations of utility and practical application, pursued learning solely or even primarily for the edification of their minds and souls?

Evidence is mixed. Anecdotal material abounds attesting to the influence of inspired teachers of liberalizing persuasions. On the one hand, there are countless stories of students within whom a genuine love of learning was kindled, of those who, reflecting back upon their college days, were persuaded they had been spiritually enlarged, intellectually stimulated, and otherwise enriched in innumerable ways having little to do directly with utilitarian considerations. On the other, bearing in mind the decidedly mixed motives drawing students to higher learning, it is difficult to imagine a time when large numbers of students sought instruction in a completely disinterested spirit. Youths of fifth-century B.C. Athens flocked to study under the sophists, but according to Plato's testimony they were impelled mainly by a desire for preference and advantage, by a felt need to acquire skills useful in the marketplace. The appeal of scribal and rhetorical schools throughout antiquity was clearly one of practicality; and those who patronized them seem to have been prompted at least as much by pecuniary interests as by absorption in intellect.

Similarly, though it has often been idealized as a disembodied community of inquiry, the fact remains that the medieval *universitas* was, more than anything else, at root a professional training facility. Its primary mission was to train clerics, physicians, specialists in civil or canon law, and (sometimes almost by default) teachers for the lower schools. Although it is true that the university provided a safe haven for pure scholarship and unfettered inquiry available nowhere else perhaps except within the confines of the monastic cloister, though the substance of the arts curriculum could be abstract in the extreme and often bore little immediate or obvious connection to the practical exigencies of life, and while the university jealously guarded its intellectual autonomy against attempts at encroachment by civil or ecclesiastical officials, it existed first and foremost to prepare young men for specific careers.

Again in modern times, in the case of the American antebellum college, for all its classical antiquarianism it is important to remember that its practical function more than anything else was to prepare clergymen for their pastoral duties (not to mention other professionals, such as physicians and lawyers, and so forth). Mastery of its curriculum could and did lead to employment. The rise of the comprehensive state land-grant institution and subsequently the emergence of the modern university in the United States, to cite other instances, were predicated on the assumption that an integral connection between learning and social life ought to be maintained, that there should be a linkage between instruction and application. The astounding growth in student enrollments universities enjoyed from the late 1860s onward, for instance, can hardly be accounted for by some vast popular swelling of interest in learning as a self-contained end.

It is also historically true, of course, that higher learning has been construed as a matter of personal adornment and refinement, disconnected in any meaningful way from occupations or careers. There is little difficulty, for example, in seeing the tendency at work among the sons of the privileged classes who sought to acquire from the rhetors of late Hellenistic times certain social graces and a superficial patina of learning. Patrons of learning in the fifteenth and sixteenth centuries who aspired to become "courtiers" after the fashion sketched out by Castiglione or later by Elyot may have been inspired by neither academic nor careerist motives. Judging from accounts of the desultory manner in which they pursued their studies, their intellectual aspirations and interests must have been modest at best. Much the same situation held true in the seventeenth and eighteenth centuries. Benjamin Franklin's criticism of Harvard as a finishing school for the idle rich, complaints throughout the antebellum period about students who were considered not serious enough about their studies, criticisms of American collegians between the 1890s and the late 1920s as coddled adolescents mainly interested in having a "good time" during their stay on campus—all do serious violence to the stereotype of budding intellectuals inhabiting the groves of academe for the sole purpose of advancing their learning. Perhaps the safest thing to say is that students in all times have pursued higher learning for a great variety of reasons, that their motives have been mixed, not pure, and that upon occasion, when they have been fortunate, they have carried away from the experience far more than they knew or imagined.

FACULTY POWER AND GOVERNANCE

Proponents of faculty power within colleges and universities are prone to bolstering their case by appeals to the past. There was a time, it is sometimes alleged, when faculty were in control, when the legitimate prerogatives of the professorate to exercise control over learning and scholarship were respected and abided by. Since that time, runs the argument, the record has been one of a more or less steady erosion of faculty power and a corresponding usurpation of authority by administrators and external authorities. If true, it is difficult to know precisely when any such state of affairs actually prevailed. Once again, the scholars' guilds of the Middle Ages tend to be most frequently invoked as illustrations of a time when teaching masters allegedly controlled their own fate and collective destiny, when all decisions rested in the hands of elected representatives of the faculty, and various assorted administrative functionaries existed solely to do their bidding.

Leaving aside for the moment significant differences between modern institutions of higher learning and medieval universities or the immediate successors, it simply was never the case that faculties enjoyed unchallenged authority or responsibility even within the institution. Except possibly for an exceedingly brief period in the late 1200s and early 1300s, and then only partially and in isolated instances, it would be difficult to identify circumstances when it could be said of faculty that they actually managed the institution's operational affairs. Furthermore, the struggle of the universities for autonomy vis-à-vis outside forces was just that—a constant struggle for control against the depredations of popes, secular monarchs, and local civic authorities, not to mention in the case of the southern Italian *studia,* an internal jockeying for power between masters' guilds or faculties and the dominant students' nations, usually with the faculty competing at a distinct disadvantage. The impact of local municipal authorities or papal factotums or court-appointed representatives of the crown upon *studia* in medieval times, for example, more nearly approximate that of state regents or boards (in the case of publicly assisted higher education); the various and sundry efforts of state legislatures to intrude upon and to define the conditions under which teaching and learning are conducted; or even in a limited sense the impact of external accrediting agencies upon academe.

Governance of the American colonial and antebellum college typically was a matter of one-man rule, usually paternalistic, sometimes autocratic. The president was in charge, and he, in turn, was overseen closely by an external board of trustees or governors. Faculty tutors served at the president's pleasure and could be dismissed at will. The situation was little changed by the end of the nineteenth century when universities came into their own. Just as faculty were closely monitored and supervised in private liberal-arts colleges and sectarian schools, those who taught in turn-of-the-century universities enjoyed few immunities and privileges. Few of the strong presidents of that era—Charles W. Eliot, Nicholas Murray Butler, Davis Starr Jordan, William Harper Rainey, and so on—brooked much opposition or tolerated significant faculty dissent.

The birth of the American Association of University Professors in 1915 was prompted precisely by a need to defend academic freedom, to bolster tenure and procedural safeguards against arbitrary dismissal of errant faculty who had incurred the displeasure of the rich or powerful, including both administrators on the inside and the external patrons to which they were sometimes beholden. It is undoubtedly true that today's administrative bureaucracies often wield power in ways faculty are apt to regard as antithetical to scholarship, teaching, and learning, doing so, moreover, at the expense of faculty influence over curricula or all-important resource allocations. Nevertheless, historical precedent affords scanty support for the argument that professors were actually once in charge and *inter alia* should now "reclaim" their rightful role in the governance of colleges and universities. The case for faculty governance, in other words, is poorly served by appeals to history, except perhaps in the negative sense of affording vivid illustrations of times when faculty lacked even whatever modest and circumscribed influence and power they enjoy today.

ACADEMIC AUTONOMY AND FREEDOM

The image or model of the college or university as a kind of secular monastery is nevertheless an enduring aspect of academic mythology. The traditional picture, sometimes drawn with great conviction, is of a sheltered enclave in which scholar-monks pursue their academic mission, preserving the accumulated wisdom and technologies of the culture, transmitting it to successive generations of students, and pushing ever outward the boundaries of ignorance and darkness. Because academe is a protected place, reason and unfettered inquiry reign supreme, sheltered by cloister walls against the intrusive influence of worldly concerns for influence, privilege, wealth, or power. As a representation of academe, the picture lends itself readily enough to caricature and ridicule, even if it encapsulates certain partial or incomplete truths. But apart from whatever other defects might be found, where the theme of sequestered free learning is least persuasive is when it is invoked in connection with academic freedom.

In colonial times, for example, anything much resembling academic freedom in its modern sense was either nonexistent or severely limited in its scope. Despite the practical necessity of practicing toleration where religious pluralism demanded it, the ideal of theological rectitude, of doctrinal soundness as the chief criterion of fitness to teach in a college was adhered to whenever and wherever possible. Harvard's first president, it is worth recalling, was dismissed from his post for having accepted the Baptist view of infant baptism. Indicative of popular thinking even toward the end of the colonial period was the rather remarkable observation of President Clapp of Yale who proclaimed, "Though every man has a right to examine and judge for himself according to truth, yet no man has a right to judge wrong." While it is true that suppression of religious heresy proved well-nigh impossible in the colonies, it should never be supposed that it was for want of trying or because toleration was looked upon as anything but a regrettable practical necessity.

In the early national period, advocates of religious freedom were ultimately successful in eliminating legal penalties for professions of unorthodox religious belief. Acceptance of a limited range of heterodoxy was easier, of course, if one was a Trinitarian Protestant Christian—the abolition of legal discrimination against Jews, Roman Catholics, Unitarians, Deists, and atheists took somewhat longer. Throughout the first half of the nineteenth century, it might be added, few colleges or universities provided congenial work places for academics imprudent enough to espouse openly certain religious, social, or political views conspicuously at variance with prevailing local norms. It is worth recalling too that before the Civil War, many easterners were reportedly most reluctant to extend support and assistance to the newer frontier institutions of higher learning being established, because they were widely perceived as hotbeds of social and economic radicalism.

Slavery probably was the single most divisive issue in early-nineteenth-century American society. Academics in the South who opposed slavery were often driven from their posts, among them the president of Mississippi College and a faculty member at Centre College who publicly dared to question the moral propriety of keeping one's fellow human beings in bondage. At the University of North Carolina, a certain Professor Hedrick was dismissed in this connection for his avowed support for a subversive organization—the Republican party. At one point even Northern colleges moved to suppress any criticism of the institution of slavery. Miami University, Kenyon College, and Lane Theological Seminary were only three of a larger number of schools where student antislavery societies were outlawed as subversive. At Lane and at Harvard, professors who were opposed to slavery lost their jobs for their views. When Harvard's distinguished alumnus Ralph Waldo Emerson delivered an abolitionist speech, he was pelted by students with rotten eggs for his trouble. On the other hand, it could work both ways, as a president of Franklin College discovered when he was forced out because of his pro-slavery views. During the Civil War, at Bowdoin and Dartmouth, presidents were dismissed for defending slavery and states' rights of secession. If to debates over slavery are added the many controversies surrounding the doctrine of evolution, and the difficulties into which professors fell for presuming to question Biblical literalism (at the Baptist Seminary in Louisville, at Vanderbilt in Tennessee, and at the Presbyterian Seminary in South Carolina, among several other places), any suggestion that academic freedom was well entrenched in nineteenth-century America begins to look like a very dubious proposition.

As has been noted, at the opening of the twentieth century there were more than a few cases where professors found themselves in trouble for having expressed what, judged by the standards of the day, were judged to be radical economic or social views. The fate of the economist at Chicago who dared to criticize the practices of the Pullman Company, whose founder was one of Chicago's leading citizens, affords an instructive case in point. Had John Dewey examined the situation a bit closer, it is doubtful whether he would have registered the opinion he did in 1902 that there was little danger to academic freedom in America. There were simply too many bona fide instances of professors who faced the threat of loss of employment when they became too outspoken in their opinions.

Again during World War I and immediately thereafter, it would be difficult to claim that professors had many opportunities to exercise the traditional prerogatives of *Lehrfreiheit* without suffering adverse consequences. In 1915, for example, Scott Nearing, a socialist professor of economics, lost his position for publicly opposing the use of child labor in coal mines. With an influential coal mine owner on the board of trustees of the institution where Nearing had been employed, the school's president did not long hesitate before demanding the offending professor's resignation.

The tendency of academics to sanitize their views or to refrain from speaking openly was amply warranted, considering the wave of nativist repression that engulfed the nation during the war. Nor could the AAUP always be relied upon to intervene on a professor's behalf. Once again a historic tendency to redraw the boundaries of acceptable professional behavior during a period of national crisis so as to reflect the prevailing political consensus reasserted itself. The distinguished psychologist James McKeen Cattell, for example, was imprudent enough to petition Congress for the passage of a law exempting unwilling wartime draftees from being forced to fight in Europe if they objected to doing so. He lost his job at Columbia as a direct result. No one intervened.

Columbia's president, Nicholas Murray Butler, undoubtedly spoke for most of his academic colleagues when he emphasized the importance of being circumspect to the graduating class of 1917: "What had been tolerated before becomes intolerable now," he declared. "What had been folly was now treason. . . . There is and will be no place in Columbia University . . . for . . . any among us who are not with whole heart and mind and strength committed to fight with us to make the world safe for democracy."

After the war, in the midst of one of the nation's periodic communist and anarchist scares, as Attorney General A. Mitchell Palmer led a national campaign to suppress dissent and to brand all unorthodox opinion as radical and disloyal, loyalty oaths were freely imposed within many of the nation's colleges and universities. The same broad trends continued into the twenties and thirties, at least to the extent that whenever any academic strayed too far beyond the boundaries of acceptable dissent, punishment was sure to follow. The sad history of what happened in higher education between 1940 and the mid-fifties when McCarthyism held sway offers yet another cautionary tale about the fragility of academic freedom in American life. Although it is true there were many instances where there was resistance, in the main, when academe was pressured to cleanse itself of suspected dissidents, colleges and universities readily acceded.

Classical forms of academic freedom, the type of civil liberty which relates to the specific work of the professor—freedom to teach, to conduct research, to publish without interference; and freedom for college teachers to exercise the same civil and political rights as other citizens without endangering their academic status—these dominated the history of academic liberty in America up until the late sixties and early seventies. Until then, except in a very limited sense, the correlative freedom of *Lernfreiheit,* students' freedom to learn, received very little attention. This latter form of academic liberty came to the fore in the midst of discussions as to whether the exercise of student freedom posed a direct threat to teachers' freedom. When campus radicals and other dissidents held administrators hostage in their offices in order to enforce their demands, called strikes to prevent classes from being held, forced major curricular changes, closed campuses, or demanded new programs, the question posed was not simply one of the legitimacy of whatever students wanted, but how those demands encroached upon teaching freedom. At the risk of considerable oversimplification, it was during the height of the period of campus riots that appreciation was registered for the reciprocal interdependence of the two types of academic liberty. Heretofore, it had been easy enough to discern in theory and practice how teachers' freedoms might intrude upon students' freedom to learn. Now the tables were turned: it became painfully obvious that unbridled demands for student freedom encroached upon teaching freedom as well.

Less often discussed has been yet another type of academic freedom: that having to do with the corporate autonomy of the institution itself, a prerogative more nearly reflective of the original medieval construction of academic freedom. Historically, the greatest threats to the academic freedom of institutions of higher learning have come from the encroachments of church or state. Arguably, in recent decades the greater threat now derives from the economic rather than the political influence of government and industry. As *The Control of the Campus,* a report issued in 1982 by the Carnegie Foundation for the Advancement of Teaching, summarized the issue, "The connection between higher education and major corporations . . . imperils colleges and universities in much the same way as the church and the state have threatened university integrity in the past. And preoccupation on the part of the academy with the priorities of business and industry may mean that . . . larger social mandates . . . will be compromised."

Contemporary institutions of higher learning depend on three main sources for funding: private gifts, research grants and contracts, and tuition payments—in other words, they depend upon outside benefactors, upon business or government, and upon the market. Dependence, as has often been argued, spells vulnerability to influence. Those upon whom colleges and universities depend for money exert influence on how the institution discharges its mission, what programs are offered, and what policies are pursued. Inevitably, colleges attempt to do whatever it is they do in ways that will ensure continued support from those upon whom they depend. Hence, the question has become one of determining whether, and in what ways, institutions of higher education can protect themselves from corrupting external influences while preserving for themselves the autonomy needed for the pursuit of learning. By the same token, the question is also one of balance between institutional independence and responsiveness to social need.

CURRICULAR CONSERVATISM

Complaints heard nowadays that colleges and universities are not responsive enough to social change, that general learning should be more diverse in its content, that colleges and universities have been exceedingly slow about opening up the curricular canon (if any such thing exists) to reflect more fully the interests and cultural contributions of minorities heretofore consigned to "invisibility" or marginality, are not without precedent. Collegiate courses of instruction have always exhibited a certain inertia, evolving at first through a process of accommodation at the periphery and only later at the core, and then almost always only as a result of strong pressure imposed from without. So far as one can ascertain, it has always been so, differing from case to case only in the degree to which accommodation took place and the rapidity with which it occurred.

The Romans were much opposed to the introduction of Hellenistic learning in the second century B.C., and went so far as to pass official proscriptions against its being taught in schools, though to little avail. Juvenal and Tacitus both railed against the apparent stagnation and deterioration of what was taught in oratorical or rhetorical schools, again without much effect. The tendency of schools to preserve and transmit knowledge no longer rooted in the social conditions that once made it vital and important is seen also in the predominance of rhetorical education in the very late Hellenistic period, long after republican government was only a memory and opportunities to apply what was learned were severely circumscribed.

The liberal arts—*artes liberales*—in their original sense, it should be observed, originally did not designate fixed fields of study so much as they referred to activities or techniques; each was conceived of, strictly speaking, as a way of *doing* something, as in the "art" of engaging in rhetorical, logical, grammatical, or literary analysis. Subsequently, as Greco-Roman learning, the *enkylios paideia* or "recurrent" general culture, passed into the medieval world, curricula were structured around what became a standardized enumeration of its primary elements: the *trivium* (grammar, logic, and rhetoric), and music, geometry, arithmetic, and astronomy, or, alternatively, philosophy (the *quadrivium*). Together they became formalized and fixed—some might say, ossified—as the basis of all instruction preparatory for professional training in the medieval university. For centuries thereafter, liberal learning was defined rigidly within the confines of the seven liberal-arts. The tendency of academic institutions to resist change, to adapt only slowly to pressures for the substitution or inclusion of new learning, is shown, for example, in the willingness of the medieval scholars' guilds to accept Aristotelian logic, but not Platonic metaphysics and other elements of learning imported from Moorish and Saracenic sources; by the initial rejection by sixteenth- and seventeenth-century universities of almost the entire corpus of Renaissance literary humanism; and the slowness or reluctance with which institutions of higher learning in the eighteenth century incorporated new scientific knowledge and discoveries.

Much of the history of collegiate curricula in America over the past century and a half revolves around the struggle to legitimate new fields of scholarly inquiry and academic instruction, a struggle marked by broad opposition to the incorporation of new professional specialties at the expense of older ones, and by a recurrent desire to preserve certain subjects or content bodies as timeless and immutable (the Yale Report of 1828, the Great Books program at the University of Chicago in the early 1930s, the spirited attack upon and defense of Western Civilization courses in the 1980s). Sometimes new learning has had to seek a place outside the academic cloister when, for whatever reasons, it was denied a place in the universities—legal training at the Inns of Court in sixteenth-century London, or literary classicism in the fifteenth-century Italian academies, the work of scientific investigation in separate clubs, societies, and academies in the seventeenth and eighteenth centuries. Today, for all their inclusivity, there are many applied technologies and practical arts not taught in colleges and universities that are offered instead in community colleges, and perhaps appropriately so. The point here is not what should be taught as part of accredited higher learning, but, rather, the historical question of how, when, and under what circumstances courses of study have evolved and devolved, have come into existence or disappeared. Overall, it seems safe to say, curricular revision has been a fitful and uneven process, invariably controversial, always a collision point for competing social interests and needs.

Likewise, the tension between commonality and diversity has been perennial. Certainly, rough parallels can be found between efforts to introduce and popularize the elective system in the early twentieth century and efforts to devise more flexible curricula emphasizing student choice in the early 1970s, over a half century later. Contrariwise, the basic form of the rationale for preserving common learning in the eighties and nineties of the twentieth century differs insignificantly from expressions of support for efforts in previous decades to accomplish the same aim. Illustrative examples might include the inauguration of general survey courses at Columbia University in the post–World War I period, the program advanced by the Harvard Redbook in the mid-1940s, or, to cite the case of Harvard once again, the inauguration of a curricular "core" in the late 1970s.

Curricular inclusivity in the special sense of representation of minority interest poses a somewhat different issue. To some extent, perhaps, the problem is historically new. Few precedents suggest themselves for any deliberate and self-conscious effort on the part of an academic community to broaden courses of study so as to treat more fully the interests, concerns, accomplishments, and contributions of the disempowered, of culturally marginal peoples. Depending upon the interpretive scheme within which the phenomenon is analyzed, a case could be made for the argument that the contemporary American effort to draw in elements from the periphery of power and cultural influence and to install them within a curricular "mainstream" has a special uniqueness about it. Which is cause and which effect—a broadening and diversification of the curriculum and the ascendancy of those whose interests historically have not been well represented—remains an interesting open question.

EDUCATIONAL AIMS AND IDEALS

Plato and Aristotle were among the first to pose the question as to whether education should primarily serve the individual or the state, whether it should be directed to the advantage of the individual or made to serve larger social ends. Phrased in the abstract as a purely philosophical issue, discussions over the aims and purposes of education might have seemed remote or fruitless. Nevertheless, all things considered, it is difficult to make sense of institutional policies and practices over time in the history of higher education without reference to the provisional answers to those queries that were accepted (if only implicitly) at some particular time and place. The Socratic ideal balanced the claims of personal development and civic rectitude, learning intended both for the perfection of self and effective participation in the life of a city-state. The Platonic perspective, in contrast, held that schooling was of such overweening importance to the welfare of the just state that it should be a public function. Cicero's *De oratore* made plain the author's conviction that oratorical learning had as its goal the production of wise statesmen. Early medieval erudition was directed to otherworldly ends, most particularly to the salvation of one's soul. Renaissance humanism enshrined secular aesthetic enrichment and expanded consciousness as a paramount goal, even as some theorists believed that from the ranks of liberally educated men would come the prudent counselors and executives of the Italian city-state.

Drawing closer to modern times, it is worth remembering how serious were the calls of Benjamin Rush and many others for a new type of education better adapted to fostering allegiance to republican ideals; and it was a goal to which many early antebellum colleges fervently pledged themselves in their founding charters. Spirited defenses of the classical curriculum competed in the nineteenth century with heartfelt appeals for more practical trade training and professional learning, symbolizing the tension between intellectualist and utilitarian aims in higher learning. From the late 1800s onward, it would be almost impossible to trace out or explain permutations in collegiate curricula without reference to the growth of scientific knowledge, the impact of the emergence of the new social-science disciplines, and the recurrent struggle between those who felt colleges and universities should be repositories of liberal culture or custodians of civic virtue and those who urged that institutions of higher learning be converted into training facilities for business and industry.

INCLUSIVITY AND ELITISM

The extent to which higher education has been an elitist phenomenon, the exclusive preserve of the rich and privileged, is historically problematic. In their formative period at least, universities seem to have attracted students from all social classes and walks of life, rich and poor alike. In many ways, students then were as heterogeneous a group as today's college students, and oftentimes were even less well prepared for their studies than their modern counterparts. Between the thirteenth and sixteenth centuries, at any rate, universities appear to have afforded many less-advantaged persons a route upward in terms of social mobility and class status. As has often been observed, the liberal arts supplied the avenue over which the sons of Europe's poor made their way into high positions in church and state. Included on the rosters of those enrolled, for example, are the names of many students whose fathers were tradesmen, merchants, and yeoman farmers.

Exclusivity sometimes correlated with geography: fragmentary records suggest that lower-class students represented a smaller percentage of enrollments in the Italian *studia* of the early Renaissance than in the Spanish universities, for example; that lower- and middle-class students were more numerous in early nineteenth-century French and German institutions of advanced learning than at Oxford and Cambridge in the same period, and so on. Again, so far as it is possible to ascertain and correlate student enrollments with socioeconomic class, degrees of inclusion or exclusion seem to have fluctuated over time, with the general trend from the late seventeenth century onward being toward exclusion. In England especially, from the early nineteenth century on into the twentieth, the commitment of the dons at Oxford and Cambridge was to social exclusivity and privilege.

In America, trends were mixed. Not nearly enough is known to permit firm judgments, but it has been suggested that the early colonial and antebellum colleges included significant percentages of enrollments drawn from working-class families and farmers. The picture grows more complicated with the advent of the so-called booster colleges and comprehensive land-grant institutions, most of which attracted an ever-increasing percentage of lower-class and middle-class students. Clearer by far in the American context has been the experience of women and minorities. Women's colleges did not make their appearance until the first third of the nineteenth century; and coeducation was not well established until the last third of the nineteenth century. African Americans enjoyed little access to higher education throughout the 1800s, and then usually their opportunities were restricted to predominantly black colleges. Not until past the midpoint of the twentieth century were blacks admitted in large numbers to predominantly white colleges and universities. Relative to their numbers as percentages of age-relevant and total populations, Hispanics fared poorly, as did Native Americans. Similarly, breaking barriers to access by religious minorities was a slow and sometimes painful process.

The second half of the twentieth century brought a major influx of women and ethnic minority students into academe, but they were distributed rather unevenly in terms of the types of institutions attended. Assuming present trends continue, as the white percentage of the population decreases relative to blacks and other minorities, non-white enrollments are predicted to climb significantly in the early twenty-first century. Nowadays much controversy attends the question of what price must be paid for the sake of greater inclusion, but few will dispute on historical grounds the apparent and not-so-simple truth that the trend in American higher education in recent decades has been away from exclusionary practices and norms of all kinds.

KNOWLEDGE AS SOCIAL CONSTRUCTION

If there is anything unambiguous about the history of higher education, it is that different types of knowledge have enjoyed varying degrees of status, prestige, and authority, and their hierarchical rankings have changed enormously over time as a function of a diverse array of social factors. In classical antiquity two quite dissimilar conceptions of education competed for acceptance: commitment to *logos* or *ratio,* "reason," and correlatively to the arts of reasoning, which framed the philosophic tradition; and a commitment to *oratio,* having to do with the arts of speech and language, which defined the oratorical or rhetorical tradition. Beginning in Greece in the fifth and fourth centuries B.C., debate opened as to which should take precedence in the education of the free citizen. Rather clearly, between the two, the Romans ultimately showed a distinct preference for the latter perspective, a view of education emphasizing public expression, political and legal discourse, and literature pertaining to the noble civic virtues upon which an orderly society was based. Over and against a stress on logic, mathematics, and philosophy characteristic of Plato, Aristotle, and their spiritual successors, Hellenistic learning was thus organized around the practical arts of grammar, dialectic, and public rhetoric.

In the thirteenth and fourteenth centuries, the ancient rhetorical tradition or model for education first came under serious challenge by medieval scholastics, at which point speculative philosophy, logic, and theology began to supersede grammar and rhetoric as leading elements within the curriculum. With the Renaissance humanist recovery of the Ciceronian educational ideal in the late 1400s and early 1500s, rhetorical and literary studies were revived and strengthened once again. To them were added Christian ethics and the social courtesies or conventions of etiquette traditionally associated with medieval knighthood. By the sixteenth century, that combination of literary training, religious piety, and courtly etiquette had given rise to an archetypical conception of the ideally-educated person as a "Christian gentleman." It was a construction of higher learning that with some modifications won ready acceptance in the first colonial colleges of America. Henceforth, throughout the seventeenth and eighteenth centuries, rhetoric, grammar, and theology were to dominate courses of study aimed at producing good citizens within a theocratic commonwealth.

The nineteenth century brought the first stirrings of protest against a curriculum defined almost exclusively by antique learning and religious piety. On one side were proponents of scientific learning and the experimental sciences. On the other appeared advocates of applied technical arts. Defenders of the rhetorical and textual arts were not easily cast aside, however; and a strong humanistic program of studies emphasizing literary and rhetorical training continued to characterize the offerings of denominational or sectarian schools and most liberal-arts colleges. However, in the universities that came to dominate the landscape of American higher education (beginning with the founding of Cornell in 1868, Johns Hopkins in 1876, Clark University in 1889, Stanford in 1891, and Chicago in 1892), the orientation was altogether different. Dedicated to specialized research and advanced professional studies, as has been shown, universities installed experimental science as a new knowledge paradigm.

Little acumen is needed to discern the results ensuing in the twentieth century. Reflective of a profound historical shift in thinking within the broader cultural milieu, the so-called "hard" experimental physical and biological sciences and their allied technologies together with mathematics now occupy places of preeminence at the top of the status hierarchy. Somewhat lower are the social-science disciplines of psychology, sociology, anthropology, together with the separate applications or "applied" subdisciplines they in turn have spawned, all of which vie for status and prestige with a range of commercial and business-related subjects (accounting, finance, administration, and so forth). Near the bottom stand the humanities (language, literature, philosophy). Ironically perhaps, today's knowledge pyramid almost perfectly inverts the disciplinary status hierarchy of centuries past.

What is at once, paradoxically, quite old and new in controversies over collegiate curricula is the basic intellectual frame of reference within which contemporary debate is increasingly conducted. Today the venerable positivist belief in the possibility of total objectivity, impartiality, and neutrality in knowledge has come in for hard times at the hands of so-called critical theorists and sociologists of knowledge, just as it did in the days of the sophists, the philosophical Cynics and Skeptics, and others of their ilk two and a half millennia ago. As Jürgen Halbermas and many others have labored to show, the ideal of scientific or philosophical objectivity in its purest forms may be largely illusory if, as is alleged, knowledge is always about power, and "truth" is in some indeterminate sense a function of interests. If the status and interests of knowers are bound up inextricably with the nature of knowledge itself, and if knowledge structures are social or cultural artifacts masquerading as immutable features of reality, any notion of the academy as a neutral field where competing truths contend on an equal basis falls into question.

From a critical-theory perspective, knowledge is socially conditioned; it is the product of communities whose regulative principles and constitutions inevitably include some and exclude others; and its reifications and codifications of information function oftentimes as obstacles to the emergence and acceptance of new knowledge-forms.

On this account it would seem to follow that any curriculum is not simply a sampling of independent and autonomous information available to society in a given historical moment, but, in a deeper sense, is an organic outgrowth of that society and the forms of consciousness it permits or allows. As society changes, so too must the curriculum—but not necessarily for reasons traditionally adduced. Rather, as John Fiske would have it, writing in *Reading the Popular* (1989), "Knowledge is never neutral, it never exists in an empiricist, objective relationship to the real. Knowledge is power, and the circulation of knowledge is part of the social distribution of power." The same point is given expression in Michael Apple's *Official Knowledge, Democratic Education in a Conservative Age* (1993): "It is naive to think of the . . . curriculum as neutral knowledge. Rather, what counts as legitimate knowledge is the result of complex power relations and struggles among identifiable class, race, gender, and religious groups."

Whatever the merits of the argument, it does seem to offer a challenging perspective for further historical inquiry. On its reading, the history of curricular change over time within colleges and universities bears close ties with a broader array of societal forces and relations than conventional interpretations have typically comprehended. Whether a critical-theory perspective can supply a more cogent accounting of how institutional change and curricular reform occur in higher education awaits further investigation.

ACADEMIC CONVENTIONS, RITES AND RITUALS

Each year countless thousands of college students don caps and gowns at commencement and join in the sort of stately processionals that characteristically mark such occasions. Pomp and circumstance lend a proper air of solemnity to the proceedings. Yet probably no more than a few of the participants have the remotest inkling of the historical derivations and origins of the pageantry in which they are engaged. Modern usage is not old: most customs trace back no more than a hundred years or so. What they do represent, however, is an outgrowth of a self-conscious nineteenth-century effort to recapture something of the spirit of Oxford and Cambridge, and behind them, the symbolism and traditions of the original universities of the Middle Ages. The master's *pileum* or *biretta* has been incarnated anew as a mortarboard; today's processional leader unknowingly imitates the ceremonial place and role of the *bedellus* of ancient times; and the long black gowns in which faculty and students now attire themselves, though quite different in style, are presumably intended to invoke associations with those worn centuries ago by medieval academics. Less well understood is the modern system under which each discipline or academic specialization is assigned its own distinctive striping: dark blue for philosophy, a light-blue color for professional education, and so on; or the different designs of academic hoods, each bearing the colors of the institution from which its wearer once graduated or is graduating. Those upon whom the bachelor's degree is conferred in all likelihood have little appreciation for how medieval nomenclature has been preserved in the identification of academic degrees, any more than do holders of the master's degree, or those to whom the Ph.D., or doctorate of philosophy (*philosophia*, "love of wisdom," comprehensive learning in general) is awarded.

Beyond the level of liturgy and ceremony stand also institutional usages and the "structural" conventions of academe which have proven so remarkably durable over time. The oral defense of a dissertation, for example, must be seen as standing in a direct line of descent from the obligatory "oration" of the colonial college, and still further back, from the medieval university disputation, or *conventus*. It is not too far-fetched to trace the lineage back even further, to the formal declamations of the rhetors' schools or even to the oral interrogations of the Mesopotamian tablet-house. Rituals of judgment, of assessment and evaluation of learning, have been a permanent feature of collegiate life in all times and places, and have been met with much the same degree of trepidation and apprehension felt by any of today's collegians contemplating final examinations. Dishonesty and cheating on tests are nothing new either: efforts to keep assessment and evaluation efforts honest by all parties involved extend back many centuries and probably always have enjoyed about the same degree of mixed success.

Fraternity and sorority initiation rites of the twentieth century loosely recapitulate the hazing to which the *bejaunus*, or "yellow-billed" fledgling scholar newly arrived at fifteenth-century Heidelberg, was subjected, or the system under which underclassmen were obliged to exhibit deference to upperclassmen in nineteenth-century British and American colleges. Contemporary student complaints over the high price of textbooks also bear an uncanny identity with officials' criticisms of the *stationarri,* or book copyists, heard in thirteenth-century Bologna.

Laments over today's unruly students partying in "Greektown" or in neighborhood bars on a Saturday night differ but little from complaints levied by Libanius of Antioch about the chaos and disorder attending gatherings of students after hours in his own time, or the popular outrage felt by townsfolk witnessing bands of drunken collegians roving along Straw Street in medieval Paris or crowding the taverns and ale-houses of Oxford and Cambridge. Instances of student intimidation of faculty and administrators during the campus unrest of the 1960s, to cite another parallel, invite rough comparison with the exactions of student courts before which Bolognese teaching masters in the early fourteenth century were hailed. Once again, one need only recall the riots and student food fights that broke out periodically at scores of antebellum colleges in order to be reminded that student misconduct and unrest have always been a more or less permanent if episodic feature of collegiate life.

The academic as an object of mingled respect and ridicule also has a long history behind it. Ironic use of the title "professor," at once signifying condescension and feigned or exaggerated deference, for example, has many historical analogues, nicely illustrated in the fun Lucian poked at the absurd pretensions of the self-important rhetors of his day, or by popular nineteenth-century images of the old-time academic as slightly dotty, absent-minded, delightfully eccentric, or woefully impractical. Criticism of scholars for their obscurantism and the unintelligibility of their writings echo down through the ages, as do attacks upon the ivory tower as a citadel of irrelevance and impracticality. Here one thinks, for example of a Hellenistic writer's dismissal of the Alexandrian *Mouseion* as a "bird cage" for scholars, or Luther's dismissal of universities as "nests of gloomy ignorance."

Perhaps, then, it is also true in higher education as it is in almost all things that, as the French have it, *Plus ça change, plus c'est la même chose*—the more things change, the more they remain the same.

Notes

Chapter I

1. A translation and summary of the text, recovered originally from the library of Assurbanipal at Nineveh, appears in Benno Landsberger, "Scribal Concepts of Education," in Carl H. Kraeling and Robert M. Adams, eds., *City Invincible: A Symposium on Urbanization and Cultural Development in the Ancient Near East* (Chicago: University of Chicago Press, 1960), pp. 99–101. See also Ake W. Sjöberg, "Examenstext A," *Zeitschrift für Assyriologie und Verwandte Gebiete* 64 (1975): 137–176.
2. See Sjöberg, "In Praise of the Scribal Art," *Journal of Cuneiform Studies* 24 (1972): 126–129.
3. Note the discussion in Christopher J. Lucas, "The Scribal Tablet-House in Ancient Mesopotamia," *History of Education Quarterly* 19 (Fall 1979): 305–332.
4. A. Leo Oppenheim, "A Note on the Scribes In Mesopotamia," in Hans G. Güterbock and Thorkild Jacobsen, eds., *Studies in Honor of Benno Landsberger on His Seventy-Fifth Birthday, April 21, 1965* (Chicago: Oriental Institute, University of Chicago Assyriological Studies No. 16, 1965), p. 253.
5. Henry Frederick Lutz, "Sumerian Temple Records of the Late Ur Dynasty," *Semitic Philology* 9 (May 31, 1928): 117–263; and Tom B. Jones, "Sumerian Administrative Documents: An Essay," in Stephen J. Lieberman, ed., *Sumerological Studies in Honor of Thorkild Jacobsen* (Chicago: Oriental Institute, University of Chicago Assyriological Studies No. 20, 1976), p. 41.
6. References to the *édubba* have been collected and summarized in Adam Falkenstein, "Der 'Sohn des Tafelhauses,'" *Welt des Orients* III (1948), pp. 174–175. Note also Sjöberg, "The Old Babylonian Eduba," in Lieberman, p. 159, note 1.
7. Samuel Noah Kramer, *The Sumerians: Their History, Culture, and Character* (Chicago: University of Chicago Press, 1963), pp. 229–248.
8. See Cyril J. Gadd, *Teachers and Students in the Oldest Schools* (London: School of Oriental and African Studies, University of London, 1956); and Kramer, *Schooldays* (Philadelphia: University Museum, University of Pennsylvania, 1949).
9. The claim that Sumero-Akkadian schools enjoy chronological precedence over their Egyptian counterparts is advanced, among others, by Kramer in *History Begins at Sumer* (Garden City, N.Y.: Doubleday, 1959), chapter 1.
10. See Lucas, op. cit., p. 326, note 2. The earliest reference of record to schooling in Egypt appears in the "Instruction of Duauf [or Khety]," dating to the early portion of the second millennium: "Instruction . . . composed for his son . . . when he voyaged up to the Residence, in order to put him in the School [or House] of Books, among the children of the magistrates." See John A. Wilson, "Scribal Concepts of Education," in Kraeling and Adams, pp. 102–104.
11. Student copy pieces, predictably, extolled the joys of scribal life, which, as noted, was touted as preferable to all others. Of scribes, it was said, "their names have become everlasting, even though they themselves are gone. . . . If doors and buildings were constructed, they are crumbled; . . . mortuary service is done . . . tombstones are covered with dirt; and . . . graves are forgotten. But [the] names [of scribes] are still pronounced because of their books which they made . . . and the memory of them lasts to the limits of eternity. Be a scribe and put it in your heart that your name may fare similarly." Quoted in Lionel Casson, *Ancient Egypt* (New York: Time-Life, 1965), p. 100. See also A. Erman (A. M. Blackman, trans.), *The Literature of the Ancient Egyptians* (London: Methuen, 1927), pp. 67, 149; and similar passages in James H. Breasted, ed., *Ancient Records of Egypt* (London: Russell & Russell, 1962), passim.
12. S. S. Laurie, *Historical Survey of Pre-Christian Education* (New York: Longmans, Green, 1907), p. 47.
13. Helpful interpretations of the Sophists are supplied in Kenneth J. Freeman, *Schools of Hellas* (New York: Macmillan, 1922), pp. 157–209; Frederick A. G. Beck, *Greek Education: 450–350*

B.C. (New York: Barnes & Noble, 1964), pp. 147–187; Werner W. Jaeger, *Paideia: The Ideals of Greek Culture*, vol. I (New York: Oxford University Press, 1945), pp. 298–321; and in James L. Jarrett, ed., *The Educational Theories of the Sophists* (New York: Teachers College, Columbia University, 1969). See also E. Dupreel, *Les sophistes: Protagoras, Gorgias, Prodicus, Hippias* (Neuchatel: Éditions du Griffon, 1948).

14. Quoted in T. V. Smith, ed., *Philosophers Speak for Themselves: From Thales to Plato* (Chicago: University of Chicago Press, 1962), p. 60.

15. Ibid., p. 60.

16. Helpful treatments of the Socratic response appear in A. E. Taylor, *Socrates* (Boston: Beacon, 1952); Francis M. Cornford, *Before and After Socrates* (Cambridge: Cambridge University Press, 1932); Robert R. Rusk and James Scotland, *Doctrines of the Great Educators*, 5th ed. (New York: St. Martin's Press, 1979), pp. 8–10; J. Anderson, *Socrates as an Educator* (Sydney: Angus and Robertson, 1962); and E. A. Havelock, "The Evidence for the Teaching of Socrates," *Transactions of the American Philological Association* 65 (1934), pp. 282–295. See Thomas C. Brickhouse and Nicholas D. Smith, *Socrates on Trial* (Princeton, N.J.: Princeton University Press, 1989); and Mary P. Nicholas, *Socrates and the Political Community: An Ancient Debate* (Albany: State University of New York Press, 1987).

17. See John E. Adamson, *The Theory of Education in Plato's Republic* (New York: Macmillan, 1903); Rupert C. Lodge, *Plato's Theory of Education* (London: Routledge & Kegan Paul, 1947); Walter Moberly, *Plato's Conception of Education and Its Meaning Today* (New York: Oxford University Press, 1944); Warner Fite, *The Platonic Legend* (New York: Charles Scribner's Sons, 1934); A. E. Taylor, *Plato: The Man and His Work*, 6th ed. (London: Methuen, 1949); G. C. Field, *Plato and His Contemporaries: A Study of Fourth-Century Life and Thought* (London: Methuen, 1948); and Richard Livingstone, *Plato and Modern Education* (London: Cambridge University Press, 1944).

18. Note the analysis in Edward J. Power, "Plato's Academy: A Halting Step Toward Higher Education," *History of Education Quarterly* 4 (September 1964): 155–166.

19. General discussions of the theoretical underpinnings of Platonic pedagogy are treated in Francis M. Cornford, *Plato's Theory of Knowledge* (London: Paul, Trench, Trubner and Company, 1949); and Norman Gully, *Plato's Theory of Knowledge* (London: Methuen, 1962).

20. For an illuminating interpretation of curricula and courses of study in the Academy, consult Harold F. Cherniss, *Aristotle's Criticism of Plato and the Academy* (Baltimore: Johns Hopkins Press, 1944); and Cherniss, *The Riddle of the Early Academy* (Berkeley: University of California Press, 1945). Especially useful is John P. Lynch, *Aristotle's School: A Study of a Greek Educational Institution* (Berkeley: University of California Press, 1972).

21. Field, p. 34; and Beck, pp. 228ff.

22. See James Bowen, *A History of Western Education*, Vol. I (New York: St. Martin's Press, 1972), pp. 133–134.

23. A dated but still useful source for Aristotle as educator is the treatment in T. Davidson, *Aristotle and Ancient Educational Ideas* (London: Heineman, 1904).

24. See Walter Jaeger, *Aristotle: Fundamentals of the History of His Development* (Oxford: Oxford University Press, 1962).

25. William K. Frankena, *Three Historical Philosophies of Education* (Glenview, Ill.: Scott, Foresman, 1965), pp. 15–79; and Robert S. Brumbaugh and Nathaniel M. Lawrence, *Philosophers on Education* (Boston: Houghton Mifflin, 1963), pp. 67ff.

26. Brief references to the career of the Aristotelian Lyceum appear in John Herman Randall, Jr., *Aristotle* (New York: Columbia University Press), passim; W. D. Ross, *Aristotle* (Cleveland: Meridian, 1959); and in D. J. Allen, *The Philosophy of Aristotle* (London: Oxford University Press, 1978). See also M. L. Clarke, *Higher Education in the Ancient World* (Albuquerque: University of New Mexico Press, 1971), p. 61.

27. A succinct summary of Aristotle's contribution to Greek educational theory and practice is included in E. B. Castle, *Ancient Education and Today* (New York: Penguin, 1964), pp. 93–101.

28. H. I. Marrou, *A History of Education in Antiquity* (New York: Mentor, 1964), pp. 91–96, 127, 135.

29. Ibid., pp. 97, 101, 228, 289, 388.

30. See R. D. Hicks, *Stoic and Epicurean* (New York: Russell and Russell, 1962).

31. Consult B. Farrington, *The Faith of Epicurus* (London: Weidenfeld and Nicolson, 1967); J. M. Rist, *Epicurus: An Introduction* (Cambridge: Cambridge University Press, 1972); G. A. Panchas, *Epicurus* (New York: Twayne, 1967); D. Clay, *Lucretius and Epicurus* (Ithaca, N.Y.: Cornell University Press, 1983); and A. A. Long, *Hellenistic Philosophy: Stoics, Epicureans, Skeptics* (London: Duckworth, 1974).

32. Clarke, op. cit., pp. 62–63.
33. Note William Boyd, *The History of Western Education* (New York: Barnes & Noble, 1960), p. 44.
34. J. B. Bury, *The Hellenistic Age* (Cambridge: Cambridge University Press, 1923), pp. 40–60. For more general discussions, consult Mikhail I. Rostovtseff, *The Social and Economic History of the Hellenistic World*, 3 vols. (Oxford: Clarendon Press, 1941); and Erich S. Gruen, *The Hellenistic World and the Coming of Rome*, vol. I (Berkeley: University of California Press, 1984), pp. 317–318.
35. Edward J. Power, *A Legacy of Learning* (Albany: State University of New York Press, 1991), pp. 62–66.
36. Marrou, p. 279. Passages quoted are adapted from the translation reproduced in James Bowen, I, pp. 161–162.
37. See Marrou, pp. 260–262; Clarke, p. 8; and Bowen, pp. 140–142.
38. Quoted in Marrou, p. 260.
39. Bowen, p. 145.
40. Relevant references include H. E. Butler, *Quintilian* (Cambridge, Mass.: Harvard University Press, 1922); H. E. Butler, *Quintilian as Educator* (New York: Twayne, 1974); W. M. Smail, *Quintilian on Education* (Oxford: Clarendon Press, 1938); and G. A. Kennedy, *Quintilian* (New York: Twayne, 1969).
41. See Libanius, *Autobiography* [Oration I] Text, translation and notes by A. F. Norman, (London: University of Hull, 1965), pp. 83, 90, 102, 105.
42. Details appear in the traditional account by Eusebius, *The Ecclesiastical History*, L. Lake, trans., vol. 2 (New York: G. P. Putnam, 1926), VI, iii, 3.
43. Clarke, chapter 6; and Marrou, p. 452. General histories of the period include Norman H. Baynes, *Byzantine Studies and Other Essays* (London: Oxford University Press, 1960); and Baynes, *The Byzantine Empire* (Oxford: Oxford University Press, 1958); Norman H. Baynes and Henry St. L. B. Moss, eds., *Byzantium: An Introduction to East Roman Civilization* (Oxford: Clarendon Press, 1962); Charles Diehl, *History of the Byzantine Empire* (Princeton: Princeton University Press, 1945); Glanville Downey, *Constantinople in the Age of Justinian* (Norman, Okla.: University of Oklahoma Press, 1960); John M. Hussey, *The Byzantine World* (New York: Harper Torchbooks, 1961); David Talbot Rice, *The Byzantines* (London: Thames and Hudson, 1962); Steven Runciman, *Byzantine Civilization* (New York: St. Martin's Press, 1966); Cecil Stewart, *Byzantine Legacy* (London: G. Allen & Unwin, 1949); and A. A. Vasiliev, *History of the Byzantine Empire: 324–1453*, 2 vols. (Madison, Wisc.: University of Wisconsin Press, 1964). Note also the brief citation in Leslie S. Domonkos, "History of Higher Education," in Lester F. Goodchild and Harold S. Wechsler, eds., *The History of Higher Education* (Needham Heights, Mass.: Ginn Press, 1989), p. 8.
44. The full extent of the decline in learning is treated in M. L. W. Laistner, *Thought and Letters in Western Europe, A.D. 500 to 900* (London: Methuen, 1931).

Chapter 2

1. See Pierre Riché, *Education and Culture in the Barbarian West, Sixth Through Eighth Centuries*, John J. Contrini, trans. (Columbia: University of South Carolina Press, 1976); Nathan Schachner, *The Medieval Universities* (New York: A. S. Barnes & Company, 1962), pp. 1–10; John Thelin, *Higher Education and Its Useful Past* (Cambridge, Mass.: Schenkman, 1982), pp. 26–28; and James Bowen, *A History of Western Education*, 3 vols. (New York: St. Martin's Press, 1975), II, pp. 5–40.
2. A relatively late expression of antipathy toward secular learning is nicely illustrated by the polemical missive of Stephen of Tournai to the Pope (c. 1192–1203) in *Chartularium universitatis Parisiensis*, I, 47–48, extracted and reproduced in Lynn Thorndike, *University Records And Life in the Middle Ages* (New York: Columbia University Press, 1944), pp. 22–24.
3. For an overview of significant cultural developments, consult the useful account supplied in Charles H. Haskins, *The Renaissance of the Twelfth Century* (Cambridge, Mass.: Harvard University Press, 1955); and Anders Piltz, *The World of Medieval Learning*, David Jones, trans. (Totowa, N.J.: Barnes and Noble, 1981), pp. 1–52.
4. *Chartularium universitatis Parisiensis*, I, 10, in Thorndike, p. 21.
5. The early medieval categorization of learning in terms of the subjects of the *trivium* and *quadrivium*, while it did not originate with Hugh of St. Victor, apparently owed much to his *Didascalicon*. See J. Taylor, trans., *The Didascalicon of Hugh of St. Victor* (New York: Columbia University Press, 1961), pp. 46–90; and Oliver H. Prior, ed., *Caxton's Mirrour of the World*

(London: Early English Text Society, 1913), pp. 33–40, in D. W. Sylvester, *Educational Documents 800–1816* (London: Methuen, 1970), pp. 5–12.

6. The evolution of the cathedral church school into the university as a recognizable institutional type is traced in Charles Homer Haskins, *The Rise of Universities* (New York: Henry Holt and Company, 1923), pp. 1–36; in Schachner, pp. 11–24; and in Helen Wieruszowski, *The Medieval University* (New York: Van Nostrand Reinhold, 1966), pp. 15–26. See also Thelin, pp. 29–30ff. and Hastings Rashdall, *The Universities of Europe in the Middle Ages,* vol. I (Oxford: Clarendon Press, 1936), pp. 3–20. Excellent original source materials for the medieval universities appear in Sylvester, pp. 52–74.

7. The career of scholastic disputation is succinctly traced in Bowen, II, pp. 143–161. See also Rashdall, I, pp. 34–54.

8. See Joan M. Ferrante, "The Education of Women in the Middle Ages in Theory, Fact, and Fantasy," in Patricia H. Labalme, ed., *Beyond Their Sex: Learned Women of the European Past* (New York: New York University Press, 1980), pp. 9–42. Striking contrasts are illustrated by Louise Collis, *Memoirs of a Medieval Woman: The Life and Times of Margery Kempe* (New York: Thomas Y. Crowell, 1964); and Eileen Power, *Medieval People* (Garden City, N.Y.: Doubleday Anchor, 1961), pp. 99–144.

9. The full tale is recounted in Étienne Gilson, *Heloise and Abelard,* L. K. Shook, trans. (Ann Arbor, Mich.: University of Michigan Press, 1960). Abbreviated accounts appear in Gabriel Compayré, *Abelard and the Origin and Early History of Universities* (New York: Charles Scribner's Sons, 1893), pp. 1–23; and in Schachner, pp. 25–36.

10. An interesting account of Perretta Petonne, an unlicensed woman surgeon who was prosecuted at Paris in 1411, appears in an extract from the *Chartularium universitatis Parisiensis,* IV, 198–199, in Thorndike, pp. 289–290.

11. Compayré, pp. 28–32; Rashdall, I, pp. 10–15; Bowen, pp. 110–113; and Dana Carleton Munro, *The Middle Ages, 395–1272* (New York: Appleton-Century-Crofts, 1922), p. 368.

12. An authoritative analysis of student nations is supplied in Pearl Kibre, *The Nations in the Medieval Universities* (Cambridge, Mass.: Mediaeval Academy of America, 1948). See also Compayré, chapter II.

13. Consult Kibre, pp. 65–115.

14. Rashdall, I, pp. 19, 215, 220–221, 247, 284; Kibre, p. 69; Thorndike, p. 72. A good account of the internal development of the University of Paris is given in Gordon Leff, *Paris and Oxford Universities in the Thirteenth and Fourteenth Centuries: An Institutional and Intellectual History* (New York: John Wiley and Sons, 1968), Parts 1, 3, and 4.

15. Schisms and conflicts among the nations at Paris, and elsewhere, are discussed in Compayré, pp. 271–277; Bowen, pp. 114–116; Schachner, pp. 340–342; Kibre, pp. 101–102; and in Rashdall, I, pp. 319–320. See also Thelin, p. 31.

16. Friedrich Heer, *The Medieval World, Europe 1100–1350,* Janet Sondheimer, trans. (New York: Mentor, 1961), p. 243.

17. The early *studia* of Bologna are treated in detail in Rashdall, I, chapter IV, pp. 87–267. Note also the discussions in Kibre, pp. 3–17; Wieruszowski, pp. 62–73; Schachner, pp. 147–185; and Haskins, *The Rise of the Universities,* pp. 10–19. Relevant primary source documents are extracted in Thorndike, pp. 163, 168, 279, 282–284. See also J. K. Hyde, "Commune, University, and Society in Early Medieval Bologna," in John W. Baldwin and Richard A. Goldthwaite, eds., *Universities In Politics: Case Studies from the Late Middle Ages and Early Modern Period* (Baltimore: Johns Hopkins Press, 1972), pp. 17–46.

18. Complaints about ill-prepared and illiterate students seeking to associate themselves with *studia* were frequent. See Daniel D. McGarry, trans., *The Metalogicon of John of Salisbury* (Berkeley: University of California Press, 1953), 3.1.

19. Conditions in "Straw Street" are represented in a contemporary document of the period, as reproduced in Thorndike, pp. 241–243. General accounts of medieval university students are supplied in Compayré, pp. 263–286; Haskins, *The Rise of the Universities,* pp. 79–126; Schachner, chapters 32–36; and in Wieruszowski, pp. 103–118.

20. An edict of 1340 at Paris sternly forbade all forms of hazing of first-year students. See *Chartularium universitatis Parisiensis,* II, 496, in Thorndike, pp. 192–193.

21. Officials repeatedly sought to curb students' excesses. Typical were the statutes of 1442 levied at Heidelberg: "No . . . student shall presume to visit the public . . . gaming houses. . . . No one shall presume by day or night to engage in gaming or to sit or tarry by night or otherwise for

any time in a brothel or house of prostitution. . . . Concerning dances at Lent or other time of year not being held by students in public and their not going about in unseemly fashion, wearing masks, and not engaging in jousts, the rector at that time always ought and has power to provide under heavy penalties." Eduard Winkelmann, *Urkundenbuch der Universität Heidelberg*, I, 1886, No. 100, p. 145, in Thorndike, p. 332. Note also a 1398 statute against oaths and blasphemy, in Thorndike, pp. 260–261.

22. A decree at Heidelberg in 1466 warned vigorously against "clamor or insolence." Further, it was stipulated, no one was to compel any first-year student to sing or "throw filth" at other students or masters. See Thorndike, No. 124, pp. 352–353.

23. Heidelberg's statutes of 1421 enjoined students against frequenting fencing schools, going out in disguise after curfew, gambling with dice, or purloining other people's domesticated birds. Further, it was commanded, "none of you shall scale your city's wall at night and no one shall make an attack on the city's gates or bridges either by forcing or ruining or destroying them in any other way, by day or night, directly or indirectly for fun or for earnest." Thorndike, I, p. 120, No. 83; and in Wieruszowski, pp. 195–196.

24. Robert F. Seybolt, trans., *The Manuale Scholarium* (Cambridge, Mass.: Harvard University Press, 1921), pp. 72–73.

25. Quoted in Haskins, *The Rise of the Universities*, pp. 104–105.

26. For other examples of correspondence between parents and students, refer to Haskins, *Studies in Medieval Culture* (Oxford: Clarendon Press, 1929), pp. 1–91; and Charles T. Wood, *The Quest for Eternity: Medieval Manners and Morals* (Garden City, N.J.: Anchor, 1971), pp. 156–157.

27. Accounts of typical courses of study and academic requirements are supplied in Friedrich Paulsen, *German Education: Past and Present*, T. Lorenz, trans. (London: T. Fisher and Unwin, 1908), pp. 24ff.; Rashdall, I, pp. 450–454, 461; F. M. Powicke, *Ways of Medieval Life and Thought* (London: Odhams Press, 1949), pp. 158–159; *Chartularium universitatis Parisiensis*, I, No. 246, pp. 277–278, in Wieruszowski, pp. 145–146; Schachner, pp. 317–339; and in Haskins, *The Rise of Universities*, pp. 37–126.

28. See Compayré, Part III, pp. 167–262.

29. The role of formal disputations in the examining process is discussed in Anne Fremantle, *Age of Faith* (New York: Time-Life, 1965), pp. 97ff. Rules for the determination in Arts (1252) at Paris appear in the *Chartularium universitatis Parisiensis*, I, pp. 227–230, in Thorndike, pp. 52–56. Examination procedures for the baccalaureat at Avignon are summarized in Thorndike, pp. 286–288. Discussions of academic rites and rituals surrounding baccalaureat trials elsewhere are given in Kibre, pp. 15, 77–78, 99–100, 142–144, 170.

30. Indicative of the usual character of such festivities, at Ferrara, a statute enacted around 1467 directed that "all attending [an academic banquet] shall conduct themselves properly and soberly and eat what is set before them with silence and modesty under the penalties constituted for doing otherwise in the present sanction." Thorndike, p. 353.

31. The organization and operations of the Faculty of Theology at Paris are summarized in Kibre, pp. 15, 26, 99, 102–103. Compayré's discussion of the same body at Paris is also still helpful; see loc. cit., pp. 199ff.

32. Treatments of medical education at Salerno and Montpellier are included in Rashdall, I, pp. 75–86; Schachner, pp. 51–55; Wieruszowski, pp. 173–177; and in Kibre, pp. 12–14, 50–51, 54, 58, 61, 122–124. Original documentation is represented in Thorndike, pp. 81–84, 253–254, 283–285, 314, 321.

33. Rashdall, II, treats the origins and growth of most of the more important Italian *studia* from the thirteenth century onward. See chapter VI, pp. 5–62.

34. For informative summaries of the teaching of civil law at Bologna, consult Schachner, pp. 174–185; and Bowen, II, pp. 125–137.

35. Quoted in Wieruszowski, p. 167. The problem addressed by the Bolognese laws of 1274 was identical with that at Paris, where in 1275 officials complained, ". . . Some of the . . . booksellers, given to insatiable cupidity, are in a way ungrateful and burdensome to the university itself, when they put obstacles in the way of procuring books whose use is essential to the students and by buying too cheaply and selling too dearly and thinking up other frauds make the same books too costly." *Chartularium universitatis Parisiensis*, I, pp. 532–534, in Thorndike, pp. 100–101, 112–117, and 119–123.

36. H. Ansley, ed., *Munimenta Academica* (1869), cited in Wieruszowski, p. 197.

37. Quoted in Haskins, *The Renaissance of the Twelfth Century*, pp. 203ff.

38. Cited in Wieruszowski, p. 166.
39. See *Chartularium universitatis Parisiensis*, III, pp. 39–40, in Thorndike, pp. 237–238. Characteristically unruly student behavior is vividly described in Heer, pp. 244–251.
40. The long and involved struggle for various university privileges and exemptions is treated succinctly in Compayré, pp. 74–95. See also Mary Martin McLaughlin, *Intellectual Freedom and Its Limitations in the University of Paris in the Thirteenth and Fourteenth Centuries* (New York: Arno Press, 1977).
41. For a discussion of royal and papal patronage, see the treatment in Schachner, pp. 42–50.
42. Geoffrey Chaucer, Prologue to *The Canterbury Tales* (various editions), lines 285–308.
43. Thelin, pp. 35–36; Haskins, *The Rise of the Universities,* chapter III.
44. Instances of student turbulence and of pitched battles between town and gown are given in Freemantle, p. 96; Compayré, pp. 272–279; Rashdall, I, pp. 334–337; and in Schachner, pp. 190, 196, 200–206, 219.
45. *The Vercelli Contract,* in Rashdall, II, Appendix III, pp. 337–340.
46. Bowen, II, p. 112; Rashdall, I, p. 338.
47. A variant translation is supplied in Wieruszowski, p. 157.
48. For an account of the origins and early development of Oxford, see Heer, pp. 251–254; and Schachner, pp. 186–190. A fuller treatment appears in Rashdall, III, pp. 140–273; and in Leff, parts 2, 3, and 5. See also J. I. Catto and Ralph Evans, eds., *Late Medieval Oxford* (New York: Oxford University Press, 1992).
49. See Rashdall, III, pp. 276–324.
50. The historical evolution of medieval colleges is traced briefly in Haskins, *The Rise of the Universities,* pp. 26–28, 32–35.
51. Quoted in Heer, pp. 241–242.
52. Rashdall, I, p. 512. See also Stephen Ferruolo, "Learning, Ambition, and Careers in the Medieval University," *History of Education Quarterly* 28 (Spring 1988): 1–22; and William J. Courtnay, "Inquiry and Inquisitions: Academic Freedom in Medieval Universities," *Church History* 58 (June 1989): 181.

Chapter 3

1. See "Spirit of the Middle Ages," *The History of Western Culture: The Medieval World* (New York: Life Educational Reprint No. 43, n.d.), p. 4; and David Knowles, *The Evolution of Medieval Thought* (New York: Vintage, 1964), passim.
2. Economic conditions in late medieval Europe are succinctly described in H. L. Adelson, *Medieval Commerce* (Princeton, N.J.: Van Nostrand, 1962).
3. Consult Roland Bainton, "Man, God, and the Church in the Age of the Renaissance," in *The Renaissance* (New York: Harper Torchbook, 1962), pp. 77–96; and Le Van Baumer, ed., "The Renaissance," in *Main Currents of Western Thought* (New York: Alfred A. Knopf, 1952), p. 109. A standard reference for Renaissance culture and learning is William Harrison Woodward, *Studies in Education During the Age of the Renaissance* (Cambridge: Cambridge University Press, 1965). Refer as well to Hugh Kearney, *Scholars and Gentlemen: Universities and Society in Pre-Industrial Britain* (Ithaca, N.Y.: Cornell University Press, 1970).
4. Jacob Burckhardt, *The Civilization of the Renaissance in Italy,* 2 vols. (New York: Harper Torchbooks, 1958).
5. For example, consult the analysis offered in Walter Ullman, *Medieval Foundations of Renaissance Humanism* (Ithaca, N.Y.: Cornell University Press, 1977). Some of the same fundamental continuities are emphasized in R. W. Southern, *Medieval Humanism and Other Essays* (Oxford: Blackwell, 1970).
6. An instructive reference for the shift in human consciousness entailed is Ernst Cassirer, et al., *Renaissance Philosophy of Man* (Chicago: University of Chicago Press, 1948).
7. Note the illustrative case study offered in A. F. Leach, *The Schools of Medieval England* (New York: Barnes and Noble, 1969), pp. 201–212.
8. See R. Weiss, *The Spread of Italian Humanism* (London: Hutchinson's University Library, 1964), chapter 1.
9. Useful biographical profiles of Petrarch are included in E. H. Wilkins, *Life of Petrarch* (Chicago: University of Chicago Press, 1958); and in Morris Bishop, *Petrarch and His World* (London: Chatto and Windus, 1964). See also Nicholas Mann, *Petrarch* (New York: Oxford University Press, 1984).

10. *Epistolae familiares*, III, quoted in Wilkins, p. 18.

11. Details are given in John H. Whitfield, *Petrarch and the Renascence* (New York: Haskell House, 1966).

12. See Woodward, *Vittorino da Feltre and Other Humanist Educators* (New York: Teachers College Press, 1976), pp. 14, 93; Hans Baron, *The Crisis of the Early Italian Renaissance*, 2 vols. (Princeton, N.J.: Princeton University Press, 1955); and Demetrius J. Geanakopolos, *Greek Scholars in Venice: Studies in the Dissemination of Greek Learning from Byzantium to Western Europe* (Cambridge, Mass.: Harvard University Press, 1962). An accessible summary profile is supplied by Ian Thomson, "Manuel Chrysoloras and the Early Italian Renaissance," *Greek, Roman and Byzantine Studies* 7 (1966): 63–82.

13. The leading role of Florence is recounted in L. Martines, *The Social World of the Florentine Humanists, 1390–1460* (London: Routledge and Kegan Paul, 1963).

14. See Wiss, passim; and Paul Oskar Kristeller, *The Classics and Renaissance Thought* (Cambridge, Mass.: Harvard University Press, 1955).

15. The account following borrows from essays by Werner L. Gundersheimer, Margaret L. King, Paul Oskar Kristeller, and Roland Bainton, in Patricia H. Labalme, ed., *Beyond Their Sex: Learned Women of the European Past* (New York: New York University Press, 1980), chapters 3–6.

16. An instructive account may be found in Mary Agnes Cannon, *The Education of Women During the Renaissance* (Washington, D.C.: Catholic University of America, 1916).

17. See Woodward, *Studies in Education*, pp. 1–78.

18. Hans Bolgar, *The Classical Heritage and Its Beneficiaries*, vol. 2 (Cambridge: Cambridge University Press, 1954), p. 487.

19. Details appear in Paul F. Grendler, *Schooling in Renaissance Italy: Literacy and Learning, 1300–1600* (Baltimore: Johns Hopkins University Press, 1989).

20. Arthur J. Dunston, *Four Centres of Classical Learning in Renaissance Italy* (Sydney: Sydney University Press, 1972).

21. Nesca A. Robb, *Neoplatonism of the Italian Renaissance* (London: Allen and Unwin, 1935), p. 58.

22. Consult Woodward, *Vittorino da Feltre*. For additional background, refer to Kate Simon, *A Renaissance Tapestry: The Gonzagas of Mantua* (New York: Harper and Row, 1988).

23. See Woodward, *Studies in Education*, pp. 244–265; and G. Bull, trans., *The Book of the Courtier* (Hammondsworth: Penguin, 1967).

24. The theme is extended in Peter Burke, *The Italian Renaissance: Culture and Society in Italy* (Princeton: Princeton University Press, 1986), pp. 177–200. Likewise relevant is the illustrative biographical profile included in Theodore K. Rabb, *Renaissance Lives: Portraits of an Age* (New York: Pantheon, 1993), pp. 75–92.

25. The outcome, however, was often quite different, as characterized by John Herman Randall, *Making of the Modern Mind* (Cambridge, Mass.: Riverside Press, 1954), p. 121.

26. Woodward, *Studies in Education*, pp. 79–103.

27. Woodward, *Desiderius Erasmus Concerning the Aim and Method of Education* (New York: Teachers College Press, 1964); and Lester K. Born, trans., *The Education of a Christian Prince* (New York: Columbia University Press, 1936).

28. Woodward, *Studies in Education*, chapter 8.

29. James Bowen, *A History of Western Education*, II (London: Methuen, 1975), pp. 264–268.

30. Quoted in Christopher J. Lucas, *Our Western Educational Heritage* (New York: Macmillan, 1972), pp. 296–297.

31. Refer to the concluding discussion in Alan B. Cobban, *Medieval Universities: Their Development and Organization* (London: Methuen, 1975). The character of the universities at Paris and Oxford, from which there were few departures in intellectual tradition, is discussed in Gordon Leff, *Paris and Oxford Universities in the Thirteenth and Fourteenth Centuries* (New York: John Wiley, 1968).

32. Bowen, II, pp. 269–290.

33. Ibid., pp. 326–328. See, for example, Joseph H. Lupton, *Life of John Colet* (Hamden, Conn.: Shoestring Press, 1961).

34. Thomas Elyot, *The Boke Named the Governour* (London: Dent, 1937). Commentary and assessment are supplied in Woodward, *Studies in Education*, chapter 13.

35. A helpful source is Ruth Kelso, *Doctrine of the English Gentleman in the Sixteenth Century* (Urbana, Ill.: University of Illinois Press, 1929).

36. Quoted and adapted from Breton's text, in Sylvester, pp. 142–143.

37. Quoted from "Legal Education in the Fifteenth Century," in Sylvester, pp. 75–77. A substantial body of literature has grown up devoted to the topic of the Inns of Court. An authoritative source is represented by W. Holdsworth, *A History of English Law*, II (London: Methuen, Sweet and Maxwell, 1945), pp. 494–512.
38. Holdsworth, pp. 494–512; IV, pp. 229–230; 263–270. See also K. Charlton, *Education in Renaissance England* (London: Routledge and Kegan Paul, 1965), chapter VI.
39. Charlton, pp. 169ff.
40. The story is recounted in Martin Brecht, *Martin Luther: His Road to Reformation, 1483–1521*, James L. Schaaf, trans. (Philadelphia: Fortress Press, 1985).
41. Gustav M. Bruce, *Luther as an Educator* (Westport, Conn.: Greenwood Press, 1979).
42. Note the profiles given in Kurt Aland, *Four Reformers: Luther, Melanchthon, Calvin, Zwingli*, James L. Schaaf, trans. (Minneapolis: Augsburg, 1979); and the interpretation given in Clyde L. Manschreck, *Melanchthon: The Quiet Reformer* (New York: Abington Press, 1958).
43. Allan P. Farrell, *The Jesuit Code of Liberal Education: Development and Scope of the Ratio Studiorum* (Milwaukee: Bruce Publishing, 1938); and Aldo Scaglione, *The Liberal Arts and the Jesuit College System* (Philadelphia: John Benjamin, 1986).
44. The full historical background is summarized nicely in Kearney, chapters 1–10.
45. See M. L. Clarke, *Classical Education in Britain* (Cambridge: Cambridge University Press, 1959), pp. 61–73.
46. Charlton, chapter IV, pp. 131–168.
47. Quotations are exerpted from F. J. Furnivall, ed., *William Harrison's Description of England* (London: Shakespeare Society, Series VI, 1877), pp. 77–78ff.; and from Sylvester, pp. 144–148.
48. See Christopher Hill, *Change and Continuity in Seventeenth Century England*, rev. ed. (New Haven, Conn.: Yale University Press, 1991), pp. 127–148.
49. Good analyses appear in David C. Lindberg and Ronald L. Numbers, eds., *God and Nature: Historical Essays on the Encounter Between Christianity and Science* (Berkeley: University of California Press, 1986).
50. See Thomas Kuhn, *The Copernican Revolution: Planetary Astronomy in the Development of Western Thought* (Cambridge, Mass.: Harvard University Press, 1952).
51. Note the relevant discussion for the sixteenth and seventeenth centuries in Charles McClelland, *State, Society and the University in Germany, 1700–1914* (Cambridge: Cambridge University Press, 1980).
52. Quoted in Felix Markham, *Oxford* (London: Weidenfeld and Nicolson, 1967), p. 84.
53. McClelland, pp. 1–132.
54. Illustrations abound in the opening sections of Friedrich Paulsen, *The German Universities and University Study*, Frank Thilly and William W. Elwang, trans. (New York: Charles Scribner's Sons, 1908). See also Donald N. Baker and Patrick J. Harrigan, eds. *The Making of Frenchmen: Current Directions in the History of Education in France, 1679–1979* (Waterloo, Ont.: Historical Reflections Press, 1980).
55. Quoted in Markham, p. 94.
56. John R. Thelin, *Higher Education and Its Useful Past* (Cambridge, Mass.: Schenckman, 1982), pp. 70–72.
57. Consult L. W. B. Brockliss, *French Higher Education in the Seventeenth and Eighteenth Centuries: A Cultural History* (New York: Oxford University Press, 1987).
58. Thelin, pp. 73–74.
59. Refer to Anthony J. LaVopa, *Grace, Talent, and Merit: Poor Students, Clerical Careers, and Professional Ideology in Eighteenth Century Germany* (Cambridge: Cambridge University Press, 1988). See also Thelin, pp. 74–76, for a general assessment.
60. Thelin, pp. 72–73.
61. For example, see Christopher Wordsworth, *Scholae Academicae, Studies of the English Universities in the Eighteenth Century* (New York: Augustus M. Kelley, 1969), pp. 82–89, 252–270.
62. Markham, pp. 64–93.
63. Charlton, chapter VII, pp. 199–225.
64. Quotations are from "The Grand Tour," in Sylvester, pp. 224–231. Similar complaints were issued by Harrison in his *Description of England*. See Furnivall, pp. 129–130.
65. Whether or not Gibbon's experience was typical or his indictment entirely fair is problematic, but his account is well worth examining in its entirety. See Edward Gibbon, *Autobiography*

(London: Humphrey Milford, Oxford University Press, n.d.), pp. 31–56. Also consult Wordsworth, pp. 5n, 12, 15.

Chapter 4

1. John Winthrop, "A Modell of Christian Charity" (1630), *Winthrop Papers* (Boston, Mass.: Massachusetts Historical Society, 1931), I, p. 295, cited in Alexander Rippa, *Education in a Free Society: An American History,* 2nd ed. (New York: David McKay, 1971), p. 18. Note the allusion in John R. Thelin, *Higher Education and Its Useful Past* (Cambridge, Mass.: Schenkman, 1982), p. 59; and the more general treatment of the establishment of New World institutions of higher learning in Oscar Handlin and Mary F. Handlin, "Colonial Seminaries, 1636–1770," in *The American College and American Culture: Socialization as a Function of Higher Education* (New York: McGraw-Hill, 1970), pp. 6ff.

2. "New England's First Fruits," in Richard Hofstadter and Wilson Smith, eds., *American Higher Education: A Documentary History,* 2 vols. (Chicago: University of Chicago Press, 1961), I, pp. 6–7. See also Nathaniel B. Schurleff and David Pulsiter, eds., *Records of the Colony of New Plymouth in New England,* 12 vols. (Boston: William White, 1855–1861), IX, pp. 20–21.

3. Consult Samuel Eliot Morison, *The Founding of Harvard College* (Cambridge, Mass.: Harvard University Press, 1935), pp. 1–6ff. A succinct account of Harvard's inception and formative years is supplied in Lawrence Cremin, *American Education: The Colonial Experience* (New York: Harper Collins, 1970), pp. 196–224.

4. W. H. Cooley and Don Williams, *International and Historical Roots Of American Higher Education* (New York: Garland Publishing, 1991), p. 74. See also "Cotton Mather's History of Harvard, 1702," in Hofstadter and Smith, I, pp. 13–19.

5. Morison, *Founding,* pp. 5–6. See also Hofstadter and Smith, I, pp. 8–10.

6. Morison, pp. 41–46.

7. Morison, pp. 5–6, 25–26, 40, 127. The theme is developed in John S. Brubacher and Willis Rudy, *Higher Education In Transition, A History of American Colleges and Universities, 1636–1976,* 3rd. ed. rev. (New York: Harper and Row, 1976), p. 3.

8. Quoted in Morison, *Harvard College in the Seventeenth Century,* vol. I (Cambridge, Mass.: Harvard University Press, 1936), p. 19.

9. Morison, *Founding,* p. 250; quoted in Thelin, p. 62.

10. Samuel Blair, *An Account of the College of New Jersey* (Woodbridge, N.J.: James Park, 1764), pp. 5–7; cited in James Bowen, *A History of Western Education,* vol. 3 (London: Methuen, 1981), pp. 275–276. Relevant institutional histories include Thomas J. Wertenbaker, *Princeton, 1746–1896* (Princeton, N. J.: Princeton University Press, 1946); Dorothy R. Dillon, *The New York Triumvirate* (New York: Columbia University Press, 1949); Walter C. Bronson, *History of Brown* (Providence, R.I.: Brown University Press, 1914); William H. S. Demarest, *A History of Rutgers College* (New Brunswick, N.J.: Rutgers University Press, 1924); James B. Conant, et al., *History and Traditions of Harvard College* (Cambridge, Mass.: Harvard University Press, 1936); Alexander Cowie, *Educational Problems at Yale College in the Eighteenth Century* (New Haven, Conn.: Yale University Press, 1936); Morison, *Three Centuries of Harvard* (Cambridge, Mass.: Harvard University Press, 1936); Leon R. Richardson, *History of Dartmouth* (Hanover, N.H.: Dartmouth College Publications, 1932); Donald Fleming, *Science and Technology in Providence, 1760–1914* (Providence, R.I.: Brown University Press, 1952); William Smith, *Account of the College, Academy, and Charitable School of Philadelphia* (Philadelphia: University of Pennsylvania Library, 1941). Consult also Robert Polk Thomson, "The Reform of the College of William and Mary, 1763–1780," *Proceedings of the American Philosophical Society* 115 (June 1971): 213ff.; and Alison B. Olson, "The Founding of Princeton University: Religion and Politics in Eighteenth-Century New Jersey," *New Jersey History* 87 (Autumn 1969): 133–150.

11. Quoted in Wertenbaker, pp. 19–20. For a similar declaration, see Courtlandt Canby, "A Note on the Influence of Oxford University on William and Mary," *William and Mary Quarterly* 21 (July 1941): 243–244.

12. The story is recounted in Frederick Rudolph, *The American College and University, A History* (Athens, Georgia: University of Georgia Press, 1990), p. 7.

13. Herbert Baxter Adams, *The College of William and Mary* (Washington, D.C.: U. S. Bureau of Education Circulation of Information No. 1, 1887), pp. 11–15.

14. Refer to Charles F. Thwing, *History of Higher Education in America* (Englewood Cliffs, N.J.: Prentice-Hall, 1906), pp. 56–57. For the early history of Yale, refer to Edwin Oviatt, *The*

Beginnings of Yale, 1701–1726 (New Haven, Conn.: Yale University Press, 1916). See also Edward C. Elliott and M. M. Chambers, *Charters and Basic Laws of Selected American Universities and Colleges* (New York: Carnegie Commission for the Advancement of Teaching, 1934), pp. 588, 593.

15. Consult Wertenbaker, pp. 396–404.
16. A helpful analysis is included in Beverly McAnear, "College Founding in the American Colonies, 1745–1775," *Mississippi Historical Review* 42 (1955): 24–44.
17. Details are given in the first volume of Leon B. Richardson, *History of Dartmouth College*, 2 vols. (Hanover, N.H.: Dartmouth College, 1932).
18. Refer to Bronson, p. 1. See also Hofstadter and Smith, pp. 134–136.
19. See Cowley and Williams, p. 84.
20. Quoted in Thelin, p. 61.
21. Edward Potts Cheyney, *History of the University of Pennsylvania, 1740–1940* (Philadelphia: University of Pennsylvania Press, 1940), p. 83.
22. John Howard Amridge, et al., *A History of Columbia University, 1754–1904* (New York: Columbia University Press, 1904), pp. 1, 32. McAnear's analysis, loc. cit., amplifies the pragmatic considerations that encouraged religious tolerance and pluralism.
23. Rudolph, p. 16.
24. Note the discussion in Brubacher and Rudy, pp. 8–12; and in Cowley and Williams, pp. 85–93.
25. Brubacher and Rudy, pp. 30–32.
26. Cowley and Williams, p. 90.
27. Morison, *Seventeenth Century*, II, p. 330.
28. Quoted in James Harold Easterby, *A History of the College of Charleston, Founded 1770* (Charleston, S.C.: n.p., 1935), p. 10.
29. Morison, *Seventeenth Century*, II, p. 433.
30. Morison, *Three Centuries*, p. 61.
31. Brubacher and Rudy, pp. 13–19; Rudolph, p. 25; Cowley and Williams, pp. 85–87; Rippa, pp. 80–81; and Thelin, pp. 59–62.
32. For an instructive illustration, see the order of studies (1642) summarized in Cremin, reproduced in Lester F. Goodchild and Harold S. Wechsler, eds., *ASHE Reader on the History of Higher Education* (Needham Heights, Mass.: Ginn Press, 1989), p. 35.
33. Refer to the discussion on clerical training and erudition in Frederick L. Weis, *The Colonial Clergy of Virginia, North Carolina and South Carolina* (Boston: Society of the Descendants of the Colonial Clergy, 1955), pp. 1–57.
34. Consult Franklin B. Dexter, "The Influence of the English Universities in the Development of New England," *A Selection from the Miscellaneous Historical Papers of Fifty Years* (New Haven, Conn.: Tuttle, Morehouse and Taylor, 1918), pp. 102–117.
35. Note the helpful account supplied in Brubacher and Rudy, pp. 13ff.
36. A relevant analysis is given in Theodore Hornberger, *Scientific Thought in the American Colleges, 1639–1800* (Austin: University of Texas Press, 1945). Note also Fleming, pp. 20–21; and Rippa, p. 81.
37. Quoted from Louis Franklin Snow, *The College Curriculum in the United States* (New York: Teachers College, Columbia University, 1907), pp. 56–60.
38. See "Statutes of Harvard, ca. 1646," in Hofstadter and Smith, pp. 8–10.
39. James J. Walsh, *Education of the Founding Fathers of the Republic* (New York: Fordham University Press, 1935), pp. 81, 85.
40. Cited in James W. Alexander, *Princeton, Old and New* (New York: Scribner, 1898), p. 48.
41. See William H. Cowley, "History of Student Residential Housing," *School and Society* 40 (December 1934): 705–710; and Brubacher and Rudy, pp. 41–42.
42. Recounted in Rudolph, p. 27.
43. Quoted in Morison, *Seventeenth Century*, I, pp. 77–78.
44. Brown University President Francis Wayland worried that in their effects residential dormitories would undermine faculty efforts to exercise needed control over students. See Theodore R. Crane, "Francis Wayland and the Residential College," *Rhode Island History* 19 (July 1960): 67–69.
45. Wertenbaker, pp. 185–187.
46. For an interesting account of the relationship between student behavior and collegiate table fare, refer to Alma D. M. Bevis, *Diets and Riots* (Boston: Marshall, Jones, 1936). Also note the antecdotes recounted in Cowley and Williams, pp. 104–106.

47. See the analysis and discussion in Brubacher and Rudy, pp. 50ff.
48. Varying interpretations of the historical significance of the American colonial college are given in Jurgen Herbst, "From Religion to Politics: Debates and Confrontations Over American College Governance in the Mid-Eighteenth Century," *Harvard Educational Review* 46 (August 1976): 397–424; Herbst, *From Crisis to Crisis: American College Government 1636–1819* (Cambridge, Mass.: Harvard University Press, 1982); Richard G. Durnin, "The Role of the Presidents in American Colleges of the Colonial Period," *History of Education Quarterly* 1 (June 1961): 23–31; and Phyllis Vine, "The Social Function of Eighteenth-Century Higher Education," *History of Education Quarterly* 16 (Winter 1976): 409–424.
49. See David W. Robson, *Educating Republicans: The College in the Era of the American Revolution, 1750–1800* (Westport, Conn.: Greenwood Press, 1985).
50. Details are supplied in Rudolph, pp. 33–35. See Wertenbaker, pp. 57–65; Van Amringe, p. 48; Adams, pp. 29, 56–57; and Morison, *Three Centuries*, pp. 148–153; Demarest, pp. 101–138; and Cheyney, pp. 115–118.
51. Noah Webster, "On the Education of Youth in America," in Rudolph, ed., *Essays on Education in the Early Republic* (Cambridge, Mass.: Belknap Press, 1965), p. 45. See also Joel Spring, *The American School, 1642–1990*, 2nd. ed. (New York: Longman, 1990), pp. 39–42.
52. Benjamin Rush, "A Plan for the Establishment of Public Schools . . . ," in Rudolph, *Essays*, pp. 10–17.
53. Quoted in James Henry Morgan, *Dickinson College: The History of One Hundred and Fifty Years 1783–1933* (Carlisle, Pa.: Dickinson College, 1933), p. 66; also cited in Rudolph, *American College and University*, p. 35.
54. Quoted in Dixon R. Fox, *Union College: An Unfinished History* (Schenectady, N.Y.: Graduate Council, Union College, 1945), p. 12.
55. Refer to Donald G. Tewksbury, *The Founding of American Colleges and Universities Before the Civil War* (New York: Bureau of Publications, Teachers College, Columbia University, 1932), p. 28.
56. See Brubacher and Rudy, pp. 33–35; Richardson, I, chapter 6; Hofstadter and Smith, pp. 202–219; William G. North, "The Political Background of the Dartmouth College Case," *New England Quarterly* 18 (June 1945): 181–203; Gordon R. Clapp, "The College Charter," *Journal of Higher Education* 5 (February 1934): 79–87; Charles G. Haines, *The Role of the Supreme Court in American Government and Politics, 1789–1835* (Berkeley: University of California Press, 1944), chapter 11; John S. Whitehead and Jurgen Herbst, "How to Think about the Dartmouth College Case," *History of Education Quarterly* 26 (Fall 1986): 333–350.
57. Quoted in Hofstadter and Rudy, p. 212; but see preceding notes, p. 202; and the bibliographic commentary in Rippa, p. 82, as to the authenticity of Webster's often-quoted summation.
58. See especially Whitehead and Herbst, pp. 333–350.
59. Background is supplied in Robert L. Church and Michael W. Sedlak, "The Antebellum College and Academy," in *Education in the United States: An Interpretive History* (New York: Free Press, 1976), pp. 23–51.
60. David W. Robson, "College Founding in the New Republic," *History of Education Quarterly* 23 (Fall 1983): 323–341.
61. Note the argument advanced in Merle E. Curti, *Growth of American Thought* (New York: Harper and Row, 1943), pp. 344–345.
62. The account here reflects the profile advanced by Tewksbury, passim.
63. Bruce Kimball, *Orators and Philosophers: A History of the Idea of Liberal Education* (New York: Teachers College Press, 1986), chapter 5.
64. Jurgen Herbst, "Church, State, and Higher Education: College Government in the American Colonies and States Before 1820," *History of Higher Education Annual* 1 (1981): 42–54; and Herbst, "The Eighteenth Century Origins of the Split Between Private and Public Higher Education in the United States," *History of Education Quarterly* 15 (Fall 1975): 273–280.
65. See Rudolph, *American College and University*, pp. 44–47. See also Louis C. Hatch, *The History of Bowdoin College* (Portland, Maine: Loring, Short and Harmon, 1927), p. 9.
66. David B. Skillman, *The Biography of a College: Being the History of the First Century of the Life of Lafayette College* (Easton, Penn.: Lafayette College, 1932), I, pp. 38ff.; Charles Henry Rammelkamp, *Illinois College: A Centennial History, 1829–1929* (New Haven: Yale University Press, 1928), p. 40; James Albert Woodburn, *History of Indiana University: 1820–1902* (Bloomington, Ind.: University of Indiana Press, 1940), pp. 51–52; James I. Osborne and Theodore G. Gronert, *Wabash College: The First Hundred Years, 1832–1932* (Crawfordsville,

Indiana: R. E. Bents, 1932), pp. 1–2; Henry M. Bullock, *A History of Emory University* (Nashville: Parthenon Press, 1936), p. 69; Elizabeth M. Farrand, *History of the University of Michigan* (Ann Arbor, Mich.: Register Publishing, 1885), p. 59.

67. Quoted in Tewksbury, p. 1.

68. Immediately prior to the Civil War, according to Tewksbury's analysis of collegiate mortality, about 182 colleges were in existence; an estimated 512 others had earlier failed. See loc. cit., pp. 15, 28.

69. Rudolph, *American College and University*, pp. 47–48. See Frederick A. P. Barnard, *Two Papers on Academic Degrees* (New York: MacGowan and Slipper, 1880), p. 18.

70. Quoted in Rudolph, *American College and University*, pp. 51–52.

71. William A. Millis, *The History of Hanover College from 1827 to 1927* (Hanover, Ind.: Hanover College, 1927), pp. 20, 31.

72. Rudolph, *American College and University*, pp. 52–53.

73. Jonas Viles, et al., *The University of Missouri: A Centennial History* (Columbia, Mo.: University of Missouri Press, 1939), p. 28.

74. Daniel J. Boorstin, *The Americans: The National Experience* (New York: Random House, 1965), pp. 153–160.

75. Quoted in Tewksbury, p. 3. For a more complete extract from Lindsley's commencement address, consult "Philip Lindsley on the Condition of the Colleges, 1837," in Hofstadter and Smith, I, pp. 243–250. See also "Philip Lindsley on the Problems of the College in a Sectarian Age, 1829," ibid., pp. 232–237.

76. Morgan, pp. 21–22.

77. Rudolph, *American College and University*, p. 48.

78. Commenting on the effects of sectarian rivalry upon the proliferation of colleges in Illinois, President Julian Monson Sturtevant of Illinois College observed in 1830, "This multiplication of colleges was exceedingly disastrous.... Every denomination must have its own institution. The small sums of money which could be gathered in a new community for educational purposes and the very limited number of students prepared to pursue the higher branches [of learning] were distributed along so many so-called colleges that it was impossible for any to attain a position worthy of the name." Reproduced in Hofstadter and Smith, I, p. 241.

79. Wertenbaker, p. 120.

80. See Church and Sedlak, pp. 23–51; Natalie A. Naylor, "The Ante-Bellum College Movement: A Reappraisal of Tewksbury's Founding of American Colleges and Universities," *History of Education Quarterly* 13 (Fall 1973): 261–274; and David Potts, "American Colleges in the Nineteenth Century: From Localism to Denominationalism," *History of Education Quarterly* 11 (Winter 1971): 363–380. Specific illustrative invocations of "Athens" include Easterby, pp. 105–106; Millis, pp. 20, 31; and Wertenbaker, p. 120; cited in Rudolph, *American College and University*, p. 50.

81. William W. Ferrier, *Origin and Development of the University of California* (Berkeley: University of California Press, 1930), p. 273.

82. Consult Noah Porter Webster, *American College and the American Public* (New Haven, Conn.: C. C. Chatfield, 1870), pp. 254–258; John D. Millet, *Financing Higher Education in the United States* (New York: Columbia University Press, 1952), p. 92; and John M. Thomas, "Report of the Commission on the Distribution of Colleges," *Bulletin of the Association of American Colleges* 7 (May 1921): 19–21.

83. Hatch, p. 19.

84. See David B. Potts, "'College Enthusiasm!' As Public Response: 1800–1860," *Harvard Educational Review* 47 (February 1977): 28–42; Brubacher and Rudy, pp. 69–74; James Findlay, "Agency, Denominations, and the Western Colleges, 1830–1860: Some Connections Between Evangelicalism and American Higher Education," *Church History* 50 (March 1981): 64–80; and James McLachlan, "The American College in the Nineteenth Century: Toward a Reappraisal," *Teachers College Record* 80 (December 1978): 286–306.

85. Note the enumeration in Rudolph, *American College and University*, pp. 52-58ff.; and the discussion in Robson, pp. 323–341; as well as "The Sectarian Status of American Colleges in 1813," in Hofstadter and Smith, I, pp. 179–189.

86. Quoted in William W. Sweet, *The American Churches* (New York: Abingdon Press, 1947), pp. 59–60. See also Sweet, *Religion in the Development of American Culture* (New York: Scribner, 1952), pp. 164–165.

87. Consult Albea Godbold, *Church Colleges of the Old South* (Durham, N.C.: Duke University Press, 1944), pp. 147–148.
88. William Sperry, *Religion in America* (Cambridge: Cambridge University Press, 1946); Kenneth S. Latourette, *The Great Century, 1800–1914* (London: Eyre and Spottiswoode, 1941), pp. 418–419. By the mid-nineteenth century, Tewksbury estimates, there were about 180 sectarian colleges in existence, of which 14 were Roman Catholic.
89. Brubacher and Rudy, pp. 69–74.
90. Cited in Rudolph, *American College and University*, p. 57.
91. "Philip Lindsley on the Problems of the College in a Sectarian Age . . . ," in Hofstadter and Smith, I, p. 233.
92. Frderick J. Kelly and Ella B. Ratcliffe, *Privately-Controlled Higher Education* (Washington, D.C.: U.S. Office of Education Bulletin No. 12, 1934), p. 22.
93. Rudolph, *Mark Hopkins and the Log, Williams College, 1836–1872* (New Haven, Conn.: Yale University Press, 1956), p. 65.
94. John Todd, *Plain Letters Addressed to a Parishioner in Behalf of the Society of Collegiate and Theological Education at the West* (New York: Leavitt, Trow, 1847), p. 22.
95. Cowley and Williams, p. 113. See Louis Schutz Boas, *Women's Education Begins* (Norton, Mass.: Wheaton College Press, 1935), pp. 11ff.
96. Patricia A. Palmieri, "From Republican Motherhood to Race Suicide: Arguments on the Higher Education of Women in the United States, 1820–1920," in Carol Lasser, ed., *Educating Men and Women Together: Coeducation in a Changing World* (Urbana: University of Illinois Press, 1987), pp. 49–64.
97. Refer to Thomas Woody, *History of Women's Education in the United States* (Lancaster, Penn.: Science Press, 1929), II, pp. 137–142; and Robert S. Fletcher, *History of Oberlin College* (Chicago: R. R. Donnelley, 1943), I, chapters 16, 24; and Helen Lefkowitz Horowitz, *Alma Mater: Design and Experience in the Women's Colleges from their 19th Century Beginnings to the 1930s* (New York: Alfred A. Knopf, 1984). An authoritative source for subsequent developments is Barbara M. Solomon, *In The Company of Educated Women: A History of Women and Higher Education in America* (New Haven, Conn.: Yale University Press, 1985).
98. Cowley and Williams, pp. 103. See John Hope Franklin, *From Slavery to Freedom* (New York: Knopf, 1947), p. 228; Charles S. Johnson, *The Negro College Graduate* (Chapel Hill, N.C.: University of North Carolina Press, 1938), p. 7.
99. Ruth D. Wilson, "Negro Colleges of Liberal Arts," *American Scholar* 19 (Autumn 1950): 462–463. Consult Dwight O. W. Holmes, *Evolution of the Negro College* (New York: Teachers College, Columbia University, 1934); Ralph L. Pearson, "Reflections on Black Colleges: The Historical Perspective of Charles S. Johnson," *History of Education Quarterly* 23 (Spring 1983): 55–68. Also useful is Lawrence B. Goodheart, "Abolitionists As Academics: The Controversy at Western Reserve College, 1832–1833," *History of Education Quarterly* 22 (Winter 1982): 421–433.
100. See Rippa, pp. 85ff.; and Walter Hugins, *Jacksonian Democracy and the Working Class: A Study of the New York Workingmen's Movement, 1829–1837* (Stanford: Stanford University Press, 1960), pp. 132–134.
101. The full text is given in LeRoy J. Halsey, ed., *The Works of Philip Lindsley, D. D.* (Philadelphia. J. P. Lippincott, 1866); the quotation is from Volume I, p. 81.
102. Quoted in George F. Smyth, *Kenyon College: Its First Century* (New Haven, Conn.: Yale University Press, 1924), pp. 42–43.
103. Cited in Rudolph, *American College and University*, pp. 217–218. For an illustration, see Thomas N. Hoover, *The History of Ohio University* (Athens, Ohio: Ohio University, 1954), p. 53. For a later revival of the movement, consult Earle D. Ross, "The Manual Labor Experiment in the Land Grant College," *Mississippi Valley Historical Review* 21 (June 1934): 513–528.
104. See Brubacher and Rudy, pp. 84–85, 88–90. Consult William D. Carrell, "American College Professors, 1750–1800," *History of Education Quarterly* 8 (Fall 1968): 289–305.
105. Recounted in Rudolph, *American College and University*, pp. 217–218, from Daniel W. Hollis, *University of South Carolina*, 2 vols. (Columbia: University of South Carolina Press, 1951–56), I, p. 189.
106. For discussion, see George Smith, *The Old Time College President* (New York: Columbia University Press, 1930); Herman Donovan, "Changing Conceptions of the College Presidency, 1795–1957," *Association of American Colleges Bulletin* 43 (March 1957): 40–52; and Dixon R. Fox, ed., *Sources of Culture in the Middle West* (Englewood Cliffs, N.J.: Prentice-Hall, 1934), pp. 56–58.

107. On faculty governance, refer to Brubacher and Rudy, pp. 30ff.; Herbst, *From Crisis to Crisis;* Samuel K. Wilson, "The Genesis of American College Government," *Thought* 1 (December 1926): 415–433. A vivid example of early nineteenth-century debate over the role of faculty in academic government is represented by an 1837 document authored by Charleston College President Jasper Adams, reproduced in Hofstadter and Smith, I, pp. 311–328.

108. Samuel A. Eliot, *A Sketch of the History of Harvard College and of Its Present State* (Boston: C. C. Little and J. Brown, 1848), p. 49, cited in Rudolph, *American College and University,* p. 167. Consult the broader discussion in John E. Kirkpatrick, *Academic Organization and Control* (Yellow Springs, Ohio: Antioch Press, 1931).

109. Rammelkamp, p. 139, cited in Rudolph, *American College and University,* p. 171.

110. Millis, pp. 21–28.

111. The examples are cited in Rudolph, *American College and University,* pp. 171–172.

112. Nashville's President Lindsley eloquently defended the contrary position. "Experience has fully proved in Europe, and in the older states of this Union," he alleged, "that large towns or cities are greatly preferable to small ones for [colleges]. All the capitals and most of the . . . cities of Europe have their universities. And wherever they have been established in small towns, the students are proverbially more riotous and ungovernable in their conduct, more boorish and savage in their manners, and more dissolute and licentious in their habits." See "Philip Lindsley on the Problems of the College . . . ," in Hofstadter and Smith, p. 235.

113. Francis Wayland, *Thoughts on the Present Collegiate System* (Boston: Gould, Kendall and Lincoln, 1842), p. 129. For commentary, see "Francis Wayland and the Residential College," *Rhode Island History* 19 (July 1960): 67–69. Note also William H. Cowley, "A History of Student Residential Housing," *School and Society* 40 (December 1934): 705–712, 758–763.

114. Cited in Brubacher and Rudy, p. 41.

115. A composite picture is drawn in Brubacher and Rudy, pp. 85–86. See as well the account in Cowley and Williams, pp. 85–87, 104–109.

116. William G. Hammond, *Remembrance of Amherst* (New York: Columbia University Press, 1946), p. 187.

117. Rudolph, *Mark Hopkins and the Log,* pp. 48–52; Brubacher and Rudy, pp. 86ff.; Francis and H. L. Wayland, *A Memoir of the Life and Labors of Francis Wayland, D. D.* (New York: Sheldon, 1867), I, pp. 35–36.

118. Student rebelliousness and protest in the early colleges are described in Cowley and Williams, pp. 104–106; in Brubacher and Rudy, pp. 50–56; and in Rudolph, *American College and University,* pp. 95–102. See Wertenbaker, p. 169; and Hollis, I, pp. 64–68, 90–91. Useful historical perspectives are offered in David F. Allmendinger, *Paupers and Scholars: The Transition of Student Life in 19th Century New England* (New York: St. Martin's Press, 1973); Henry D. Sheldon, *Student Life and Customs* (New York: Arno Press, 1971); and Anthony Esler, *Bombs, Beards, and Barricades: 150 Years of Youth in Revolt* (New York: Stewin and Day, 1972).

119. See Clarence P. Shedd, *Two Centuries of Student Christian Movements: Their Origin and Intercollegiate Life* (New York: Association Press, 1934), pp. 13, 25–31, 40, 76–77, 126ff.; Cowley and Williams, pp. 102–103; Brubacher and Rudy, pp. 42–45; Rudolph, *American College and University,* pp. 78ff.

120. William O. Carr, *Amherst Diary, 1853–1857* (Guilford, Conn.: Shore Line Times Publishing, 1940), pp. 15–18.

121. Charles W. Lomas, "The Lighter Side of the Literary Society," *Quarterly Journal of Speech* 39 (February 1953): 45–48; and Henry D. Sheldon, *History and Pedagogy of American Student Societies* (Englewood Cliffs, N.J.: Prentice-Hall, 1907), pp. 89–94; and David Potter, *Debating in Colonial Chartered Colleges* (New York: Teachers College, Columbia University, 1944).

122. Thomas S. Harting, *College Literary Societies: Their Contribution to Higher Education in the United States, 1815–1876* (New York: Pageant Press, 1971), pp. 317ff.; and James McLachlin, "American Student Societies in the Early 19th Century," in Lawrence Stone, ed., *The University in Society,* 2 vols. (Princeton: Princeton University Press, 1974), II, pp. 449–494.

123. Saul Sack, "Student Life in the Nineteenth Century," *Pennsylvania Magazine of History and Biography* (July 1961): 270–273.

124. Wertenbaker, p. 138; Sheldon, p. 147.

125. See Lily Jay Silver, "Phi Beta Kappa and the Nation," *Education* 74 (March 1954): 401–413; William T. Hastings, "Phi Beta Kappa as a Secret Society," *Key Reporter* 31 (Autumn 1965); Wayne Musgrave, *College Fraternities* (New York: Interfraternity Conference, 1923), pp. 88–93;

William Baird, *Manual of College Fraternities* (New York: College Fraternity Publishing, 1915), pp. 6–35; H. L. Kellogg, ed., *College Secret Societies* (Chicago: Ezra A. Cook, 1874).

126. Quoted in Rudolph, *Mark Hopkins and the Log*, p. 110.
127. Cited in Brubacher and Rudy, p. 127.
128. Discussions of the curricular reform movements of the period appear in Elbert V. Wills, *The Growth of American Higher Education* (Philadelphia: Dorrance, 1936), pp. 173–180; R. Freeman Butts, *The College Charts Its Course* (New York: McGraw-Hill, 1939), pp. 132–134; and in Milton H. Turk, "Without Classical Studies," *Journal of Higher Education* 4 (October 1933): 339–346. Refer to Brubacher and Rudy, pp. 101–104; Rudolph, *American College and University*, chapter 6, pp. 110–116; and Cowley and Williams, pp. 115–118.
129. Wertenbaker, p. 123.
130. See William T. Foster, *Administration of the College Curriculum* (Boston: Houghton Mifflin, 1911), pp. 26–28; and Rudolph, *American College and University*, p. 113.
131. On Jefferson's reforms at William and Mary College in the late 1770s, consult Philip A. Bruce, *History of the University of Virginia* (New York: Macmillan, 1920), I, pp. 223ff. Responses to innovations introduced subsequent to the founding of the University of Virginia are commented upon in George P. Schmidt, "Crosscurrents in American Colleges," *American Historical Review* 42 (October 1936): 57–58. Also relevant is Orie W. Long, *Thomas Jefferson and George Ticknor* (Williamstown, Mass.: McClelland Press, 1933). Useful source materials on Jefferson at Virginia are reproduced in Hofstadter and Smith, I, pp. 175–176, 193–202, 224–231, and 266–268. Tricknor's work at Harvard is treated ibid., pp. 268–273.
132. Ralph Waldo Emerson, "The American Scholar," in Frederick I. Carpenter, ed., *Emerson: Representative Selections* (New York: American Book, 1934), pp. 64–70.
133. Francis Wayland, *The Education Demanded by the People of the United States* (Boston: Phillips, Sampson, 1855), pp. 28–29. For commentary, see William G. Roelker, *Francis Wayland: A Neglected Pioneer of Higher Education* (Worcester, Mass.: American Antiquarian Society, 1944).
134. Henry Tappan, *University Education* (New York: Putnam, 1851), p. 64.
135. "Original Papers in Relation to a Course of Liberal Education," *American Journal of Science and Arts* 15 (January 1829): 297–351. Significant portions of the document are reproduced in Hofstadter and Smith, pp. 274–291; and in Goodchild and Wechsler, pp. 171–178.
136. "Original Papers," pp. 300ff.
137. Ibid., p. 310.
138. Ibid., p. 323.
139. Quoted in Rudolph, *American College and University*, p. 135.
140. Hollis, I, p. iv.
141. William Lathrop Kingsley, ed., *Yale College: A Sketch of Its History*, 2 vols. (New York: Holt, 1879), I, pp. 150–152.
142. John William Draper, *The Indebtedness of the City of New York to its University: An Address to the Alumni of the University of the City of New York at their Twenty-First Anniversary, 28th June, 1835* (New York: The University, 1853), pp. 20–24.
143. Quoted in Wertenbaker, p. 95.
144. Quoted in Rudolph, *Mark Hopkins and the Log*, p. 137.
145. Ferrier, p. 34.
146. Coulter, p. 201.
147. Tappan, p. 64.
148. Consult James Findlay, "The Society for Promotion of Collegiate Education at the West and Western Colleges," *History of Education Quarterly* 17 (Spring 1977): 31–62.
149. Francis Wayland, *Report to the Corporation of Brown University on Changes in the System of College Education, Read March 28, 1850* (Providence, R.I.: Brown University, 1850). See Rudolph, *American College and University*, p. 238.
150. Wayland, p. 34.

Chapter 5

1. James B. Angell, *Selected Addresses* (New York: Longmans, Green, 1912), pp. 7, 27.
2. Quoted in Walter P. Rogers, *Andrew D. White and the Modern University* (Ithaca, N.Y.: Cornell University Press, 1942), p. 4.
3. Noah Porter, "Inaugural Address," in *Addresses at the Inauguration of Professor Noah Porter, D.D., LL.D., as President of Yale College, Wednesday, October 11, 1871* (p. 27), quoted in Laurence R. Veysey, *The Emergence of the Modern University* (Chicago: University of Chicago Press, 1965), p. 1.

4. See Jurgen Herbst, "Diversification in American Higher Education," in Conrad H. Jarausch, ed., *The Transformation of Higher Learning 1860–1930* (Chicago: University of Chicago Press, 1983), pp. 196–206; and Richard Storr, *The Beginnings of Graduate Education In America* (Chicago: University of Chicago Press, 1953), pp. 1–66.

5. See Colin B. Burke, "The Expansion of American Higher Education," in Jarausch, p. 111.

6. A graphic overview is given in Joseph M. Stetar, "In Search of a Direction: Southern Higher Education After the Civil War," *History of Education Quarterly* 25 (Fall 1985): 341–368.

7. James B. Sellers, *History of the University of Alabama*, 2 vols. (University: University of Alabama Press, 1953), I, pp. 292ff.

8. Kemp P. Battle, *The Struggle and the Story of the Rebirth of the University* (Chapel Hill, N.C.: University of North Carolina Press, 1901), pp. 3–10ff.

9. Daniel W. Hollis, *University of South Carolina*, 2 vols. (Columbia, S.C.: University of South Carolina Press, 1951), pp. 214–222.

10. George W. Paschal, *History of Wake Forest College*, 2 vols. (Wake Forest, N.C.: Wake Forest College, 1935), II, pp. 2–22.

11. Daniel Read, "Historical Sketch of the University of Missouri," *Historical Sketches of the Universities and Colleges of the United States* (Washington, D.C.: United States Bureau of Education, 1883), pp. 40ff.

12. Christopher J. Lucas, *School of the Schoolmasters* (Columbia, Missouri: College of Education, University of Missouri, 1989), p. 9.

13. See John A. Garraty, *The American Nation Since 1865* (New York: Harper and Row, 1966), pp. 11–32.

14. Refer to William H. Cowley, "European Influence Upon American Higher Education," *Educational Record* 20 (April 1939): 165–190.

15. Storr, pp. 125–130.

16. As Laurence Veysey aptly remarks, discussing such aging college presidents as William A. Stearns of Amherst, Woolsey of Yale, and Mark Hopkins of Williams, "The only course of action which these men could urge was to hold on, perhaps making minor concessions, and hope that their institutions would be able to survive. These were tired men. . . ." (p. 9).

17. A cogent description of the new leadership coming to power in the early state universities is offered in Frederick Rudolph, *The American College and University: A History* (Athens, Ga.: University of Georgia Press, 1990), pp. 348–350.

18. For illustrative declarations, consult Andrew Dickson White, *Autobiography* (Englewood Cliffs, N.J.: Prentice-Hall, 1905), I, p. 291; James A. Angell, *Reminiscences* (New York: David McKay, 1912), p. 102; Solon J. Buck, ed., *William Watts Folwell, The Autobiography and Letters of a Pioneer of Culture* (Minneapolis: University of Minnesota Press, 1933), p. 88; and Nicholas Murray Butler, *Across the Busy Years* (New York: Scribner, 1935), I, p. 126.

19. Charles Kendall Adams, "The Relations of Higher Education to National Prosperity," in C. S. Northrup, et al., eds., *Representative Phi Beta Kappa Orations* (1915); cited in Veysey, p. 4.

20. T. H. Safford, "Why Does the Number of Students in American Colleges Fail to Keep Pace with the Population?" *The Academy* 3 (1888): 485.

21. Quoted in "Is the Higher Education Growing Unpopular?" *New York Teacher and American Educational Monthly* 8 (1871): 35.

22. Quoted in Samuel Eliot Morison, ed., *The Development of Harvard University Since the Inauguration of President Eliot, 1869–1929* (Cambridge, Mass.: Harvard University Press, 1930), p. lxxii.

23. John W. Burgess, *The American University: When Shall It Be? Where Shall It Be? What Shall It Be?* (1884), p. 5; quoted in Rudolph, p. 330.

24. Refer to Hugh Hawkins, "University Identity: The Teaching and Research Functions," in Alexandra Oleson and John Voss, eds., *The Organization of Knowledge in Modern America, 1860–1920* (Baltimore: Johns Hopkins University Press, 1979), pp. 285–312; and see the discussion in Rudolph, pp. 332ff.

25. Jonas Viles, et. al., *The University of Missouri: A Centennial History* (Columbia, Mo.: University of Missouri Press, 1939), p. 108.

26. The founding of Johns Hopkins University is described in John Calvin French, *A History of the University Founded by Johns Hopkins* (Baltimore: Johns Hopkins Press, 1946); and in Hugh Hawkins, *Pioneer: A History of the Johns Hopkins University, 1874–1889* (Ithaca, N.Y.: Cornell University Press, 1960).

27. Daniel C. Gilman, *The Building of the University: An Inaugural Address Delivered at Oakland, November 7th, 1872* (1872), p. 6; cited in Rudolph, p. 333.
28. The comment is referenced in M. A. DeWolfe Howe, ed., *John Jay Chapman and His Letters* (Boston: Houghton Mifflin, 1937), pp. 96–97.
29. F. H. Stoddard, "Inductive Work in College Classes," *Proceedings of the Annual Convention, College Association of the Middle States and Maryland, 1890* (1890), p. 78.
30. F. W. Kelsey, "The Study of Latin in Collegiate Education," *Education* 3 (January 1883): 270.
31. Quoted in Allan Nevins, *The State Universities and Democracy* (Urbana: University of Illinois Press, 1962), p. 35.
32. President Eliot's remarks, included in Harvard's *Annual Report* for 1898–99, were advanced in support of the campaign to create the Harvard Business School. On a related issue, see Eliot, "The New Education," *Atlantic Monthly* 23 (February–March 1869): 202–220, 365–366. Note also Hugh Hawkins, "Charles W. Eliot, University Reform, and Religious Faith in America, 1869–1909," *Journal of American History* 51 (September 1964): 191–213. A more complete exposition and interpretation of Eliot's views are given in Hawkins, *Between Harvard and America: The Educational Leadership of Charles W. Eliot* (New York: Oxford University Press, 1972). Likewise noteworthy is Edward Cotton, *Life of Charles W. Eliot* (Boston: Small, Maynard, 1926).
33. Rogers, pp. 47ff. See David Starr Jordan, *The Days of a Man*, 2 vols. (Yonkers, N.Y.: World Book, 1922), I, p. 80. White's basic views remained substantially unchanged in the years following his inauguration. See Andrew D. White, *Autobiography of Andrew Dickson White*, 2 vols. (Englewood Cliffs, N.J.: Prentice-Hall, 1905).
34. The point is well illustrated in Veysey, pp. 63–66.
35. See E. E. Brown, "The University in Its Relation to the People," *National Education Association, Proceedings, 1892* 31 (1892), pp. 398–399, 402–405.
36. Refer to John S. Brubacher and Willis Rudy, *Higher Education in Transition,* 3rd. ed. rev. (New York: Harper and Row, 1976), pp. 116ff.
37. An authoritative source for curricular reform is Rudolph, *Curriculum: A History of the American Undergraduate Course of Study Since 1636* (San Francisco: Jossey-Bass, 1977). See especially chapters 4 and 5. Consult also Douglas Sloan, "Harmony, Chaos, and Consensus: The American College Curriculum," *Teachers College Record* 73 (December 1971): 221–251; and Edward D. Eddy, *Colleges for Our Land and Time: The Land-Grant Idea in American Education* (New York: Harper, 1957), pp. 54, 88.
38. Quoted in Rogers, p. 108.
39. See Eddy, passim; and Earle D. Ross, *Democracy's College: The Land-Grant Movement in the Formative Stage* (Ames, Iowa: Iowa State College Press, 1942); Ross, "Contributions of Land-Grant Colleges and Universities to Higher Education," in William W. Brickman and Stanley Lehrer, eds., *A Century of Higher Education: Classical Citadel to Collegiate Colossus* (New York: Society for the Advancement of Education, 1962), pp. 94–109; and James L. Morrill, *The Ongoing State University* (Minneapolis: University of Minnesota Press, 1960).
40. Historical background is given in Frederick B. Mumford, *The Land Grant College Movement* (Columbia, Mo.: University of Missouri Press, 1940); and in Richard A. Hatch, *An Early View of the Land Grant Colleges* (Urbana, Ill.: University of Illinois Press, 1967). The account following benefits from Eldon L. Johnson, "Misconceptions About the Early Land-Grant Colleges," *Journal of Higher Education* 52 (July/August 1981); reprinted in Lester F. Goodchild and Harold S. Wechsler, eds., *ASHE Reader on the History of Higher Education* (Needham Heights, Mass.: Ginn Press, 1989), pp. 211–225; and George N. Rainsford, *Congress and Higher Education in the Nineteenth Century* (Knoxville, Tenn.: University of Tennessee Press, 1972), pp. 3–98.
41. See George W. Knight, *History of Land Grants for Education in the Northwest Territory* (New York: G. P. Putnam, 1885); and Knight, "Higher Education in the Northwest Territory," *Annual Report of the U.S. Commissioner of Education for 1888* (Washington, D.C.: United States Bureau of Education, 1889), pp. 1039–1047.
42. David S. Hill, *Control of Tax-Supported Higher Education* (New York: Carnegie Foundation, 1934), pp. 29–30.
43. An interesting case study is offered by Daniel W. Lang, "The People's College, the Mechanics Mutual Protection and the Agricultural College Act," *History of Education Quarterly* 18 (Fall 1978): 295–321.
44. Such refrains were to be echoed almost unchanged in the next century as state colleges across the country sought to transform themselves into regional state universities.

45. General background references for land-grant legislation include: Elizabeth A. Osborne, ed., *From the Office-Files of S. W. Johnson* (New Haven, Conn.: Yale University Press, 1913); Alfred C. True, *A History of Agricultural Education in the United States 1785–1925* (Washington, D.C.: United States Department of Agriculture, Miscellaneous Publication No. 36, 1929); and True, *History of Agricultural Experimentation and Research* (Washington, D.C.: United States Department of Agriculture, Miscellaneous Publication No. 251, 1937). Refer also to S. Willis Rudy, "The `Revolution' in American Higher Education, 1865–1900," *Harvard Educational Review* 21 (Summer 1951): 155–173; Earle D. Ross, "The `Father' of the Land-Grant College," *Agricultural History* 12 (April 1938): 151–186; and Ross, "The Manual Labor Experiment in the Land-Grant College," *Mississippi Valley Historical Review* 21 (March 1935): 513–528.

46. Eddy, p. 27; Ross, *Democracy's College,* p. 47. Morrill's biography, showcasing his commitment to agricultural and industrial education, is given by William B. Parker, *The Life and Public Service of Justin Smith Morrill* (Boston: Houghton Mifflin, 1924).

47. The prominent role of Evan Pugh of Pennsylvania and Jonathan B. Turner of Illinois in fending off critics and garnering support is recounted, respectively, in Margaret T. Riley, "Evan Pugh of Pennsylvania State University," *Pennsylvania History* (October 1960): 340–359; and Mary T. Carriel, *Jonathan Baldwin Turner* (Urbana, Illinois: University of Illinois Press, 1961).

48. Quoted in Eddy, pp. 31–32.

49. A major portion of the legislative text is reproduced in Richard Hofstadter and Wilson Smith, eds., *American Higher Education, A Documentary History,* 2 vols. (Chicago: University of Chicago Press, 1961), II, pp. 568–569.

50. See Rudolph, *American College and University,* pp. 253ff.; and Arthur J. Klein, ed., *Survey of Land Grant Colleges* (Washington, D.C.: United States Government Printing Office, 1930), I, pp. 19–22. Developing institutional patterns subsequent to the enactment of the first Morrill Act are treated in Ross, *Democracy's College;* and in Richard G. Axt, *The Federal Government and the Financing of Higher Education* (New York: Columbia University Press, 1952), pp. 59–60.

51. Examples are cited in Johnson; in Nevins, pp. 36–137; and in Ross, "Manual Labor Experiment," pp. 513–552. See also W. O. Thompson, "Spirit of the Land-Grant Institutions, " *Proceedings of the Association of Land Grant Colleges* 45 (February 1931), pp. 106ff.

52. Nevins, pp. 40–47.

53. Illustrations are cited in Philip M. Marston, ed., *History of the University of New Hampshire, 1866–1941* (Durham, N.H.: Record, 1941), p. 58; Daniel Read, "Historical Sketches of the Universities and Colleges in the United States," in F. B. Hough, ed., *Contributions to the History of Education* (Washington, D.C.: United States Bureau of Education, 1883), p. 25; Wayland F. Dunaway, *History of the Pennsylvania State College* (Lancaster, Penn.: Lancaster Press, 1946), p. 25; Walter Stemmons, *Connecticut Agricultural College: A History* (Storrs, Conn.: Conecticut Agricultural College, 1931), p. 144; Samuel Proctor, *The University of Florida: Its Early Years, 1853–1906* (Gainesville: University of Florida, 1958), p. 278; Madison Kuhn, *Michigan State: The First Hundred Years, 1855–1955* (East Lansing: Michigan State University Press, 1955), p. 23; J. D. Walters, *History of the Kansas State Agricultural College* (Manhattan, Kans.: Kansas State Agricultural College, 1909), p. 22; and John H. Reynolds and David Y. Thomas, *History of the University of Arkansas* (Fayetteville: University of Arkansas, 1910), pp. 74, 137.

54. Quoted in Norman Foerster, *The American State University* (Chapel Hill, N.C.: University of North Carolina Press, 1937), pp. 24–25.

55. Cited in Daniel W. Hollis, *University of South Carolina,* 2 vols. (Columbia, S.C.: University of South Carolina Press, 1951), II, p. 91.

56. Viles, pp. 159–160.

57. Refer to Johnson, passim; and consult H. J. Carman and R. G. Tugwell, "The Significance of American Agricultural History," *Agricultural History* 12 (April 1938): 101; and to P. W. Bidwell and J. I. Falconer, *History of Agriculture in the Northern United States, 1620–1860* (Washington, D.C.: Carnegie Institution, 1925), p. 452.

58. Nevins, pp. 88–90.

59. Note the discussions in Wellford Addis, "Technological Instruction in the Land Grant Colleges," *Annual Report of the U. S. Commissioner of Education for 1895* (Washington, D.C.: United States Bureau of Education, 1896), pp. 1189–1210; and Addis, "Agriculture and Mechanical Colleges," *Annual Report of the U.S. Commissioner of Education for 1898* (Washington, D.C.: United States Bureau of Education, 1899), pp 1969–1990. Consult also: George S. Emmerson, *Engineering Education: A Social History* (New York: Crane, Russak, 1973); Monte A.

Calvert, *The Mechanical Engineer in America, 1830–1910: Professional Cultures in Conflict* (Baltimore: Johns Hopkins University Press, 1967); Daniel Calhoun, *The American Civil Engineer* (Cambridge, Mass.: Massachusetts Institute of Technology Press, 1960); H. G. Good, "New Data on Early Engineering Education," *Journal of Educational Research* 29 (September 1935): 37–46; and Earle D. Ross, "Letters of an Engineering Student in the 1880s," *Annals of Iowa* 35 (Fall 1960): 434–453.

60. Refer to the account given in Michael Bezilla, *Engineering at Penn State: A Century of the Land-Grant Tradition* (University Park, Penn.: Pennsylvania State University Press, 1981); and the relevant examples cited passim in Emmerson and Calvert. How technical education developed an internal dynamic and autonomy all its own in the nineteenth century is well illustrated in James K. Finch, *Trends in Engineering Education: The Columbia Experience* (New York: Columbia University Press, 1948).

61. Nineteenth-century tensions between proponents of liberal education and supporters of technical training is treated in Earle D. Ross, *A History of Iowa State College of Agriculture and Mechanic Arts* (Ames: Iowa State College Press, 1942), pp. 382–402.

62. Quoted in William W. Ferrier, *Origin and Development of the University of California* (Berkeley: Sather Gate, 1930), pp. 62–63.

63. Viles, p. 100.

64. James E. Pollard, *History of the Ohio State University, The Story of Its First Seventy-five Years, 1873–1948* (Columbus: Ohio State University Press, 1954), pp. 16–35.

65. Ross, *Democracy's College*, pp. 90–91.

66. Stemmons, p. 48. Preceding quotations are cited in Rudolph, *American College and University*, pp. 256, 262–263.

67. See Brubacher and Rudy, pp. 241–263.

68. Ibid., pp. 156, 243, 244.

69. Refer to Claude M. Fuess, *The College Board, Its First Fifty Years* (New York: Columbia University Press, 1950), pp. 6ff. Also, refer to the treatments in Rudolph, *American College and University*, pp. 281–284.

70. Rudolph, *American College and University*, p. 264.

71. Quoted in Walters, p. 58.

72. James Bryce, *The American Commonwealth*, 2 vols. (New York: Macmillan, 1889), II, pp. 550–551; and Bryce, *University and Historical Addresses* (New York: Macmillan, 1913), pp. 160–163.

73. Helpful references on the historical origins and development of municipal colleges and universities include: Maurice Berube, *The Urban University in America* (Westport, Conn.: Greenwood Press, 1978); Roscoe H. Eckelberry, *The History of the Municipal University in the United States* (Washington, D.C.: United States Bureau of Education Bulletin No. 2, 1932); and National Association of Municipal Universities, *The University and the Municipality* (Washington, D.C.: United States Bureau of Education Publication No. 38, 1915).

74. See Parke R. Kolbe, *Urban Influences on Higher Education in England and the United States* (New York: Macmillan, 1928).

75. Consult Charles E. Bevry, *Responsiveness: The Place of the Urban University* (Philadelphia: Temple University, 1936).

76. The account following borrows from Patricia A. Palmieri, "From Republican Motherhood to Race Suicide: Arguments on the Higher Education of Women in the United States, 1820–1920," in Carol Lasser, ed., *Coeducation in a Changing World* (Urbana: University of Illinois Press, 1987), pp. 49–64.

77. Thus, some nineteenth-century proponents of expanded educational opportunities for women urged coeducation; others argued vigorously for separate women's colleges. See Lynn White, Jr., *Educating Our Daughters* (New York: Harper and Row, 1950), p. 50.

78. Note the interpretation advanced in Linda Kerber, *Women of the Republic: Intellect and Ideology in Revolutionary America* (Chapel Hill, N.C.: University of North Carolina Press, 1980). The founding of Mt. Holyoke is recounted in Arthur C. Cole, *A Hundred Years of Mount Holyoke College: The Evolution of an Educational Ideal* (New Haven, Conn.: Yale University Press, 1940). See Sarah D. Stow, *History of Mount Holyoke Seminary, South Hadley, Massachusetts, During Its First Half Century, 1837–1887* (Springfield, Mass.: Springfield Printing, 1887); Anne Scott, "The Diffusion of Feminist Values from Troy Female Seminary, 1822–1872," *History of Education Quarterly* 19 (Spring 1979): 3–26; and Thomas Woody, *History of Women's Education in the United States*, 2 vols. (Lancaster, Penn.: Science Press, 1929), II, pp. 137–142.

79. But see Scott; and compare with Oliver C. Carmichael, "Change in Higher Education," *Bulletin of the Association of American Colleges* 32 (October 1946): 355–356; and Roberta Wein, "Women's Colleges and Domesticity, 1875–1918," *History of Education Quarterly* 14 (Spring 1974): 31–47.

80. A popular belief that too much learning posed a threat to virtuous womanhood is discussed in Barbara Welter, "The Cult of True Womanhood," in *Dimity Convictions: The American Woman in the Nineteenth Century* (Athens, Ohio: Ohio University Press, 1976), pp. 21–41. A quintessential expression of opposition to women's higher learning was supplied by Edward Clarke, *Sex in Education, or A Fair Chance for the Girls* (Boston: J. R. Osgood, 1874), passim.

81. Quoted in Woody, II, pp. 144–148.

82. See Charles W. Barber, *Elmira College: The First Hundred Years* (New York: McGraw-Hill, 1955); and Gilbert Meltser, *The Beginnings of Elmira College, 1851–1862* (Elmira, N.Y.: Commercial Press, 1941); and Ann Miller, *Women of Bryn Mawr, 1876–1975* (Boulder: Westview, 1976).

83. See Woody, II, pp. 140–150; and also Louise S. Boas, *Women's Education Begins: The Rise of Women's Colleges* (Norton: Wheaton College, 1935). Institutional histories of some of the more prominent early women's colleges include: Elizabeth D. Henscom and Helen F. Greene, *Sophie Smith and the Beginnings of Smith College* (Northampton, Mass.: Smith College, 1925); Laurenus C. Seelye, *The Early History of Smith College, 1871–1910* (Boston: Houghton Mifflin, 1923); Dorothy A. Plum and George B. Dowell, *The Great Experiment: A Chronicle of Vassar* (Poughkeepsie, N.Y.: n.p., 1961); and Plum and Dowell, *The Magnificent Enterprise: A Chronicle of Vassar College* (Poughkeepsie, N.Y.: n.p., 1961); James M. Taylor and Elizabeth H. Haight, *Vassar* (New York: Oxford University Press, 1915); Florence Converse, *The Story of Wellesley* (Boston: Little, Brown, 1915); Converse, *Wellesley College: A Chronicle of the Years 1875–1939* (Wellesley, Mass.: Hathaway House, 1939); Alice Payne Heckett, *Wellesley, Part of the American Story* (New York: E. P. Dutton, 1949).

84. Although the precise circumstances differed from school to school, coordinate colleges shared a common commitment to higher education for women. In the views of some, a "separatist" approach was desirable; for others, the idea of a coordinate college was—in varying degrees— an artifact of male exclusion. See the accounts in Adelaide H. Thierry, *When Radcliffe Was Teenage* (Boston: Bruce Humphries, 1959); Annie N. Mayer, *Barnard Beginnings* (Boston: Houghton Mifflin, 1935); Alice D. Miller and Susan Myers, *Barnard College, The First Fifty Years* (New York: Columbia University, 1939); Helen H. Kitzmiller, *One Hundred Years of Western Reserve* (Hudson, Ohio: Jane W. Ellsworth Foundation, 1926). Note the discussion in Newcomer, *A Century of Higher Education for American Women* (New York: Harper and Row, 1959), pp. 40–50.

85. The pioneering role of Oberlin in coeducation is retold in Robert S. Fletcher, *History of Oberlin College from Its Foundation Through the Civil War*, 2 vols. (Oberlin, Ohio: Oberlin College, 1943), I, chapters 16, 24; II, p. 718. See as well Fletcher, "The First Coeds," *American Scholar* 7 (Winter 1938): 76–86.

86. See Newcomer, pp. 21–32; Woody, II, pp. 52, 151–157ff., 203, 210; Anna Brackett, ed., *Education of American Girls* (New York: Putnam, 1874), pp. 202–209, 315–317; and John Raymond, "The Demand of the Age for the Liberal Education of Women and How It Should Be Met," in James Orton, ed., *The Liberal Education of Women* (New York: A. S. Barnes, 1873), pp. 27–58.

87. Sources include Reginald Snell, *Co-education in its Historical and Theoretical Setting* (London: Hogarth, 1938); Anna T. Smith, "Co-education in the Schools and Colleges of the United States," in *U. S. Commissioner of Education Annual Report for 1903* (Washington, D.C.: United States Bureau of Education, 1905), pp. 1047–1078; and Marion Talbot, *More than Lore* (Chicago: University of Chicago Press, 1936).

88. Cited in Rudolph, *American College and University*, p. 326.

89. Woody, II, p. 242.

90. Specific case studies include Helen M. Olin, *The Women of a State University* (New York: Putnam's, 1909); and Dorothy McGuigan, *A Dangerous Experiment: 100 Years of Women at the University of Michigan* (Ann Arbor: University of Michigan Press, 1970).

91. Newcomer, p. 46–49ff.

92. For example, see ibid., pp. 13–14.

93. Read, "Historical Sketch," pp. 40ff.

94. Rogers, p. 228; cited in Rudolph, *American College and University*, p. 328.

95. Pollard, p. 149.

96. Lynn D. Gordon, "Co-Education on Two Campuses: Berkeley and Chicago, 1890–1912," in Mary Kelly, ed., *Woman's Being, Woman's Place: Female Identity and Vocation in American History* (Boston: G. K. Hall, 1979), reproduced in Goodchild and Wechsler, p. 354. The presumption typified in the *Blue and Gold* yearbook that female college students were destined for domesticity or teaching careers is effectively explored in Nancy Hoffman, *Women's True Profession* (New York: Feminist Press, 1981).

97. Gordon, in Goodchild and Wechsler, p. 354.

98. Ibid., p. 355, from "B. I. Wheeler's 'Opening Address, August 22, 1904,' " *Benjamin Ide Wheeler Writings and Papers* (Berkeley: University of California Archives).

99. Gordon, in Goodchild and Wechsler, p. 356; quoted from Talbot, *The Education of Women* (Chicago: University of Chicago Press, 1910), p. 22.

100. John Hope Franklin, *From Slavery to Freedom* (New York: Knopf, 1947), p. 228. See C. G. Woodson, *The Education of the Negro Prior to 1861* (New York: Arno Press, 1968).

101. Charles S. Johnson, *The Negro College Graduate* (Chapel Hill, N.C.: University of North Carolina, 1938), p. 7.

102. Ruth O. Wilson, "Negro Colleges of Liberal Arts, 1866–1950," *American Scholar* 19 (Autumn 1950); 462–463; and James D. Anderson, *The Education of Blacks in the South, 1860–1935* (Chapel Hill, N.C.: University of North Carolina Press, 1988), pp. 238–278. Refer as well to Frederick A. McGinnis, *A History and an Interpretation of Wilberforce University* (Wilberforce, Ohio: Brown, 1941); and Edward Webb, *Lincoln University, Pennsylvania: Its History and Work* (Philadelphia: Allen, Lane and Scott, 1890).

103. Quoted in Earle H. West, *The Black American and Education* (Columbus, Ohio: Charles E. Merrill, 1972), pp. 92–93. See also C. Van Woodward, *The Strange Career of Jim Crow*, rev. ed. (New York: Oxford University Press, 1966); and Woodward, *Origins of the New South, 1877–1913* (Baton Rouge, La.: Louisiana State University Press, 1951).

104. Wilson, pp. 462–464.

105. A relevant discussion appears in Donald Spivey, *Schooling for the New Slavery: Black Industrial Education, 1868–1915* (Westport, Conn.: Greenwood Press, 1978). See Jennings L. Wagoner, Jr., "The American Compromise: Charles W. Eliot, Black Education, and the New South," in Ronald K. Goodenow and Arthur O. White, eds., *Education and the Rise of the New South* (Boston: G. K. Hall, 1981), pp. 26–46; Paul M. Gaston, *The New South Creed: A Study in Southern Mythmaking* (New York: Alfred A. Knopf, 1970); and Paul H. Buck, *The Road to Reunion, 1865–1900* (New York: Vintage, 1959).

106. Dwight O. W. Holmes, *Evolution of the Negro College* (New York: Teachers College, Columbia University, 1934); and Holmes, "Seventy Years of the Negro College," *Phylon* 10 (Fourth Quarter, 1949): 307–313; Stephen J. Peeps, "Northern Philanthropy and the Emergence of Black Higher Education," *Journal of Negro Education* 50 (Summer 1981): 251–269.

107. John Sekora, "The Emergence of Negro Higher Education in America, A Review," *Race* 10 (July 1968): 79–87.

108. General background materials are supplied in Thomas Jesse Jones, ed., *Negro Education: A Study of the Private and Higher Schools for Colored People in the United States,* 2 vols. (New York: Arno Press, 1969).

109. Holmes, pp. 49–54; Wilson, p. 466.

110. James McPherson, "White Liberals and Black Power in Negro Education, 1865–1915," *American Historical Review* 75 (June 1970): 1357–1386. Consult Alan Pifer, *The Higher Education of Blacks in the United States* (New York: Carnegie Corporation of New York, 1973), pp. 11–12; and Frank Bowles and Frank A. DeCosta, *Between Two Worlds: A Profile of Negro Higher Education* (New York: McGraw-Hill, 1971), pp. 28ff.

111. See Anderson, pp. 239–242; DeCosta, pp. 28–34; Holmes, *Negro College,* pp. 4–15.

112. See Franklin, p. 538; Wilson, pp. 465–466; Kenneth H. Ashworth, *Scholars and Statesmen* (San Francisco: Jossey-Bass, 1972), pp. 80–81; Janet Henderson and John Hart, "The Development and Spacial Patterns of Black Colleges," *Southeastern Geography* 11 (November 1971): 133–144; and Willard Range, *The Rise and Progress of Negro Colleges in Georgia, 1865–1949* (Atlanta: University of Georgia Press, 1951).

113. Some indvidual school histories include: M. Guy Dunham, *The Centennial History of Alcorn Agricultural and Mechanical College* (Hattiesburg, Miss.: University and College Press of Mississippi, 1971); Walter Dyson, *The Founding of Howard University* (Washington, D.C.: Howard University Press, 1921); Dyson, *Howard University: The Capstone of Negro Education, A*

History: 1867–1940 (Washington, D.C.: The Graduate School, Howard University, 1941); Rayford W. Logan, *Howard University: The First Hundred Years, 1867–1967* (New York: New York University Press, 1969); B. Baldwin Densby, *A Brief History of Jackson College: A Typical Story of the Survival of Education Among Negroes in the South* (Jackson, Miss.: Jackson College, 1953); Benjamin G. Brawley, *History of Morehouse College* (Atlanta: Morehouse College, 1917); Solon T. Kimball, *The Talledega Story: A Study in Community Process* (University: University of Alabama Press, 1954); Frederick Chambers, *Historical Study of Arkansas Agricultural, Mechanical, and Normal College, 1873–1943* (Muncie, Ind.: Ball State University, 1970); Cecil L. Spellman, *Rough Steps on My Stairway: The Life History of a Negro Educator* (New York: Exposition Press, 1953); Clarence A. Bacote, *The Story of Atlanta University: A Century of Service 1865–1965* (Atlanta: Atlanta University Press, 1969); E. H. Fitchett, "The Role of Claflin College in Negro Life in South Carolina," *Journal of Negro Education* 12 (Winter 1943): 42–68; Joe M. Richardson, "Fisk University, the First Critical Years," *Tennessee Historical Quarterly* 29 (Spring 1970): 24–41; John J. Mullowney, *America Gives a Chance* (Tampa, Fla.: Tribune Press, 1940); L. P. Jackson, "The Origin of Hampton Institute," *Journal of Negro History* 10 (April 1925): 131–149; Wilmoth A. Carter, *Shaw's Universe* (Washington, D.C.: National Publishing, 1973).

114. Anderson, pp. 240–241.

115. Ibid., p. 244.

116. Ibid., pp. 247–248. "Except in the rarest of instances," Baldwin declared, "I am bitterly opposed to the so-called higher education of Negroes."

117. West, pp. 113ff.

118. See August Meier, *Negro Thought in America, 1880–1915: Racial Ideologies in the Age of Booker T. Washington* (Ann Arbor: University of Michigan Press, 1963), pp. 85–118. Relevant reading includes Washington's *Up from Slavery: An Autobiography* (New York: Doubelday, 1953), pp. 204ff.; and Washington, *Character Building: Being Addresses Delivered on Sunday Evenings to the Students of Tuskegee Institute* (New York: Doubleday, Page, 1902). Consult Louis R. Harlan, *Booker T. Washington: The Wizard of Tuskegee, 1901–1915* (Oxford: Oxford University Press, 1983).

119. Refer to E. Davidson Washington, ed., *Selected Speeches of Booker T. Washington* (Garden City, N.Y.: Doubleday, Doran, 1932).

120. For example, see Rena L. Vassar, ed., *Social History of American Education*, 2 vols. (Chicago: Rand McNally, 1965), II, p. 72.

121. For an assessment of the relatively low academic standards prevalent among predominantly black land-grant institutions, consult Ashworth, pp. 80ff.

122. See Samuel Shannon, "Land Grant College Legislation and Black Tennesseans: A Case Study in the Politics of Education," *History of Education Quarterly* 22 (Summer 1982): 139–158.

123. See Garraty, p. 67.

124. W. E. B. DuBois, "The Talented Tenth," from *The Negro Problem: A Series of Articles by Representative Negroes of Today* (New York: James Pott, 1903), p. 75.

125. See Rudolph, *American College and University*, pp. 290–306.

126. Eliot's remarks are included in David Andrew Weaver, ed., *Builders of American Universities: Inaugural Addresses* (Alton, Ill.: Shurtleff Press, 1950), pp. 16, 23ff.; reproduced in Charles W. Eliot, *Educational Reform* (Englewood Cliffs, N. J.: Prentice-Hall, 1898), p. 1.

127. On the changes introduced at Harvard, consult LeBaron R. Briggs, "President Eliot, as Seen by a Disciple," *Atlantic Monthly* 144 (November 1929): 597; also refer to Hugh Hawkins, "Charles W. Eliot, University Reform, and Religious Faith in America, 1869–1909," pp. 191–201.

128. Eliot, in Weaver, p. 24.

129. For examples, see R. M. Wenley, "The Classics and the Elective System," *School Review* 18 (October 1910): 518; Andrew F. West, "Must the Classics Go?" *North American Review* 138 (February 1884): 152–159; James McCosh, *New Departure in College Education* (New York: Scribner, 1885), p. 4; Noah Porter, *The American College and the American Public*, 2nd. ed. (New Haven, Conn.: C. C. Chatfield, 1870), pp. 15–16; Richard R. Bowker, "The College of Today," *Princeton Review* 13 (January 1884): 93.

130. McCosh, pp. 4, 12, 22.

131. Woody, II, p. 220.

132. Porter, p. 103.

133. West, *A Review of President Eliot's Report on Elective Studies* (New York: J. K. Lees, 1886), p. 14.

134. See Hazen C. Carpenter, "Emerson, Eliot, and the Elective System," *New England Quarterly* 24 (March 1951): 13–34; D. E. Phillips, "The Elective System in American Education," *Pedagogical*

Seminary 8 (June 1901): 210–212; Charles F. Adams, Jr., *A College Fetish* (Boston: Lee and Shepard, 1883), pp. 18ff.; William S. Gray, *Provision for the Individual in College Education* (Chicago: University of Chicago Press, 1932), pp. 14ff.; and George W. Pierson, "The Elective System and the Difficulties of College Planning, 1870–1940," *Journal of General Education* 4 (April 1950): 165. Discussions and notes are supplied in Brubacher and Rudy, pp. 111–116; and in Veysey, p. 119.

135. Porter, pp. 35–36.

136. W. B. Kolesnik, *Mental Discipline in Modern Education* (Madison, Wisc.: University of Wisconsin Press, 1958), pp. 10–30, 90–110ff.

137. C. B. Hulbert, *The Distinctive Idea in Education* (New York: J. B. Alden, 1890), p. 11.

138. See Porter, pp. 103–105; Hulbert, p. 34. Source materials on the controversy surrounding the elective system at Harvard are included in Hofstadter and Smith, II, Part 8, pp. 697–747.

139. George F. Magoun, "The Making of a Christian College," *Education* 11 (February 1891): 335–336.

140. J. W. Strong, "The Relation of the Christian College," *National Education Association Proceedings* (1887), p. 153.

141. Quoted in Veysey, p. 34.

142. Charles W. Dabney, *The Old College and the New* (n.p., 1896), p. 9.

143. Arthur J. Hope, *Notre Dame: One Hundred Years* (Notre Dame, Ind.: [Notre Dame] University Press, 1943), p. 198.

144. Charles H. Rammelkamp, *Illinois College: A Centennial History 1829–1929* (New Haven, Conn.: Yale University Press, 1928), pp. 383–384.

145. William Warren Sweet, *Indiana Asbury-DePauw University, 1837–1937: A Hundred Years of Higher Education in the Middle West* (New York: Abingdon Press, 1937), pp. 153–154. See Rudolph, *American College and University*, pp. 297–302.

146. Consult A. P. Brigham, "Present Status of the Elective System in American Colleges," *Educational Review* 14 (November 1897): 360–369; and F. W. Clarke, "The Evolution of the American University," *Forum* 32 (September 1901): 94–104; H. C. Goddard, et al., "The American College Course," *Educational Review* 26 (September 1903): 169–170. See especially Rudolph, *American College and University*, chapter 14, pp. 287–306.

147. David Star Jordan, *The Voice of the Scholar* (San Francisco: Paul Elder, 1903), p. 58.

148. A helpful discussion of academic nomenclature and institutional types is given in John R. Thelin, *Higher Education and Its Useful Past* (Cambridge, Mass.: Schenckman, 1982), pp. 83–105. See also Everett Walters, "Graduate Education, 1862–1962," in Brickman and Lehrer, pp. 124–137.

149. Refer to Richard Hofstadter and C. DeWitt Hardy, *Development and Scope of Higher Education in the United States* (New York: Columbia University Press, 1952); Margaret Clapp, ed., *The Modern University* (Ithaca, N.Y.: Cornell University Press, 1950); Foerster; and Storr, passim.

150. Thelin, pp. 83–103; Walter C. Eells, "Earned Doctorates in American Institutions of Higher Education, 1861–1955," *Higher Education* 12 (March 1956): 109–114; Eells and Harold Haswell, *Academic Degrees* (Washington, D.C.: United States Printing Office, 1961); Adolph E. Meyer, "The Farce of Honorary Degrees, 1650–1949," *American Mercury* 67 (July 1948): 104–110; Francesco Cordasco, *Daniel Coit Gilman and the Protean Ph.D.: The Shaping of American Graduate Education* (Leiden, Netherlands: Brill, 1960); Bernard Berelson, *Graduate Education in the United States* (New York: McGraw-Hill, 1960).

151. See Cowley, 165–190; Charles F. Thwing, *The American and the German University: 100 Years of History* (New York: Macmillan, 1928); Friedrich Paulsen, *German Education, Past and Present*, E. D. Perry, trans. (London: T. Fisher Unwin, 1908), pp. 182ff.; M. M. Curtis, "The Present Condition of German Universities," *Educational Review* 2 (June 1891): 28–37ff.

152. G. Stanley Hall, "Philosophy in the United States," *Popular Science Monthly* 1 (1879), Supplement, p. 67.

153. On academic freedom issues, consult Richard Hofstadter and Walter P. Metzger, *Development of Academic Freedom in the United States* (New York: Columbia University Press, 1955), pp. 386ff. On American interest in Germanic academic norms and values in the 1880s, note H. M. Kennedy, "Studying in Germany," *Popular Science Monthly* 26 (April 1889): 347–352. See especially, Samuel Sheldon, "Why Our Science Students Go to Germany," *Atlantic Monthly* 63 (April 1889): 463–466; and A. C. Armstrong, Jr., "German Culture and the Universities: A Retrospect," *Educational Review* 45 (April 1913): 325–328.

154. Quoted in William F. Russell, ed., *Rise of a University: The Later Days of Old Columbia College,* 2 vols. (New York: Columbia University Press, 1937), I, p. 379.

155. The text of Gilman's address appears in Weaver, pp. 295–326. See also, ibid., pp. 327–331.

156. Gilman, *The Benefits Which Society Derives from Universities* (Baltimore: Johns Hopkins University, 1885), pp. 15–19, 31–33. For Gilman's view on intellectual freedom, refer to Hawkins, *Pioneer,* pp. 22–23.

157. See Abraham Flexner, *Daniel Coit Gilman: Creator of the American Type University* (New York: Harcourt Brace Jovanovich, 1946); and Fabian Franklin, *The Life of Daniel Coit Gilman* (New York: Dodd, Mead, 1910).

158. Brubacher and Rudy, p. 179.

159. Johns Hopkins University, *Celebration of the Twenty-Fifth Anniversary of the Founding of the University, and Inauguration of Ira Remsen as President* (Baltimore: Johns Hopkins University Press, 1902), p. 105.

160. W. Carson Ryan, *Studies in Early Graduate Education* (New York: Carnegie Foundation for the Advancement of Teaching, 1939), p. 126.

161. See G. Stanley Hall, "Inaugural Address," in Weaver, p. 370.

162. Patrick H. Ahern, *The Catholic University of America, 1837–1896: The Rectorship of John J. Keane* (Washington, D.C.: Catholic University of America Press, 1948).

163. Edwin Mims, *History of Vanderbilt University* (Nashville, Tenn.: Vanderbilt University Press, 1946), pp. 63–64.

164. Israel C. Russell, "Research in State Universities," *Science* 19 (June 1904): 853.

165. Thomas J. Wertenbaker, *Princeton, 1746–1896* (Princeton, N.J.: Princeton University Press, 1946), pp. 302–303, 339–340.

166. The incident is recounted in John Hugh Reynolds and David Y. Thomas, *History of the University of Arkansas* (Fayetteville: University of Arkansas Press, 1910), p. 125.

167. See William H. Glasson, "The College Professor in Public Service," *South Atlantic Quarterly* I (July 1902): 247–255; and Storr, "The Public Conscience of the University, 1775–1956," *Harvard Educational Review* 26 (Winter 1956): 71–84.

168. Vernon Cartensen, "The Origin and Early Development of the Wisconsin Idea," *Wisconsin Magazine of History* 39 (Spring 1956): 181–187; Charles McCarthy, *The Wisconsin Idea* (New York: Macmillan, 1912); and J. David Hoeveler, Jr., "The University and the Social Gospel: The Intellectual Origins of the 'Wisconsin Idea,'" *Wisconsin Magazine of History* 59 (Summer 1976): 282–298.

169. See Frederic C. Howe, *Wisconsin: An Experiment in Democracy* (New York: Scribner, 1912); Maurice M. Vance, *Charles Richard Van Hise: Scientist Progressive* (Madison: State Historical Society of Wisconsin, 1960); A. Stephen Stephan, "University Extension in America," *Harvard Educational Review* 18 (Spring 1948): 100ff.

170. Edmund J. James, "Function of the State University," *Science* 22 (November 17, 1905): 625–628; Lotus D. Coffman, *The State University: Its Work and Problems* (Minneapolis: University of Minnesota Press, 1934).

171. Angell, "The Old College and the New University," in *Selected Addresses* (New York: David McKay, 1912), p. 150.

172. James, p. 625.

173. Excellent treatments of the topic are given in Chapter 18, "The Rise of Football," in Rudolph, *American College and University,* pp. 373–393; and in Brubacher and Rudy, pp. 131–136. The following summary account draws upon some of the same source materials.

174. Informative references on the history of collegiate athletics include W. Carson Ryan, Jr., *The Literature of American School and College Athletics* (New York: Carnegie Foundation for the Advancement of Teaching, 1929); Howard J. Savage, *American College Athletics* (New York: Carnegie Foundation for the Advancement of Teaching, 1929); William J. Peterson, "University Football Through the Years," *Palimpsest* 38 (October 1957): 389–446; and Allison Danzig, *The History of American Football* (Englewood Cliffs, N.J.: Prentice-Hall, 1956).

175. For an interesting example, see Benjamin Moran, "The Harvard-Oxford Boat Race of 1869," *Massachusetts History Society Proceedings* 50 (1917): 184–188.

176. Savage, pp. 13–20.

177. See David Riesman and Reuel Denney, "Football in America: A Study in Culture Diffusion," *American Quarterly* 3 (Winter 1951): 309–325.

178. Quoted in Kent Sagendorph, *Michigan: The Story of the University* (New York: E. P. Dutton, 1948), p. 150; and cited in Rudolph, *American College and University,* pp. 373–374.

179. Amos Alonzo Stagg, *Touchdown!* (New York: McKay, 1927), p. 70.
180. Ibid., pp. 150–153; Wertenbaker, p. 357; Rudolph, *American College and University*, p. 375.
181. Stagg, pp. 50–51, 71–82, 180–181; Savage, pp. 20, 22–29; Clarence Birdseye, *Individual Training in Our Colleges* (New York: Macmillan, 1907), pp. 158–164.
182. Henry D. Sheldon, *History and Pedagogy of American Student Societies* (Englewood Cliffs, N.J.: Prentice-Hall, 1907), p. 238.
183. Ryan, p. 130.
184. Note A. Lawrence Lowell, "College Rank and Distinction in Life," *Atlantic Monthly* 92 (October 1903), p. 519. See also John F. Crowell, *Personal Reflections* (Durham, N.C.: Duke University Press, 1939), pp. 45–46, 230–231; Walter Camp, *Book of College Sports* (Englewood Cliffs, N.J.: Prentice-Hall, 1910), pp. 2–8; E. Benjamin Andrews, "The General Tendencies of College Athletics," *National Education Association Proceedings* (1904), pp. 549–557; William H. P. Faunce, "Character in Athletics," *National Education Association Proceedings* (1904), pp. 558–565; and Savage, pp. 28–29.
185. Arthur Twining Hadley, "Wealth and Democracy in American Colleges," *Harper's Monthly* 113 (August 1906): 450–453.
186. See Veysey, pp. 197ff.
187. Ibid., pp. 233–235, 264–268, 317–338.
188. Andrew Fleming West, quoted in Rudolph, *American College and University*, p. 402.
189. Veysey, pp. 302–304, 319–320.
190. Ibid., p. 372. See also Thomas W. Goodspeed, *A History of the University of Chicago Founded by John D. Rockefeller: The First Quarter Century* (Chicago: University of Chicago Press, 1916), p. 138.
191. Jacob Gould Schurman, "The Reaction of Graduate Work on the Other Work of the University," *Journal of Proceedings and Addresses of the Association of American Universities* 7 (1906), p. 60. See also Hugh Hawkins, "University Identity," pp. 285–312.
192. Walter P. Metzger, "A Spectre Is Haunting American Scholars: The Spectre of 'Professionalism,'" *Educational Research* 16 (August/September 1987): 10ff.
193. Veysey, pp. 186–187; Robert MacDougall, "University Training and the Doctoral Degree," *Education* 24 (January 1904): 261–276; W. A. Merrill, "The Practical Value of a Liberal Education," *Education* 10 (March 1890): 441.
194. William DeWitt Hyde, "The Place of the College in the Social System," *School Review* 12 (1904): 796.

Chapter 6

1. Henry Seidel Canby, *Alma Mater: The Gothic Age of the American College* (New York: Farrar, Straus & Giroux, 1936), pp. 81–82.
2. To speak of an "overall climate" is something of an historiographical fiction, but the general theme is amplified to good advantage in Laurence R. Veysey, *The Emergence of the American University* (Chicago: University of Chicago Press, 1965), pp. 342ff.
3. For an illustrative retrospective view by a major participant-observer, refer to Daniel Coit Gilman, "The Launching of a University" in *Scribner's Magazine* 31 (March 1902): 327–331, later expanded into a book of the same title. Portions of the 1906 revised text appear as "Daniel Coit Gilman Reviews the Accomplishments of the University Era, 1869–1902," in Richard Hofstadter and Wilson Smith, eds., *American Higher Education, A Documentary History*, 2 vols. (Chicago: University of Chicago Press, 1961), II, pp. 595–601.
4. Quoted in Veysey, p. 344.
5. J. R. Wheeler, "The Idea of a College and of a University," *Columbia University Quarterly* 10 (December 1907): 12. This somewhat disingenuous argument, now hallowed by much reiteration, is now advanced oftentimes virtually unchanged in similar contemporary pronouncements.
6. On the contrast between the "old-time college" and the modern university, see Walter P. Metzger, *Academic Freedom in the Age of the University* (New York: Columbia University Press, 1955), pp. 4–5.
7. Relevant commentary includes Frank Thilly, "What Is a University?" *Educational Review* 22 (December 1901): 500; R. M. Wenley, "The Classics and the Elective System," *School Review* 18 (October 1910): 518; Webster Cook, "Evolution and Education," *Education* 9 (February 1889): 372; Robert MacDougall, "University Training and the Doctoral Degree," *Education* 24 (January 1904): 261–276; and A. Lawrence Lowell, *At War with Academic Traditions in America*

(Cambridge, Mass.: Harvard University Press, 1934), pp. 5–7, 40–41, 108–109, 116, 239–240. Also refer to Russell Thomas, *The Search for a Common Learning: General Education, 1800–1960* (New York: McGraw Hill, 1962), pp. 24–25, 62ff.

8. The assertion that regional schools embraced a research-dominated model may be too strong. Nevertheless, it does seem defensible to claim that, in contrast with most private liberal-arts colleges, many public-assisted regional schools in recent decades have sought to redefine themselves as multipurpose universities. Consult George P. Schmidt, "A Century of the Liberal Arts College," in William W. Brickman and Stanley Lehrer, eds., *A Century of Higher Education: Classical Citadel to Collegiate Colossus* (New York: Society for the Advancement of Education, 1962), pp. 50–66. See also Archie M. Palmer, ed., *The Liberal Arts College Movement* (New York: Little and Ives, 1930); and Schmidt, *The Liberal Arts College: A Chapter in American Cultural History* (New Brunswick, N.J.: Rutgers University Press, 1957). Note as well the trenchant analysis in James Axtell, "The Death of the Liberal Arts College," *History of Education Quarterly* 11 (Winter 1971): 339–352.

9. J. P. Gordy, *The Rise of the Normal-School Idea in the United States* (Washington, D.C.: United States Bureau of Education, 1891); Wesley E. Armstrong, "Teacher Education, 1839–1953," *Higher Education* 10 (April 1954): 123–131; William F. Russell, "A Century of Teacher Education," *Teachers College Record* 4 (March 1940): 481–492; and Paul Woodring, "A Century of Teacher Education," in Brickman and Lehrer, pp. 154–165.

10. Two somewhat different perspectives are offered, respectively, in Charles A. Harper, *A Century of Public Teacher Education: State Teachers Colleges as They Evolved from Normal Schools* (Washington, D.C.: American Association of Teachers Colleges, 1939); and Paul Mattingley, *The Classless Profession: American Schoolmen in the 19th Century* (New York: New York University Press, 1975).

11. Karl W. Bigelow, "The Passing of the Teachers College, 1938–1956," *Teachers College Record* 58 (May 1957): 409–417; and see Merle L. Borrowman, *The Liberal and Technical in Teacher Education* (New York: Teachers College, Columbia University, 1956).

12. Consult Lawrence A. Cremin, "The Education of the Educating Profession," *Research Bulletin: Horace Mann Institute* 18 (March 1978): 1–8; and John S. Brubacher and Willis Rudy, *Higher Education in Transition: A History of American Colleges and Universities*, 3rd. ed. rev. (New York: Harper and Row, 1976), pp. 198–210.

13. An encapsulated summary is given in Frederick Rudolph, *The American College and University: A History* (Athens, Ga.: University of Georgia Press, 1990), chapter 20, pp. 417–439. Besides Rudolph's excellent discussion, see Herman Donovan, "Changing Conceptions of the College Presidency, 1795–1957," *Association of American Colleges Bulletin* 43 (March 1957): 40–52; Walter C. Eells and Earnest V. Hollis, *The College Presidency, 1900–1960* (Washington, D.C.: United States Office of Education, 1961); and George Schmidt, *The Old Time College President* (New York: Columbia University Press, 1930).

14. Cited in James E. Pollard, *History of the Ohio State University: The Story of Its First Seventy-Five Years, 1873–1948* (Columbus, Ohio: Ohio State University Press, 1952), p. 136.

15. Thorstein Veblen, *The Higher Learning in America* (New York: B. W. Huebsch, 1918), cited by Rudolph, pp. 418–419.

16. Note the characterizations drawn by Schmidt in *The Old-Time College President*, passim.

17. Veysey, pp. 305–312ff. See also Frank P. Graves, "The Need of Training for the College Presidency," *Forum* 32 (February 1902): 680–685.

18. Schmidt, pp. 184–187.

19. Rudolph, p. 419.

20. Ibid., p. 420. The same pattern is attested to in Ross's *Democracy's College* (Ames, Iowa: Iowa State College Press, 1942), pp. 104ff.; Homer P. Rainey, "Some Facts About College Presidents," *School and Society* 30 (October 1929): 581–582; John A. Perkins and Margaret H. Perkins, "From These Leadership Must Come," *School and Society* 70 (September 1949): 162–164; and Brubacher and Rudy, pp. 365–376.

21. Brubacher and Rudy, p. 366.

22. G. M. Stratton, "Externalism in American Universities," *Atlantic Monthly* 100 (October 1907): 518.

23. Quoted in Rudolph, p. 421.

24. The potential implications are discussed in Richard Hofstadter and Walter P. Metzger, *The Development of Academic Freedom in the United States* (New York: Columbia University Press, 1955), pp. 453–454.

25. The theme is developed at some length in Merle Curti, *Philanthropy in the Shaping of American Higher Education* (New Brunswick, N.J.: Rutgers University Press, 1965). Note as well the treatments in William T. Laprade, "Funds and Foundations: A Neglected Phase of Higher Education, 1867–1952," *American Association of University Professors Bulletin* 38 (Winter 1952): 559–576; Jesse B. Sears, *Philanthropy in the History of American Higher Education* (Washington, D.C.: United States Bureau of Education No. 26); and in Warren Weaver, *United States Philanthropic Foundations: Their History, Structure, Management, and Record* (New York: Harper and Row, 1967).

26. Cited in Rudolph, p. 433.

27. Ibid., p. 433.

28. National Education Association, National Council of Education, *Report of the Committee of Ten on Secondary School Studies* (1893); National Education Association, *Report of the Committee on College Education Requirements* (1899); and National Education Association, *Report of the Committee of Nine on the Articulation of High School and College* (1911). For discussion, particularly on the effort to standardize collegiate admission prerequisites, see Lawrence A. Cremin, "The Revolution in American Secondary Education, 1893–1918," *Teachers College Record* 56 (March 1955): 296ff. See also Charles W. Eliot, "The Fundamental Assumptions in the Report of the Committee of Ten," *Educational Review* 30 (November 1905): 333–335.

29. Claude M. Fuess, *The College Board: Its First Fifty Years* (New York: College Entrance Examination Board, 1950), pp. 9–25.

30. Ibid., pp. 23–25; and refer to the account in Rudolph, pp. 437–438.

31. Brubacher and Rudy, pp. 364–365. For further background, consult Webster S. Stover, Alumni Stimulation (New York: Teachers College, Columbia University, 1930); and Percy Marks, "The Pestiferous Alumni," *Harper's Magazine* 153 (July 1926): 144–149; and Henry S. Pritchett, "The Influence of Alumni on Their Colleges," in *Annual Report* (1923), Carnegie Foundation for the Advancement of Teaching, pp. 38ff.

32. Brubacher and Rudy, p. 363.

33. Ibid., pp. 367–371; and Veysey, pp. 387–388.

34. Refer to Earl J. McGrath, "The Control of Higher Education, 1860-1930," *Educational Record* 17 (April 1936): 259–272; Samuel K. Wilson, "The Genesis of American College Government," *Thought* 1 (December 1926): 415–433; George C. Bogart, "Faculty Participation in American University Government: A History," *American Association of University Professors Bulletin* 31 (Spring 1945): 72–82; and James B. Conant, "Academic Patronage and Superintendence," *Harvard Educational Review* 8 (May 1938): 312–334.

35. John J. Chapman, "The Harvard Classics and Harvard," *Science* 30 (October 1, 1909): 440.

36. John Dewey, "Academic Freedom," *Educational Review* 23 (January 1902): 11.

37. The point is discussed in Veysey, pp. 346–347. See Thorstein Veblen, *The Higher Learning in America* (New York: B. W. Huebsch, 1918); and the short extract in Hofstadter and Smith, pp. 818–832.

38. Quoted and referenced in Rudolph, p. 423.

39. Veysey, p. 353, citing "Despotism in College Administration," *The Nation* 70 (April 26, 1900): 318; and Andrew S. Draper, "The University Presidency," *Atlantic Monthly* 47 (1906): 36.

40. Quoted in Veysey, p. 268.

41. See William Kent, "The Ideal University Administration," *Science* 28 (July 3, 1908): 8–10; J. J. Stevenson, "The Status of American College Professors," *Popular Science Monthly* 66 (December 1904): 122–130; and "An Academic Scientist's Plea for More Efficient University Control, 1902," in Hofstadter and Smith, pp. 761–771.

42. "The Point of View," *Scribner's Magazine* 42 (July 1907): 123. See "J. McKeen Cattell on Reforming University Control, 1913," in Hofstadter and Smith, pp. 784–808.

43. John Jay Chapman, "Professorial Ethics," *Science* 32 (July 1, 1910): 6.

44. See Leo Rockwell, "Academic Freedom: German Origin and American Development," *Bulletin of the American Association of University Professors* 36 (Summer 1950): 225–236; and "Andrew D. White on Faculty Status in the 1870's and 1880's," in Hofstadter and Smith, pp. 751–752.

45. "G. Stanley Hall on Academic Unrest Before World War I," in Hofstadter and Smith, pp. 771–773; "Alexander Winchell's Encounter with Bishop McTyeire, 1878," ibid., pp. 846–848; "Andrew D. White's Comment on the Winchell Case, 1878," ibid., pp. 848–849; "Noah Porter Objects to William Graham Sumner's Use of Herbert Spencer in Undergraduate Courses, 1879," ibid., pp. 849–850; and "Sumner's Review of His Controversy with Porter, 1881," ibid., pp. 850–857.

46. See Hofstadter and Metzger, "The Development of Academic Freedom," pp. 383–497; "The Wisconsin Regents Speak for Academic Freedom," in Hofstadter and Smith, pp. 859–860; Howard C. Warren, "Academic Freedom," *Atlantic Monthly* 114 (November 1914): 693–694; Merle Curti and Vernon R. Cartensen, *The University of Wisconsin: A History*, 2 vols. (Madison: University of Wisconsin Press, 1949), I, pp. 508–527. See also Richard T. Ely, *The Ground Under Our Feet: An Autobiography* (New York: Macmillan, 1938), pp. 218ff.

47. Thomas Elmer Will, "A Menace to Freedom," *Arena* 26 (September 1901): 244–257.

48. Edward A. Ross, *Seventy Years of It* (Englewood Cliffs, N.J.: Prentice-Hall, 1936), pp. 94ff.

49. Orrin Leslie Elliott, *Stanford University: The First Twenty-five Years* (Stanford: Stanford University Press, 1937), pp. 326–378.

50. Stephen B. L. Penrose, "The Organization of a Standard College," *Educational Review* 44 (September 1912): 119.

51. See Arthur T. Hadley, "Academic Freedom in Theory and Practice," *Atlantic Monthly* 91 (February–March 1903): 152–160, 334–344; and by an anonymous author, "The Perplexities of a College President," *Atlantic Monthly* 85 (April 1900): 483–493.

52. Andrew S. Draper, "The American Type of University," *Science* 26 (July 12, 1907): 41.

53. W. O. Thompson, "In What Sense and to What Extent Is Freedom of Teaching in State Colleges and Universities Expedient and Permissible?" *National Association of State Universities in the United States of America, Transactions and Proceedings* (1910), pp. 66, 75, 87. Also refer to Veysey, pp. 408–409.

54. Alton B. Parker, "Rights of Donors," *Educational Review* 23 (January 1902): 19–21.

55. Ira W. Howerth, "An Ethnic View of Higher Education," *Educational Review* 20 (November 1900): 352. Note the relevant discussion in Veysey, pp. 416–418.

56. Canby, *Alma Mater*, p. 153. See also Joseph Jastrow, "The Academic Career as Affected by Administration," *Science* 23 (April 13, 1906): 566–567; and "Charles A. Beard Notifies Nicholas Murray Butler of His Resignation from Columbia, 1917," in Hofstadter and Smith, pp. 883–884; and refer, ibid., pp. 885–892.

57. Veblen, *The Higher Learning*, pp. 174–175; James McKeen Cattell, "Concerning the American University," *Popular Science Monthly* 61 (June 1902): 180–182; Cattell, *University Control* (New York: Science Press, 1913); and W. C. Lawton, "The Decay of Academic Courage," *Educational Review* 32 (November 1906): 400.

58. For example, see Arthur O. Lovejoy, "Professional Association or Trade Union," *American Association of University Professors Bulletin* 24 (May 1938): 409–417; Earl E. Cummings and Harold A. Larrabe, "Individual vs. College Bargaining for Professors," *American Association of University Professors Bulletin* 24 (October 1938): 487–496.

59. Quoted from *School and Society* 3 (January 1916): 175, cited in Brubacher and Rudy, p. 320.

60. "General Declaration of Principles," *American Association of University Professors Bulletin* 1 (December 1915): 20–29; and in Hofstadter and Smith, pp. 860–878. See Louis Joughin, ed., *Academic Freedom and Tenure* (Madison: University of Wisconsin Press, 1967).

61. For example, consult "Report of Self-Survey Committee on the American Association of University Professors," *American Association of University Professors Bulletin* 51 (May 1965): 110, 116–117.

62. Lowell, *At War with Academic Traditions*, pp. 266–272; and see as a case study Carol S. Gruber, "Academic Freedom at Columbia University, 1917–1918: The Case of James McKeen Cattell," *American Association of University Professors Bulletin* 58 (September 1972): 297–305. Consult also Metzger, *Professors on Guard: The First AAUP Investigations* (New York: Arno Press, 1977); and William Summerscales, *Affirmation and Dissent: Columbia's Response to the Crisis of World War One* (New York: Teachers College Press, 1970).

63. Hofstadter and Metzger, pp. 482–500ff.; Brubacher and Rudy, pp. 322–323.

64. See "Statement of Committee B of the American Association of University Professors," *American Association of University Professors Bulletin* 23 (January 1937): 26–32.

65. The full text of the 1940 *Statement of Principles*, accompanied by interpretive commentary, appears in Lester F. Goodchild and Harold S. Wechsler, eds., *ASHE Reader on The History of Higher Education* (Needham Heights, Mass.: Ginn Press, 1989), pp. 26–32.

66. An interesting analysis of undergraduate college students in the early 1900s is given in Veysey, pp. 268–283.

67. Randolph S. Bourne, "The College: An Undergraduate View," *Atlantic Monthly* 58 (October 1911): 668.

68. Varying perspectives are afforded in R. C. Angell, *The Campus: A Study of Contemporary Undergraduate Life in the American University* (New York: Appleton-Century, 1928); Richard Angelo, "Students at the University of Pennsylvania and Temple College, 1873–1906," *History of Education Quarterly* 19 (Summer 1979): 179–206; John Bascom, "Changes in College Life," *Atlantic Monthly* 91 (June 1903): 749–758; Canby, *Alma Mater*, pp. 89–90; E. M. Coulter, *College Life in the Old South* (Athens, Ga.: University of Georgia Press, 1951); Christian Gauss, *Life in College* (New York: Scribner, 1930). For a slightly later period, see Carol S. Gruber, *Mars and Minerva: World War One and the Uses of the Higher Learning in America* (Baton Rouge: Louisiana State University Press, 1975).

69. See I. G. Wyllie, "The Businessman Looks at the Higher Learning," *Journal of Higher Education* 23 (June 1952): 295–300.

70. Calvin Thomas, "The New Program of Studies at Columbia College," *Educational Review* 29 (April 1905): 335.

71. Veysey, pp. 277–278. See F. H. Giddings, "Student Life in New York," *Columbia University Quarterly* 3 (1900): 3; G. Stanley Hall, "Student Customs," *American Antiquarian Society: Proceedings* (1900–1901): 85–91.

72. Eugene Babbitt, "College Words and Phrases," *Dialect Notes* 2 (1900): 3–70.

73. Edwin E. Slosson, *Great American Universities* (New York: Macmillan, 1910), pp. 75–77.

74. Ross, *Democracy's College*, p. 151.

75. Woodrow Wilson, "What Is a College For?" *Scribner's Magazine* 46 (October 1909): 574.

76. Wilson, in *Harvard Annual Report* (1899–1900), p. 11.

77. Randolph Bourne, "The College," *Atlantic Monthly* 58 (October 1911): 669.

78. Upton Sinclair, *The Goose-step: A Study of American Education* (New York: Albert and Charles Boni, 1936), pp. 90–91; also cited by Rudolph, p. 402.

79. For the immediate postwar period, consult Samuel P. Capon, "The Effect of The World War, 1914–1918, on American Colleges and Universities," *Educational Review* 21 (1939): 40–48; and see Gruber, *Mars and Minerva*.

80. Richard G. Axt, *The Federal Government and Financing Higher Education* (New York: Columbia University Press, 1952), pp. 79–81.

81. See Maxine Davis, *The Lost Generation* (New York: Macmillan, 1936); Howard Bell, *Youth Tell Their Story* (Washington, D.C.: American Council on Education, 1938); and "The Case Against the Younger Generation," *Literary Digest* 17 (June 1922): 40–51.

82. Philip Altbach and P. Peterson, "Before Berkeley: Historical Perspectives on American Student Activism," *Annals of the American Academy of Political and Social Science* (May 1971), 395, p. 6; Alexander W. Astin, et al., "Overview of the Unrest Era," in Astin, et al., eds. *The Power of Protest* (San Francisco: Jossey-Bass, 1975), pp. 17–18; and Ralph Brax, *The First Student Movements: Student Activism in the United States during the 1930s* (Port Washington: Kennikat, 1981).

83. Arthur G. Beach, *A Pioneer College: The Story of Marietta* (Chicago: John F. Caneo, 1935), p. 293.

84. Eugenie A. Leonard, *Origins of Personnel Services in American Higher Education* (Minneapolis: University of Minnesota Press, 1955); Archibald McIntosh, *Behind the Academic Curtain* (New York: Harper and Row, 1948); C. Gilbert Wrenn and Reginald Bell, *Student Personnel Problems* (New York: Farrar, Straus & Giroux, 1942), pp. 2–6; William H. Cowley, "Intelligence Is Not Enough," *Journal of Higher Education* 8 (December 1937): 469–477; and Cowley, "The College Guarantees Satisfaction," *Educational Record* 16 (January 1935): 42–43.

85. See Brubacher and Rudy, pp. 330–344.

86. Gilman, *Launching of a University* (New York: Dodd, Mead, 1916), pp. 53ff.

87. Note, for example, the prediction ventured in William Rainey Harper, *The Trend in Higher Education* (Chicago: University of Chicago Press, 1905), pp. 320–325.

88. Varying analyses, for different periods, are given in Guido H. Marx, "Some Trends in Higher Education," *Science* 29 (May 14, 1909): 764–767; William T. Harris, "The Use of Higher Education," *Educational Review* 16 (September 1898): 161; Slossen, *Great American Universities*, pp. 208, 475; Veysey, pp. 1–2, 4; Henry G. Badger, "Higher Education Statistics: 1870–1952," *Higher Education* 11 (September 1954): 10–15; Toby Oxtoby, et al., "Enrollment and Graduation Trends from Grade School to Ph.D., 1899–1973," *School and Society* 76 (1955): 225–231; and Raymond Walters, *Four Decades of U.S. Collegiate Enrollments* (New York: Society for the Advancement of Education, 1960).

89. See William B. Furie, "Jewish Education in the United States, 1654–1955," in Theodore Friedman, ed., *Jewish Life in America* (New York: Horizon Press, 1955), pp. 227–245; and

Solomon Zeitland, "Jewish Learning in America," *Jewish Quarterly Review* 45 (1955): 582–616. Consult also Sherry Gorelick, *City College and the Jewish Poor, 1880–1924* (New Brunswick, N.J.: Rutgers University Press, 1981).

90. Harold S. Wechsler, "An Academic Gresham's Law: Group Repulsion as a Theme in American Higher Education," quoted in Goodchild and Wechsler, p. 393.

91. Vincent Sheean, *Personal History* (Garden City, N.Y.: Doubleday, Doran, 1936), p. 14.

92. Quoted in Helen R. Olin, *The Women of a State University: An Illustration of the Working of Coeducation in the Middle West* (New York: G. P. Putnam's Sons, 1909), pp. 101–102.

93. Mabel Newcomer, *A Century of Higher Education for American Women* (New York: Harper and Brothers, 1959), p. 46.

94. Wechsler, p. 392.

95. Newcomer, pp. 45–49; and Patricia A. Graham, "Expansion and Exclusion: A History of Women in American Higher Education," *Signs* 3 (Summer 1978): 759–773.

96. Marjorie Hope Nicholson, "The Rights and Privileges Pertaining Thereto," *Journal of the American Association of University Women* 31 (April 1938): 136. Also, for an illustration, see Ethel P. Howe, "Accepting the Universe," *Atlantic Monthly* 129 (April 1922): 453.

97. See Jill Conway, "Perspectives on the History of Women's Education in the United States," *History of Education Quarterly* 14 (Spring 1974): 1–12; and Mary Roth Walsh, *Doctors Wanted: No Women Need Apply* (New Haven, Conn.: Yale University Press, 1977).

98. Frank Bowles and Frank A. DeCosta, *Between Two Worlds: A Profile of Negro Higher Education* (New York: McGraw-Hill, 1971), p. 57; and Frank J. Kelly, *National Survey of the Higher Education of Negroes* (Washington, D.C.: United States Office of Education, 1942-43), pp. 13–29. See also Ruth D. Wilson, "Negro Colleges of Liberal Arts," *American Scholar* 19 (Autumn 1950): 462–463.

99. Dwight O. W. Holmes, *Evolution of the Negro College* (New York: Teachers College, Columbia University, 1934); Kenneth H. Ashworth, *Scholars and Statesmen* (San Francisco: Jossey Bass, 1972), pp. 80ff. Consult also James D. Anderson, "Training the Apostles of Liberal Culture: Black Higher Education, 1900–1935," in Anderson, *The Education of Blacks in the South, 1860–1935* (Chapel Hill, N.C.: University of North Carolina Press, 1988), p. 238.

100. Jennings L. Wagoner, Jr., "The American Compromise: Charles W. Eliot, Black Education, and the New South," in Ronald K. Goodenow and Arthur D. White, eds., *Education and the Rise of the New South* (Boston: G. K. Hall, 1981), pp. 26ff.

101. Quoted by Anderson, p. 276.

102. Ibid., p. 277.

103. Wechsler, p. 396.

104. For an example of the larger, enduring national pattern in subsequent years, refer to Donald E. Muir, "The First Years of Desegregation: Patterns of Acceptance of Black Students on a Deep South Campus," *Social Forces* 49 (March 1971): 371–378.

105. Edythe Hargrove, "How I Feel as a Negro at a White College," *Journal of Negro Education* 11 (October 1942): 484.

106. Felix C. Robb and James W. Tyler, "The Law and Segregation in Southern Higher Education: A Chronology," *Educational Forum* 16 (May 1952): 475–480.

107. Note, for example, Frederick P. Kappel's review of Eliot's *University Administration*, in *Educational Review* 37 (January 1909): 94.

108. See Veysey, pp. 255ff.; "Alexander Meiklejohn Defines the Liberal College, 1912," from *The Liberal College* (1920), in Hofstadter and Smith, pp. 896–903; Russell Thomas, *The Search For A Common Learning: General Education, 1800–1960* (New York: McGraw-Hill, 1962), pp. 62ff.; Meiklejohn, "The Unity of the Curriculum," *New Republic* 32 (October 25, 1922): 2–3; Lewis B. Mayhew, ed., *General Education: An Account and Appraisal* (New York: Harper and Row, 1960), pp. 11–24; Lowell, *At War With Academic Traditions*, pp. 5-7; Willis Rudy, *The Evolving Liberal Arts Curriculum: A Historical Review of Basic Themes* (New York: Bureau of Publications, Teachers College, Columbia University, 1960), p. 1; Archie M. Palmer, ed., *The Liberal Arts College Movement* (New York: Little and Ives, 1930).

109. See Mowat G. Fraser, *The College of the Future* (New York: Columbia University Press, 1937), chapter 9; Bliss Perry, *And Gladly Teach* (Boston: Houghton Mifflin, 1935), chapters 3, 4, 7; and Woodrow Wilson, "The Preceptorial System at Princeton," *Educational Review* 39 (April 1910): 385–390.

110. Andrew D. White, "Old and New University Problems," *Cornell Alumni News* 10 (1908): 445–446; cited in Veysey, p. 255.

111. Quoted in Veysey, p. 242.
112. R. S. Baker and W. E. Dodd, eds., *Woodrow Wilson, College and State: Educational, Literary and Political Papers (1875–1913)*, (1925), I, p. 496, cited in Veysey, p. 216.
113. Lowell, *At War With Academic Traditions*, pp. 108–109, 116.
114. A good summary overview is supplied in Rudolph, *Curriculum: A History of the American Undergraduate Course of Study Since 1636* (San Francisco: Jossey-Bass, 1977), pp. 227–244.
115. John Dewey, *The Educational Situation* (Chicago: University of Chicago Press, 1902), pp. 85–86.
116. See Meiklejohn, "The Unity of the Curriculum," pp. 2–3; M. L. Burton, "The Undergraduate Course," *New Republic* 32 (October 25, 1922): 9; Louis T. Benezet, *General Education in the Progressive College* (New York: Teachers College Press, 1943); William T. Foster, "Our Democratic American Colleges," *Nation* 88 (April 1, 1909): 325; and Foster, "The Gentleman's Grade," *Educational Review* 33 (April 1907): 386–392.
117. Dwight C. Miner, ed., *A History of Columbia College on Morningside* (New York: Columbia University Press, 1954), pp. 46–53. See Rudolph, *American College and University*, pp. 455–456; and "The Columbia College Faculty Devises a Course in Contemporary Civilization, 1919," in Hofstadter and Smith, pp. 904–905. Also, refer to Norman F. Coleman, "How We Teach at Reed College," *Bulletin of the Association of American Colleges* 14 (November 1928), pp. 407–408.
118. A helpful reference for collegiate experimentation of the period is represented by Hoyt Trowbridge, "Forty Years of General Education," *Journal of General Education* 11 (July 1958): 161–169.
119. Meiklejohn, "The Unity of the Curriculum," pp. 2–3.
120. See Frank Aydelotte, *Breaking the Academic Lock Step: The Development of Honors Work in American Colleges and Universities* (New York: Harper and Row, 1944); and Aydellote, *An Adventure in Education* (New York: Macmillan, 1941), p. 224. See as well Burton R. Clark, *The Distinctive College* (Chicago: Aldine, 1970), chapter 7; and Algo D. Henderson and Dorothy Hall, *Antioch College: Its Design for Liberal Education* (New York: Harper, 1946).
121. Refer to Rudolph, *American College and University*, p. 478. See James Gray, *The University of Minnesota, 1851–1951* (Minneapolis: University of Minnesota Press, 1951), pp. 308–322.
122. For further details and a full-fledged narrative description, refer to Chauncey S. Boucher, *The Chicago College Plan* (Chicago: University of Chicago Press, 1935); and Reuben Frodin, *The Idea and Practice of General Education* (Chicago: University of Chicago Press, 1951), pp. 87–122.
123. Note Rudolph, *American College and University*, pp. 479–480.
124. Ibid., p. 479. See Robert Maynard Hutchins, *The Higher Learning In America* (New Haven, Conn.: Yale University Press, 1936; reissued 1962). References and quotations are from the 1962 reprint edition.
125. Hutchins, pp. 4–12.
126. Ibid., p. 36.
127. Ibid., p. 47.
128. Ibid., pp. 66–67.
129. Ibid., pp. xiii–xiv.
130. David Boroff, "St. John's College: Four Years with the Great Books," *Saturday Review* 46 (March 23, 1963): 58–61; Donald P. Cottrell, "General Education in Experimental Liberal Arts Colleges," in Guy Montrose Whipple, ed., *General Education In The American College, Part II, The Thirty-Eighth Yearbook of the National Society For The Study Of Education* (Bloomington, Ind.: Public School Publishing, 1939), pp. 206-207; Christopher Jencks and David Riesman, *The Academic Revolution* (New York: Doubleday, 1968), pp. 494ff.; F. R. Leavis, "Great Books and a Liberal Education," *Commentary* 16 (September 1953): 224–232; Gerald Grant and David Riesman, "St. John's And the Great Books," *Change* 6 (May 1974): 30; and Harry D. Gideonse, *The Higher Learning in a Democracy* (New York: Holt, Rinehart and Winston, 1937), pp. 2–6, 8–10, 19–27, 30–34; John Dewey, "President Hutchins' Proposals To Remake Higher Education," *The Social Frontier* 3 (January 1937): 103–104.
131. Quoted in Leon B. Richardson, *A Study of the Liberal College: A Report to the President of Dartmouth College* (Hanover, N.H.: Dartmouth College, 1924), p. 15.
132. See Brubacher and Rudy, pp. 250–260; Veysey, p. 338n.; Jacques Barzun, "College to University—and After," *American Scholar* 33 (Spring 1964), pp. 212–220; Charles W. Eliot, *Educational Reform* (Englewood Cliffs, N.J.: Prentice-Hall, 1898), pp. 151–176; William R. Harper, "The Length of the College Course," *Educational Review* 26 (September 1903): 134–140; Lewis W. Smith, "Early Junior College—Harper's Influence," *Junior College Journal* 11 (May 1941): 516ff.; Charles K. Adams, "The Next Step in Education," *Forum* 10 (February,

1891): 629-630; William H. Cowley, "The War on the College," *Atlantic Monthly* 169 (June 1942): 721; Walter C. Eells, "Abolition of the Lower Division: Early History," *Junior College Journal* 6 (January 1936): 194–195.

133. See Rudolph, *Curriculum*, pp. 197, 200, 274, 284–286; and David O. Levine, *The American College and the Culture of Aspiration, 1915–1940* (Ithaca, N.Y.: Cornell University Press, 1986). Also note Goodchild and Wechsler, pp. 401–412.

134. Quotations are from Levine, in Goodchild and Wechsler, p. 403.

135. Background is supplied in Jesse P. Bogue and Shirley Sanders, "Analysis of Junior College Growth, 1896–1949," *Junior College Journal* 19 (February 1949): 311–319; Walter C. Eells, *The Junior College* (Boston: Houghton Mifflin, 1931); Gregory Goodwin, *A Social Panacea: History of the Community-Junior College Ideology* (Los Angeles: ERIC Clearinghouse for Junior Colleges, 1973); Walter J. Greenleaf, *Junior Colleges* (Washington, D.C.: United States Bureau of Education, 1936).

136. See Bogue, *The Community College* (New York: McGraw-Hill, 1950); and Leland L. Medsker, "Changes in Junior Colleges and Technical Institutes," in Logan Wilson, ed., *Emerging Patterns in American Higher Education* (Washington, D.C.: American Council on Education, 1965), pp. 79–84.

137. See Algo D. Henderson and Jean Glidden Henderson, *Higher Education in America* (San Francisco: Jossey-Bass, 1974), pp. 50–52.

138. The full text of Lowell's remarks appear in Lowell, "Universities, Graduate Schools, and Colleges," *Atlantic Monthly* 150 (August 1932): 219–221.

139. See Elbert K. Fretwell, *Founding Public Junior Colleges* (New York: Teachers College, Columbia University, 1954), chapter 2; and Leland L. Medsker and Dale Tillery, *Breaking The Access Barriers* (New York: McGraw-Hill, 1971), pp. 18ff.

140. A. Monroe Stowe, *Modernizing the College* (New York: Alfred A. Knopf, 1926), pp. 55–56. It is significant, perhaps, that in recent decades many two-year colleges have sought to claim the (presumably) more prestigious appellation "community colleges" for themselves. The change undoubtedly reflects both ideological forces at work and institutional aspirations to enhanced status.

Chapter 7

1. See Willis Rudy, *The College of the City of New York: A History, 1847–1947* (New York: City College Press, 1949), pp. 450–452.

2. John Dewey and Horace M. Kallen, eds., *The Bertrand Russell Case* (New York: Viking Press, 1941), p. 20.

3. Ibid., p. 19.

4. Ibid., pp. 22, 213–225.

5. See "Academic Freedom and National Security," *American Association of University Professors Bulletin* 42 (Spring 1956): 99.

6. Ellen W. Schrecker, *No Ivory Tower: McCarthyism and the Universities* (New York: Oxford University Press, 1986).

7. An informative study of the period is provided in Jane Sanders, *Cold War on Campus* (Seattle: University of Washington Press, 1979).

8. See Rudy, pp. 451–452.

9. Relevant illustrations and commentaries appear in Allen A. Zoll, *Our American Heritage* (New York: National Council for American Education, 1950), p. 12; Robert C. Morris, "The Right Wing Critics of Education: Yesterday and Today," *Educational Leadership* 35 (May 1978): 625; and Morris, "Thunder on the Right: Past and Present," *Education* 99 (Winter 1978): 168–169; William Van Til, *Education: A Beginning* (Boston: Houghton Mifflin, 1974), p. 161; Mary Anne Raywid, *The Axe-Grinders: Critics of Our Public Schools* (New York: Macmillan, 1962), pp. 1, 2; and Robert A. Skaife, "They Oppose Progress," *Nation's Schools* 47 (February 1951): 32.

10. Conant's position was echoed by Sidney Hook, *Heresy—Yes; Conspiracy—No!* (New York: John Day, 1953). A contrasting position was advanced in Alexander Meiklejohn, *Political Freedom: The Constitutional Powers of the People* (New York: Harper and Row, 1960), pp. 3–4, 59–60, 86.

11. See "Statement of Committee on Cultural Freedom," in Dewey and Kallen, pp. 226–227.

12. This essentially was the position defended by Hook in *Heresy—Yes; Conspiracy—No!*

13. Note, as an example, David P. Gardner, *The California Oath Controversy* (Berkeley: University of California Press, 1967).

14. Refer to Paul F. Lazarsfeld and Wagner Thielens, *The Academic Mind* (New York: Free Press, 1958); Robert K. Carr, "Academic Freedom, the A.A.U.P., and the United States Supreme

Court," *American Association of University Professors Bulletin* 45 (March 1959): 5–24; Robert E. Summers, *Freedom and Loyalty in Our Colleges* (New York: H. W. Wilson, 1954); and the concluding section of Walter P. Metzger, *Academic Freedom in the Age of the University* (New York: Columbia University Press, 1955).

15. Henry G. Badger, "Higher Education Statistics: 1870–1952," *Higher Education* 11 (September 1954): 10–15.

16. Toby Oxtoby, et al., "Enrollment and Graduation Trends from Grade School to Ph.D., 1899–1973," *School and Society* 76 (1955): 225–231.

17. Raymond Walters, *Four Decades of U.S. Collegiate Enrollments* (New York: Society for the Advancement of Education, 1960); and Calvin B. T. Lee, *The Campus Scene, 1900–79* (New York: David McKay, 1970), pp. 75ff.

18. Walters, "Statistics of Attendance in American Universities and Colleges, 1949," *School and Society* 70 (December 1949): 392; Educational Policies Commission, *Higher Education in a Decade of Decision* (Washington, D.C.: National Education Association, 1957), pp. 4–5, 31–32; Charles J. Anderson, *A Fact Book on Higher Education* (Washington, D.C.: American Council on Education, 1968), p. 809; Martin Trow, "American Higher Education: Past, Present, and Future," *Educational Researcher* 15 (April 1988): 13–15.

19. The remainder of the statistical profile following is compiled from previously cited sources and from successive editions of the *Fact Book on Higher Education*. Consult Anderson, et al., *1989–90 Fact Book on Higher Education* (New York: Macmillan, 1989), pp. 5–9, 133–145. Also, most current figures and projections are derived in part from Thomas D. Snyder, et al., *Digest of Educational Statistics 1993* (Washington, D.C.: National Center for Educational Statistics, October 1993), pp. 172–223.

20. Snyder, passim.; and Anderson, pp. 7–8.

21. Snyder, passim.; and Anderson, pp. 6, 9.

22. See also Michael A. Olivas, "Indian, Chicano, and Puerto Rican Colleges: Status and Issues," *Bilingual Review* 9 (January–April 1982): 36–58.

23. James E. Russell, *Federal Activities in Higher Education After the Second World War* (New York: King's Crown Press, 1951); and for further background, see Lawrence Gladieu, *Congress and the Colleges* (Lexington, Mass.: D. C. Heath, 1976).

24. An overview is given in Walter C. Hobbs, *Government Regulation of Higher Education* (Cambridge, Mass.: Ballinger, 1978).

25. Keith W. Olson, *The G.I. Bill, the Veterans, and the Colleges* (Lexington: University Press of Kentucky, 1974).

26. For a cogent analysis of the framing of several major federal policy initiatives affecting higher education in the postwar era, see Janet C. Kerr, "From Truman to Johnson: Ad Hoc Policy Formulation in Higher Education," *Review of Higher Education* 8 (Fall 1984): 15–84.

27. Trow, pp. 15ff.

28. For a sampling of the controversy surrounding federal aid to higher education, including the 1957 Report, refer to Gail Kennedy, ed., *Education for Democracy, The Debate over the Report of the President's Commission on Higher Education* (Lexington, Mass.: D. C. Heath, 1952); American Council on Education, and National Education Association Educational Policies Commission, *Federal-State Relations in Education* (Washington, D.C.: National Education Association, 1945), pp. 45–47 and John K. Norton, "The Need for Federal Aid for Education," *School and Society* 77 (March 17, 1956): 87–88.

29. Ernst Becker, "Financing Higher Education: A Review of Trends and Projections," in United States Office of Education, *Trends in Post-Secondary Education* (Washington, D.C.: United States Government Printing Office, 1970), pp. 97–180; Theodore Schultz, "Resources for Higher Education: An Economist's View," *Journal of Political Economy* 76 (May–June 1968): 327–347; Earl F. Cheit, *The New Depression in Higher Education* (New York: McGraw-Hill, 1971).

30. Henry Rosovsky, *The University: An Owner's Manual* (New York: W. W. Norton and Company, 1990), p. 14.

31. Page Smith, *Killing the Spirit: Higher Education in America* (New York: Viking Penguin, 1990), pp. 1, 10–11, 13.

32. *Ibid.,* pp. 2, 13.

33. Somewhat dated but still useful for tracing the beginnings of coordinated state systems of higher education is John S. Brubacher and Willis Rudy, *Higher Education in Transition,* 3rd. ed. rev. (New York: Harper and Row, 1976), pp. 384–386.

34. Ibid., pp. 408–410; and John Hardin Best, "The Revolution of Markets and Management: Toward a History of American Higher Education Since 1945," *History of Education Quarterly* 28 (Summer 1988): 177–191.

35. The interpretation follows Best's analysis, ibid., pp. 178ff.; and see Trow, passim.

36. The growing influence of corporate business norms upon American academe is discussed in Laurence R. Veysey, *The Emergence of the American University* (Chicago: University of Chicago Press, 1965), pp. 258–259, 302–303, 305–309, 315–317, 351–353. A quite different but related perspective is supplied in Bruce Wilshire, *The Moral Collapse of the University* (Albany: State University of New York, 1990).

37. Smith, pp. 14–16, 59, 207–208.

38. Trow, p. 18.

39. See Frank Bowles and Frank A. DeCosta, *Between Two Worlds: A Profile of Negro Higher Education* (New York: McGraw-Hill, 1971), pp. 61–80.

40. Martin D. Jenkins, "Enrollment in Institutions of Higher Education of Negroes," *Journal of Negro Education* 9 (April 1940): 268–270.

41. See Hurley H. Doddy, "The Progress of the Negro in Higher Education," *Journal of Negro Education* 32 (Fall 1963): 485–492.

42. Phineas Indritz, "The Meaning of the School Decisions: The Breakthrough on the Legal Front of Racial Segregation," *Journal of Negro Education* 23 (Summer 1954): 355–363; and Guy B. Johnson, "Desegregation in Southern Higher Education," *Higher Education* 20 (June 1964): 5–7.

43. Southern Education Reporting Service, *Statistical Summary, 1964–65* (Nashville: Southern Education Reporting Service, 1965), p. 4.

44. Ibid., p. 4.

45. Reed Sarratt, *The Ordeal of Desegregation* (New York: Harper and Row, 1966), pp. 127–128.

46. Southern Education Reporting Service, *Statistical Summary,* p. 14. See James H. Meredith, *Three Years in Mississippi* (Bloomington: Indiana University Press, 1966).

47. Johnson, pp. 5–7.

48. Figures cited were compiled by the Carnegie Commission on Higher Education from multiple sources, including Marjorie O. Chandler and M. C. Rice, *Opening Fall Enrollment in Higher Education, 1967* (Washington, D.C.: United States Office of Education, 1967), pp. 52–134. Consult also "White, Negro Undergraduates at Colleges," *Chronicle of Higher Education* (April 22, 1968): 3–4.

49. W. R. Allen, "Black Colleges v. White Colleges," *Change* 19 (May/June 1987): 28–31.

50. Figures cited are compiled from various statistical summaries in S. Arbeiter, "Black Enrollments: The Case of the Missing Students," *Change* 19 (May/June 1987): 14–19; N. Joyce Payne, "The Role of Black Colleges in an Expanding Economy," *Educational Record* 68 (Fall 1987/Winter 1988): 104–106; and Jacqueline Fleming, *Blacks in College* (San Francisco: Jossey-Bass, 1984), passim.

51. Gail E. Thomas and Susan Hill, "Black Institutions in U.S. Higher Education: Present Roles, Contributions, Future Projections," *Journal of College Student Personnel* 28 (November 1987): 496–503.

52. William B. Harvey and Lea E. Williams, "Historically Black Colleges: Models for Increasing Minority Representation," *Education and Urban Society* 21 (May 1989): 328–340; F. G. Jenifer, "The Supreme Court Must Act to Preserve and Strengthen Historically Black Colleges," *Chronicle of Higher Education* 38 (October 16, 1991): A60; Reginald Wilson, "Can Black Colleges Solve the Problem of Access for Black Students?" *American Journal of Education* 98 (August 1990): 443–457.

53. Albert N. Whiting, "Black Colleges, An Alternative Strategy for Survival," *Change* 20 (March/April 1988): 10–11.

54. Bailey's comment and all subsequent quotations relative to black colleges represent written responses to a narrative survey reported in Paula Roper and Christopher J. Lucas, "Academic Leaders on the Role and Future of Black Colleges and Universities," *Journal of Thought* 29 (Summer 1994): 33–46. See also Jill M. Constantine, "The 'Added Value' of Historically Black Colleges," *Academe* 80 (May/June 1994): 12–17.

55. Significant documents include Ernest L. Boyer, *College: The Undergraduate Experience in America* (New York: Harper and Row, 1987); Boyer, *Common Learning: A Carnegie Colloquium on General Education* (Princeton, N.J.: Carnegie Foundation for the Advancement of Learning, 1981); Association of American Colleges, *Integrity in the College Curriculum: A Report to the Academic*

Community: The Findings and Recommendations of the Project on Redefining the Meaning and Purpose of Baccalaureate Degrees (Washington, D.C.: Association of American Colleges, 1985); William J. Bennett, *To Reclaim a Legacy: A Report on the Humanities in Higher Education* (Washington, D.C.: National Endowment for the Humanities, 1984); Herant A. Katchadourian and John Boli, *Careerism and Intellectualism Among College Students: Patterns of Academic and Career Choice in the Undergraduate Years* (San Francisco: Jossey-Bass, 1985); Jerry G. Gaff, *General Education Today: A Critical Analysis of Controversies, Practices, and Reforms* (San Francisco: Jossey-Bass, 1983): David L. Wee, *On General Education: Outlines for Reform* (New Haven, Conn.: Society for Values in Higher Education, 1981).

56. Bruce A. Kimball, "The Historical and Cultural Dimensions of the Recent Reports on Undergraduate Education," *American Journal of Education* 98 (May 1988): 293–322.

57. Refer to Douglas Sloan, "Harmony, Chaos, and Consensus: The American College Curriculum," *Teachers College Record* 73 (December 1971): 221–251; Frederick Rudolph, *Curriculum: A History of the Undergraduate Course of Study Since 1636* (San Francisco: Jossey-Bass, 1977), pp. 245–289; Robert Blackburn et al., *Changing Practices in Undergraduate Education* (Berkeley: Carnegie Council on Policy Studies in Higher Education, 1976); Arthur Levine and John Weingart, *Reform of Undergraduate Education* (San Francisco: Jossey-Bass, 1973): Willis Rudy, *The Evolving Liberal Arts Curriculum: A Historical Review of Basic Themes* (New York: Teachers College, Columbia University, 1960).

58. Consult Elizabeth Minnich et al., eds., *Reconstructing the Academy: Women's Education and Women's Studies* (Chicago: University of Chicago Press, 1988).

59. Guy Montrose Whipple, ed., *General Education In The American College, Part II, The Thirty-Eighth Yearbook of the National Society for the Study of Education* (Bloomington, Ill.: Public School Publishing, 1939).

60. Alvin E. Eurich, "A Renewed Emphasis Upon General Education," in Whipple, p. 6.

61. Two representative works of the genre include Mark Van Doren, *Liberal Education* (New York: Holt, Rinehart & Winston, 1943); and Jacques Maritain, *Education at the Crossroads* (New Haven, Conn.: Yale University Press, 1934).

62. Eurich, p. 6.

63. John Dale Russell, "General Education in the Liberal Arts Colleges," in Whipple, pp. 171–192.

64. Henry M. Wriston, "A Critical Appraisal of Experiments in General Education," in Whipple, pp. 307–308.

65. Ernest L. Boyer and Arthur Levine, "A Quest for Common Learning," *Change* 13 (April 1981): 30.

66. Report of the Harvard Committee, *General Education in a Free Society* (Cambridge, Mass.: Harvard University Press, 1945).

67. Ibid., p. 4.

68. Ibid., p. 39.

69. Ibid., pp. 40, 51, 64, 195.

70. Ibid., p. 93.

71. Horace M. Kallen, *The Education of Free Men* (New York: Farrar, Straus & Giroux, 1949), pp. 88–89, 316–318.

72. Ibid., p. 317.

73. Ibid., pp. 319, 323, 325–326.

74. See T. R. McConnell, "General Education: An Analysis," in Nelson B. Henry, ed., *General Education: The Fifty-First Yearbook of the National Society for the Study of Education, Part I* (Chicago: University of Chicago Press, 1952), pp. 4–13; Horace T. Morse, "Liberal and General Education: A Problem of Differentiation," in James G. Rice, ed., *General Education: Current Ideas and Concerns* (Washington, D.C.: Association for Higher Education, National Education Association, 1964), pp. 7–12; and Morse, "Liberal and General Education: Partisans or Partners?" *Junior College Journal* 24 (March 1954): 395–399.

75. Gresham Riley, "The Reform of General Education," *Liberal Education* 66 (Fall 1980): 299.

76. Robert E. Mason, *Contemporary Educational Theory* (New York: David McKay, 1972), pp. 138ff.

77. John W. Gardner, *Excellence* (New York: Harper and Row, 1961), p. xiv.

78. Daniel Bell, *The Reforming of General Education* (New York: Columbia University Press, 1966).

79. Ibid., pp. 8, 68.

80. Ibid., p. 141.

81. Ibid., p. 166.

82. See also Daniel Bell, "A Second Look at General Education," *Seminar Reports* I (December 7, 1973), p. 4; and Bell, "The Reform of General Education," in Robert A. Goldwin, ed., *Education and Modern Democracy* (Chicago: Rand McNally, 1967), p. 103.

83. Wayne C. Booth, ed., *The Knowledge Most Worth Having* (Chicago: University of Chicago Press, 1976).

84. Richard McKeon, "The Battle of the Books," in Booth, pp. 183ff.

85. Refer to Philip G. Altbach, *Student Politics in America: A Historical Analysis* (New York: McGraw-Hill, 1974); and Seymour M. Lipset, *Rebellion in the University: A History of Student Activism in America* (London: Routledge & Kegan Paul, 1972).

86. On February 2, 1960, the *New York Times* reported, "A group of well dressed Negro college students staged a sitdown strike in a downtown Woolworth store today and vowed to continue it in relays until Negroes were served at the lunch counters." The students were quoted as declaring, "We believe, since we buy books and papers in the other part of the store, we should get served in this part." See W. H. Cowley and Don Williams, *International and Historical Roots of American Higher Education* (New York: Garland Publishing, 1991), p. 194.

87. See Nathan Glazer, "'Student Power' in Berkeley," in Daniel Bell and Irving Kristol, *Confrontation: The Student Rebellion and the Universities* (New York: Basic Books, 1969), pp. 3–21; and Alexander W. Astin, et al., *The Power of Protest* (San Francisco: Jossey-Bass, 1975), pp. 20–22.

88. See, for example, Nathan Tarcov, "Four Crucial Years at Cornell," in Glazer, pp. 128–144; and "Three Sample Protests," in Astin, pp. 88–144.

89. Sale Kirkpatrick, *SDS* (New York: Random House, 1973).

90. For a chronology of events and an interpretation, see Bell, "Columbia and the New Left," and Roger Starr, "The Case of the Columbia Gym," in Glazer, pp. 67–127.

91. Scranton Commission, *Report of the President's Commission on Campus Unrest* (Washington, D.C.: United States Government Printing Office, 1970), p. 36.

92. For example, see John H. Bunzel, "Black Studies at San Francisco State," in Glazer, pp. 22–44; and "Overview of the Unrest," in Astin, pp. 22–24.

93. Campus ferment provoked a staggering body of literature within a very short time span. See Jacquelyn Estrada, ed., *The University Under Siege* (Los Angeles: Nash Publishing, 1971); Helen Lefkowitz Horowitz, *Campus Life: Undergraduate Cultures From the End of the Eighteenth Century to the Present* (New York: Alfred A. Knopf, 1987), pp. 220–244; Julian Foster and Durward Long, *Protest!: Student Activism in America* (New York: William Morrow, 1970); Donald E. Phillips, *Student Protest, 1960–1969: An Analysis of the Issues and Speeches* (Washington, D.C.: University Press of America, 1980); Jack D. Douglas, *Youth in Turmoil* (Chevy Chase, Md.: National Institute of Mental Health, 1970); Donald L. Rogan, *Campus Apocalypse: The Student Search Today* (New York: Seabury Press, 1969); Donald Light, Jr., and John Spiegel, *The Dynamics of University Protest* (Chicago: Nelson-Hall, 1977); John R. Searle, *The Campus War* (New York: World Publishing, 1971); Art Seidenbaum, *Confrontation on Campus: Student Challenge in California* (Los Angeles: Ward Ritche Press, 1969); Seymour M. Lipset and Philip Altbach, *Students in Revolt* (Boston: Houghton Mifflin, 1969); Glazer, *Remembering the Answers: Essays On The American Student Revolt* (New York: Basic Books, 1970); William McGill, *The Year of the Monkey: Revolt on Campus, 1968–1969* (New York: McGraw-Hill, 1982); David Westby, *The Student Movement in the United States During the 1960s* (Lewisburg, Penn.: Bucknell University Press, 1976).

94. Edward J. Bloustein, *The University and the Counterculture* (New Brunswick, N.J.: Rutgers University Press, 1972), pp. 59.

95. See Samuel Lubell, "That 'Generation Gap,'" in Bell and Kristol, pp. 58–66.

96. Bloustein, p. 95.

97. Richard E. Peterson and John A. Bilorusky, *May, 1970: The Campus Aftermath of Cambodia and Kent State* (Berkeley: Carnegie Commission on Higher Education, 1971); and Scott Bills, ed., *Kent State, May 4: Echoes through a Decade* (Kent, Ohio: Kent State University Press, 1982).

98. Astin, pp. 34–35.

99. The full text of the report is given in Blackburn.

100. See Horowitz, pp. 245–262.

101. Astin, p. 35.

Chapter 8

1. See B. Frank Brown, ed., *Education for Responsible Citizenship: The Report of the National Task Force on Citizenship Education* (New York: McGraw-Hill, 1977); Robert A. Dahl, *After the*

Revolution?: Authority in a Good Society (New Haven, Conn.: Yale University Press, 1970); Edwin O. Reischauer, *Toward the 21st Century: Education for a Changing World* (New York: Vintage, 1973); National Assembly on Foreign Languages and International Studies, *Toward Education with a Global Perspective* (Washington, D.C.: Association of American Colleges, 1981); Council on Learning, *Task Force Statement on Education and Worldview* (New York: Council on Learning, 1981); Working Group on the Successor Generation, *The Successor Generation: Its Challenges and Responsibilities* (Washington, D.C.: Atlantic Council of the United States, 1981).

2. Willis D. Weatherford, "Commission on Liberal Learning," *Liberal Education* 57 (March, 1971): 37.

3. Carnegie Foundation for the Advancement of Teaching, *Missions of the College Curriculum* (San Francisco: Jossey-Bass, 1977), p. 11.

4. Clark Kerr, *Uses of the University* (New York: Harper and Row, 1972).

5. Robert Paul Wolff, *The Ideal of the University* (Boston: Beacon Press, 1969); Brand Blanchard, *The Uses of a Liberal Education* (LaSalle, Ill.: Open Court, 1973); Christopher Jencks and David Riesman, *The Academic Revolution* (Chicago: University of Chicago Press, 1968, 1977).

6. See Robert H. Chambers, "Educating for Perspective—A Proposal," *Change* 13 (September 1981): 46.

7. Barry O'Connell, "Where Does Harvard Lead Us?" *Change* 10 (September 1978): 38.

8. Edward Joseph Shoben, Jr., "The Liberal Arts and Contemporary Society: The 1970's," *Liberal Education* 56 (March 1970): 28–38; and Frank R. Harrison, "The Pervasive Peanut," *Modern Age* 23 (Winter 1979): 78.

9. Herbert I. London, "The Politics of the Core Curriculum," *Change* 10 (September 1978): 11.

10. Page Smith, *Killing the Spirit: Higher Education in America* (New York: Viking Penguin, 1990), pp. 1, 5–6, 77–78, 143, 282, 294, 297.

11. London, pp. 11ff.

12. O'Connell, pp. 30–31ff.

13. Specific examples include Ernest L. Boyer and Arthur Levine, *A Quest for Common Learning* (New York: Carnegie Foundation for the Advancement of Teaching, 1981); William J. Bennett, *To Reclaim a Legacy: A Report on the Humanities in Higher Education* (Washington, D.C.: National Endowment for the Humanities, 1984); Association of American Colleges, *Integrity in the College Curriculum: A Report to the Academic Community* (Washington, D.C.: Association of American Colleges, 1985); E. D. Hirsch, Jr., *Cultural Literacy* (New York: Random House, 1987); and Allan Bloom, *The Closing of the American Mind* (New York: Simon and Schuster, 1987).

14. For examples, refer to Sidney Hook, et al., eds., *The Idea of a Modern University* (Buffalo: Prometheus, 1974); C. Wegener, *Liberal Education and the Modern University* (Chicago: University of Chicago Press, 1978); Michael Simpson, "The Case for the Liberal Arts," *Liberal Education* 66 (Fall 1980): 315–319; and David G. Winter, et al., *A New Case for the Liberal Arts* (San Francisco: Jossey-Bass, 1981).

15. See Paul Berman, ed., *Debating P.C.: The Controversy Over Political Correctness On College Campuses* (New York: Dell / Bantam Doubleday, 1992).

16. John Searle, "The Storm Over the University," in Berman, pp. 85–123.

17. Irving Howe, "The Value of the Canon," in Berman, pp. 153–171.

18. Dinesh D'Souza, *Illiberal Education: The Politics of Race and Sex on Campus* (New York: Free Press, 1991).

19. Ibid., p. 220. The quotation is from the 1992 Vintage edition.

20. Ibid., p. 230.

21. See Henry Louis Gates, Jr., "Whose Canon Is It, Anyway?" in Berman, pp. 190–200.

22. Catharine R. Stimpson, "On Differences: Modern Language Association Presidential Address," in Berman, p. 45.

23. See Dinesh D'Souza and Robert MacNeil, "The Big Chill? Interview with Dinesh D'Souza," in Berman, p. 31.

24. Roger Kimball, *Tenured Radicals: How Politics Has Corrupted Our Higher Education* (New York: Harper Collins, 1990).

25. D'Souza, *Illiberal Education,* pp. 60–65ff.

26. Note the discussion in Edward W. Said, "The Politics of Knowledge," in Berman, pp. 172–189.

27. Michael Apple, *Official Knowledge: Democratic Education in a Conservative Age* (New York: Routledge, Chapman and Hall, 1993).

28. Quoted in Courtney Leatherman, "Conservative Scholars' Group Draws Increasingly Diverse Voices to Its Cause," *Chronicle of Higher Education* (April 28, 1993): A15–16.

29. Quoted ibid., p. A16.
30. George H. Douglas, *Education Without Impact: How Our Universities Fail the Young* (New York: Birch Lane / Carol Publishing Group, 1992).
31. Benjamin R. Barber, *An Aristocracy of Everyone: The Politics of Education and the Future of America* (New York: Ballantine Books, 1992), p. 9.
32. Douglas, p. xii.
33. Smith, pp. 1–2.
34. Charles Sykes, *Profscam: Professors and the Demise of Higher Education* (Washington, D.C.: Regnery Gateway, 1988); and Sykes, *The Hollow Men: Politics and Corruption in Higher Education* (Washington, D.C.: Regnery Gateway, 1990).
35 Smith, pp. 12–13.
36. Barber, p. 197.
37. Ibid., pp. 196–209.
38. Ibid., p. 203.
39. Ibid., pp. 204–205.
40. Ibid., p. 205.
41. Ibid., p. 196.
42. Ibid., p. 197.
43. Robert N. Bellah, et al., *Habits of the Heart: Individualism and Commitment in American Life* (Berkeley: University of California Press, 1985).
44. Bellah, pp. 298–299.
45. Quoted in Daniel Callahan and Sissela Bok, eds., *Ethics Training in Higher Education* (New York: Plenum Press, 1980), p. 4.
46. Bellah, pp. 299–301.
47. Bellah, et al., *The Good Society* (New York: Vintage, 1992).
48. Douglas, pp. 4, 34, 58, 165–167.
49. See Pierre Bourdieu and Jean-Claude Passeron, *Reproduction in Education, Society and Culture* (Los Angeles: Sage, 1979).
50. Douglas, p. 90.
51. Henry Rosovsky, *The University, An Owner's Manual* (New York: W. W. Norton and Company, 1990), pp. 84–98.
52. Ibid., p. 93.
53. Smith, pp. 7, 20, 179, 197–198.
54. Barber, p. 196.
55. Douglas, pp. 68–70, 85–89, 93, 95, 100–101.
56. Barber, pp. 200ff.
57. See ibid., chapter 4, "Radical Excesses and Post-Modernism," pp. 107–150.
58. Douglas, pp. xiii–xiv.
59. Ibid., pp. 9–18.
60. William Johnson Cory, *Eton Reform* (London: Longman, Green, Longman, & Roberts, 1861), pp. 6–7.
61. Douglas, p. 12.
62. Note the interesting discussion in this connection in John R. Thelin, *Higher Education And Its Useful Past* (Cambridge, Mass.: Schenkman, 1982), pp. 157–160.
63. Still other factors of a more fundamental character are alluded to in Bruce Wilshire, *The Moral Collapse of the University, Professionalism, Purity, and Alienation* (Albany: State University of New York Press, 1990), pp. 72–83, 171–174.
64. Edward B. Fiske, *Selective Guide to Colleges* (New York: New York Times Books, 1985), p. xiii; cited in Rosovsky, p. 60n. For historical background, consult "Mostly Stable: College and University Enrollments: 1985–91," *Chronicle of Higher Education* (November 25, 1987): A29; Kenneth Young, *Access to Higher Education: A History* (Washington, D.C.: American Association of State Colleges and Universities, 1971); and Richard I. Ferrin, *A Decade of Change in Free Access to Higher Education* (New York: College Entrance Examination Board, 1971).
65. Rosovsky cites one conspicuous example at Harvard in 1968, p. 23. Similar capitulations took place in many other colleges and universities across the nation. See Douglas, pp. 105–114ff.
66. Douglas, pp. 114.
67. See, for example, Christopher Shea, "Grade Inflation's Consequences," *Chronicle of Higher Education* 40 (January 5, 1994): A45–A46; and Arthur Levine, "To Deflate Grade Inflation, Simplify the System," *Chronicle of Higher Education* 40 (January 19, 1994): B3.

68. John Leo, "A for Effort. Or for Showing Up," *US News & World Report* 115 (October 18, 1993): 22.

69. Quoted in Leo, p. 22. Consult William Cole, "By Rewarding Mediocrity, We Discourage Excellence," *Chronicle of Higher Education* 39 (January 6, 1993): B1–B2.

70. Steven M. Cahn, *Saints and Scamps: Ethics in Academia,* rev. ed. (Lanham, Md.: Rowman & Littlefield, 1994), pp. 30–33.

71. See William D. Schaefer, *Education Without Compromise, From Chaos to Coherence in Higher Education* (San Francisco: Jossey-Bass, 1990), passim.

72. Ibid., p. xii.

73. Ibid., pp. 18ff.

74. Ibid., pp. 23–25.

75. Ibid., pp. 123–124.

76. C. P. Snow, *The Two Cultures and the Scientific Revolution* (Cambridge: Cambridge University Press, 1959).

77. Allan Bloom, *The Closing of the American Mind* (New York: Simon and Shuster, 1987).

78. Hirsch, pp. 2–18ff.

79. Mortimer Adler, *The Paideia Proposal* (New York: Macmillan, 1982), pp. 42–43.

80. E. D. Hirsch, Jr., "Cultural Literacy: Let's Get Specific," *NEA Today* 6 (January 1988): 15–21.

Sources and References

GENERAL REFERENCES

Brubacher, John S., and Willis Rudy. *Higher Education in Transition, A History of American Colleges and Universities, 1636–1976,* 3rd. ed. rev. New York: Harper & Row, 1976.

Chambers, Frederick. *Black Higher Education in the United States.* Westport, Conn.: Greenwood Press, 1978.

Cowley, W. H., and Don Williams. *International and Historical Roots of American Higher Education.* New York: Garland, 1991.

Faragher, John M., and Florence Howe, eds. *Women and Higher Education in American History: Essays from the Mount Holyoke College Sesquicentennial Symposia.* New York: Norton, 1988.

Goodchild, Lester F., and Harold S. Wechsler, eds. *The ASHE Reader in the History of Higher Education.* Needham, Mass.: Ginn Press, 1989.

Henry, David Dodds. *Challenges Past, Challenges Present: An Analysis of American Higher Education Since 1930.* San Francisco: Jossey-Bass, 1975.

Hoftstadter, Richard, and C. DeWitt Hardy. *The Development and Scope of Higher Education in the United States.* New York: Columbia University Press, 1952.

Hofstadter, Richard, and W. Smith. *American Higher Education: A Documentary History.* Chicago: University of Chicago Press, 1961.

Rudolph, Frederick. *Curriculum: A History of the American Undergraduate Course of Study Since 1636.* San Francisco: Jossey-Bass, 1977.

———. *The American College and University: A History.* New York: Vintage, 1965.

Solomon, Barbara. *In the Company of Educated Women: A History of Women and Higher Education in America.* New Haven, Conn.: Yale University Press, 1985.

Thelin, John R. *Higher Education and Its Useful Past.* Cambridge, Mass.: Schenkman, 1982.

Veysey, Laurence R. *The Emergence of the American University.* Chicago: University of Chicago Press, 1965.

1. HIGHER LEARNING IN ANTIQUITY

Bowen, James. *A History of Western Education,* vol. I. New York: St. Martin's Press, 1972.

Brickhouse, Thomas C., and Nicholas D. Smith. *Socrates on Trial.* Princeton, N.J.: Princeton University Press, 1989.

Castle, E. B. *Ancient Education and Today.* New York: Penguin, 1964.

Clarke, Martin L. *Higher Education in the Ancient World.* Albuquerque, N.M.: University of New Mexico Press, 1971.

Gadd, Cyril J. *Teachers and Students in the Oldest Schools.* London: School of Oriental and African Studies, University of London, 1956.

Laurie, S. S. *Historical Survey of Pre-Christian Education.* New York: Longmans, Green, 1907.

Lynch, John P. *Aristotle's School.* Berkeley: University of California Press, 1972.

Marrou, Henri. *A History of Education in Antiquity.* New York: Mentor, 1964.

2. FROM CATHEDRAL CHURCH SCHOOLS TO UNIVERSITIES

Baldwin, John W., and Richard A. Goldwaite, eds. *Universities in Politics: Case Studies from the Late Middle Ages and Early Modern Period.* Baltimore: Johns Hopkins Press, 1972.

Bowen, James. *A History of Western Education*, vol. II. New York: St. Martin's Press, 1975.

Compayré, Gabriel. *Abelard and the Origin and Early History of Universities*. New York: Charles Scribner's Sons, 1910.

Daly, Lowrie J. *The Medieval University 1200–1400*. New York: Sheed and Ward, 1961.

Haskins, Charles H. *The Rise of Universities*. New York: Henry Holt and Company, 1923.

Kibre, Pearl. *Nations in the Mediaeval European Universities*. Cambridge, MA.: Mediaeval Academy of America, Publication No. 49, 1948.

Labalme, Patricia H., ed. *Beyond Their Sex: Learned Women of the European Past*. New York: New York University Press, 1984.

Leff, Gordon. *Paris and Oxford Universities in the Thirteenth and Fourteenth Centuries: An Institutional and Intellectual History*. New York: John Wiley and Sons, 1968.

Piltz, Anders. *The World of Medieval Learning*, David Jones, trans. Totawa, N.J.: Barnes and Noble, 1981.

Powicke, F. M., and A. B. Emden, eds. *Rashdall's Medieval Universities*, 3 vols. Oxford: Clarendon Press, 1936.

Radcliff-Umstead, Douglas, ed. *The University World: A Synoptic View of Higher Education*. Pittsburgh, Penn.: Medieval and Renaissance Studies Committee, Vol II, University of Pittsburgh, 1973.

Schachner, Nathan. *The Medieval Universities*. New York: A. S. Barnes & Company, 1938.

Thorndike, Lynn, *University Records and Life in the Middle Ages*. New York: Columbia University Press, 1944.

Wieruszoksi, Helene. *The Medieval University*. New York: D. Van Nostrand, 1966.

3. POST-MEDIEVAL ACADEME: EVOLUTION AND ESTRANGEMENT

Blockliss, L. W. B. *French Higher Education in the Seventeenth and Eighteenth Century: A Cultural History*. New York: Oxford University Press, 1987.

Charleton, K. *Education in Renaissance England*. London: Routledge & Kegan Paul, 1965.

Clarke, Martin L. *Classical Education in Great Britain, 1500–1900*. Cambridge: Cambridge University Press, 1959.

Dunston, Arthur J. *Four Centres of Classical Learning in Renaissance Italy*. Sydney: Sydney University Press, 1972.

Grendler, Paul F. *Schooling in Renaissance Italy: Literacy and Learning, 1300–1600*. Baltimore: Johns Hopkins University Press, 1989.

Kearney, Hugh. *Scholars and Gentlemen: Universities and Society in Pre-Industrial Britain*. Ithaca: Cornell University Press, 1970.

LaVopa, Anthony J. *Grace, Talent, and Merit: Poor Students, Clerical Careers, and Professional Ideology in Eighteenth Century Germany*. Cambridge: Cambridge University Press, 1988.

Leach, A. F. *Educational Charters and Documents*. Cambridge: Cambridge University Press, 1911.

Lucki, Emil. *History of the Renaissance, 1350–1550, Book III: Education, Learning and Thought*. Salt Lake City: University of Utah Press, 1963.

Markham, Felix. *Oxford*. London: Weidenfeld and Nicholson, 1967.

Paulsen, Friedrich. *German Education: Past and Present*. London: T. Fisher & Unwin, 1908.

Smith, J. W. Ashley. *The Birth of Modern Education: The Contribution of the Dissenting Academies*. London: Independent Press, 1954.

Sylvester, D. W. *Educational Documents 800–1816*. London: Methuen & Company, 1970.

Woodward, W. H. *Studies in Education During the Age of the Renaissance*. Cambridge: Cambridge University Press, 1965.

Wordsworth, Christopher. *Scholae Academicae: Studies at the English Universities in the Eighteenth Century*. New York: Augustus M. Kelley, 1969.

4. THE AMERICAN COLONIAL AND ANTEBELLUM COLLEGE

Allmendinger, David F. *Paupers and Scholars: The Transition of Student Life in 19th Century New England*. New York: St. Martin's Press, 1973.

Axt, Richard G. *The Federal Government and the Financing of Higher Education.* New York: Columbia University Press, 1952.

Boas, Louis Schutz. *Women's Education Begins.* Norton, Mass.: Wheaton College Press, 1935.

Butts, R. Freeman. *The College Charts Its Course.* New York: McGraw-Hill, 1939.

Canby, Henry S. *Alma Mater: The Gothic Age of the American College.* New York: Farrar Straus & Giroux, 1936.

Cremin, Lawrence. *American Education: The Colonial Experience.* New York: HarperCollins, 1970.

Gummere, Richard M. *The American Colonial Mind and the Classical Tradition.* Cambridge, Mass.: Harvard University Press, 1963.

Hansen, Allen O. *Liberalism and American Education in the Eighteenth Century.* New York: Macmillan, 1926.

Harding, Thomas S. *College Literary Societies: Their Contribution to Higher Education in the United States, 1815–1876.* New York: Pageant Press, 1971.

Hofstadter, Richard, and Wilson Smith, eds. *American Higher Education: A Documentary History,* Vol. I. Chicago: University of Chicago Press, 1961.

Hornberger, Theodore. *Scientific Thought in the American Colleges, 1639–1800.* Austin, Tex.: University of Texas Press, 1945.

Herbst, Jurgen. *From Crisis to Crisis: American College Government 1636–1819.* Cambridge, Mass.: Harvard University Press, 1982.

Kelly, Robert L. *The American Colleges and the Social Order.* New York: Macmillan, 1940.

Meiklejohn, Alexander. *The Liberal College.* Boston: Marshall Jones, 1920.

Miller, Perry. *The New England Mind: The Seventeenth Century.* New York: Macmillan, 1939.

Morison, Samuel Eliot. *Three Centuries of Harvard.* Cambridge, Mass.: Harvard University Press, 1936.

———. *The Intellectual Life of Colonial New England.* Ithaca, N.Y.: Cornell University Press, 1956.

Potter, David. *Debating in Colonial Chartered Colleges.* New York: Teachers College, Columbia University, 1944.

Robson, David W. *Educating Republicans: The College in the Era of the American Revolution, 1750–1800.* Westport, Conn.: Greenwood Press, 1985.

Rudolph, Frederick. *Mark Hopkins and the Log.* New Haven, Conn.: Yale University Press, 1956; reissued.

Schmidt, George P. *The Liberal Arts College: A Chapter in American Cultural History.* New Brunswick, N.J.: Rutgers University Press, 1957.

Sheldon, Henry D. *History and Pedagogy of American Student Societies.* Englewood Cliffs, N.J.: Prentice Hall, 1901.

Smallwood, Mary L. *An Historical Study of Examinations and Grading Systems in Early American Universities* (New York: Johnson Reprint Corporation, 1969.

Smith, George. *The Old Time College President.* New York: Columbia University Press, 1930.

Storr, Richard J. *The Beginnings of Graduate Education in America.* Chicago: University of Chicago Press, 1953.

Tewksbury, Donald G. *The Founding of American Colleges and Universities Before the Civil War.* New York: Bureau of Publications, Teachers College, Columbia University, 1932.

Thwing, Charles F. *History of Higher Education in America.* Englewood Cliffs, N.J.: Prentice-Hall, 1906.

Wills, Elbert V. *The Growth of American Higher Education.* Philadelphia: Dorrance, 1936.

Woody, Thomas. *History of Women's Education in the United States.* Lancaster, Penn.: Science Press, 1929.

5. THE EVOLVING AMERICAN UNIVERSITY

Becker, Carl L. *Cornell University: The Founders and the Founding.* Ithaca, N.Y.: Cornell University Press, 1944.

Berelson, Bernard. *Graduate Education in the United States.* New York: McGraw-Hill, 1960.

Brickman, William W., and Stanley Lehrer, eds. *A Century of Higher Education: Classical Citadel to Collegiate Colossus.* New York: Society for the Advancement of Education, 1962.

Clapp, Margaret, ed. *The Modern University.* Ithaca, N.Y.: Cornell University Press, 1950.

Curti, Merle, and Vernon Carstensen. *The University of Wisconsin, A History 1848–1925,* vol. 1. Madison, Wisc.: University of Wisconsin Press, 1949.

Eckelberry, Roscoe H. *A History of the Municipal University of the United States.* Washington, D.C.: U. S. Office of Education, 1932.

Eddy, E. D., Jr. *Colleges for Our Land and Time: The Land Grant Idea in Education.* New York: Harper, 1956.

Fitch, George. *At Good Old Siwash.* Boston: Little, Brown, 1911.

Foerster, Norman. *The American State University.* Chapel Hill: University of North Carolina Press, 1937.

Hawkins, Hugh. *Harvard and America: The Educational Leadership of Charles W. Eliot.* New York: Oxford University Press, 1972.

———. *Pioneer: A History of the Johns Hopkins University, 1874–1889.* Ithaca, N.Y.: Cornell University Press, 1960.

Henderson, Algo D. *Policies and Practices in Higher Education.* New York: Harper & Row, 1960.

Hudson, Jay W. *The College and New America.* Englewood Cliffs, N.J.: Prentice-Hall, 1920.

Hofstadter, Richard, and Walter P. Metzger. *Development of Academic Freedom in the United States.* New York: Columbia University Press, 1955.

Howe, Frederic C. *Wisconsin, An Experiment in Democracy.* New York: Scribner, 1912.

Jarausch, Konrad H., ed. *The Transformation of Higher Learning 1860–1930.* Chicago: University of Chicago Press, 1983.

Miller, Howard S. *Dollars for Research: Science and Its Patrons in Nineteenth-Century America.* Seattle: University of Washington Press, 1970.

Nevins, Allan. *The State Universities and Democracy.* Urbana, Ill.: University of Illinois Press, 1962.

Newcomer, Mabel. *A Century of Higher Education for American Women.* New York: Harper & Brothers, 1959.

Rainsford, G. N. *Congress and Higher Education in the Nineteenth Century.* Knoxville: University of Tennessee Press, 1972.

Rogers, Walter P. *Andrew D. White and the Modern University.* Ithaca, N.Y.: Cornell University Press, 1942.

Ross, Earle D. *Democracy's College: The Land-Grant Movement in the Formative Stage.* Ames, Iowa: Iowa State College Press, 1942.

Sanford, Nevitt, ed. *The American College.* New York: Wiley, 1962.

Slosson, E. E. *Great American Universities.* New York: Macmillan, 1910.

Storr, Richard J. *Harper's University: The Beginnings.* Chicago: University of Chicago Press, 1966.

———. *The Beginnings of Graduate Education in America.* Chicago: University of Chicago Press, 1953.

Weaver, David A. *Builders of American Universities: Inaugural Addresses.* Alton, Ill.: Shurtleff College Press, 1950.

6. AMERICAN ACADEME IN THE EARLY TWENTIETH CENTURY

Anderson, James D. *The Education of Blacks in the South, 1860–1935.* Chapel Hill, N.C.: University of North Carolina Press, 1988.

Angell, James B. *Reminiscences.* New York: McKay, 1912.

Aydelotte, Frank. *Breaking the Academic Lockstep: The Development of Honors Work in American Colleges and Universities.* New York: Harper & Row, 1944.

————. *An Adventure in Education.* New York: Macmillan, 1941.

Benezet, Louis T. *General Education in the Progressive College.* New York: Teachers College, Columbia University Press, 1943.

Bogue, Jesse P. *The Community College.* New York: McGraw-Hill, 1950.

Boucher, Chauncey S. *The Chicago College Plan.* Chicago: Chicago University Press, 1935.

Brax, Ralph. *The First Student Movement: Student Activism in the United States During the 1930s* Port Washington: Kennikat, 1981.

Canby, Henry S. *Alma Mater.* New York: Farrar, Straus & Giroux, 1936.

————. *College Sons and College Fathers.* New York: Harper & Row, 1915.

Dewey, John. *The Educational Situation.* Chicago: Chicago University Press, 1902.

Duffus, Robert L. *Democracy Enters College.* New York: Scribner, 1936.

Eells, Walter C. *The Junior College.* Boston: Houghton Mifflin, 1936.

Elliott, Edward C., and Merritt M. Chambers. *The Colleges and the Courts.* New York: Carnegie Foundation, 1936.

Foerster, Norman. *The American State University.* Chapel Hill: University of North Carolina Press, 1937.

Fraser, Mowat G. *The College of the Future.* New York: Columbia University Press, 1937.

Fretwell, Elbert K. *Founding Public Junior Colleges.* New York: Teachers College, Columbia University, 1954.

Frodin, Reuben. *The Idea and Practice of General Education.* Chicago: Chicago University Press, 1951.

Gauss, Christian. *Life in College.* New York: Scribner, 1930.

Gilman, Daniel Coit. *Launching of a University.* New York: Dodd, Mead, 1906.

Gruber, Carol S. *Mars and Minerva: World War One and the Uses of the Higher Learning in America.* Baton Rouge: Louisiana State University Press, 1975.

Hall, G. Stanley. *Adolescence.* Englewood Cliffs, N.J.: Prentice-Hall, 1904.

Harper, William Rainey. *The Trend in Higher Education.* Chicago: University of Chicago Press, 1905.

Holmes, Dwight O. W. *Evolution of the Negro College.* New York: Teachers College, Columbia University, 1934.

Hutchins, Robert M. *The Higher Learning in America.* New Haven, Conn.: Yale University Press, 1936.

Kallen, Horace. *College Prolongs Infancy.* New York: John Day, 1932.

Leonard, Eugenie A. *Origins of Personnel Services in American Higher Education.* Minneapolis: University of Minnesota Press, 1955.

Levine, David O. *The American College and the Culture of Aspiration, 1915–1940.* Ithaca, N.Y.: Cornell University Press, 1986.

Lowell, Lawrence, A. *At War with Academic Traditions in America.* Cambridge, Mass.: Harvard University Press, 1934.

McConn, Max. *College or Kindergarten.* New York: New Republic, 1928.

Meiklejohn, Alexander. *The Experimental College.* New York: Harper & Row, 1932.

Metzger, Walter P. *Academic Freedom in the Age of the University.* New York: Columbia University Press, 1955.

Newcomer, Mabel. *A Century of Higher Education for American Women.* New York: Harper and Brothers, 1959.

Sheean, Vincent. *Personal History.* Garden City, N.J.: Doubleday Doran, 1936.

Sinclair, Upton. *The Goose-Step: A Study of American Education.* New York: Albert and Charles Boni, 1936.

Slosson, Edwin E. *Great American Universities.* New York: Macmillan, 1910.

Thomas, Russell. *The Search for a Common Learning: General Education, 1800–1960.* New York: McGraw-Hill, 1962.

Veblen, Thorstein. *The Higher Learning in America.* New York: Viking, 1935.

Wilkins, Ernest H. *The Changing College.* Chicago: Chicago University Press, 1927.

Willie, Charles V., and Arkine S. McCord. *Black Students at White Colleges.* New York: Praeger, 1972.

7. POSTWAR HIGHER LEARNING IN AMERICA

Bander, Edward J., ed. *Turmoil on the Campus.* New York: H. W. Wilson, 1970.

Bell, Daniel. *The Reforming of General Education.* New York: Columbia University Press, 1966.

Bloustein, Edward J. *The University and the Counterculture.* New Brunswick, N.J.: Rutgers University Press, 1972.

Boyer, Ernest L. *College: The Undergraduate Experience in America.* New York: Harper and Row, 1987.

————, and Arthur Levine. *A Quest for Common Learning.* Washington, D.C.: Carnegie Foundation for the Advancement of Teaching, 1981.

Carnegie Commission on Higher Education. *Priorities for Action: Final Report of the Carnegie Commission on Higher Education.* New York: McGraw Hill, 1973.

Carnegie Council on Policy Studies in Higher Education. *Three Thousand Futures: The Next Twenty Years for Higher Education.* San Francisco: Jossey-Bass/Carnegie Council on Policy Studies in Higher Education, 1980.

Dickman, Howard, ed. *The Imperiled Academy.* New Brunswick, N.J.: Transaction, 1993.

Dressel, Paul L., and Lewis B. Mayhew. *General Education: Explorations in Evaluation.* Washington, D.C.: American Council on Education, 1954.

Frodin, Reuben. *The Idea and Practice of General Education.* Chicago: University of Chicago Press, 1951.

Glazer, Nathan. *Remembering the Answers: Essays on the American Student Revolt.* New York: Basic Books, 1970.

Greene, Theodore. *Liberal Education Reconsidered.* Cambridge, Mass.: Harvard University Press, 1953.

Harvard University Committee on the Objective of a General Education in a Free Society. *General Education in a Free Society.* Cambridge, Mass.: Harvard University Press, 1945.

Heath, D. H. *Growing Up in College: Liberal Education and Maturity.* San Francisco: Jossey-Bass, 1968.

Hodgkinson, H. L. *Institutions in Transition: A Study of Change in Higher Education.* Berkeley: Carnegie Commission on Higher Education, 1970.

Kallen, Horace M. *The Education of Free Men.* New York: Farrar, Straus & Giroux, 1949.

Katchadourian, Herant A., and John Boli. *Careerism and Intellectualism Among College Students: Patterns of Academic and Career Choice in the Undergraduate Years.* San Francisco: Jossey-Bass, 1985.

Kenniston, Kenneth. *Youth and Dissent.* New York: Harcourt Brace Jovanovich, 1971.

Kerr, Clark. *The Uses of the University.* New York: Harper and Row, 1972.

Kirk, Russell. *Decadence and Renewal in the Higher Learning.* South Bend, Ind.: Regnery, 1978.

Lipset, Seymour Martin. *Rebellion in the University.* New Brunswick, N.J.: Transaction, 1993.

Mayhew, Lewis B., ed. *General Education: An Account and Appraisal.* New York: Harper and Row, 1960.

————. *Higher Education in the Revolutionary Decades.* Berkeley, Calif.: McCutchan Publishing Corporation, 1967.

Minnich, Elizabeth et al., eds. *Reconstructing the Academy: Women's Education and Women's Studies.* Chicago: University of Chicago Press, 1988.

Niblett, W. R., ed. *Higher Education: Demand and Response.* San Francisco: Jossey-Bass, 1970.

Parsons, Talcott, and Gerald M. Platt. *The American University.* Cambridge, Mass.: Harvard University Press, 1973.

Rice, James G., ed. *General Education: Current Ideas and Concerns.* Washington, D.C.: Association for Higher Education, National Education Association, 1964.

Rosovsky, Henry. *The University: An Owner's Manual.* New York: W. W. Norton, 1990.

Sarratt, R. *The Ordeal of Segregation.* New York: Harper and Row, 1966.

Smith, Page. *Killing the Spirit: Higher Education in America.* New York: Viking Penguin, 1990.

Stadtmun, Verne A. *Academic Adaptations: Higher Education Prepares for the 1980s and 1990s.* San Francisco: Jossey-Bass, 1980.

Wechsler, Harold S. *The Qualified Student: A History of Selective College Admission in America, 1870–1970.* New York: Wiley-Interscience, 1977.

Whipple, Guy Montrose, ed. *General Education in the American College, Part II, The Thirty-Eighth Yearbook of the National Society for the Study of Education.* Bloomington, Ill.: Public School Publishing Company, 1939.

Wilshire, Bruce. *The Moral Collapse of the University.* Albany: State University of New York Press, 1990.

Wilson, Logan. *American Academics: Then and Now.* New York: Oxford University Press, 1979.

8. ANOTHER SEASON OF DISCONTENT: THE CRITICS

Adler, Mortimer. *The Paideia Proposal.* New York: Macmillan, 1982.

Apple, Michael. *Official Knowledge: Democratic Education in a Conservative Age.* New York: Routledge, 1993.

Barber, Benamin R. *An Aristocracy of Everyone: The Politics of Education and the Future of America.* New York: Ballantine Books, 1992.

Bellah, Robert N., et al. *Habits of the Heart: Individualism and Commitment in American Life.* Berkeley: University of California Press, 1985.

————. *The Good Society.* New York: Vintage, 1992.

Benda, Julien. *The Betrayal of the Intellectuals,* trans. Richard Aldington. New York: Norton, 1969.

Bennett, William J. *To Reclaim a Legacy: A Report on the Humanities in Higher Education.* Washington, D.C.: National Endowment for the Humanities, 1984.

Berman, Paul, ed. *Debating P.C.: The Controversy Over Political Correctness on College Campuses.* New York: Dell, 1992.

Blanshard, Brand. *The Uses of a Liberal Education.* LaSalle, Ill.: Open Court, 1973.

Bloom, Allan. *The Closing of the American Mind* (New York: Simon and Schuster, 1987.

Bok, Derek. *Beyond the Ivory Tower: Social Responsibilities of the Modern University.* Cambridge, Mass.: Harvard University Press, 1982.

————. *Higher Learning.* Cambridge, Mass.: Harvard University Press, 1986.

Boorstin, Daniel. *The Americans: The National Experience.* New York: Random House, 1965.

Boyer, Ernest L. *Campus Life: In Search of Community.* Princeton, N.J.: Carnegie Foundation for the Advancement of Teaching, 1990.

Cory, William J.. *Eton Reform.* London: Longman, Green, Longman, & Roberts, 1861.

Douglas, George H.. *Education Without Impact.* New York: Birch Lane Press, 1992.

D'Souza, Dinesh. *Illiberal Education: The Politics of Race and Sex on Campus.* New York: Free Press, 1991.

Hirsch, E. D., Jr. *Cultural Literacy.* Boston: Houghton-Mifflin, 1987.

Horowitz, Helen Lefkowitz. *Campus Life: Undergraduate Culture from the End of the Eighteenth Century to the Present.* New York: Knopf, 1987.

Jacoby, Russell. *The Last Intellectuals: American Culture in the Age of Academe.* New York: Basic Books, 1987.

Jencks, Christopher, and David Riesman. *The Academic Revolution.* Chicago: University of Chicago Press, 1977.

Kerr, Clark. *The Uses of the University.* Cambridge, Mass.: Harvard University Press, 1963.

Kimball, Roger. *Tenured Radicals.* New York: Harper Collins, 1990.

Silber, John. *Shooting Straight: What's Wrong with America.* New York: Harper & Row, 1990.

Smith, Page. *Killing the Spirit: Higher Education in America.* New York: Viking Penguin, 1990.

Snow, C. P. *The Two Cultures and the Scientific Revolution.* Cambridge, Mass.: Cambridge University Press, 1959.

Sykes, Charles. *The Hollow Men: Politics and Corruption in Higher Education.* Washington: Regnery Gateway, 1990.

————. *Profscam: Professors and the Demise of Higher Education.* Washington: Regnery Gateway, 1988.

Toch, Thomas. *In the Name of Excellence.* New York: Oxford University Press, 1991.

Veblen, Thorstein. *The Higher Learning in America.* New York: B. W. Huebsch, 1918.

Wolff, Robert Paul. *The Ideal of the University.* Boston: Beacon Press, 1969.

9. EPILOGUE: IN HISTORICAL RETROSPECT

Bourdieu, Pierre, and Jean-Claude Passeron. *Reproduction in Education, Society and Culture.* Los Angles: Sage, 1979.

Kaplan, Craig, and Ellen Schrecker, eds. *Regulating the Intellectuals.* New York: Praeger, 1983.

MacIver, Robert M. *Academic Freedom in Our Time.* New York: Columbia University Press, 1955.

Index